THE ARDEN SHAKESPEARE
GENERAL EDITOR: RICHARD PROUDFOOT

ANTONY AND CLEOPATRA

THE ARDEN SHAKESPEARE

THE ARDEN EDITION OF THE
WORKS OF WILLIAM SHAKESPEARE

ANTONY AND
CLEOPATRA

Edited by
M. R. RIDLEY

ROUTLEDGE

LONDON and NEW YORK

The general editors of the Arden Shakespeare have been
W. J. Craig (1899–1906), R. H. Case (1909–44),
Una Ellis-Fermor (1946–58), Harold F. Brooks (1952–82),
Harold Jenkins (1958–82) and Brian Morris (1975–82)

Present general editor: Richard Proudfoot

This edition of *Antony and Cleopatra* by M. R. Ridley
first published in 1954 by
Methuen & Co. Ltd
Reprinted with minor corrections 1961, 1965 and 1967
Reprinted 1974

First published as a University Paperback in 1965
Reprinted fourteen times
Reprinted 1987

Reprinted 1988, 1989
by Routledge
11 New Fetter Lane, London EC4P 4EE
29 West 35th Street, New York NY 10001

ISBN (hardbound) 0 416 47290 7
ISBN (paperback) 0 415 02680 6

Printed and bound in Great Britain by
Richard Clay Ltd, Bungay, Suffolk

CONTENTS

PREFACE TO REVISED EDITION

'NOTHING recently written on Shakespeare, I venture to say, shows more thorough scholarship or better judgement than Mr Case's edition in the Arden series.' That is the comment of an exacting critic[1] on the first edition of *Antony and Cleopatra* in the Arden series. It was well justified, and the task of the reviser forty-five years later is correspondingly lightened, the sphere of his duties strictly circumscribed. When work is as sound and comprehensive as Case's introduction and the great bulk of his notes, tinkering with it is both needless and, I think, silly, as though one should set to work to renovate a period piece of furniture. Case's edition shows by its excellences how far English Shakespearean scholarship had at the time advanced, and by its limitations what fields of critical enquiry were still waiting for succeeding scholars to explore.

I can best explain what I have taken the reviser's job to be, and what I have done, with the reasons for it, under three heads: the text; the apparatus criticus; the introduction, notes, and appendices.

I. THE TEXT

Verbally the present text is much the same as that of the original (Arden) edition—which is to say much the same as that of all modern editions—except that in several places the Folio reading has been retained against a commonly accepted emendation. The punctuation, however, has been drastically revised.

The only authoritative text of the play is that of the First Folio. Dover Wilson[2] and Greg[3] agree that the copy for it was pretty certainly Shakespeare's own manuscript. The text is for the most part a good one, with two noticeable defects, (*a*) a considerable amount of mislineation (mainly in short speeches) and (*b*) some odd vagaries in the spelling of proper names.

As to (*a*) Greg says that this 'seems mainly due to the author running on half-lines to economize space', and Dover Wilson

1. A. C. Bradley, *Oxford Lectures on Poetry* (1909), p. 307, note C.
2. *Antony and Cleopatra*, in *New Shakespeare* edition (1951), p. 127.
3. *The Editorial Problem* (1942), p. 148.

accepts this explanation, supporting it 'by the fact that... speeches of one and a half to two and a half lines account for practically all the mislining'. I do not think that the explanation is very convincing. In the first place, it is somewhat too much of a 'blanket' explanation, not reckoning with the different kinds of mislineation which the F text presents. But apart from that, so far as the half-lines are concerned, it does not seem to me to square with the observable facts. If Greg means, as I think he must, that when a speech ended with a half-line Shakespeare was apt to run the half-line on at the end of the preceding complete line, then surely what we should expect to find in F is hypermetric lines in which the unwanted foot or two come at the end. For example, taking Cæsar's speech at II. ii. 37–40, we might expect it to end not with

> Did practise on my state, your being in Egypt
> Might be my question.

but with a single 'line'

> Did practise on my state, your being in Egypt might be my question.

But in fact that kind of hypermetric line is rare, and much commoner is the kind in which the unwanted foot or two are at the beginning of the line, as for example, II. ii. 70–3, printed thus in modern editions

>   for that you must
>   But say, I could not help it.
> *Cæs.*   I wrote to you:
>   When rioting in Alexandria you
>   Did pocket up my letters. ...

But which appears in F as

>   for that you must,
>   But say I could not help it.
> *Cæs.* I wrote to you, when rioting in Alexandria you
>   Did pocket up my letters. ...

thus producing an impossible first line for Cæsar. What I think is clear is that the F compositor certainly, and Shakespeare almost certainly, did not use the modern typographical device whereby, when one speech ends and the next begins in the middle of a line, the second speech is indented, as at the opening of II. i.

> *Pom.* If the great gods be just, they shall assist
>   The deeds of justest men.
> *Mene.*   Know, worthy Pompey,
>   That what ...

I suspect that Shakespeare wrote the second line there as

The deeds of justest men.   *Mene.* Know worthy *Pompey*

but the F compositor, whenever he found himself confronted by a
fresh speech-heading, invariably started a new line, and sometimes, with unhappy results, did the best he could to divide the
speech into some sort of lines. (The point about how Shakespeare
wrote the line above, and others like it, has some importance, apart
from the question of mislineation. In F both speech-headings and
proper names are in italic, and it is natural to suppose that Shakespeare indicated that this should be so. But if italic speech-headings
were apt to occur in the middle of lines there is obvious danger of
confusion between them and italic proper names in the text.)

The question of mislineation is treated at greater length in
Appendix II; I have there devoted a good deal of space to exempli-
fying the kinds of mislineation which F presents, and in notes on
II. v. 31–2 and 105–10 I have discussed two typical passages in
detail. I have done this for two reasons. First, for reasons given in
the relevant section (p. xx below), I have omitted all references to
mislineation from the apparatus criticus, and it is desirable that the
reader who is interested in such things should be able to see examples of what happened more clearly than he can reconstruct
them from summary notes. Second, it is important, I think, for the
modern reader to realize that 'correction of frequent mislineation'
does not imply a drastic revision of the original text, the sort of
revision of which he is suspicious (as with much cavalier emendation of words he is very rightly suspicious) that it may be taking him
further from, rather than nearer to, what Shakespeare intended. It
will be noticed from the examples, firstly, that a good deal of the
so-called mislineation is not really *mis*lineation at all, but what one
might call absence of lineation, consequent on the absence of an
accepted modern typographical device, and secondly, that almost
all the real mislineation can be easily, and for the most part with
certainty, corrected.

To turn now to (*b*), the mis-spelling of proper names. F presents
us with such oddities as 'Scicion'[1] for Sicyon, 'Towrus' for Taurus,
and 'Ventigius' for Ventidius, not to mention 'Cleopater' three
times in Act II for Cleopatra.[2] The mis-spellings are almost all corrected by whoever prepared the copy for F2, and they are intrin-

1. See note on I. ii. 110.

2. It rather looks as though something had happened in Act II. Two of the
three *Cleopater*'s come within a hundred lines of one another in scene ii, and all
three *Ventigius*'s within ten lines in scene iii, though in III. i he is three times spelt
correctly.

sically of small importance, but there is some interest in speculating how they arose. Dover Wilson says: 'Working presumably with North under his eye, Shakespeare was nevertheless restrained by no habits of "correctness" or consistency so long as the names sounded all right on the stage.' I find this very hard to swallow. Why should Shakespeare, working 'with North under his eye', and often adhering to North very closely, go out of his way to alter words which were staring at him out of the page? It is no easier to write 'Towrus' than 'Taurus' or to give Ventidius a 'g' instead of his proper 'd'. If we are to make Shakespeare responsible for the errors I can only suggest that he was *not* working with North under his eye, but knew him so well, almost by heart, that he could versify him without reference to the book, and when he came to a proper name relied on his memory of how he had heard it 'in his head'. But this will hardly work with 'Cleopater'. The other, and I think much more probable, explanation is that these are 'auditory' errors. I know that the hypothesis that copy was sometimes read to the compositor is at present somewhat blown upon, and that such external evidence as there is for it is readily (I think much too readily) dismissed. But it is quite clear that some errors in Shakespearean texts depend on an auditory link at *some* point in the chain of transmission, though not necessarily on the link between copy and compositor. For example, the famous 'a dog so bade in office' for 'a dog's obey'd in office'[1] is not accountable for by any misreading, but only by mishearing. And some at least of these proper names seem to me the results of mishearing, in particular 'Ventigius', because he is not by any means always mis-spelt, and I do not see why Shakespeare should have been inconsistent. But some people naturally pronounce an '-idius' ending so that it sounds like '-igius'. 'Towrus', by the way, is interesting, on the 'auditory' supposition, since it implies an 'Italian' pronunciation, whereas Henslowe's 'Fostus' for 'Faustus' implies the English.[2]

Punctuation. Since Case's edition first appeared a great deal more attention has been paid to the punctuation of the early Quarto and First Folio texts than had been paid by earlier editors, who felt themselves free to play any old Harry they chose with the original punctuation. This increased attention was largely due to Percy Simpson's *Shakespearian Punctuation* (1911). To this book, something of a landmark in Shakespearean scholarship, I will return later, but for the moment it is worth while to ask why earlier editors felt justified in allowing themselves such freedom. The assumption that punctuation could be properly treated much more high-handedly

---

1. *Lr*, IV. vi. 164.   2. And see note on *Cicelie* at II. vi. 45.

than words arose, I think, in part from a misconception which has nothing to do with Simpson's thesis, and which can be examined without reference to it. To editors accustomed to a style of punctuation mainly 'syntactical', a guide to logical comprehension, the punctuation of early Shakespeare texts inevitably seemed very strange, and it was not unnatural that instead of looking for a principle behind it they dismissed it as haphazard and careless, and rectified it according to their own principles.[1] But the idea that punctuation is anyway much more likely to have been carelessly handled than words depends on a misconception of how a compositor works. The compositor is a man who is trying to turn, as accurately as he can, the 'copy' in front of him into something which, when duly dealt with by the printer, will reproduce that copy in a printed page. Before the invention of linotype or monotype machines the compositor did this by selecting, one by one, from the 'cases' in front of him a series of pieces of type corresponding to the marks on the paper of the copy. Whether these 'marks' are letters or marks of punctuation is a matter of indifference to him; each must be represented by its appropriate piece of type. He does not say 'so long as I get the letters right it does not matter what happens to the punctuation'. Give him the following four marks in the manuscript, *end:*, and he is no more likely to set a comma instead of the colon than to set an *e* for the *d* (in an Elizabethan printing-house he was in fact a good deal less likely, since in Elizabethan script *e* and *d* were very easily confused, so that we have *end* for an undoubted *due* in Sonnet LXIX). It is true that there may be with punctuation slightly more danger of 'foul case', and also that punctuation seems to suffer somewhat readily from the malady known as 'transposed pointing' where the compositor's eye registers the right symbol but puts it in the wrong place, or registers the right pair of symbols but transposes their positions.[2] But in

1. The attitude of almost all these editors, and most of their successors, is well expressed by Johnson, and his statement is significant, since it comes from an editor who, so far as the verbal text was concerned, was extremely conservative, and never emended himself or accepted the emendations of others except where he considered that there was overwhelming cause. 'In restoring the authour's works to their integrity. I have considered the punctuation as wholly in my power; for what could be their care of colons and commas. who corrupted words and sentences. Whatever could be done by adjusting points is therefore silently performed....' The right answer to Johnson's rhetorical question, 'what care...', as I have tried to suggest, is 'about the same' instead of the one which he implies, 'none'.

2. Here is an example of 'wrong place'. *Coriolanus*, I. ix. 6 reads 'And gladly quaked hear more; where the dull tribunes'. A modern compositor, working under good conditions and from the printed page, none the less produced a line that made nonsense: 'And gladly quaked hear more where; the dull tri-

general the 'expectation of error' should not be much higher with
punctuation than with letters, unless the fault lies with the original
copy.

If we put it at double we are putting it high. But editors till quite
recently have put it far higher than that. For purposes of comparison I selected quite arbitrarily the last twenty lines of the first,
third, and fifth acts of *Antony and Cleopatra*, as they appear in the
Folio and in three modern editions, the Arden (Case), the single
volume Oxford (Craig), and the New Shakespeare (Dover Wilson). (The details of the three passages, together with some further
examples, are given in Appendix III.) In these three passages F
has comparatively few errors. There are four obvious misprints of
words, and two, possibly four, in punctuation in sixty lines, so that
the balance between errors in words and those in punctuation is
about level—which is what with reasonable care on the compositor's part one would expect. But two of the modern editors
allow themselves about ten times, and the third about eight times,
greater freedom in altering the punctuation than in altering words.
Further, the alterations are not all in one direction, since, though
the majority make the punctuation heavier, an appreciable number (about a third of the total) make it lighter. This has two effects;
it slows up the general rate of delivery, but it also makes the tempo
more monotonous and often destroys an effect of which Shake-

---

bunes'. And here is, I think, an almost certain example of the transposition of
symbols in an early text which has not, I judge, been previously observed. In
MND., III. ii. 382–7, all three early texts (except for a *dxile* in F) read as follows
(spelling modernized but punctuation retained):
> damned spirits all,
> That in crossways and floods have burial,
> Already to their wormy beds are gone;
> For fear lest day should look their shames upon,
> They wilfully themselves exile from light,
> And must for aye consort with black-brow'd night.

That is not nonsensical or ungrammatical, but it is not wholly satisfactory. The
semi-colon breaks the second couplet awkwardly, *exile* is an odd word for a hurried departure, and *wilfully* even odder when we are told in the next line that
they *must* whether they will or no. Assume a transposed pointing and the commonest of all errors, the *e : d*, and we have a reading in which the rhythm is better
and the point of the everlasting consort with night as punishment for the wilful
exile from light is made.
> damned spirits all,
> That in crossways and floods have burial,
> Already to their wormy beds are gone,
> For fear lest day should look their shames upon;
> They wilfully themselves exil'd from light,
> And must for aye consort with black-brow'd night.

speare—if for the moment we assume that the punctuation is his—
was fond, that namely of giving three or four rapidly running
phrases, separated only by commas, and following them by the
heaviest pause at his command, a full stop. Shakespeare, that is,
was writing for dramatic delivery, while his editors re-write him
for logical comprehension from the page. Many readers must have
noticed that the actor frequently does not deliver his lines in the
least as his modern text has carefully prepared them for him, but
reverts—often no doubt simply from his actor's just instinct, and
not from consultation of the Folio—to the delivery that Shakespeare intended for him, and indicated as his intention.

But in the last few lines above I have of course been begging, or
partly begging, a main question. Have we any justification for
assuming that the punctuation which the early texts represent, or
occasionally mis-represent, was Shakespeare's? Simpson's main
thesis, in the book already mentioned, was this, that 'Shakespearian' punctuation was not, like ours, an aid to understanding
the syntactical construction of a sentence, but rather a guide to
how the sentence should be delivered. It was 'dramatic' or 'rhetorical' rather than logical, and was, largely for that reason,
usually considerably lighter than ours. Further, since it was not
confined within the comparatively narrow limits of syntactical
exposition, it was an instrument which could be used to indicate
considerable and often subtle varieties of interpretation. It was a
dramatic tool, not a grammatical one.

Of the fundamental soundness of Simpson's general idea there
is, I think, little doubt, and of its importance, if sound, no doubt at
all. But it is true that in the natural enthusiasm created by the
application of a new idea a good deal of nonsense was talked, and
attempts were made, for example, to justify every apparently intrusive comma by over-subtle argument which would not stand up to
examination. As a result there has been a strong reaction, and
some critics, eager to pounce on absurdities of detailed example,
have been led—I think misled—into dismissing the whole theory
as moonshine.[1]

Two distinct questions arise. Is the punctuation of the early
texts an approximation to Shakespeare's own? If not, has it any
connection with theatrical performance, or is it the compositor's
own, following 'house-style' (if any), or his own temporary whim?
Now those critics who hold that, except in a few special instances, it
is idle to descry Shakespeare's, or any other playwright's, own in-

---

1. There is a balanced criticism of the theory in Chambers's *William Shakespeare*, I, pp. 190–6. I think he misses one point.

tentions in the punctuation of the early texts, can justifiably point
to the famous three pages of *Sir Thomas More*, which are most inadequately punctuated, and to some, though not all, of the other
extant dramatic manuscripts of the period. But they seem tacitly to
assume that if the punctuation is not the author's, then it is the
compositor's. This is surely not so, and the view, I think, depends
on a failure to imagine what must have happened to an author's
manuscript after it was delivered to the players. Sir Edmund
Chambers gives a clear account[1] of the operations of the man he
calls the 'stage-reviser'—the man, that is, who prepared the manuscript for direct use in the theatre, checking entries and exits, am-
plifying, if necessary, the stage-directions, and so on. But even
Chambers does no more than glance by implication at another
operation which this man must, so far as I can see, have conducted
if it had not already been done. Before the play can go into pro-
duction, each actor must be handed a transcript of his part. But no
actor can efficiently study an unpunctuated, or very inadequately
punctuated, part. Hence someone, whether the author himself or
the 'stage-reviser' (probably identical with the book-keeper), must
complete the punctuation before these transcripts are made and
handed out. And if the author is in close contact with the players
(as, for example, Shakespeare and Heywood were) my guess is that
the 'someone' is likely to have been the author himself. But at least
it seems moderately certain that the printed punctuation is the
compositor's attempt to reproduce what was before him, and that
that was at least contemporary theatrical punctuation.

But can we with any justification suppose that the punctuation
of the original manuscript was Shakespeare's own? The probability, now generally accepted, that the manuscript which went to the
printer was either Shakespeare's own original, or at worst at only
one remove from that, does not much help us, since it can always be
argued that though the words were his the punctuation was not,
but was inserted by someone else. We are reduced therefore to an
examination of a few bits of direct evidence and to a consideration
of likelihood. The question to which we are trying to find what
must be at best a largely conjectural answer, is 'Was Shakespeare a
careless punctuator?'

In the first place it is demonstrable and generally admitted that
on occasion he was extremely careful. The passage in *MND.*, v. i.
108–16 is punctuated (i.e. mis-punctuated, beyond the range of the
wildest compositor's nightmare) to indicate the breathless mis-
delivery of the prologist; and the comments of Theseus and

1. *Op. cit.*, pp. 108–23.

Lysander put this beyond doubt. Chambers also admits as examples of care on Shakespeare's part 'Pistol's gabble when he eats the leek or the pace of Margaret's tongue in *Much Ado About Nothing*' (*H5*, v. i. 47, *Ado*, III. iv. 78 onwards—both passages are unhappily over-punctuated in most modern editions). But I think that he misses the significance of the two passages, especially Pistol's. The carefulness of the author, which is admitted, is shown not in punctuation, but in *non*-punctuation. To secure a particular effect he deliberately omits normal punctuation. But, if the whole manuscript had been very inadequately punctuated, no one, whether compositor or transcriber, would have noticed anything out of the way or suspected any particular intention on Shakespeare's part; as a result, surely, in would have gone some form of punctuation. Either then Shakespeare inserted specific directions that these passages were to be left almost unpunctuated, or these passages were at variance with his normal practice. I think the second alternative the more likely.

This is partly because I find it hard to accept the view that Shakespeare was 'normally a rapid writer, who did not trouble about punctuation, but occasionally became more careful'. Rapid he may have been, and probably was; but why therefore assume that he did not trouble about punctuation? After all, punctuation (of whatever type) is a tool of any writer's trade, and Shakespeare was a skilled workman; more, he was a skilled *dramatic* workman, who knew precisely the effects he wanted produced by the spoken word. There seems to be a curious *non sequitur* which lurks in a good deal of writing on the subject, and every now and then emerges. 'A few writers are always careless in punctuation; many writers are occasionally careless; therefore most writers are always careless.' Stated in those terms the absurdity is of course apparent, but there does seem a tendency to assume that writers are a careless race, and careless in particular about their stops. It is of course impossible to prove a negative, but the example of Keats is interesting. He was, so far as one can judge, a rapid worker; though in the heat of composition he would correct and correct till he got what he wanted, he disliked cold-blooded revision; and in the ordinary run of his letters he was if not a careless at least a very limited punctuator—for long stretches there will be nothing but full stops and dashes. But when, in these same letters, he is being Keats the deliberate poet, when he wants to be sure that a poem he cares about will be rightly read, he is very far from either careless or limited. Some of the less important poems in the letters are inadequately punctuated, but look at the verse epistle to his brother (letter 2 in M.

Buxton Forman's 3rd edition), at the *Ode to Psyche* (letter 123), and *To Autumn* (letter 152). All are punctuated with the greatest care, and so are many others, and not infrequently the punctuation is more effective than that of the printed text. I find it hard to believe that Shakespeare was more careless than Keats, and even harder to believe that by carelessness he robbed himself of a device by the use of which he could go some way towards securing what he wanted.

I think therefore that in the punctuation of the early texts we have, pretty certainly, at least 'playhouse' punctuation, and very possibly a great deal of Shakespeare's own. If this is so, it means that no modern editor can neglect the Q and F punctuation. I should go further, and be prepared to say that no editor can desert it without very careful consideration, and if he does so, does so at his peril. An alteration in the original punctuation should be regarded as no less an emendation than a change in a word, and should be felt to need the same kind of justification. The justification may often be much easier to find, but that is no excuse for not looking for it.

For these reasons I have in the text which follows retained an unusually high proportion of the F punctuation, and I think that any readers who are interested in the subject, and will compare the following passages in this edition with the same passages in others, will appreciate the difference in effect: I. iii. 71–3, and v. ii. 193–5. These passages, together with further examples, are given in full in Appendix III, and attention is drawn in the notes on a number of lines to the way in which the usual modern emendation of the F punctuation has wrecked the intended sense.

Stage directions, scene-divisions, etc. I have retained wherever possible the stage-directions of F, which are more complete and satisfactory than in many plays; I have made the minimum of addition to them (from the copious store provided by the early editors) where, for example, a necessary exit has been omitted, or where the indication of 'business' is helpful to the reader, and in a number of places I have, for reasons given in the notes, not accepted the usual modifications of them, since I think that Shakespeare's stage-directions, particularly in the matter of the order in which characters enter, not infrequently have a significance which facile modification has obscured.

I have retained the usual scene-divisions. They are convenient for reference, and so long as we remember that to the Elizabethans a new scene did not mean new scenery, but simply the sequence of the exit of one group of characters, a momentarily bare stage, and the entry of a new group, the retention does not do much harm. In two places (III. viii–x and IV. x–xii) I have tried to indicate something of the Elizabethan continuity by omitting the vexatious 'another part of the plain' indication of locality.

Indications of locality at the beginning of scenes I have, with some hesitation, retained in their simplest form. I dislike most of them, and I think we lose appreciably by not becoming accustomed, in Shakespeare and other Elizabethan drama, to 'non-localized' scenes—some characters meet 'somewhere' to transact some necessary business of the play, and where the 'somewhere' is may often be of small importance. But the modern reader expects them, and is perhaps needlessly distracted by their absence, since, if he insists on knowing where he is, he wastes time, better spent on listening to the characters, in trying to deduce it from the text. But I have bracketed them, as well as the scene divisions, as a continued reminder that they do not occur in F. And I have omitted any notice of them from the apparatus criticus. It seems to me of the least possible importance whether it was Rowe, or Hanmer, or Capell who inserted this or that example of them. All that matters is that F has *none* of them.

The Text (*verbally*). Here there is little to be said. There is a comparatively small number of instances of obvious corruption, of which the curative emendations have been, since their promulgation, almost universally accepted. These are commented on in the apparatus criticus and the notes. There are a few other passages where I am inclined to think that something has gone wrong, and where I have made speculative suggestions. I am far from confident of any of the suggestions—certainly not nearly confident enough to promote them to the text—but there are two or three places where I am fairly confident that the possibility of corruption is at least worth consideration, whatever the cure may be.[1]

2. THE APPARATUS CRITICUS

This I have considerably lightened. In an edition such as this, which does not pretend to present an exhaustive apparatus, like that of the Furness *Variorum*, it is, I think, important that what is given should be readily comprehensible, and should not obscure salient points by a cloud of minor ones.

I have therefore cut out all record of mislineations, and transferred the consideration of this problem to Appendix II. It is next to impossible for anyone, without long practice, to construct, from

1. E.g. I. i. 41; I. iii. 80; II. i. 22; II. vi. 54; III. x. 32; IV. ii. 30–1. And at I. i. 50 I have substituted a new (so far as I know) emendation for the hitherto accepted one.

the abbreviated notes of an apparatus, a picture of what the F text in fact looks like, or to deduce from a series of such notes the types of mislineating which occur. The study of this problem—which in any case is of comparatively small importance—can be conducted only by an examination of a copy, or a facsimile, of the Folio. But something can be done by an examination of a number of examples, if they are given *in extenso*.

I have cut out almost all variants in proper names, and transferred this feature also of F to the introduction (p. x above). All that matters here is that some proper names are regularly, and some occasionally, mis-spelt, that F2 corrected most of them (indicating that some trouble was taken in preparing the copy for F2), and that mis-spellings of at least two names come in blocks. This last point, probably the least unimportant of the three, is hard to emphasize in an apparatus. I have, however, left in the apparatus an occasional example, as a reminder.

I have also cut out, for reasons given above, in the section on 'Stage directions, etc.', all record of the various indications of locality inserted by editors.

I have made one change which I think is perhaps more important than it looks, namely, the excision throughout of the symbol Ff. Since Furness in the Variorum edition, printing the F1 text, meant by Ff an agreement of F2, F3, and F4, whereas Case in the original Arden edition meant an agreement of all the four Folios, the symbol is confusing anyway. But I think it is much worse than confusing, since it is apt to suggest to a reader not versed in textual problems that all four folios together have in some way or other a superior and overriding authority which F alone has not. And this is not so. The successive Folios, like successive Quartos, each printed from the last, occasionally emend, and occasionally introduce new errors, but none of them has any 'authority', which only consultation of the original manuscript could have given. Johnson was wiser about this than many of his predecessors and successors: 'In his enumeration of editions, he [Theobald] mentions the two first folios as of high, and the third folio as of middle authority; but the truth is, that the first is equivalent to all others, and that the rest only deviate from it by the printer's negligence.' (A slight overstatement, since the latter Folios do occasionally emend.) For the same reason emendations in the later Folios derive no superior probability over those of later editions from greater proximity of date to the first Folio, and these emendations are to be judged by precisely the same standards as one would apply to an emendation of 1953, with one small qualification. The second Folio, printed nine years after the first, is less likely than eighteenth-century editions to contain emendations which a more intimate knowledge of Elizabethan idiom would have shown to be needless, and such emendations as it may make are more likely to be consonant with that idiom.[1]

The present apparatus criticus therefore contains the following: (a) adequate material for the study of all the major and most of the minor textual cruces, giving the original reading and a selection from the often very numerous suggested emendations; (b) a record of additions to (other than those of locality), and departures from, the stage-directions of F; (c) a limited number of quite minor errors, and occasional oddities of spelling, in F, selected so far as possible for their relevance to the textual study of other plays as well as this— e.g. errors which depend on the common *e : d*, or the equally common minim, confusion, or, in spelling, F's *bin* for *been*, which may have some bearing on, e.g. the odd *cliffe-cleefe* variant in *Hamlet*; (d) a few examples of the needless or wild conjecture, included simply as warning illustrations of the *cacoethes emendandi*.

It is apparent, therefore, that the apparatus is eclectic; eclectic to some extent it must be, for reasons already given, but is also sometimes so in a fashion, and on a principle, which are, I know, open to criticism. In constructing the apparatus, and deciding what to include and what to omit, I have tried to keep in mind two main types of reader, the student who is in the early or prentice days of his study of textual problems, and the ordinary reader who is mainly concerned with reading the plays as plays, who relies therefore on his edition primarily for discussion of points of meaning or dramatic presentation, but who is prepared every now and again to be interested in a technical problem. For both classes it is desirable to let the important things stand out, and not embed them in a mass of minor ones. Hence, for example, I have often, after giving the name of the editor who first made the emendation, said 'and many other edd.' instead of giving a string of names, which would be significant only to the mature scholar, already well-versed, or wanting to be better versed, in the habit of mind of this or that editor. But there is a type of what one may call 'recurrent variant' which raises a problem. Many of these variants are matters of spelling, and some may be significant and some not. For example, the Folio's very frequent *loose* for *lose* is no more than a normal Elizabethan spelling, and is, I think rightly, silently modernized, in common with others of the same kind. On the

---

1. Whoever prepared the copy for F2 took a good deal of trouble over his job. Apart from the proper names, he made a number of needless, and sometimes pedantic, changes, but also a number of sensible, if pedestrian, emendations.

other hand the Folio's frequent *bin* for *been* has some significance
with regard to Elizabethan pronunciation, and therefore, possibly,
with regard to problems elsewhere. But to record every occurrence
of *bin* would be not only tiresome to the reader but, in an apparatus
of this scope, disproportionate. I have therefore given only one
instance of *bin*. I do not think that this is misleading so long as it is
made clear (whether in the apparatus itself, as with *bin*, or in notes
or introduction, as with mis-spelt proper names) that the instance
recorded is not an isolated one, but is given as an example.

I have occasionally, following Case's example, admitted an
explanatory word or two, when this seemed the way to direct the
reader's attention to what matters and save him from wasting time
on what does not.

There is one last point to which attention should be drawn. A
mark of punctuation which in the text follows a word or phrase
included in the apparatus is recorded only when it is the point, or
one of the points, at issue (e.g. 'chaps,' at III. v. 13). But to this rule
there is, for typographical reasons, one general exception. Words
which in the text are printed in italic type (i.e. stage-directions)
appear in italic also in the apparatus: but so do the names of
editors. This, in the absence of some recognized symbol to separate
the words cited from the name of the editor concerned has sometimes odd results. I have therefore retained in the apparatus the
full stop which closes stage-directions. This is admittedly inconsistent, but it avoids such entries as '*They wake Rowe*' or '*Noise
within Capell*'.

3. INTRODUCTION, NOTES, AND APPENDICES

The introduction, for reasons already explained, I have left
almost as it stood, venturing only on half a dozen minor verbal
alterations where I thought that Case had not made his meaning as
clear as he would have wished. Any matter of my own is by way of
addition, not alteration, and is indicated by being included between a † and [R].

In the notes I have allowed myself a freer, but only slightly freer,
hand. I have added, without comment, a certain number of
glosses where Case had left unglossed a word or phrase which
might puzzle a modern reader. I have occasionally (again without
comment) cut out one of Case's more recondite illustrations—I
think that Case's wealth and range of knowledge sometimes
defeats its own ends and bewilders or wearies the reader instead of
illuminating him—but on the other side I have on occasion given
in full a Shakespearean illustration to which Case gave only a

reference. Illustrations from a man's own work are always, I think, more valuable than those from others, and it is only, in my experience, the rarely assiduous student who will look up a casual reference. Lastly, I have re-written some notes, and made additions, whether by way of amplification or doubt, to others, as well as making a few suggestions of my own. It will not, I hope, be vexatious to the reader to find all the modifications or additions in this last category indicated by the same symbols († ... [R]). Where so much has been left untouched I see no reason why I should foist on to Case, by the absence of any such indication, the responsibility for comment with which he might have seriously disagreed.

Appendices. I have incorporated most of Case's Appendix I in the notes on the passages concerned, but I have left standing the long note on the arm-gaunt steed. This unhappy animal has caused more trouble than he is worth, but the note is worth retaining, partly as an example of painstaking scholarship, and partly as an example (even an awful example) of the vagaries of emenders. I have cut out altogether his Appendix II. It was a presentation, almost as exhaustive as the five pages of the Furness *Variorum*, of the many explanations and emendations of II. ii. 206–8. Since most of the expositors expose little but themselves, and demonstrate little but the fact that determined resolution can always find difficulties where no difficulties are, the presentation of their labours throws little light on a passage which we have, I think, as Shakespeare wrote it and the Folio correctly presented it.

I have added three appendices of my own, one on the mislineation of F, one containing examples of punctuation, and one on the staging of certain scenes.

My thanks are due to Dr H. F. Brooks for his scholarly and generous help, particularly with the apparatus, but also in making a number of illuminating suggestions about isolated points of text and interpretation.

M. R. R.

INTRODUCTION

(R. H. CASE: 1906)

This edition of *Antony and Cleopatra* presents the first folio text with the majority of those emendations which in course of time have secured almost universal assent, no others, whether accepted in one or more editions or merely suggested, possessing, in the editor's judgement, that probability only short of certainty which alone justifies adoption. Certain changes countenanced by the best editions have, on the other hand, been rejected in favour of the original readings, and are here briefly indicated.

The plurals in *-th* and *-s*, so extremely common in the literature of the period, have been restored wherever they occur in the folio; and similarly other slight variations from modern grammar: obsolete forms of words (mere differences of spelling excepted) are invariably given in place of following the usual eclectic plan: the folio forms of names, where they correspond with those of North and are consequently not press errors, are retained; and finally, also, besides the folio readings in certain places, its sense-affecting punctuation in the following passages, for reasons given in the notes in each case: I. i. 4, v. 74–5; II. ii. 71–2; III. xiii. 74; IV. xv. 73; V. ii. 291.

With regard to interpretation of identical readings, many instances of greater or less variation from the usually accepted senses will be found. The obstinate cruces of the play have been fully discussed, and, as a choice of evils, no ascertained difficulties have been avoided, though in cases of ambiguity where language is so freely wielded as in *Antony and Cleopatra*, it is a question whether a reader's cursory impressions are not less likely to mislead than laboured analyses. A particular aim has been to illustrate as far as possible from new sources, with acknowledgment of all illustrations —save sometimes those from Shakespeare—owed to their employment by others. In the critical apparatus, all material differences from the first folio text, including the re-arrangement of the lines, are recorded; and any corrections or variations worth noting in the later folios have been extracted from the collation in the Cambridge

Shakespeare. This has also been used to determine the originators of emendations; but the editions and independent commentaries have been themselves examined.

The composition of *Antony and Cleopatra* is assigned to 1607, or the early part of 1608, for which dates the external evidence is the second of the following entries[1] in the Stationers' Registers (see Arber's *Transcript*, iii. 167*b*) under date 20 May 1608:

> Edward Blount. Entred for his copie vnder thandes of Sir George Buck knight and Master Warden Seton A booke called. *The booke of* PERICLES *prynce of Tyre* . . . vj^d.
> Edward Blunt Entred also for his copie by the lyke Aucthoritie. A booke Called. ANTHONY. *and* CLEOPATRA . . . vj^d.

Next year (1609) *Pericles* was published in quarto by another publisher, but the second entry either bore no fruit, or any resulting impression has disappeared. It is reasonably taken to refer to Shakespeare's play, which was registered by Master Blounte and Isaak Jaggard on 8 November 1623—in that case, for the second time—among 'Master William Shakspeers *Comedyes Histories, and Tragedyes* soe manie of the said Copies as are not formerly entred to other men, *viz*^t.' [Here follow sixteen plays under the several headings, the *Tragedies* being *Coriolanus, Timon of Athens, Julius Cæsar, Mackbeth, Anthonie and Cleopatra, Cymbeline* (see Arber's *Transcript*, iv. 69).] The play appeared in that year in the first folio, where it is placed between *Othello* and *Cymbeline*, and is consequently last but one in the book.

If, however, what I now put forward is not merely matter of coincidence, 1608 may be ruled out entirely and 1606 be granted a possibility beside 1607. Daniel's *Cleopatra* appeared in 1594, in that year's edition of his *Delia*: it was reprinted with some deletions and modifications in the *Poeticall Essayes* of 1599, in the folio editions of *Workes*, 1601 and 1602, and again in *Certaine Small Workes Heretofore Devulged by Samuel Daniel*, in 1605. In the next edition of *Certaine Small Workes*, however, namely that of 1607, an altered text appeared, which was repeated in the issues of 1609 and 1611, and also by itself in 1611. The *verso* of the general title-page of 1607 declared the play to be 'newly altred', and the question is: what induced Daniel to reconstitute his play between 1605 and 1607? Was it merely due to re-reading Plutarch with a maturer eye, and a growing preference for dialogue as against relation; or had the author been stimulated by a new treatment of the story to improve his own version, and guided in some respects in so doing? There is at least

1. † Probably 'blocking entries'; see Pollard, *Shakespeare Folios and Quartos* (1909), p. 78, and *Shakespeare's Fight with the Pirates* (1920), pp. 26–52. [R]

a probability that a sudden remodelling of old work, once already textually revised, may be accounted for on the latter score.

Dr Grosart, in his edition of Daniel (1885-6), drew attention to the additions of 1607 for the first time, as he thought, but Langbaine had long ago said—though apparently with muddling reference to the 1623 quarto: 'this later Copy infinitly differs from the former, and far exceeds it; the Language being not only corrected, but it having another advantage in the Opinion of a Modern Poet,(ᶜ) since that which is only dully recited in the first Edition, is in the last represented' (*An Account of the Dramatick Poets*, 1691, p. 101). Dr Grosart printed the additions before his reproduction of the earlier version as it reappeared in 1623, after Daniel's death, but without any hint of the comparison which I am suggesting. I have verified his statements by examining the various editions.

Cleopatra, especially as first written and first altered a few years later, is a stately rhymed tragedy after the Senecan model. It takes up the story of Cleopatra after Antony's death, and sadly dilutes its tragic force by pursuit of moral rather than romantic themes, in reflection on their conduct and its reward from Cæsar by the traitors Rodon and Seleucus, and on the faults and fortunes of Egypt by the philosophers Philostratus and Arius. It has, here and there in the earlier version, resemblances more or less slight to passages in *Antony and Cleopatra*, of which, omitting such as are traceable to the common source in Plutarch, the chief may be noticed here. The numbers I assign to the lines quoted are those of Dr Grosart's edition, which run consecutively throughout the play.

In Act I, l. 54, compare 'I have both hands, and will, and I can die' with IV. xv. 49 *post*, 'My resolution and my hands I'll trust'; also in ll. 69-70, 'That I should passe whereas *Octavia* stands, To view my misery', etc., the same dislike to submit to the gaze of her rival in Rome that Cleopatra expresses in IV. xv. 27-9, and v. ii. 54-5 *post*. In Act v, sc. ii, ll. 1475 *et seq.*, Cleopatra is described as sitting in all her pomp:

> as if sh' had wonne
> *Cæsar*, and all the world beside, this day:
> Euen as she was when on thy cristall streames,
> Clear *Cydnos*, she did shew what earth could shew; etc.

Compare v. ii. 227-8 *post*, 'I am again for Cydnus, To meet Mark Antony', and *ibid*. 345-6 *post*, 'As she would catch another Antony In her strong toil of grace.'

Though, on the whole, I think Shakespeare had, as was natural, Daniel's and other predecessors' work before him, however small

'(ᶜ) Mr. *Crown's* Epistle to *Andromache*.'

his use of it, such resemblances in thought, as, for instance, the effective retrospect to *Cydnus* here, might easily occur independently to writers of the same age exercising their genius on the same subject; and, if we take this view, their existence makes a little against the weight of any correspondences we may have to consider in the remodelled play. This, however, stands upon a different basis. It draws somewhat nearer to the contemporary drama by replacing relation and soliloquy to a great extent by dialogue, so that not only is the play more dramatic, but characters familiar to us in *Antony and Cleopatra* now play a greater part, viz. Charmian and Iras; others, Dercetas and Diomedes, are employed for the first time; Gallus becomes an interlocutor where he was but mentioned. It introduces the incident of 'Dircetus' bringing Antony's sword to Cæsar (see v. i *post*); and, by means of his relation, the story of the events preceding Antony's death, on the lines followed by Shakespeare in IV. xii (latter part), xiii, xiv, xv *post*, though of course with the comparative brevity of a narration. This constitutes a new scene of Act I, and is a detail in which Daniel had not previously thought fit to follow the example of the Countess of Pembroke. Further: the new scene contains certain noticeable expressions. The second line is, 'Will Antony yet struggle being undone?' and the second and third lines of Shakespeare's Act v *post*, on the same occasion:

> Being so frustrate, tell him, he mocks
> The pauses that he makes.

Again, 'Dircetus' says (l. 4): 'His worke is ended. *Anthony* hath done.' Compare *post*, IV. xiv. 35: 'Unarm Eros, the long day's task is done.' 'Dircetus', describing Antony's last efforts with his forces, uses the phrase, 'Had brought them to their worke', a possible reminiscence of Antony's 'I'll bring you to't' in IV. iv. 34 *post*. Further—always remembering that I am not recording resemblances which may be due to Plutarch—there is a significant use of a similar conceit in both plays on the occasion of Antony's being drawn up into the monument: compare Daniel's (p. 8, Grosart):

> When shee afresh renewes
> Her hold, and with r'inforced power doth straine,
> And all the weight of her weake bodie laies,
> Whose surcharg'd heart more than her body wayes.

with IV. xv. 33–4 *post*:

> Our strength is all gone into heaviness,
> That makes the weight.

The rest of the alterations of the play furnish nothing very material in the way of coincident thought, and remove some of the resemblances of the older version. The question rests on the parallels just given, the introduction of events from Plutarch treated also in certain scenes of *Antony and Cleopatra*, and the re-modelling of the play in more dramatic form; and though this evidence is by no means overwhelming, so far as it goes it is consistent with a hypothesis that Daniel re-wrote his play because he had seen another treatment of the theme, namely, Shakespeare's, and just so much probability follows that we should finally exclude 1608 in considering the date of *Antony and Cleopatra*, and admit 1606 to competition with 1607. Unfortunately, the Stationers' Registers do not appear to contain any entry which would enable us to determine whether Daniel's altered text came early or late in the latter year.

The fact is slightly corroborative of Daniel's imitation that he is thought to have similarly profited by Shakespeare's *Richard II*, owing to changes made in the second edition of his *Civil Warres*, 1595.[1] His name is maliciously associated with Shakespeare's in *The Returne from Parnassus* (assigned to 1598 by Fleay, *Chronicle of the English Drama*, ii), III. i. 1015, *et seq.*, p. 57, in Macray's edition, and in the later play of the same name, acted 1601 or 1602, he is exhorted to use his own wit and 'scorne base imitation'.[2] I am, of course, not interpreting his revision of *Cleopatra* in any such way here.

Finally, in connection with the date of *Antony and Cleopatra*, some resemblances which occur in other plays are perhaps worth mentioning. In *Nobody and Somebody*, entered in the Stationers' Registers in 1606, and, though an older play, probably revised at that time (see Simpson, *School of Shakespeare*, i, p. 272, and Fleay, as before, under Heywood, No. 31), King Archigallo resembles Antony in a certain point:

> There's *Elydure*
> Your elder brother next unto the king:
> He plies his booke; when shall you see him trace
> Lascivious *Archigallo* through the streets,
> And fight with common hacksters hand to hand
> To wrest from them their goods and dignities?[3]

1. It should be observed that whether Daniel's second edition (dated, like the first, 1595) or Shakespeare's *Richard II* appeared first, is quite uncertain; and that *1 Henry IV*, 1596–7, probably owes some detail to Daniel, as Dr Moorman has shown: see his Introduction to that play in *The Warwick Shakespeare*. As regards *Cleopatra*, however, adoption in a late text of a more dramatic method and detail previously ignored suggests, at least, a new model.

2. I. ii. 244–6, ed. Macray, 1886, p. 85.

3. Ll. 34–9. *School of Shakespeare*, i. 278.

and in Barnabe Barnes's *The Divils Charter*, first played 2 February 1607, entered 16 October, and printed same year after being 're-vised, corrected, and augmented', this passage occurs:

> *He draweth out of his boxes aspiks.*
> Come out here now you *Cleopatraes* birds.
> Fed fat and plump with proud *Egiptian* slime,
> Of seauen mouth'd *Nylus* but now turn'd leane:
> > *He putteth to either of their*
> > *brests an* Aspike.
> Take your repast vpon these Princely paps.
> Now *Ptolamies* wife is highly magnified,
> Ensigning these faire princely twins their death,
> And you my louely boys competitors,
> With *Cleopatra* share in death and fate.
>
> . . . .
>
> I see their coulors chang and death sittes heauy.
> On their fayre foreheads with his leaden mace.
> My birds are glutted with this sacrefice.
> > *He taketh of the* Aspiks *and put*
> > *teth them vp in his box.*
> What now proud wormes? how tasts yon princes blood.
> The slaues be plump and round; into your nest,
> Is there no token of the serpents draught,
> All cleere and safe well now faire boyes good-night.[1]

A passage in Chapman's *Bussy D'Ambois*, which furnishes two important parallels with our text (see on IV. xii. 37, xiv. 2–7 *post*) exists substantially in the first edition, which appeared in 1607. This play, in Mr Fleay's opinion, was written late in 1604,[2] and produced the next year.

The internal evidence for the date of composition is not thrown out of correspondence by the slight recession of date suggested. It depends on the complete change in metrical style approached through the plays since Hamlet, which deprives Shakespeare's blank verse of much music in its effort to become a more spacious continent of his multiplying thought; the increased percentage of lines in which the sense is carried on to the next without pause, and the consequent increase of stops within lines; the employment of the weak ending, prominent for the first time in *Macbeth* and now much more strikingly so; the increased use of the double or feminine end-

---

1. See McKerrow's edition in *Materialen zur Kunde des älteren Englischen Dramas*, 1904, ll. 2546–69, p. [71].

2. Chapman's latest editor, Mr T. M. Parrott, maintains this date, approximately, against appeals to Henslowe's *Diary* in support of 1598 for a first version. See his article in *Modern Language Review*, January 1908.

ing. Dependence on elocution to make a pause within a line metrically equivalent to a syllable, or a long line musical, is frequent in this play, and there is a free disposition of accent which gives grip and strength at the cost of some ruggedness; but all this does but deceive the sense of space; ellipse and ambiguous phrase show that no relaxation of metrical restraints could accommodate the ideas and images demanding utterance. The theme of the play, ethically considered as the consequence of grave defect in a nature generously endowed with noble traits, has been compared with those of *Macbeth* and *Coriolanus*, between which it has taken its place on the different considerations already stated.

Shakespeare's debt to Plutarch, Amyot, and Sir Thomas North, through the medium of the last named and especially to him, has been displayed in its real extent and with fine enthusiasm by Mr Wyndham, in his introduction to the reprint of North's *Plutarch* in the Tudor Translations. It has been necessary here only to make it as readily traceable as possible, by appending full extracts from the life of Antonius, and by giving complete references to them throughout the notes, sometimes for whole scenes, sometimes for particular passages, as the case demanded. The space they leave at my disposal will be divided between a few not very orthodox impressions of *Antony and Cleopatra*, whose excuse for non-suppression must be that they have survived long concern with the play, and some account of the other English plays on the same subject.

Since Coleridge's famous criticism of *Antony and Cleopatra* in his *Notes and Lectures*, there has been no danger of the play's being under-rated, and the impression received from many examens in which this criticism is cited is that there is a tendency for its doubt to be ignored and its limitations obscured. Coleridge expressed a 'doubt . . . whether the *Antony and Cleopatra* is not, in all exhibitions of a giant power in its strength and vigour of maturity, a formidable rival of the *Macbeth, Lear, Hamlet,* and *Othello*'; but even if we replace the doubt by an absolute certainty, there remains the fact that a special point of comparison is indicated, viz. 'all exhibitions of a giant power in its strength and vigour of maturity'. It is in this respect only that comparison is possible with the other plays named by Coleridge,[1] for, in the first place, *Antony and Cleopatra* belongs to a type of play defective in construction and absorbing centre of interest. The Chronicle play has its compensations: we see in

1. Here, and perhaps again, I may seem to have conveyed and mismanaged a hint from an article on *Antony and Cleopatra*, of far wider scope than these impressions, in the *Quarterly Review* for April 1906, by Professor A. C. Bradley; but in these respects I set down 'mine own rudeness rudely' months previously, and owe homage, not acknowledgment.

Antony and Cleopatra vivid presentation of the earlier processes which lead to tragedy, set before us in a series of significant pictures; but historical fact is lopped and telescoped only so far as is indispensable to a stage-plot, and it does not in this case provide any rousing incident till the play is far advanced. Secondly, there is in the theme at its intensest, and the characters at their deepest, a defect of tragedy in comparison with that of the greater plays. The world-tragedy—admitting for the sake of argument Dr Brandes' contention that the play is really and intentionally 'the picture of a world-catastrophe'—is here too little insistently obvious, and depends too much for its effect on the constitution of a reader's mind, to surround the sufferers with a deeper gloom than their destiny can bestow. The magnanimity of Antony sets him above fate at last, and the death of Cleopatra is her triumph. We see these lovers hasten to reunion 'where souls do couch on flowers'; there is what meeting for Othello and Desdemona?

> O ill-starr'd wench!
> Pale as thy smock! when we shall meet at compt,
> This look of thine will hurl my soul from heaven
> And fiends will snatch at it.

The appalling situations of Macbeth or Othello, set between retrospect and prospect of horror, have no parallel here, and the despairs of Antony and Cleopatra are never as theirs: the profundities of tragic feeling which awe us in their words belong to an abyss of which the two who have been erected to rivalry with them know nothing. The utterance of the latter, for all its magnificence of poetry and pathos, is more conscious, and has in it something of the luxury of woe: it is of their own plane of enchantment, where 'all the haunt' is indeed theirs; it is not humanly heart-rending, nor language of despair fit for a Hall of Eblis.

An extraordinarily vivid presentment in Elizabethan terms of events and characters of the ancient world, with truth to life as its one restraining condition, *Antony and Cleopatra* is almost as far removed from the tragedies as it is from the decorous treatment of the same theme by the Senecan school of poets. The ethical value of that theme is considerable, and has its due weight. Events enforce it, and draw from Enobarbus witty sarcasms, from Antony many a bitter reflection on his own folly. But this is all: the riotous life of pleasure betrays its charm beside its cost, and the ultimate effects of all the moralist would condemn are moral and not immoral. There is a temporary 'diminution in our captain's brain' as a permanent one in his fortunes, but all that is great in him, his heart-winning magnanimity in its various manifestations, is conspicuous as ever, and to this is now added the capacity for devotion and self-forgetfulness which he pitifully lacked before. It is absurd to shake our heads over Antony's love because, in the sharp reversal of the situation of himself and Cleopatra with respect to one another, he pays for the mortifications and distresses he had once inflicted on her, in frenzied doubts of a fidelity suspiciously unstable in our eyes as well as his. It must be tested by the unselfish devotion at the supreme hour which renders it incapable of differentiation from a virtuous passion and which (at first sight, at any rate) is in such striking contrast with Cleopatra's care for her own safety when love and pity should have exiled every other thought.

It is said that Shakespeare softened or suppressed Antony's worst traits as he found them in North; but his instanced cruelties and oppressions precede as much of the story as is retold in the play, and a dramatist must have gone out of his way to reveal in him anything beyond what we gather from his treacherous and cold-blooded treatment of Octavia. It is even questionable whether his good qualities are not more conspicuous in Shakespeare than in Plutarch only because of the diminished size of the canvas; but the former certainly gives them full dramatic effect, and from the first we are attracted by glimpses of the 'noble minde', 'the rare and singular gifts', with which Plutarch loves to 'soften to the heart' Antonius' story.

In this play, as in life, things extraneous to passion strengthen its hold for good or evil. In all probability, Antony must have returned to Cleopatra, but two factors besides infatuation are assigned, the 'holy cold and still conversation' of Octavia, and, very definitely, the supposed subjection of his genius to Cæsar's. Similarly, something *apparently* stronger than her love for Antony, yet, perhaps, connected with it—her royal determination to endure no bonds nor ignominy—seem to transform Cleopatra after his death and to allow that passion to gain depth and dignity under its powerful shelter. She deceives Cæsar with exultant cunning, and throughout, in her unswerving purpose, in the tolerance with which she suffers the garrulous clown, in the wonderful language of her exultation, free now from all suspicious notes, she exerts, in this dilation to a tragic figure, a fascination which some may have so far heard more about than felt.

To create his Cleopatra, Shakespeare to some extent forsook Plutarch. His Queen of Egypt is a figure of coarser fibre than that which moves in the prose narrative, even allowing for the strong lights of dialogue; and the arts of irritating perverseness employed in I. iii, where Cleopatra's conduct is not indicated in Plutarch, are of harder cast than 'the flickering enticements' with which, at a later time, the latter shows her seeking to keep Antony from Octavia; when she seemed to languish for love, contrived that Antony should often find her weeping, and then made show of hiding her tears, 'as if she were unwilling that he should see her weepe'. The original, with its subtlety preserved or augmented, is outgone in this draught of a type of the sex as well vehement and full-blooded as full of wiles and caprices, in whom qualities of brain and energetic life strike more than 'the courteous nature that tempered her words and deeds', and the gift of 'words . . . marvelous pleasant' less than its reverse; but the wondrous charm for which the character in its earlier manifestations is praised so unstintedly, seems, in the main, to be unconsciously transferred from the incomparable descriptions of Enobarbus. Of course it does not matter how the illusion is produced, except as a question for the critic; but Cleopatra, as self-revealed merely, does not, I venture to think, altogether justify the somewhat Lepidian 'kneel down, kneel down, and wonder' attitude of her admirers. Johnson spoke of 'the feminine arts, some of which are too low, which distinguish Cleopatra', but an earlier and kinder critic has set the tune of comment, and the most fastidious almost outvie his 'vilest things become themselves in her'.

If we apply to Cleopatra, and extend, her own metaphor for Antony, one way we look on majesty ('Isis else defend!'), the other way is painted in hues that belong to Madam Cæsarean's; but full front she is 'a very woman', and the question suggests itself: did Shakespeare intend to leave her a problem for this excellent reason? or was he unable to make up his own mind about her? We may probably dismiss from consideration any idea of the play's being incomplete as it stands, or even of vagueness due to haste.

We do not even know whether Cleopatra paltered with Cæsar after Actium, and there are ill-sounding notes in her protestations like the tuneless strings in a neglected instrument. We undoubtedly receive an impression, which I hinted at just now, and which seems to go unquestioned, that Shakespeare intentionally represented Cleopatra less favourably than Plutarch in dealing with the motive of her death. Such an impression goes for much, and the fewer the touches that produce it, the greater the writer's art; but even if the inquiry be narrowed to this last respect, it is worth making.

In Plutarch, there is no direct mention of what is so strongly enforced in Shakespeare, and previously in Daniel, Cleopatra's dread of being made part of Cæsar's triumph in Rome. He merely states the fact that Cleopatra would not open the gates of the monument, and later, that Dolabella, as she had requested him, informed her that Cæsar would within three days send her away before him with her children. In a moving speech at Antony's tomb, she lays stress on her preservation by Cæsar only that he may triumph over Antony: there is no word of her own fear of ignominy, and she implores Antony to help her to foil this attempt to triumph over him, and to save her from the misery she endures in living without him. Before this, Plutarch has already told us of her self-disfigurement for grief and her attempt to make the resulting fever fatal by the aid of starvation, from which she was only deterred by Cæsar's threat of slaying her children—a threat as little permanently effective as in Shakespeare, however, for Dolabella's news determines her action in Plutarch as in him.

Shakespeare's omissions throw into strong relief his development of the mere hint of a second motive for self-destruction, but it is not absolutely certain that he meant us to infer that this second motive was the only efficient one, and that Cleopatra would gladly have survived. He inserts in the final scene with Antony (l. 49) and after his death (l. 79 *et seq.*) expressions on the part of Cleopatra of determination to die, which rest as much or more on the desire not to outlive Antony as on the unwillingness to endure ignominy. He gives us no right to judge this determination weakened, for it is her first thought when we meet her next, and she reveals then, and in the ensuing scene with Proculeius, no incipient hope of life with grace at Cæsar's hands. She has her dagger ready when she is seized, her thought of starvation leaps to her lips, and the fact that, on such an occasion, what she naturally bursts out with is her dread and hatred of the triumph, does not exclude the continuance of her unwillingness to outlive Antony. Cæsar's lies cause her no hesitation, as they might be expected to do if she really cared to survive, or was only moved by fear of disgrace: her directions are at once given to Charmian (v. ii. 191), and this *precedes* Dolabella's final and positive information of Cæsar's purpose. Here, if anywhere, there is token of omission or confusion. Dolabella had previously assured her that Cæsar would lead her in triumph, and he had not, as he now says, been either commanded or sworn to obtain confirmation of that intention.

We have now once more a recurrence to the theme of Cæsar's triumph, this time partly to stimulate Iras (as Antony himself had used it to induce Eros to kill him), and it would be the height of absurdity to underrate the force of the desire to escape it as a motive in Cleopatra. I am only endeavouring to ascertain how far we are justified in regarding this, and this only, as what enabled her to 'be noble' to herself; and perhaps the best plea I can put in for her love is an appeal to the first appearance of these 'triumph' passages. It seems as if Shakespeare felt the necessity of accounting for Cleopatra's refusal to open the gates of the monument, and did so in a way which we interpret adversely to her; but let us recollect the lovers' last previous parting, and admit a doubt whether we should not, like Antony, 'weep for' our 'pardon'. In language as forcible as he could make it, which has not the remotest suggestion in Plutarch, Antony had at once declared his belief in Cleopatra's willingness to grace Cæsar's triumph, and the miserable part she would play in it. Such words would surely haunt her; and by her action and the echo of them now, even of the reference to Octavia— a feminine touch, which, if it were not an echo, would go far to overthrow my plea—she took the readiest way to prove their untruth, and to assure Antony that she would help no triumph over him,[1] nor let what he had so jealously engrossed suffer ignominy. If it were so, all was indeed—

> well done, and fitting for a princess
> Descended of so many royal kings.

The familiar of these great figures, Enobarbus, a keen-sighted mocking observer, with lapses into tiresome forced wit, and exaltations into the finest poetry, proves to have understood every one but himself, and knows neither the strength of the ties that bind him to Antony, nor his risk of remorse, nor his inability to bear it. With him, too, there is something extraneous that helps to determine his fate: we must add to remorse the small favour shown to master-leavers by Cæsar, neither so honourable nor adequate a help as the ague which carries him off in Plutarch. Cæsar himself, though cold and hard in contrast with his generous rival, is not heartless. The generous apostrophe to Antony into which he sugdenly breaks in I. iv, the warning appeal in III. ii, beginning: 'Most noble Antony, Let not the piece of virtue', etc., forbid our taking this view; and above all the pathos worthy of mighty rivals, lords of the world, in his lament:

> O Antony!
> I have followed thee to this; but we do lance
> Diseases in our bodies: I must perforce
> Have shown to thee such a declining day,

---

1. There is some significance in the language of the various passages. To Antony, she will not *brooch* Cæsar's triumph; to Proculeius and Iras later, it is indignities she dwells upon.

Or look on thine: we could not stall together
In the whole world: . . .

Finally, I retain some impression that *Antony and Cleopatra* was rather hastily written, with as much advantageous as injurious result if this had anything to do with the daring language and treatment, the 'happy valiancy' that Coleridge admired. Haste may have caused some peculiarities of construction, and caused the ready utilization of similar thoughts and illustrations when they cropped up in parallel cases: the number of reminiscences in *Antony and Cleopatra* has been noted and is sometimes put down to profound art. By supposing haste also, we may account for the occasional occurrence of common-place exaggeration.

The English plays on the same subject would almost provide material for a study of the forms of English tragedy. The Countess of Pembroke translated Garnier's *Marc-Antoine*, as *The Trajedie of Antonie*, into a monotonous blank verse, with here and there a few eloquent lines (sometimes affording illustrations for our text), and, in the choruses, short measures, often intricately rhymed, which served as models for Daniel in his *Cleopatra*, 1594. This latter play—which occupied me in the beginning of this introduction—is occasionally placed first owing to the date of impress of *Antonie* (1595); but *Antonie* was finished 'At Ramsbury 26. of November 1590', and was the cause, according to Daniel's dedication, of his digression from Delia's unkindness to a less absorbing subject. Till Shakespeare rescued it, the theme remained in the possession of the classical school: Fulke Greville, Lord Brooke, tells us in his life of Sidney,[1] that his tragedies 'were in their first creation three; Whereof Antonie and Cleopatra, according to their irregular passions, in forsaking empire to follow sensuality, were sacrificed in the fire. The executioner the author him selfe'. It appears that it did not thus regrettably perish as being inferior to his other plays, but owing to 'Many members in that creature—by the opinion of those few eyes which saw it—having some childish wantonness in them, apt enough to be construed or strained to a personating of vices in the present governors and government'.

Lord Brooke was followed by Samuel Brandon, whose work has survived and is named for re-issue in the admirable series edited by Professor Bang, of Louvain, *Materialen zur Kunde des älteren Englischen Dramas*. I have not seen this Senecan play, *The Virtuous Octavia*, 1598, but Mr Craig has kindly examined for me the copy in the Dyce Library at South Kensington, and has come to the conclusion, as I have done with regard to the other early plays, that

---

1. Chap. xiv, *Works*, ed. Grosart, iv. 155.

Shakespeare had cast an eye over his predecessor's work. There are two or three expressions recalling the like in other plays of Shakespeare, and for *Antony and Cleopatra*, putting aside as before coincidences traceable to Plutarch, there is a possible hint for Cæsar's description of Octavia's prevented welcome in an account of her reception at Athens, where, says 'Geminus (a Captaine)':

> Long before we could approach the gates
> Of that faire citty, we encountered were
> With people of all ages and estates,
> Who in their handes did boughes of laurel bear,
> Some on their knees with joy and wonder filled,
> Salute the empress; some rich gifts present,
> Some strew'd the way with flowers and some distill'd
> Their sweet perfumes along the fieldes we went. . . .
> Their loud applauses pierced the very skies,
> Extoll'd Octavia past the reach of fame,
> And silent Echo, waken'd with their cries,
> Taught all the neighbour hills to blesse her name.

The play is thus—save, of course, in its choruses—written in quatrains, like Daniel's *Cleopatra*. The scene is entirely in Rome, but the action (licentiously for such a play) covers a far longer period than that of the latter, and its dilutions promise to be less dry, two virtuous ladies and a wanton, for example, replacing Daniel's philosophers, and discussing constancy and variety in love. One of the former, in a later dialogue, excuses Antony's conduct on the ground of an affinity between him and Cleopatra as inevitable as that of the loadstone for iron.

After Shakespeare, Fletcher tried his hand on the delineation of Cleopatra, with some slight debt to him; but Cleopatra in 'the salad days' of her intrigue with Cæsar; and in the prologue to his play, *The False One* (*circa* 1620, according to Fleay), he pleads this as an excuse for meddling with the theme. The first to challenge comparison upon the same ground was Thomas May, the translator of Lucan, for whom, as a historical poet, much was said by Headley, and might be repeated. His *Cleopatra* was acted in 1626, printed in 1639, and its scheme is interesting, as coming between Shakespeare and Dryden, and showing how a learned and conscientious Caroline poet stood towards Elizabethan drama. May does not quite dismiss the comic element: he smooths out the actual representation of battle and sea-fight, but his time is partly coextensive with Shakespeare's, as he takes up the theme before the Actium disaster. Otherwise, his play disappoints, and its language irritates by balking expectation of just the little better that makes all the difference. But I except the *Thyreus* scene,[1] in which his

1. The scene is fine enough and inaccessible enough for rescue for comparison
here:

An.   Hands on that Thyreus there, to prison with him.
Thy.   To prison!
Ant.   Yes; away with him I say.
Thy.   *Cæsar* would not have us'd your messenger
           So ill.
An.   Thou wert no messenger to me.
Cle.   For my sake dearest Lord.
An.   O for your sake?
           I cry you mercy Lady, bear him hence.   [*Exit Thyreus.*
           I had forgot that *Thyreus* was your servant.
           But what strange act should he perform for you?
           Is it to help you to a happier friend?
Cle.   Can you suspect it? was my truest love
           So ill bestow'd? Can he, for whose dear sake
           A Queen so highly born as I preferr'd
           Love before fame, and fondly did neglect
           All names of honour when false *Fulvia*,
           And proud *Octavia* had the name of wives,
           Requite me thus? ungrateful *Anthony*:
           For now the fury of a wronged love
           Justly provokes my speech.
Ant.   Oh *Cleopatra*,
           It is not *Thyreus* but this heart of mine
           That suffers now, deep wounded with the thought
           Of thy inconstancie; did Fortune leave
           One only comfort to my wretched state
           And what a false one? for what conference
           Couldst thou so oft, and in such privacie
           With *Cæsar's* servant hold, if true to me?
           Which with the rack I could enforce from him.
           But that I scorn to do.
Cle.   You do not scorn
           To wrong with base unworthie jealousies
           A faithfull heart: but if you think me false
           Heer sheath your sword: make me the subject rather
           Of manly rage then childish jealousie.
           It is a nobler crime, and fitter farre
           For you to act, easier for me to suffer.
           For live suspected I nor can nor will.
           The lovely Aspe, which I with care have kept
           And was intended a preservative
           'Gainst *Cæsar's* crueltie, I now must use
           Against *Antonius* basenesse a worse fo
           Than Cæsar is: farewell, till death approve
           That I was true, and you unjust in love.
Ant.   Stay *Cleopatra*, dearest Love, forgive me
           Let not so small a winde have power to shake
           A love so grown as ours: I did not think
           That thou wert false: my heart gave no consent

usually colourless Antony achieves a kind of despairing pathos. His Cleopatra is false a while, but repents when she finds Cæsar proof against her charms.

The rhymed heroic play now claimed the subject. Sir Charles Sedley's *Antony and Cleopatra* was acted at the Duke's Theatre, with Betterton as Antony, in 1676 or 1677, and printed in the latter year, reappearing in 1702 as *Beauty the Conqueror* or *The Death of Marc Antony*. Sir Walter Scott (Dryden's *Works*, 1808, v. 293) and Dr A. W. Ward, in his *History of English Dramatic Literature*, treat it with severity, but it cannot be accused of rant, and takes its place among the heroic plays in which tragedy turns on manlike aims and passions rather than on strained points of honour. The story is taken up after Actium, the number of actors reduced, Cleopatra refined, and comedy expelled, while the plot is complicated by new loves; those of Mæcenas for Octavia, of Photinus, the ambitious traitor of the piece, for Iras, of Thyreus for Cleopatra. Antony and Cleopatra are, according to the kind, heroic and faithful lovers, and Canidius and other Romans prefer death to faithlessness or surrender. The play is full of life and bustle, combat and siege, and the whole can appeal, if we forget Shakespeare, who influences it in a general way.

In the meantime, or possibly owing to Sedley's example, the subject attracted the former champion of the heroic play: Dryden's *All for Love* was acted and printed in 1678. In it he abandoned rhyme and restored to the drama the art of writing good blank verse; this, too, without reproducing that of any previous writer or coming under the spell of Milton. The figures he drew deserve their own observance, but, thanks to critics less generous than himself, are seen only forlornly following Cæsar's triumph.

In *All for Love*, a close observance of the unities and restriction to few characters does not prevent the contrivance of an interesting series of events, to the development of which every scene contributes. The plot and characters show Dryden still influenced to some extent by the love and honour scheme of the heroic play. Cleopatra, save that she would sooner see her hero ruined with her than secure without her, is fidelity itself, and rejects Cæsar's ample offers; Antony is torn either way by the truth of Cleopatra and the generosity of Octavia. Love triumphs almost by accident, when jealousy and a natural collapse of Octavia's patience is vigorously

To what my tongue so rashly uttered
Nor could I have outliv'd so sad a thought.
Let *Thyreus* be releast, and sent to *Cæsar*.

marshalled to its aid. *All for Love* certainly contains some imitation and reminiscence of *Antony and Cleopatra*, but Dryden said truly that he had not copied his author servilely, and his play can be read and enjoyed as a study in a different manner, for its different conception of character, and its fine poetry, without the least compulsory reference to an all-belittling standard.

In preparing this edition I have been without the help of any on the same or a greater scale; but my obligations are many, as appears in the notes, and to the eighteenth-century editors of course incalculable. I owe to Mr Craig, the general editor of this Shakespeare, the most cordial thanks for help and encouragement throughout; and Mr Henry Cuningham, the editor of *A Midsummer-Night's Dream* in the same series, obliged me by investigating some material points at the British Museum. From my friend Mr J. Roy Coventry I had a useful loan of some of the early critical editions, and from Mr T. Harkness Graham, Assistant Librarian in the University of Liverpool, a most generous gift of time and scrupulous care in reading and correcting the whole of the proofs, and in verifying the numerous references, which will owe much of their exactness to him.

The following summarizes Mr Daniel's Time-Analysis of the play: twelve days are represented on the stage with intervals after the first, third, fourth, fifth, sixth, seventh, and ninth, the historic time being about ten years, 40 to 30 B.C.:

> Day 1. I. i–iv.
> „ 2. I. v, II. i–iii.
> „ 3. II. iv.
> „ 4. II. v–vii.
> „ 5. III. i, ii, iii.
> „ 6. III. iv, v.
> „ 7. III. vi.
> „ 8. III. vii.
> „ 9. III. viii–x.
> „ 10. III. xi–xiii, IV. i–iii.
> „ 11. IV. iv–ix.
> „ 12. IV. x–xv, V. i, ii.   [R. H. C.]

† I have little to add to this introduction. Three judgements on the play and the characters deserve to have attention drawn to them. Bradley's article in the *Quarterly*, at which Case glances on p. xxix, was later republished in his *Oxford Lectures on Poetry* (1909). It is probably the finest piece of concentrated criticism which even this great critic achieved. (I say 'great critic' because, though his

reputation is at the moment suffering from a natural, and perhaps salutary, reaction, I cannot believe that his stature can long remain obscured.) In 1944 Lord David Cecil published a lecture on *Antony and Cleopatra* in which he presents the interest as 'largely political'. Shakespeare, he thinks, 'conceived his play as a piece of history', and though there is a single presiding theme, 'this theme is not love, it is success'. He must find the play much duller than most of us do, but so odd a judgement, coming from a usually sane and sensitive critic, has at least the merit of making one think. Lastly, there is Dover Wilson's introduction to the play in the *New Shakespeare*. It exhibits, I think, a generous error to which he is liable: if he admires a character he cannot bear it to be less than almost wholly admirable; and this predisposition colours his judgement of both Antony and Cleopatra. But in the course of it he performs two signal services. The first is to draw attention to Dr Tarn's presentation of Cleopatra in the *Cambridge Ancient History*, vol. x, ch. 2. The other is to discuss the Seleucus scene, and emphasize the interpretation of it which I am sure is the right one, but which, since Stahr is now little read, and in any case was not writing about Shakespeare's play but about Plutarch's Cleopatra, is apt to escape the modern reader and producer. Stahr[1] pointed out that Plutarch says, at the end of the account of Cæsar's interview with Cleopatra, 'and so he took his leave of her, supposing he had deceived her, but indeed he was deceived himself' (North's translation); and North underlines this and makes the design explicit, by a marginal comment, 'Cleopatra finely deceiveth Octavius Cæsar *as though she desired to live*' (italics mine). That is to say, the whole scene with Seleucus is a put-up job, possibly even rehearsed beforehand. The easiest way of convincing Cæsar that she desires to live is to be exposed as having retained, and omitted from her declaration, half her fortune, to support not only life, but life in something like her former state.

This interpretation has two dramatic advantages. It prevents Cleopatra's assault on Seleucus being no more than an undignified repetition of the earlier scene with the messenger—a drop in tone which at this point of the play is hardly tolerable. And it gives us the pleasure of watching Cæsar out-played, not only walking headlong into the trap but (in ll. 183–8) thinking himself clever as he does so, so that Cleopatra's 'My master, and my lord!' can carry its full charge of irony, since she knows that he is already the ass, unpolicied. The only trouble about the interpretation is whether it can be made plain to the audience, since if it cannot it is not what Shake-

1. A. Stahr, *Cleopatra* (1864), and see Furness, *Variorum* edition, pp. xiii–xiv.

speare the practical playwright intended. But I think it can be done.[1] In the first place, the more quick-witted of the audience will wonder why Cleopatra brings in Seleucus at all—and it is her doing, not Cæsar's, that he is introduced. If Cæsar will not take her own word for her 'brief' he is not likely to take that of a subordinate official, presumably under her thumb. 'Hullo,' says the suspicious spectator, 'there is more here than meets the eye.' But I think the vital point is the way in which the actress playing Cleopatra delivers the words 'Speak the truth, Seleucus'. They are his cue. After that both he and Cleopatra, by slight exaggeration, he of his fears and she of her tantrums and her humiliation, indicate that they are playing a game.

But if the interpretation is right in itself, I think that in the application of it Dover Wilson overplays his hand. He is so anxious to establish Cleopatra's unswerving nobility, to show that her resolution to follow Antony at once never wavered, that he takes this interpretation of the Seleucus scene as proof positive of the unwavering resolution, and he also neglects an awkward interval and the conversation with Proculeius. Now that conversation, though it is possible to get round it, cannot safely be neglected; and the Seleucus scene turns out, on examination, to be irrelevant to the main issue. No one denies that Cleopatra contemplates suicide as at least a possibility. Even if she is only going to be driven to it as a last resort, still she will, when convinced of its necessity, need time for its achievement, and this time, she hopes, the scene with Seleucus will provide. If she finds that she can make satisfactory terms, little will have been lost; if she cannot, everything will have been gained. That is to say, the 'put-up-job' interpretation of the Seleucus scene fits as neatly and as dramatically into either reading of Cleopatra's state of mind as into the other.

It is perhaps worth while examining for a moment the stages in Cleopatra's progress towards suicide. In the first place, at any time we like anterior to the climax of the play, she has pursued infinite conclusions of easy ways to die. In a crisis, therefore, her thoughts will not be exercised by the mechanics of suicide, but only by its necessity or desirability; and we guess that the compulsion will need to be strong that drives her to it. Under the immediate shock of Antony's death she rises to a mood of exaltation; the odds is gone, the world is a dull place, we have no friend but resolution and the briefest end, so let us act after the high Roman fashion, rush into the secret house of death and make death proud to take us.

---

1. Dover Wilson says 'the episode can readily be played so as to bring it out to the audience', but makes no attempt to show how.

There is no mistake about that. But is it cynical to suggest that even here she does not exactly 'rush' into the house of death, as Antony did or tried to do, but gains time even from her own resolution on the grounds of burying Antony? There is then an interval, during which we have no clue to her thoughts except that she sends the 'poor Egyptian' to Cæsar to enquire his 'intents'. When next we see her (v. ii) she is again contemplating suicide, though in more philosophic fashion. She then has an interview with Proculeius, in which she expresses submission, states her terms, and suggests an interview with Cæsar. When captured by the guard she attempts suicide, and gives as reason for the attempt the hateful prospect of Cæsar's triumph—not a word of Antony. Her last message now to Cæsar is 'I would die.' Left alone with Dolabella she pays tribute to Antony, and having got Dolabella well-tempered she comes out with the direct question, 'Know you what Cæsar means to do with me?' and forces an answer from him. She has no time to comment on it before Cæsar enters. She plays her scene with Cæsar and Seleucus, and after Cæsar has gone despatches Charmian, presumably to arrange for the introduction of the asps. While Charmian is away she receives from Dolabella further confirmation of Cæsar's intentions and paints for herself and Iras a picture of the degrading circumstances of Cæsar's intended triumph. From the moment of Charmian's return not only is her 'resolution' indeed 'placed' and she 'marble-constant' but Antony at last is the expressed motive for the resolution. She is again for Cydnus to meet him, she claims him as her husband, and she will not, if she can help it, let Iras reach him first.

That, I think, is a fair statement of what the text shows us. Nothing can detract from Cleopatra's royal splendour at the end; but we should not allow our eyes to be so dazzled by it that we cannot examine what happens, or does not happen, earlier. There is, first, the short conversation with Proculeius before her capture. This reads to me like an honest attempt at negotiation. I admit that it may be construed as a dishonest playing for time; but if her resolution had been constant the time should not have needed to be played for. Far more crucial than the interview with Proculeius is the interval between the end of iv. xv and the opening of v. ii, an interval from which the supporters of the unwavering purpose resolutely avert their eyes, and do their best to avert the eyes of their readers. Dover Wilson, for example, says 'She announces it [the resolution] at the end of 4.15 immediately after Antony's own death, reiterates it at the opening of 5.2, and is only forced to postpone it by her unexpected capture and the interview with Cæsar.'

'Only forced to postpone it' seems to me a piece of clever but somewhat disingenuous special pleading. It is true *of the moment*; but what has Cleopatra been doing with the interval before this moment? There is as yet, so far as we know, no guard through whom the bearer of the asps has to be brought in, and so nothing in the world to prevent her arranging for his arrival when she chooses. I think that after her first moment of exaltation she would make terms with Cæsar if she could make her own, and is brought back to her original resolution only by her later conviction of Cæsar's intentions.

I have laboured the point only because I think that Shakespeare's portrayal of Cleopatra at the end of the play is far more subtly penetrating, and more unsparing, than some of his critics would like it to be.

What little else I have to say, particularly about the 'echoes' of which the play is so full, and which Case dismisses rather summarily on p. xxxiv, I have said some fifteen years ago.[1] And since the re-writing, merely for the sake of re-writing, of something which, whether well or ill said, was at least as clear as the writer could make it, is an unprofitable business, I am, by the courtesy of Messrs J. M. Dent & Sons, repeating it, with a few minor modifications.

To read this play is like watching a great tragic actor playing, as it were for his amusement and relaxation, a lighter part that is very far inside his compass. There is no carelessness about it; every touch is as perfect as imagination and long-trained technique can make it; but the perfection is achieved with a felicity of ease which is enthralling.

In two ways the play is sharply differentiated from the 'four great' tragedies. In the first place it is a love tragedy. Shakespeare opened his tragic career (if we may not unreasonably leave *Titus* out of the reckoning) with *Romeo and Juliet*, and he closed it (if again we may omit *Coriolanus* as being of a somewhat different order of play) with *Antony and Cleopatra*. These are both love tragedies, the one of youth, the other of maturity, and the fact that only twelve or thirteen years divide them shows the bitter rapidity of the maturing. In the second place we are left at the end of *Antony and Cleopatra* with less sense of waste than at the end of any of the others, not excepting *Romeo and Juliet*. When Antony says 'the nobleness of life is to do thus' we know that for himself, and perhaps also for Cleopatra, he is stating the mere truth; but unless his values were wrong it would not be the truth. Their passion ennobles them as nothing

1. *Shakespeare's Plays, a Commentary* (Dent, 1936).

else ever has or ever could, but also as, if they were themselves nobler, it would not. The world loses little by their passing; and indeed we know that for the world it is better that the course of the Roman State should on, cracking their link asunder. Finally the play has little dramatic tension, none of the complication followed by explication of plot which marks the others.

But all this is not to say that Shakespeare tried to write a tragedy like *Othello* or *Lear* and failed. He tried to write a drama of a different order, and royally succeeded. The different order may be also an inferior order, but there is no question about the success. The play is a brilliant *tour de force*, perhaps Shakespeare's high-water-mark of sheer technical brilliance. He is handling recalcitrant material. The story of Antony and Cleopatra as narrated by Plutarch or elsewhere, is not in its essence dramatic at all. There is no proper forward progress, and so no plot; there is merely a series of oscillations on the part of Antony. Under various influences—a weak loyalty to Octavia, a rather stronger loyalty to Rome, and, by far the strongest, the love of being a great fighting general and leading to victory his adoring troops—Antony swings like a compass needle; but he always comes to rest again pointing to the inevitable north. And not only is this story not essentially dramatic, but it is in danger of being a trifle sordid. The spectacle of a man of at least considerable qualities wasting them in an infatuation is not an ennobling spectacle, certainly not a tragic one. If this subject is to be lifted to any sort of greatness, something must be added to it, and Shakespeare met the difficulty in the only way in which it could be met (and which Dryden missed realizing) by giving to Antony a greatness other than that of his character. We must be made to feel him as a man whose fate matters to the world, to the course of history from then till now; we must ourselves stand under the arch of the ranged empire; we must not only be *told* that he is the triple pillar of the world, we must *see* him so, or we care little whether or not he is transformed into a strumpet's fool; but show him to us as the great triumvir, in consultation with Octavius and the slight, unmeritable Lepidus, and we realize that his fall may cause the world to totter. And so Shakespeare neglects the unities, and hurries us about in space and time (bringing in, for example, stray captains from Syria) so that we feel the surge of great events, and Antony's greatness among them, as determined things hold their way to destiny. And the greater, even in this historical sense, that Antony can be made, the greater, by a natural, if illogical, process, do we feel to be the woman who so enslaves him; and, moving further round the same circle, the greater that

Cleopatra becomes the less do we experience either wonder or distress at Antony's subjugation.

On the two main characters opinions have differed widely, as was indeed to be expected, human nature being what it is. A critic who sees mainly one side of Antony finds a man 'of the most noble and high spirit, capable at times of a thoroughly soldier-like life, and full of kind and generous feelings'. That is well said, and is true. Another, with his eyes rather on Antony's morals than his soldier-ship, sees that he is 'dissolute and voluptuous, and Cleopatra's depravity is congenial to his nature'; that is also true, except that depravity is hardly the right word, and that it is only to one side of his nature that the 'depravity' appeals. A third gives himself away by announcing that 'the passion of Antony for Cleopatra is too obviously spurious to command our sympathy'(!). A fourth sees well round the subject from its various angles: 'Antony appears as the soldier and the voluptuary, swayed alternately by love, by regret, by ambition, at one moment the great ruler of the divided world, at the next flinging his future away at the dictation of a passionate caprice.' That I think is both justly and clearly said, and leaves little to add. Antony has a magnificant virility about him, to which both men and women react; but he is a creature of impulse, he has no eye for the stars, and cannot steer a course; he wants what he wants strongly, and he wants it immediately; he is gener-ous, and even his faults are on the grand scale; he can descend to folly, but never to meanness.

Cleopatra gravels the critics of later ages as completely as she did those of her own. She is 'a brilliant antithesis' (whatever that may mean), 'a compound of contradictions', or (perhaps the best ex-ample of the meaningless verbiage of befuddled bewilderment) 'this glorious riddle, whose dazzling complexity continually mocks and eludes us'. She is often described as 'the courtesan of genius', but to take that phrase in isolation is fair neither to Cleopatra nor to the penetrating criticism from which it is isolated. 'Cleopatra is the greatest of the enchantresses. She has wit, grace, humour; the intoxication of sex breathes from her; she unites the passion of a great temperament with the fathomless coquetry of a courtesan of genius. . . . It is this magnificence which invests Cleopatra's crimin-ality with a kind of sublimity, so vast is the scale of her being, and so tremendous the force of her passions.' That also, I think, is just. It is easy to miss the cutting and balanced precision of Shakespeare's delineation of Cleopatra. If only we will hear, it is as though we were members of a jury, listening to the summing-up of the most dispassionate and brilliant of judges. When once we have read the play it is hard not to reflect back upon the Cleopatra of the first four acts the light and colour of the Cleopatra of the last. In the last act she is the great queen, and is indeed fire and air; no doubt she would have made terms with Cæsar if she could have made her own, but, seeing that she cannot, she will follow Antony, and if she is to die, she will die indeed painlessly, but she will do it after the high Roman fashion; and Death would be a poor creature if he was not proud to take her. But if our eyes are not dazzled by this reflection we shall recognize that it would be hard to find anywhere in literature a more unsparing picture of the professional courtesan than Shakespeare's picture of Cleopatra in the first four acts. Her aim indeed is not ignoble; she is genuinely, and perhaps for the first time in her life, in love; Antony at last realizes her ideal; but the methods by which she achieves her aim and holds him are those of the past-mistress in her ancient art, learnt and perfected to the last finesse of technique in years in which she hung the scalps of Cæsar and Pompey, amongst others, at her belt. The bafflement of the critics, or some of them, about her seems to depend on a confusion of complexity with variety. She is infinitely varied, but not in the least complex; she is as single-minded in pursuit of her aim as Lady Macbeth in pursuit of hers, and all the quick shifts of temper are little more than part of her brilliant technique. Perhaps in the end the best description of her is Enobarbus' simple 'a wonderful piece of work'. That at least avoids any idle questionings as to the morality or immorality of the love of Antony and Cleopatra.

For, unless we suffer from a kind of moral myopia, we are little troubled as we read, and even less as we see, by questions of worthiness or unworthiness, still less of morality and immorality. We have been transported to a world in which such disputes seem to lose their meaning. Admittedly it is far from the noblest kind of world, as the two main figures are far from human nature at its noblest. But, being what they are, they are by their mutual passion lifted to the highest pitch to which they are capable of soaring. It is the merest fatuity of moralizing to deny the name of 'love' to their passion, and write it off as 'mere lust'. No doubt it is not the highest kind of love; it is completely an *égoisme à deux*, and has no power to inspire to anything outside itself; but it has in it something that should be an element in the highest kind of love; and at least it is the passion of human beings and not of animals, of the spirit as well as of the body. It was not by her beauty (of which by all accounts the gods had not been lavish) but by her superb vitality that Cleopatra took Antony captive and held him.

And it is by that same vitality that she takes us captive also. We may attempt to analyse the play, to apply critical criteria to it, to examine the characters, and so on; and no doubt we are right to do so, and by so doing help our appreciation of the play. But in the end these intellectual exercises and their results drift down the wind like the idle thistledown that for this play they are; we know in our hearts that what in this play Shakespeare has to offer us is a thrill, a quickening of the pulses, a brief experience in a region where there is an unimagined vividness of life; and we surrender, with Antony, if anything so vitalizing can be called surrender, to the 'strong toil of grace'.

Octavius is an unattractive figure, but one worth study, not so much for himself as because he draws our wandering attention to a noticeable feature of the play. In the first three acts, by touch on subtle touch, the relentless power of Rome is forced on our subconscious notice. We are made to feel that it is something against whose ineluctable march no individuals, however great, can for one moment stand. Octavius, like the equally unattractive Aeneas, is the typical Roman; and at the end he, the 'cold Cæsar', is more than himself: he is Rome, looking down, with a just and not unsympathetic estimation, on the 'pair so famous' over whom her chariot wheels have rolled.

When all is said, the peculiar glory of this play is not in its dramatic quality at all. It is in its poetry. It is full, to begin with, of phrases in Shakespeare's best later manner, where the whole force depends on the use of a word, or a juxtaposition of words, which would startle us if we were not aware of their inevitable rightness before we have time to be startled. For example:

> the odds is gone,
> And there is nothing left remarkable
> Beneath the visiting moon.   (IV. xv. 66)

Again, it is full of echoes, like:

> *Ant.* Unarm, Eros, the long day's task is done,
> And we must sleep.   (IV. xiv. 35)

> *Iras.* Finish, good lady, the bright day is done,
> And we are for the dark.   (V. ii. 192)

Or

> *Ant.*   I will be
> A bridegroom in my death, and run into 't
> As to a lover's bed.   (IV. xiv. 99)

> *Cleo.* The stroke of death is as a lover's pinch,
> Which hurts, and is desir'd.   (V. ii. 294)

Or

> *Cleo.* And when thou hast done this chare, I'll give thee leave
>   To play till doomsday. (v. ii. 230)
> *Char.*   Your crown's awry,
>   I'll mend it, and then play. (v. ii. 317)

Or the triple chime on 'royal' in the last scene, where Shakespeare is stressing Cleopatra the queen:

> *Char.*   Downy windows, close,
>   And golden Phoebus, never be beheld
>   Of eyes again so royal! (v. ii. 315)
> *Char.* It is well done, and fitting for a princess
>   Descended of so many royal kings. (v. ii. 325)
> *Cæs.*   Bravest at the last
>   She levell'd at our purposes, and being royal
>   Took her own way. (v. ii. 333)

Finally, we have here beyond question Shakespeare's topmost achievement in dramatic poetry, that kind of poetry which apart from its context is little remarkable, but in its dramatic setting is indefinably moving. The earlier plays are full of pure lyric poetry which is quite irrelevant to the action of the play, and not infrequently even out of character for the person who speaks it; and even down to the end of Shakespeare's dramatic career, down to *The Tempest*, with its cloud-capped towers, there will occur passages which can be lifted with little loss from their contexts. But in this play, with the sole exception of the description of Cleopatra's barge, most incongruously put into the mouth of the prosaically, however penetratingly, common-sensical Enobarbus, there is hardly a line which is not in character, and perhaps no considerable memorable passage which can stand by itself, none that can be excerpted, without losing half its force; while there is passage after passage, line after line, of which the force in its setting is electric. To take two examples only:

> I am dying, Egypt, dying: (IV. xv. 41)

Four (or three) very ordinary words, and a proper name, as they stand prosaic enough; but spoken by the dying Antony, to his royal lover, his serpent of old Nile, they are potent and poignant magic. Or again:

> Dost thou not see my baby at my breast,
> That sucks the nurse asleep? (v. ii. 308)

Write that for its natural context, the description, let us say, of a happy and carefree mother, and it is a piece of quiet competence that no one will think of twice. Put those same words in the mouth of the great queen, standing in her full and final majesty, robed and crowned for the stroke of her last fatal lover, with the asp at the breast that had suckled her children, and the world catches its breath.   [R]

References to passages in other plays of Shakespeare's are to the single volume Oxford edition (ed. W. J. Craig).

For the other writers chiefly referred to the following list of editions may be useful. In selecting the editions I have been guided not only by intrinsic excellence but in part by considerations of accessibility and ease of reference. Some otherwise admirable editions have no line-numbering, and it is a vexatious business to try to locate a brief passage with nothing but act and scene to help one.

Beaumont and Fletcher	Variorum edition (Bell & Bullen, 1904–12) so far as available; for other plays the Glover-Waller edn. (C.U.P. 1905–12).
Chapman	Plays, ed. Parrott (Routledge, 1910); Poems, ed. Shepherd (Chatto & Windus, 1875).
'Doubtful' plays	*Shakespeare Apocrypha*, ed. Tucker Brooke (Clarendon Press, 1908).
Gammer Gurton's Needle	*Representative English Comedies*, ed. C. M. Gayley (Macmillan Co., New York, 1903).
Jonson	ed. Herford and Simpson (Clarendon Press, 1925–52).
Kyd	ed. Boas (Clarendon Press, 1901).
Lyly	ed. Warwick Bond (Clarendon Press, 1902).
Marlowe	ed. Tucker Brooke (Clarendon Press, 1910).
Marston	ed. Bullen (Nimmo, 1887).
Middleton	ed. Bullen (Nimmo, 1885–6).
Nashe	ed. McKerrow (Clarendon Press, 1905–12).
Peele	ed. Bullen (Nimmo, 1888).
Ralph Roister Doister	as for *Gammer Gurton's Needle*.
Webster	ed. F. L. Lucas (Chatto & Windus, 1927).

ANTONY AND CLEOPATRA

DRAMATIS PERSONÆ[1]

ANTONY,
OCTAVIUS CÆSAR, } *triumvirs.*
LEPIDUS,

SEXTUS POMPEIUS.

DOMITIUS ENOBARBUS,
VENTIDIUS,
EROS,
SCARUS, } *friends of Antony.*
DECRETAS
DEMETRIUS,
PHILO,

MÆCENAS,
AGRIPPA,
DOLABELLA,
PROCULEIUS, } *friends of Cæsar.*
THIDIAS,
GALLUS,

MENAS,
MENECRATES, } *friends of Pompey.*
VARRIUS,

TARUS, *lieutenant-general to Cæsar.*
CANIDIUS, *lieutenant-general to Antony.*
SILIUS, *an officer in Ventidius' army.*
A 'schoolmaster' *acting as ambassador from Antony to Cæsar.*
ALEXAS,
MARDIAN, *a eunuch,* } *attendants on Cleopatra.*
DIOMEDES,
SELEUCUS, *treasurer to Cleopatra.*
A *soothsayer.*
A *Clown.*

CLEOPATRA, *queen of Egypt.*
OCTAVIA, *Cæsar's sister.*
CHARMIAN, } *attendants on Cleopatra.*
IRAS,

Officers, Soldiers, Messengers, and other attendants.

SCENE: *In several parts of the Roman empire.*

---

1. There is no list of *dramatis personæ* in F. It is first given (more or less) by Rowe, and expanded and emended by later editors. For Decretas and Thidias, instead of the more usual Dercetas and Thyreus, see notes on IV. xiv. 104 S.D. and III. xii. 31 respectively.

2

ANTONY AND CLEOPATRA

ACT I

SCENE I.—[*Alexandria. A room in Cleopatra's palace.*]

Enter DEMETRIUS *and* PHILO.

Phi. Nay, but this dotage of our general's
    O'erflows the measure: those his goodly eyes,
    That o'er the files and musters of the war
    Have glow'd like plated Mars, now bend, now turn
    The office and devotion of their view   5
    Upon a tawny front: his captain's heart,
    Which in the scuffles of great fights hath burst
    The buckles on his breast, reneges all temper,

ACT I
Scene 1
Act I. Scene I.] *Acts and scenes not marked, save here, in* F.

1. *general's*] Cf. *John*, II. i. 65: 'a bastard of the king's,' and I. ii. 71 *post*. The double genitive still occurs in colloquial usage.

4. *plated*] See *R2*, I. iii. 28: 'Thus *plated* in habiliments of war,' and Heywood, *The Silver Age* (*Works*, Pearson, iii. 132): 'Were his head brasse, or his breast doubly *plated* / With best Vulcanian armour Lemnos yeelds;' etc.

bend, now turn] This is the pointing of F. Editors place a comma after *turn*, but *bend* may be independent, expressing a contrast to the fiery outlook inferred in *glow'd*, and without influence on *the office*, etc. Cf. Jonson, *The Poetaster*, v. ii. 92: 'Nor do her eyes once *bend* to taste sweet sleep.'

5. *office*] service, as in *R2*, II. ii. 136: 'for little *office*, / The hateful commons will perform for us.' There seems no reason to deprive *devotion* of its separate

force, as some do, by regarding *office and devotion* as a hendiadys, equivalent to 'devoted service.'

6. *front*] forehead, and so face.

8. *reneges all temper*] refuses *or* renounces all self-restraint. Fletcher's *Maid's Tragedy* concludes with: 'May this a fair example be to me, / To rule with *temper*:' etc. A late instance of *renegue* is in Ferrand Spence's *Lucian*, 1684, ii. 43: '*Lucian.* . . . What say you, *Diogenes*, know you this Dapper Blade? He's of your Pond. *Diogenes*. I *renegue* him for mine.' Steevens quotes *Lr*, II. ii. 82, '*Renege*, affirm,' and Stanyhurst's Virgil, *Æneis*, 1582, bk II: 'Too liue now longer, Troy burnt, hee flatlye *reneaged*' (see Arber's repr., p. 64, and also pp. 75, 143). For the pronunciation, Halliwell quotes Sylvester's Du Bartas [*The Battail of Ivry*, lines 33–4] and adopts the spelling

3

And is become the bellows and the fan
To cool a gipsy's lust.

Flourish. Enter ANTONY, CLEOPATRA, *her Ladies, the Train,
with Eunuchs fanning her.*

Look, where they come: 10
Take but good note, and you shall see in him
The triple pillar of the world transform'd
Into a strumpet's fool: behold and see.
Cleo. If it be love indeed, tell me how much.
Ant. There's beggary in the love that can be reckon'd.   15
Cleo. I'll set a bourn how far to be belov'd.
Ant. Then must thou needs find out new heaven, new earth.

Enter an Attendant.

17. S.D. *Enter an Attendant*] Capell; *Enter a Messenger. F.*

suggested by Coleridge in *Notes and Lectures, reneagues*: 'All Europe nigh (all sorts of Rights *reneg'd*) / Against the Truth and Thee unholy leagu'd.'

9–10. *bellows . . . To cool*] Johnson suggests *to kindle and to cool*, misled by the usual use of the bellows; for which, as a cooling implement, Steevens quotes Lyly's *Midas*, v. ii. 84: 'methinks *Venus* and Nature stande with each of them a paire of *bellowes*, the one cooling my lowe birth, the other kindling my loftie affections.' Malone cites also Spenser, *Faerie Queene*, II. ix. 30: 'But to delay the heat, least by mischaunce / It might breake out and set the whole on fyre, / There added was by goodly ordinaunce / An huge great payre of *bellowes*, which did styre / Continually, and cooling breath inspyre.'

10. *gipsy's*] Not colour only but conduct is aimed at in the word. For its contemptuous or insulting application to any woman, see Shirley, *The Traitor*, II. i: '*Gipsy*, use better language, / Or I'll forget your sex.' See also on IV. xii. 28 *post*, on the word and its further supposed application to Cleopatra.

12. *triple pillar*] applied to Antony as

one of the three, the Triumvirs, who governed the world between them. Cf. Sir Thomas Browne, *Religio Medici*, section xix: 'I have therefore always endeavoured to compose those feuds and angry dissensions between Affection, Faith and Reason; for there is in our soul a kind of Triumvirate, a Triple Government of Three Competitors, which distracts the Peace of this our Commonwealth not less than did that other the state of *Rome*.' For *triple* = third, cf. *All's W.*, II. i. III: 'Which . . . He bade me store up, as a *triple* eye,' etc.

13. *strumpet's fool*] There were professional fools whose places entitled them to this description. Such is the fool in *Tim.* See Douce, *Illustrations of Shakes.*, 1807, i. 151; ii. 73, 304 *et seq.*

15. *There's beggary . . . reckon'd*] Steevens furnishes references to *Rom.*, II. vi. 32: 'they are but *beggars* that can count their worth'; Martial, lib. vi, ep. 34: '[Basia] pauca cupit, qui numerare potest'; *beggary* is niggardliness, meanness, cf. *Cym.*, I. vi. 115.

16. *bourn*] boundary, as in *Ham.*, III. i. 79.

17. S.D. Enter an Attendant] The 'messengers' are waiting outside.

Att. News, my good lord, from Rome.
Ant.   Grates me, the sum.
Cleo. Nay, hear them, Antony:
      Fulvia perchance is angry; or who knows   20
      If the scarce-bearded Cæsar have not sent
      His powerful mandate to you, 'Do this, or this;
      Take in that kingdom, and enfranchise that;
      Perform't, or else we damn thee.'
Ant.   How, my love?
Cleo. Perchance? nay, and most like: 25
      You must not stay here longer, your dismission
      Is come from Cæsar, therefore hear it, Antony.
      Where's Fulvia's process? Cæsar's I would say. Both?
      Call in the messengers. As I am Egypt's queen,
      Thou blushest, Antony, and that blood of thine   30
      Is Cæsar's homager: else so thy cheek pays shame
      When shrill-tongued Fulvia scolds. The messengers!
Ant. Let Rome in Tiber melt, and the wide arch

18. *Att.*] *Capell; Mes.* F.

18. *Grates me, the sum*] offends me: be brief. See Middleton, *No Wit [Help] Like a Woman's*, i. i. 9: 'but I'm *grated* [=*vexed*] / In a dear, absolute friend,' etc. F's comma (as against many editors' colon) gives Antony's impatience.

19. *them*] i.e. the news. *News* is sometimes singular, as in iii. vii. 54 *post*; *Lr*, iv. ii. 87; sometimes plural, as in *Rom.*, ii. v. 22.

23. *Take in*] subdue, occupy. See iii. vii. 23 *post*, on which Steevens quotes Chapman's Homer, *Iliad*, ii. 10. The expression occurs again and again in that book, e.g. line 22: 'Thy strong hand the broad-way'd town of Troy / Shall now *take in*.'

enfranchise] set free.

26. *dismission*] similarly for *dismissal* in *Cym.*, ii. iii. 57.

28. *Fulvia*] Antony's wife.

process] summons; the name of the whole course of proceedings in a cause, being so applied, according to Minshew, because the calling into court '*is the* beginning *or the* principall part

thereof, *by which the rest of the* business is directed,' etc. See Forman's *Diary* (ed. Halliwell, 1849), under 1590: 'The 26. of Julii I was served with *proces* to apeare at the Star chamber, before the counsell'; Overbury, *Characters*, 1616, *An Apparatour*: 'Thus lives he in a golden age, till Death by a *processe*, summons him to appeare.'

31. *homager*] vassal. So Browne, *Britannia's Pastorals*, i. iii. 742: 'A many *homagers* to Tamar's crown.'

else so . . .] or else (even more humiliating) it is your usual reaction to Fulvia's reproaches.

32. *shrill-tongued Fulvia*] See North, *post*, p. 242.

33. *Let Rome . . . melt*] Cf. ii. v. 78 *post*.

33–4. *arch . . . rang'd empire fall!*] *rang'd* is probably ordered, having its parts in due succession. The main conception is elusive. Should the mind momentarily image a structure supported by a vast arch, or 'a fabric standing on pillars' (Johnson), or the

Of the rang'd empire fall! Here is my space,
Kingdoms are clay: our dungy earth alike   35
Feeds beast as man; the nobleness of life
Is to do thus: when such a mutual pair,   [*Embracing*.
And such a twain can do't, in which I bind,
On pain of punishment, the world to weet
We stand up peerless.

Cleo.   Excellent falsehood!   40
Why did he marry Fulvia, and not love her?
I'll seem the fool I am not; Antony
Will be himself.

Ant.   But stirr'd by Cleopatra.

---

34. rang'd] raing'd *F*.   37. *Embracing*] *Pope*; *not in F*.

mighty vault of a great hall or nave?
The alternative would be to suppose
the words imply an arch only, itself the
empire, with Rome as keystone, and
the extent on either side implied in
rang'd. The well-known passage in
Cor., III. i. 203: 'That is the way to lay
the city flat; / To bring the roof to the
foundation, / And. bury all, which yet
distinctly *ranges*, / In heaps and piles of
ruin;' is cited in *OED* under: 'Of
things, especially buildings and their
parts, . . . to stretch out or run in a line,
to extend.' I find in Laneham's *Letter*,
etc., 1575 (Ballad Society, 1871, p.
50), in the account of a large building
used as an aviary, the architrave described as '*raunging* about the Cage.'
Malone having remarked that *range*
was apparently 'applied, in a peculiar
way, to mason-work in our author's
time,' and having quoted Spenser,
Faerie Queene, II. ix. 29, 'With many
raunges reard along the wall,' without
a hint that these *raunges*, however con-
structed, were merely kitchen ranges,
Steevens subjoined: 'What in ancient
mason's or bricklayer's work was de-
nominated a *range*, is now called a
course.' Rowe read *the rais'd empire*.
Bearing on the possibility of a misprint, Mr Craig notes that the spelling
raing'd is exceptional.

35. *dungy*] Cf. *Wint.*, II. i. 155–6:
'There's not a grain of it [honesty] the

face to sweeten / Of the whole *dungy*
earth.'

37. *a mutual pair*] i.e. a pair who
interchange equal love.

39. *to weet*] to wit, i.e. to know. So
Spenser, *Faerie Queene*, III. i. 19, and
often. See also *Gammer Gurton's Needle*,
II. iii. 10: 'Tush, man, is Gammers
neele found? that chould gladly *weete*.'

40–2. *Excellent . . . not*] Johnson
marked this as an aside, a plausible
though not convincing conjecture.

Excellent] †surpassing; here, as
often, in uncomplimentary sense; cf.
R3, IV. iv. 52, '*excellent* grand tyrant',
and *Lr*, I. ii. 132, '*excellent* foppery.'
I suspect that we should read a
comma after *Why*. Cleopatra is not
asking why Antony married Fulvia,
but saying: 'The fact that he married
her proves that he loved her.' [R]

42–3. *Antony . . . Cleopatra*] It is
slightly in favour of a previous aside
(see last note) that 'Antony will be
himself' (i.e. noble, peerless as he is),
may revert to *peerless*, the whole being
equivalent to Antony will show himself noble, as he is. *Ant.* Only if inspired by Cleopatra. This is, in any
case, substantially the usual interpretation. Johnson, taking *but* in its excep-
tive sense (cf. III. xi. 47 *post*), understood: 'Antony will recollect his
thoughts,' 'Unless kept in commotion
by Cleopatra'; and I have sometimes

Now for the love of Love, and her soft hours,
Let's not confound the time with conference harsh: 45
There's not a minute of our lives should stretch
Without some pleasure now. What sport to-night?
Cleo. Hear the ambassadors.
Ant.   Fie, wrangling queen!
Whom every thing becomes, to chide, to laugh,
To weep: how every passion fully strives   50
To make itself, in thee, fair and admired!
No messenger but thine, and all alone,
To-night we'll wander through the streets, and note
The qualities of people. Come, my queen,
Last night you did desire it. Speak not to us.   55
                    [*Exeunt Ant. and Cleo. with their Train.*
Dem. Is Cæsar with Antonius priz'd so slight?
Phi. Sir, sometimes, when he is not Antony,
He comes too short of that great property
Which still should go with Antony.
Dem.   I am full sorry
That he approves the common liar, who   60

---

47. now] *F*; new *Warburton.*   50. how] who *F*; whose *F2. See note.*   55. S.D.
Exeunt . . .] *Capell; Exeunt with the Traine. F.*

thought that Cleopatra's reference
might be to Antony's conduct at the
moment; and the sense: Antony will
be Antony, play the lover, embrace.
Ant. Yes, unless angered by Cleopatra.
What follows is a plea against such
angering. Cf. Beaumont and Fletcher,
Philaster, I. i. 268: 'Be more yourself, as
you respect our favour; / You'll stir us
else:' etc.

45. *confound*] waste. See I. iv. 28 *post*,
and *Cor.*, I. vi. 17.

50. *how*] †F's *who* is clearly impossible, and F2's emendation, *whose*, has
been universally accepted. But it is not
wholly satisfactory, and I suggest *how*.
It is graphically a trifle easier, assuming the transposition of one letter by
the compositor rather than the omission of two, and it regularizes somewhat confused syntax, since *in thee* is
redundant after *whose*. This second
argument goes for little, since the

redundancy is not un-Shakespearean,
but I think that the picture with *how* is
the better of the two. The passions are
not Cleopatra's possessions, but independent things, looking for someone in
whom to display themselves to the best
advantage, and finding their show-
ground in Cleopatra. [R]

52. *No . . . thine:* etc.] For Antony's
treatment of ambassadors, see North,
post, p. 244; for the rest, *ibid.*, p. 249.

54. *qualities*] characters or characteristics. The word is also frequent in the
sense function, profession, as in *Ham.*,
II. ii. 461. Cf. Whetstone, *Promos and
Cassandra*, v. i (*Six Old Plays*, Nichols,
i. 49): 'but now tell me / What *quality*
hast, that I may use thee? / *Rosk.* I am
a Barbour.'

55. *Speak . . . us*] to the messenger
who waited for the news.

58. *property*] distinctive quality.

60. *approves*] corroborates. So in *Lr*,

Thus speaks of him at Rome; but I will hope
Of better deeds to-morrow. Rest you happy!   [*Exeunt.*

[SCENE II.—*The same. Another room.*]

Enter ENOBARBUS, LAMPRIUS, *a Soothsayer,* RANNIUS, LUCILLIUS,
CHARMIAN, IRAS, MARDIAN *the Eunuch,* and ALEXAS.

Char. Lord Alexas, sweet Alexas, most any thing Alexas,

Scene II

1. Lord] *Johnson;* L. F.

II. ii. 167: 'Good king, that must
approve the common saw'; *Ham.*, I. i.
29: 'He may *approve* our eyes,' i.e. con-
firm their witness. Malone rather unnecessarily takes 'the common liar' to
be Fame.

61–2. *hope Of*] So in *Meas.*, III. i. 1:
'So then you *hope of* pardon from Lord
Angelo?'

62. *Rest you happy*] Cf. 'Rest you
merry,' *Rom.*, I. ii. 65; 'Sit you merry,
sir,' Johnson, *Bartholomew Fair*, IV. vi.
55, said ironically to Waspe when he is
put in the stocks. The full phrase
appears in *AYL.*, v. i. 66: 'God rest
you merry, sir.'

Scene II

S.D. Enter . . .] †Of the nine characters in F's entry (or eight if we take
'Lamprius' to be the name of the
soothsayer) four (or three) have nothing to say throughout the scene, and
three of the names occur nowhere else
in the play. The usual way, since
Steevens, of treating this entry has
been to excise Lamprius, Rannius,
Lucilius, and Mardian, to bring in
Charmian, Iras, Alexas, and the soothsayer together, and defer Enobarbus'
entry till after line 10. I do not think
that this at all represents Shakespeare's
intention. And it is a good example of
what happens when one starts playing
fast and loose with Shakespeare's
stage-directions, and neglects to keep
an eye on the stage. In the first place it

makes something near nonsense of
Charmian's opening question; if a
group of four people enter together it
is merely silly for one to ask a second
where the fourth member of the quar-
tet is; and Alexas' 'Soothsayer!' is
clearly in the nature of a summons.
(This no doubt could be met by giving
the soothsayer his entry after line 6.)
In the second place there is no reason
why Enobarbus should not be among
the first entrants. No doubt, again, he
could enter after line 10, throwing his
order over his shoulder as he comes in,
but he is then left up in the air, since
the others neglect him, and he has no
more to say till line 44, which would
not matter with a character on already
but is dramatically clumsy with a
fresh entrant. With this in mind it is
worth examining F's entry again, and
in particular the *order* of it, since I
think that the order of a Shakespearean entry is sometimes significant (see
note on II. vi below, and compare
Hamlet's first entry (in Q2), universally and disastrously emended by all
editors from F inclusive downwards
till Dover Wilson saw the dramatic
point and restored the Quarto reading). The characters fall into two
groups, one of Enobarbus, a soothsayer, and two (or three) non-speaking
figures who, from their names, are
presumably Romans; and an Egyptian
group, of Cleopatra's waiting women,
Mardian, and Alexas. (There is just

almost most absolute Alexas, where's the soothsayer
that you prais'd so to the queen? O that I knew this
husband, which, you say, must charge his horns with
garlands!   5

4. charge] *Theobald (Warburton and Southern MS)*; change *F.*

this much to be said for thinking Lamprius to be the soothsayer that this
would give the two speaking characters first, followed by the two
supers.) Dover Wilson saw this, and
brings in 'Enobarbus and three other
Romans talking with a Soothsayer,'
and then 'a little after,' the Egyptian
group. I do not think that this is a
possible interpretation of F's entry. A
scene-opening in which the entrants
are engaged in an inaudible conversation is surely unparalleled in Shakespeare (on the modern stage even a
silent entry can be covered by business, arranging cushions or a coffee
tray or what not, but this sort of cover
is not possible on the Elizabethan
stage; Shakespeare often covers an
entry with *irrelevant* conversation till
the characters are well down stage,
but he invariably gives the entrants
something to say). I do not understand
why Wilson, having gone seven-
eighths of the way, failed to make the
final step to what seems the obvious
solution. The two groups come in
simultaneously, but by different doors.
The entry of both is covered by the
brisk conversation of one, Enobarbus
is there to give his order, and the
soothsayer is where we want him, in
the non-Egyptian group, so that
Alexas can call him over. [R] (Plutarch gives his 'grandfather Lampryas'
as the authority for one of his stories.
See *post*, p. 248. He does not mention
Rannius or Lucillius.)

1–5. *Lord . . . garlands*] This speech
has a suspicion of mutilated verse
about it. Capell (omitting *Lord*) printed as six lines of verse. S. Walker conjectures verse, lines 3–5: 'O . . .
garlands!'

4–5. *charge . . . garlands*] This reading

is taken to imply cuckoldom for Charmian's wished husband—which is
Alexas' prediction—but cuckoldom
garlanded, i.e. rich and honourable
(Warburton) or contented (Malone)
or triumphant (Steevens), an idea
which Charmian herself would more
probably contribute. Steevens might
have quoted *Jack Drum's Entertainment*
(1616), v. 334 (Simpson's *School of
Shakspere*, ii. 207): 'I'le weare this
Crowne [a compulsory 'Coronet of
Cuckolds,' line 316 *ante*] and triumph
in this horne.' I doubt these inferences,
'rich,' etc. Quite possibly the horns are
credited in advance, and *must charge*,
etc., merely means must marry me,
wear the bridegroom's chaplet. Cf.
Sylvester's *Du Bartas, The Magnificence*
(1621 ed., p. 462): 'A *Garland*, . . . The
Royall Bride-groom's radiant brow
bedights.' Or may the jest be, after all,
only the equivalent (with cuckoldom
thrown in) of modern banter, in an
allusion to the *victim*, and the phrase =
must come as a sacrifice to the altar?
Cf. D'Avenant, *Gondibert* (1651), III.
iii. 61: 'Who lets this guilded Sacrifice
proceed / To *Hymen's* Altar, by the
king adorn'd, / As Priests give Victims
Garlands ere they bleed.' Some would
retain *change*. Steevens quotes *Cym.*,
I. v. 55; *Paradise Lost*, iv. 892 ('to *change*
Torment with ease') for *change with* =
change for, and interprets much as the
advocates of *charge*. Thiselton has:
'take his horns in exchange for [wed-
ding] garlands,' aptly comparing Jonson, 'To Celia' (*The Forest*, ix): 'But
might I of Jove's nectar sup, / I would
not *change* for thine.' Upton's 'new
dress and adorn' or Johnson's suggestion 'dress, or dress with changes of
garlands,' reappears in Staunton, who
reads *change* as = 'vary or garnish';

Alex. Soothsayer!

Sooth. Your will?

Char. Is this the man? Is't you, sir, that know things?

Sooth. In nature's infinite book of secrecy
    A little I can read.

Alex.   Show him your hand.   10

Eno. Bring in the banquet quickly; wine enough,
    Cleopatra's health to drink.

Char. Good sir, give me good fortune.

Sooth. I make not, but foresee.

Char. Pray then, foresee me one.   15

Sooth. You shall be yet far fairer than you are.

Char. He means in flesh.

Iras. No, you shall paint when you are old.

Char. Wrinkles forbid!

Alex. Vex not his prescience, be attentive.   20

Char. Hush!

Sooth. You shall be more beloving than belov'd.

Char. I had rather heat my liver with drinking.

---

20. prescience] *F*; patience *F3*.

Schmidt gives *change* = 'make of another appearance,' and cf. *Cor.*, v. iii. 152 (F reading), on which Malone relied as an unmistakable instance of *change* in error for *charge*.

16. *fairer . . . are*] Mr Craig points out that the soothsayer, whose later deliverances (II. iii *post*) are so pregnant, probably does not speak idly in this scene, and that the present prediction is perhaps fulfilled in Charmian's *character*, by the fairer, nobler qualities displayed in Act v (or the fame resulting from them) which made her mistress call her 'noble' (v. ii. 229 *post*), and Cæsar exclaim of her last movements: 'O noble weakness' (v. ii. 342 *post*).

17. *in flesh*] Charmian takes *fair* in the sense 'plump, in good condition'. Cf. *AYL.*, I. i. 11: 'His horses are bred better; for, besides that they are *fair* with their feeding,' etc. (Craig).

20. *his prescience*] Delius thinks this a title like *his worship*, used jocosely.

22. *You . . . belov'd*] 'i.e. [as the soothsayer means it, not as Charmian takes it] You shall expend all your love on your queen and mistress, and so will not gain the affection of male admirers' (Craig). Or possibly it refers to the love between Charmian and her mistress. The further *direct* predictions may be conveniently noted here as literally true, viz., those in lines 31, 33–4, and that to Iras in line 52: 'Your fortunes are alike.'

23. *heat . . . drinking*] So in *Mer.V.*, I. i. 81: 'And let my liver rather *heat* with wine.' The same effect was formerly attributed to love, whence Charmian's expression of preference. Cf. *Tp.*, IV. i. 55–6, and Webster, *Appius and Virginia*, IV. i. 255, where the lust of Appius is aimed at: 'We have not such hot livers: mark you that.' That love has its seat in the liver was an opinion of the ancients, and is amusingly discussed in Prior's *Alma*, i. 351

Alex. Nay, hear him.

Char. Good now, some excellent fortune! Let me be mar-   25
ried to three kings in a forenoon, and widow them
all: let me have a child at fifty, to whom Herod of
Jewry may do homage. Find me to marry me with
Octavius Cæsar, and companion me with my mistress.   30

Sooth. You shall outlive the lady whom you serve.

Char. O excellent, I love long life better than figs.

et seq. Unlike the generality, Phineas Fletcher (*The Purple Island*, III. x, and his note thereon) gives the liver a Platonic tenant: 'Not Cupid's self but Cupid's better brother: . . . / By whose command we either love our kinde, / Or with most perfect love affect the minde'; etc.

27. *let me . . . fifty*] On this jesting wish of Charmian to be one of very few mothers, Steevens observes: 'This is one of Shakespeare's natural touches. Few circumstances are more flattering to the fair sex than breeding at an advanced period of life.' Cf. the jest in *Histriomastix*, Act VI. 192 (Simpson, *School of Shakspere*, ii. 82), where, when his unpaid hostess says: 'Go to, I'll bear no longer,' Posthast replies: 'What, and be under fifty?'

27–8. *Herod of Jewry*] As Steevens pointed out, Charmian bespeaks a son powerful enough to subdue even the fiercest of blustering tyrants. Herod is the type of these in the Miracle plays. The York play of *The Coming of the Three Kings to Herod* opens with a rant in which Herod claims the clouds, Saturn, Sun and Moon, etc., as his subjects; and in that of the Nativity, in the Coventry series, occurs the direction: 'Here Erode ragis in thys pagond and in the strete also.' See III. iii. 3 *post*; *Wiv.*, II. i. 20: 'What a *Herod of Jewry* is this!' and *Ham.*, III. ii. 16, of rant: 'It out-herods Herod.' Furness cites, and unwillingly inclines to accept, the suggestion of Th. Zielinski (*Philologus*, p. 19) that in Charmian's speech, the child is Christ, and the

three Kings are the three wise men, or three Kings [of Cologne] as they were usually called.

28. *Find*] i.e. in the lines of the hand, as Delius notes. See line 10 *ante*.

32. *I . . . figs*] a proverbial expression, say Steevens and Schmidt, regrettably without references to distinguish the assertion from an easy surmise. I can only doubtfully suggest possible clues for the choice of figs (if, indeed, there was any occult reason for it) in (1) 'The Fig-tree is more fruitful than other trees, for it beareth fruit three or four times in one year,' etc. (Charmian's mind was running on fruitfulness); 'Figs do away rivels [i.e. wrinkles] of old men, if they ate thereof among their meat' (see 'Wrinkles forbid!' line 19 above), *Bartholomew* (Berthelet, 1535), *De Proprietatibus Rerum*, bk xvii, §61; (2) the poisoned fig of Spain so often alluded to as a secret means of removing an enemy, e.g. by Shirley, *The Maid's Revenge*, III. ii. (*Works*, 1833, i. 141): 'A rat! give him his bane: . . . our own country figs shall do it rarely'; (3) the following passages, particularly the second, from Sir T. Browne, *A Letter to a Friend*, etc., 1690 (*Religio Medici*, etc., Canterbury, 1894, p. 138): 'Upon my first visit I was bold to tell them who had not let fall all hopes of his recovery, that in my sad opinion he was not like to behold a grasshopper, much less to pluck another fig; . . . for he lived not unto the middle of May, and confirmed the observation of *Hippocrates* of that mortal time of the year when the leaves of

Sooth. You have seen and prov'd a fairer former fortune
   Than that which is to approach.

Char. Then belike my children shall have no names: pri-   35
   thee, how many boys and wenches must I have?

Sooth. If every of your wishes had a womb,
   And fertile every wish, a million.

Char. Out, fool! I forgive thee for a witch.

Alex. You think none but your sheets are privy to your   40
   wishes.

Char. Nay, come, tell Iras hers.

Alex. We'll know all our fortunes.

Eno. Mine, and most of our fortunes to-night, shall be—
   drunk to bed.   45

Iras. There's a palm presages chastity, if nothing else.

Char. E'en as the o'erflowing Nilus presageth famine.

Iras. Go, you wild bedfellow, you cannot soothsay.

Char. Nay, if an oily palm be not a fruitful prognostica-

---

38. fertile] *Theobald (Warburton); foretell F.*

---

the fig-tree resemble a Daw's claw.'
Perhaps, as there is more in the soothsayer's words than meets the eye, so
we ought not to forget here the basket
of figs which brings death to Charmian,
v. ii *post*, though Warburton has been
ridiculed for detecting an omen.

35. *Then . . . names*] Then, I suppose,
my children will be bastards. Steevens
quotes *Gent.*, III. i. 324: '*Speed.* She hath
many nameless virtues. *Launce.* That's
as much as to say, bastard virtues, that
indeed know not their fathers and
therefore have no names.' See also
Beaumont and Fletcher, *A King and
No King*, III. i. 175: 'else I shall live /
Like sinfull issues that are left in
streets / By their regardless Mothers,
and no name / Will be found for me.'

37. *every*] similarly a pronoun in
AYL., v. iv. 179: '*Every* of this happy
number.'

38. *fertile*] The frequent spelling
fertill supports the emendation. Pope
reads *foretold*, Collier MS *fruitful*. Johnson thought *foretell* might stand, explaining, on the supposition of an unlikely ellipse: 'And [if] I should foretel

all those wishes, I should foretel a
million of children.' Malone objects
that the supposition of wombs without
a second fertility would not be a
sufficient hypothesis.

39. *I . . . witch*] Professor Herford
says: '*for a witch*, i.e. as being a wizard,
and hence privileged to utter home-
truths'; and a frank admission would
not be unlike the Charmian who has
just said: 'Then belike my children,'
etc. On the other hand, there is much
to be said for repudiation, and the
usual explanation, which = I'll
answer for your being no witch, if this
is a sample of your skill. The phrase is
not unlike, 'I'll warrant him for drown-
ing' (*Tp.*, I. i. 51); '*R. Royster.* Except
I have hir to my Wife, I shall runne
madde. *M. Mery.* Nay unwise perhaps,
but I warrant you for madde' (*Roister
Doister*, I. ii. 79). Steevens quotes 'a
common proverbial reproach to silly
ignorant females: "You'll never be
burnt for a witch."' The gender of
witch was formerly common; it is
masculine again in *Cym.*, I. vi. 166.

49. *oily palm*] A moist palm was sup-

tion, I cannot scratch mine ear. Prithee tell her but 50
a worky-day fortune.

Sooth. Your fortunes are alike.

Iras. But how, but how? give me particulars.

Sooth. I have said.

Iras. Am I not an inch of fortune better than she? 55

Char. Well, if you were but an inch of fortune better than
I, wnere would you choose it?

Iras. Not in my husband's nose.

Char. Our worser thoughts heavens mend! Alexas,—
come, his fortune, his fortune! O, let him marry a 60
woman that cannot go, sweet Isis, I beseech thee,

59–60. Alexas,—come] *Theobald; Alexas.* Come, *F, apparently assigning the speech
from* Come *onward to Alexas.*

---

posed to indicate a wanton disposition.
See Middleton, *Blurt Master Constable*,
I. ii. 20: '*Lazarillo.* A woman, Pilcher,
the moist-handed Madonna Imperia,
a most rare and divine creature. *Pilch.*
A most rascally damned courtesan.'
Malone quotes *Oth.*, III. iv. 37: 'This
hand is moist, my lady,' and 39: 'This
argues fruitfulness and liberal heart';
but see the whole passage, 37–44, and
Ven., 25–6. See also Overbury's *Characters*, under 'A very whore.'

49–50. *fruitful prognostication*] pres-
age of fertility.

51. *worky-day*] ordinary. Cf. *AYL.*,
I. iii. 12: 'working-day world.' The
noun occurs in *Two Wise Men and All
the Rest Fools*, 1619, II. i: 'I ha' more
weeds grown in one Holy-day than in
three worky-days.'

58. *Not . . . nose*] The author of
Tristram Shandy may be consulted here.
See bk III, chap. xxxi; bk v, chap. i *ad
fin.* Cf. also *The Unnatural Combat*, IV. ii
(Gifford's *Massinger*, ed. Cuningham,
p. 58a): 'It hath just your eyes; and
such a promising *nose*, / That, if the
sign deceive me not, in time / 'Twill
prove a notable striker, like his
father.'

59–60. *Alexas,—come*] † The F reading is an interesting example of the
confusion that may be caused by the

italicization of proper names in text as
well as in speech-headings. The compositor presumably found the proper
name indicated for italicization in his
copy and took it for a speech-heading.
It is even possible, I think, that he did
not at first regard it as a speech-heading, but, having barely room for it in
the line after *mend*, started a new line
with it and inadvertently inset it level
with the speech-headings, since it is
noticeable (and Rolfe noted it) that
this is the only place where the name
is given in full as a speech-heading, and
not in the abbreviated form *Alex.* [R]

61. *that cannot go*] *Go* is constantly
employed for walk, etc., and go up-
right, as opposed to creep, especially in
a varying proverb: 'blood (kind, love,
bairns, etc.) will creep where it (they)
cannot go,' in print as early as 1481
(Caxton, *Reynard the Fox*, ed. Arber,
p. 70): 'one shal alway seke on his
frendis, though he haue angred them,
for blood must krepe, where it *can not
goo*.' Does Charmian, then, mean here
an old, crippled, or bed-rid woman,
whom, on second thoughts, she wills to
die and give place to a series of worse
in another kind, who will cuckold
Alexas as she could not? Another common sense of *go* is 'be pregnant,' and
go = go with child, actually occurs

and let her die too, and give him a worse, and let
worse follow worse, till the worst of all follow him
laughing to his grave, fifty-fold a cuckold! Good Isis,
hear me this prayer, though thou deny me a matter   65
of more weight: good Isis, I beseech thee!

Iras. Amen, dear goddess, hear that prayer of the people!
for, as it is a heart-breaking to see a handsome man
loose-wiv'd, so it is a deadly sorrow to behold a
foul knave uncuckolded: therefore, dear Isis, keep   70
decorum, and fortune him accordingly!

Char. Amen.

Alex. Lo now, if it lay in their hands to make me a
cuckold, they would make themselves whores, but
they'ld do't.   75

Eno. Hush, here comes Antony.

Enter CLEOPATRA.

Char.   Not he, the queen.

Cleo. Saw you my lord?

Eno.   No, lady.

Cleo.   Was he not here?

Char. No, madam.

Cleo. He was dispos'd to mirth; but on the sudden

---

76. S.D. *Enter Cleopatra*] *after* do 't, *line* 75, F.   77. Saw you my lord?] *F2;*
Saue you, my lord. *F.*

---

without the time-expression which
usually makes the sense unmistakable,
in *A Cure for a Cuckold,* II. iii. 102: 'And,
Urse, how goes all at home? or cannot
all *go* yet? lank still! will 't never be
full sea at our wharf? *Wife.* Alas, husband! *Comp[ass].* A lass, or a lad,
wench, I should be glad of both.' In
LLL., v. ii. 676–7, Costard says: 'The
party is *gone*; fellow Hector, she is
gone: she is two months on her way.'
Charmian, who wished to bear at
fifty (see line 27 *ante*), would account
sterility a severe wish, not to mention
that it would imprecate on Alexas one
of the things that are said to be never
satisfied. Thiselton—the only commentator, I believe, to offer an expla-

nation—makes 'that cannot go' =
'that is never satisfied,' without remark or evidence to support his view.

Isis] originally the Egyptian goddess
of the earth and fertility, later of the
moon. See Spenser, *Faerie Queene,* v.
vii. 4: 'They wore rich Mitres shaped
like the Moone, / To shew that *Isis*
doth the Moone portend;' etc.

67. *that prayer . . . people*] 'seems
to mean "that universal prayer"'
(Thiselton).

76. S.D.] F puts the entry before
Enobarbus' remark at the beginning
of the line, but this is hardly possible,
since the actual presence of Cleopatra
on the stage would make the remark
nonsensical.

A Roman thought hath struck him. Enobarbus! 80
Eno. Madam.
Cleo. Seek him, and bring him hither. Where's Alexas?
Alex. Here at your service. My lord approaches.
Cleo. We will not look upon him: go with us. [*Exeunt.*

Enter ANTONY, *with a Messenger.*

Mess. Fulvia thy wife first came into the field. 85
Ant. Against my brother Lucius?
Mess. Ay:
But soon that war had end, and the time's state
Made friends of them, jointing their force 'gainst Cæsar,
Whose better issue in the war, from Italy, 90
Upon the first encounter, drave them.
Ant.   Well, what worst?
Mess. The nature of bad news infects the teller.
Ant. When it concerns the fool or coward. On:
Things that are past are done, with me. 'Tis thus,
Who tells me true, though in his tale lie death, 95
I hear him as he flatter'd.
Mess.   Labienus—
This is stiff news—hath with his Parthian force

80. *A Roman thought*] perhaps a thought such as Roman virtue would inspire, and not merely, as Schmidt explains it, 'A thought of Rome.'

84. S.D.] Again F puts the entry a line earlier. It is impossible to place it rightly, since Cleopatra's exit and Antony's entry are simultaneous.

85–91. *Fulvia*, etc.] See North, *post*, p. 249.

89. *jointing*] The past part. of the same verb occurs in *Cym.*, v. iv. 143; v. v. 441.

92. *The nature . . . teller*] So in *2H4*, I. i. 100: 'Yet the first bringer of un-welcome news / Hath but a losing office, and his tongue,' etc. Cf. also II. v. 85–6 *post*.

94. *done, with me. 'Tis thus*] Dover Wilson, adopting a suggestion of Capt. E. G. Spencer-Churchill, repunctu-ates *done. With me, 'tis thus.*

96. *as he flatter'd*] as (readily as) if he . . .

96–101. *Labienus . . . Whilst*] †F prints thus:

Labienus (this is stiffe-newes)
Hath with his Parthian Force
Extended Asia: from Euphrates
 his conquering
Banner shooke, from Syria to Lydia,
And to Ionia, whil'st—,

a typical example of F mislineation, corrected by most editors as in text here, though Pope, followed by Theo-bald, tried a different, and rhythmi-cally much duller, arrangement. But there has been a conspiracy of most editors, including Case and Dover Wilson, to tinker also with F's punctu-ation and read:

Extended Asia from Euphrates,
His conquering banner shook from
 Syria

Extended Asia: from Euphrates
His conquering banner shook, from Syria
To Lydia, and to Ionia: 100
Whilst—
Ant.   Antony, thou wouldst say,—
Mess.   O, my lord!
Ant. Speak to me home, mince not the general tongue:
Name Cleopatra as she is call'd in Rome;
Rail thou in Fulvia's phrase, and taunt my faults
With such full licence, as both truth and malice   105
Have power to utter. O then we bring forth weeds,
When our quick minds lie still, and our ills told us

107. minds] *Hanmer* (*Warburton*); windes *F.*

To Lydia and to Ionia, whilst . . .
which (apart from producing two
rhythmically repetitive lines) misses
the point that Shakespeare was merely
versifying North's 'Labienus conquered all Asia with the armie of the
Parthians, from the river of Euphrates,
and from Syria, unto the contries of
Lydia and Ionia' (p. 249, *post*). [R]
  98. *Extended*] seized upon. *Extent* is a
legal phrase from the words of a writ—
extendi facias—authorizing full valuation of land before seizure. See *AYL.*,
III. i. 17: 'let my officers . . . /Make an
extent upon his house and lands';
Nashe, *The Unfortunate Traveller*, II,
p. 311, line 11: 'Ere the officers come
to *extend*, Ile bestow a hundred pound
on a doale of bread,' etc.
  Asia . . . Euphrates] *Asia* a trisyllable
and *Euphrates*, as usually at this period,
'Euphrātes'. So Drayton, in a passage
(of which Steevens quotes line 2) recalling the famous lines of Denham in
Cooper's Hill: 'Give me those lines,
(whose touch the skilful eare to please) /
That gliding flow in state, like swelling
Euphrates,' etc. *Polyolbion*, pt ii, 1622,
Song xxi.
  102. *home*] directly (cf. 'strike home')
as in *Cym.*, III. v. 92.
  mince] diminish, fine down. Now
used only in '*mince* the matter *or*
matters', as in *Oth.*, II. iii. 249; but

compare Charles Cotton, *Poems* (1689),
p. 182: 'The man, upon this, comes
me running again, / But yet *minced* his
Message, and was not so plain,' [i.e. so
peremptory].
  104. *Fulvia's phrase*] See on I. i. 32
ante.
  107. *minds*] So most editors, the
sense of this passage being thus either:
(1) we accumulate faults when our
reason forgets its natural activity and
exerts no corrective force; and to be
told of these is as salutary as earing
(ploughing) to weed-grown fields; or
(2) when our *minds*, with their gift of
fertility, lie idle and uncultivated, they
produce evil growths; and, etc.
Ascham, *Toxophilus*, 1545 (Arber,
1868, p. 93), similarly appeals to the
value of ploughing for eradicating
weeds, in support of his receipt against
the weeds of the mind: '. . . euen as
plowing of a good grounde for wheate,
doth not onely make it mete for the
seede, but also riueth and plucketh vp
by the rootes, all thistles, brambles and
weedes . . .: Euen so shulde the teaching of youth to shote, not only make
them shote well, but also plucke awaye
by the rootes all other desyre to
noughtye pastymes, as disynge,' etc.
See also next note; and for *quick*, compare Ascham, as before, p. 40:
'Muche musike . . . recreateth and

Is as our earing. Fare thee well awhile.
Mess. At your noble pleasure.   [*Exit.*

Enter another Messenger.

Ant. From Sicyon how the news? Speak there!   110

110. Sicyon how the news?] *F* (Scicion); Sicyon ho, the news! *Dyce.*

maketh *quycke* a mannes *mynde*'; also *H5*, IV. i. 20: 'And when the *mind* is *quickened.*' On *winds*, which several editors retain, Johnson says: 'The sense is, that man, not agitated by censure, like soil not ventilated by *quick winds*, produces more evil than good.' See *3H6*, II. vi. 21: 'For what doth cherish weeds but gentle air?' quoted by Steevens. Capell thought *quick winds = friends*. Another explanation, beginning with a suggestion of Blackstone, is technical: Steevens thinks *quick winds* = teeming fallows, because 'the ridges left in lands turned up by the plough, that they may sweeten during their fallow state, are still called *wind-rows.*' In Collier *winds* = (perhaps) *wints*, 'in Kent and Surrey two furrows ploughed by the horses going to one end of the field and back again.' He refers to Cooper's *Glossary of Provincialisms*, etc. (Sussex, 1836), and Holloway, *Gen. Prov. Dict.* (1838).

108. *earing*] ploughing. See I. iv. 49 *post*; Herbert, *A Priest to the Temple* (1652), chap. xxxiv: 'the usuall seasons of summer and winter, *earing* and harvest'; *Arden of Feversham*, III. v. 24: 'For Greene doth *ear* the land and weed thee up, / To make my harvest nothing but pure corn.'

109-14.] † I have retained F's S.D.s since I am not clear that the seeming difficulties justify the drastic changes which have been followed by almost all editors. Rowe cut out the S.D. at line 109 altogether, and Capell turned the messengers of lines 111 and 112 into attendants. This runs smoothly enough, but the 'Enter another Messenger' at line 109 is obstinately there and I do not think that F is at all

impossible as it stands. The entering messenger finds that he has come from the wrong place, and calls to a group at the door to see whether there is another messenger who will give Antony what he wants; a second messenger in the group, eager to please, reports that there is such a messenger, waiting. I think that this perhaps gives better the general bustle of the scene, with messengers from various places coming with news, than the somewhat formal business with attendants summoning messengers in their proper turn.

And I retain F's 'how the news.' Antony's speech is usually given as 'From Sicyon, ho, the news!', and admittedly 'how' often in Shakespearean text stands for 'ho'. But 'how the news?' is a quite possible phrase (cf. Shallow's 'How a score of ewes now?' in *2H4*, III. ii. 55) and fits rather better than 'ho' if we retain F's entries. [R]

110. *Sicyon*] † F's *Scicion* may easily be no more than a blunder—the sort of repeating of a letter to which we are all liable with an unfamiliar name. But it may also be quite reasonably adduced as evidence supporting the view that the copy for this play was Shakespeare's autograph, in view of the fact that 'scilens' (for 'silence') occurs in the 'addition' to *Sir Thomas More*, and 'Scilens' occurs eighteen times in Q1 of *2H4* as the name of the character whom we know as Silence.

Perhaps I may without impertinence interject a word about the famous three pages in *Sir Thomas More* which are so often alluded to in discussion of textual problems. It has not, I think, been *proved* (indeed it is a

First Mess. The man from Sicyon,—is there such an one?
Sec. Mess. He stays upon your will.
Ant.   Let him appear.
    These strong Egyptian fetters I must break,
    Or lose myself in dotage.

                 Enter another Messenger, with a letter.

                              What are you?
Third. Mess. Fulvia thy wife is dead.
Ant.   Where died she?   115
Third Mess. In Sicyon:
    Her length of sickness, with what else more serious
    Importeth thee to know, this bears.   [*Gives a letter.*
Ant.   Forbear me.
                                   [*Exeunt Messengers.*
    There's a great spirit gone! Thus did I desire it:
    What our contempts doth often hurl from us,   120
    We wish it ours again. The present pleasure,
    By revolution lowering, does become

---

118. *Gives a letter*] *Johnson; not in F.
Staunton and some other edd.*

120. doth] *F;* do *F2;* contempt doth

thing hardly susceptible of proof) that
they are in Shakespeare's autograph,
though I think that the cumulative
evidence makes it much more likely
that they are than that they are not.
Arguments, therefore, which use the
three pages as conclusive evidence of
Shakespeare's practice in such things
as spelling, punctuation, or italicization of proper names are based on an
assumption and not on a fact. On
the other hand, I think the evidence
makes it almost certain that even if the
pages are not Shakespeare's autograph
they are in a hand so nearly identical
with his that in considering such things
as 'probability of error'—that whole
section of the field of emendation
which depends on the probable formation of letters in the original—we can
safely operate as though the three
pages had Shakespeare's signature on
them. [R]

112. *stays upon*] So in *All's W.,* III. v.

45: 'I thank you and will *stay upon* your
leisure.'
115. *Fulvia . . . dead*] See North, *post,*
p. 250.
118. S.D. Exeunt . . .] I think Dover
Wilson is clearly right that Antony
should here be left alone. F has no S.D.
120. *contempts doth*] As the old Southern plural in -*th* occurs elsewhere in F,
and very frequently in contemporary
writings, in the verbs *do* and *have,* I
have retained it. Cf. in F, p. 174, *Mer.
V.,* III. ii. 33: 'I, but I feare, you speake
vpon the racke, / Where men enforced
doth speake anything.' So Queen Elizabeth (Harington's *Nugæ Antiquæ* (1769),
i. 59): 'But clouds of joys untry'd/*Doth*
cloke aspyring mynds.' It is scarce in
the case of other verbs, but see Sidney's
Apologie for Poetrie (ed. Arber, p.
31): 'the generalities that contayneth
it.'
122. *By revolution lowering*] carried to
a lower and lower pitch in our estima-

The opposite of itself: she's good, being gone,
The hand could pluck her back that shov'd her on.
I must from this enchanting queen break off,   125
Ten thousand harms, more than the ills I know,
My idleness doth hatch. Ho now, Enobarbus!

Re-enter ENOBARBUS.

Eno. What's your pleasure, sir?
Ant. I must with haste from hence.

tion by the changes in ourselves and
circumstances which accompany the
revolution of time, or of 'the Wheel of
things', as Sir T. Browne calls it
(*Christian Morals*, §16). Warburton saw
an allusion to the sun's diurnal course
and its termination opposite to the
point of rising; but the figure is no
doubt merely that of the turning of a
wheel, so often and variously applied.
See *Lr*, v. iii. 176, of the correspondence between a vicious act and its
final consequences: 'The wheel is
come full circle'; *Tw.N.*, v. i. 388:
'and thus the whirligig of time brings
in his revenges.' In the present case
the wheel has not come full circle:
'Opinions do find, after certain revo-
lutions [of time], men and minds like
those that first begat them' (Sir
Thomas Browne, *Religio Medici*, §6),
and by and by the advantages of
losing Fulvia would again find a mind
in Antony to appreciate them; at the
moment, appreciation of these advantages is at its greatest distance in the
revolution.

123. *she's good, being gone*] Cf. *All's
W.*, v. iii. 60: 'Crying "That's good
that's gone."'

124. *could*] would be ready to. The
line resembles one in Lyly's *The
Woman in the Moone*, ii. i. 139: 'Whether
thou drawe me on, or put me back.'

125. *I must . . . off*] Cf. Countess of
Pembroke's *Antonie* (1595), i. 83:
'Thou breakest at length from thence
as one encharmed / Breaks from the
enchanter that him firmly held, / For

thy first reason, (spoiling of their
force / The poisoned cups of thy fair
sorceress) / Recured thy spirit;' etc.

127-8. †F reads as follows: 'My
idlenesse doth hatch. / *Enter Enobarbus*. / How now *Enobarbus*.' This is
precisely parallel to ii. i. 27, where
Varrius' entry interrupts a speech (as
indicated by a long dash in F), and he
is greeted with 'How now *Varrius*?' At
first sight there seems to be little that
needs doing with either passage; insert
a comma after 'now' in both, and give
F's question mark after Varrius after
Enobarbus also, and all is well. But in
fact all is not at all well, since, though
the text is the same in the two passages, the situation is not. Varrius
enters hurriedly with news, whereas
Enobarbus, as seems clearly implied
by his first words, enters in answer to a
summons. This has led most editors to
shift the entry of Enobarbus to half a
line later, but retaining 'How now',
and led Capell and (independently)
Dyce to read 'Ho, Enobarbus!' 'How'
is not infrequently printed for 'Ho' (cf.
iv. xiv. 104 *post*) and Dyce makes the
just comment: 'It would be impossible,
I presume, to point out, in any old
writer, an instance of "How now!"
used as *the exclamation of a person summoning another into his presence.*'

The crucial point is Enobarbus'
'What's your pleasure?' which is almost nonsensical as a reply to a question ('How now?'), but natural as the
reply to a summons, and, though
reluctant to tamper with F, I think

Eno. Why, then we kill all our women. We see how   130
   mortal an unkindness is to them; if they suffer our
   departure, death's the word.

Ant. I must be gone.

Eno. Under a compelling occasion let women die: it
   were pity to cast them away for nothing, though   135
   between them and a great cause, they should be
   esteemed nothing. Cleopatra catching but the least
   noise of this, dies instantly. I have seen her die
   twenty times upon far poorer moment: I do think
   there is mettle in death, which commits some   140
   loving act upon her, she hath such a celerity in
   dying.

Ant. She is cunning past man's thought.

Eno. Alack, sir, no, her passions are made of nothing but
   the finest part of pure love. We cannot call her   145
   winds and waters sighs and tears; they are greater
   storms and tempests than almanacs can report.
   This cannot be cunning in her; if it be, she makes a
   shower of rain as well as Jove.

Ant. Would I had never seen her!   150

Eno. O, sir, you had then left unseen a wonderful piece

---

134. a compelling occasion] *Rowe;* a compelling an occasion *F;* so . . . an . . .
Nicholson conj.; as . . . an . . . *Anon. conj.*

---

that Capell and Dyce were probably
right, and that those who go half-way,
retaining the words but shifting the
S.D., are certainly wrong, making
poor sense either way, as is the usual
fate of such compromises. (I have retained F's 'now', since, though it
makes the line hypermetrical, it is not
impossible, but Capell and Dyce may
well have been right in omitting it, on
the grounds that, as Furness suggests,
a compositor, taking 'How' to mean
'How' and not 'Ho' might easily insert
the natural 'now'.) [R]

132. *death's the word*] So in *Cym.,* v.
iv. 155: 'Hanging is the word, sir.'

138. *noise*] rumour. Cf. *Troil.,* I. ii.
12. 'The *noise* goes, this: there is,'
etc.

139. *upon . . . moment*] for causes
much less weighty.

139–42. *I do . . . dying*] Enobarbus
pictures death as a vigorous lover to
whom Cleopatra yields willingly.

145–6. *We . . . tears*] Malone suspected an inversion on all fours with
'To make your house our Tower' (*H8,*
v. i. 107) and equivalent to 'we cannot
call her sighs and tears, winds,' etc.;
but this is failing to think in Enobarbus' fashion. For an elaboration of a
similar metaphor, see *Rom.,* III. v. 131–
8; and for what follows, the storms and
tempests of almanacs, cf. Ben Jonson,
E.M.O., I. iii. 51, where the grain-
hoarding chuff Sordido rejoices in the
almanac prediction: 'great tempest of
rain, thunder and lightning.'

of work, which not to have been blest withal, would
have discredited your travel.

Ant. Fulvia is dead.

Eno. Sir?   155

Ant. Fulvia is dead.

Eno. Fulvia?

Ant. Dead.

Eno. Why, sir, give the gods a thankful sacrifice. When
it pleaseth their deities to take the wife of a man   160
from him, it shows to man the tailors of the earth;
comforting therein, that when old robes are worn
out, there are members to make new. If there were
no more women but Fulvia, then had you indeed
a cut, and the case to be lamented: this grief is   165
crown'd with consolation, your old smock brings
forth a new petticoat, and indeed the tears live in an
onion, that should water this sorrow.

Ant. The business she hath broached in the state
Cannot endure my absence.   170

Eno. And the business you have broach'd here cannot be
without you, especially that of Cleopatra's, which
wholly depends on your abode.

153. *discredited your travel*] proved
you a bad sight-seer.

159–63. *When . . . new*] Malone explains: 'When the deities are pleased
to take a man's wife from him, this act
of theirs makes them appear to man
like the tailors of the earth; affording
this comfortable reflection, that the
deities have made other women to
supply the place of his former wife; as
the tailor, when one robe is worn out,
supplies him with another.' It is possible that the bereaving deities are
neither called nor resembled to 'the
tailors of the earth': these may be
merely reproductive man. In the following passage, the bereaved lover,
Pan, is apparently the *workman* (see
Goodwin's Browne, *Britannia's Pastorals*, II. iv. 672): 'If thou the best of
women didst forego, / Weigh if thou
found'st her, or didst make her so; /
If she were found so, know there's

more than one; / If made, the workman lives, though she be gone.'

165. *cut*] blow. So Lady Kix, of her
childlessness after seven years' marriage: 'Can any woman have a greater
cut?' (Middleton, *A Chaste Maid in
Cheapside*, II. i. 135).

167–8. *the tears . . . sorrow*] i.e. an
onion would bring to your eyes all the
tears that this sorrow deserves. Cf. *The
Noble Soldier*, 1634 (Bullen's *Old Plays*,
i. 268), quoted in part by Steevens: 'If
you had buried nine husbands, so
much water as you might squeeze out
of an Onyon had been teares enow to
cast away upon fellowes that cannot
thanke you'; see also *Shr.*, Ind., i. 124–
8. *Onion-ey'd* occurs IV. ii. 35 *post.*

172. *that of Cleopatra's*] Hanmer read
Cleopatra: but see on I. i. 1 *ante.*

173. *abode*] stay. See *Cym.*, I. vi. 53;
Fairfax, *Godfrey of Bulloigne*, 1600,
p. 98: 'Thus spake the king, and soone

Ant. No more light answers. Let our officers
    Have notice what we purpose. I shall break   175
    The cause of our expedience to the queen,
    And get her leave to part. For not alone
    The death of Fulvia, with more urgent touches,
    Do strongly speak to us; but the letters too
    Of many our contriving friends in Rome   180
    Petition us at home. Sextus Pompeius
    Hath given the dare to Cæsar, and commands
    The empire of the sea. Our slippery people,
    Whose love is never link'd to the deserver
    Till his deserts are past, begin to throw   185
    Pompey the Great, and all his dignities
    Upon his son, who high in name and power,
    Higher than both in blood and life, stands up
    For the main soldier: whose quality, going on,

174. light] *F;* like *F2.*   177. leave] *Pope;* loue *F.*   182. Hath] *F2;* Haue *F.*

without *aboad* / The troupe went forth in shining armour clad,' etc.

176. *expedience*] The word usually means *haste* in Shakespeare (cf. *R2,* ii. i. 287) and may very well = *haste* here, as Dyce explains it, for the departure was to be sudden. It is, however, generally explained as *expedition* with Warburton, and compared with *2H4,* i. i. 33, where 'this dear expedience' *seems* to stand for the expedition to the Holy Land. But even there, it probably rather means 'matter demanding haste,' else why the next line: 'My liege, this *haste* was hot in question'?

177. *leave to part*] Several editors retain *love,* understanding with Steevens: 'And prevail on her love to consent to our separation'; but strong probability favours *leave,* and Malone remarked a similar misprint (*loves* for *leaves*) in *Tit.,* iii. i. 291 : part = depart, as often.

178. *more urgent touches*] 'things that touch us more sensibly, more pressing motives' (Johnson).

180. *many . . . contriving friends*] many

who occupy themselves in my interests. The usual sense of *contrive* is plot, conspire, as in *Cæs.,* ii. iii. 6: 'If not, the Fates with traitors do *contrive*'; and S. Walker scents a Latinism here for 'spending the time', 'sojourning'. Cf. *Shr.,* i. ii. 279: 'Please ye we may *contrive* this afternoon.' The difference of the cases, however, makes the point very doubtful, and even in the instance just quoted this sense is questioned by Schmidt. For the position of *many,* cf. *Tim.,* iii. vi. 11 : '*many* my near occasions.'

181. *Petition . . . home*] beg for my presence in Rome.

181–90. *Sextus Pompeius,* etc.] See North, *post,* p. 251; i. iii. 45, etc.; i. iv. 36, etc., *post.* The clause 'Whose . . . past,' lines 184–5, has been taken of Pompey the Great, but would be less true of him, and seems to be definitely confirmed to Sextus by i. iv. 43 *post;* 'the ebb'd man, ne'er lov'd till ne'er worth love.'

188. *blood and life*] high mettle and vital energy.

189. *quality*] nature and condition,

The sides o' the world may danger. Much is breeding,
Which like the courser's hair, hath yet but life,   191
And not a serpent's poison. Say our pleasure,
To such whose places under us require,
Our quick remove from hence.
Eno. I shall do't.   [*Exeunt.*

193. whose places . . . require] whose places under us, require *F;* whose place is under us, requires *F2;* who've places . . . requires *Mason conj.*   195. *Exeunt*] *not in F.*

including their potentialities. Some, however, connect it more especially with 'the main soldier,' as, e.g., Delius: 'If Pompey progresses pre-eminently in this *role* of soldier,' etc. See also on I. i. 54 *ante.* It is worth noting that *quality* in *2H4,* IV. iii. 36, 'Because you are not of our *quality,*/But stand against us like an enemy,' is explained 'party.' It is given in *OED* as the sole known instance, but this sense, if admissible, would suit the passage before us. So Kinnear takes it.

190. *The sides . . . danger*] So in *Cym.,* III. i. 49–51: 'Cæsar's ambition / Which swelled so much that it did almost stretch / The sides of the world.' See also on I. iii. 16 and IV. xiv. 39 *post.*

191. *the courser's hair*] In a passage in Holinshed's Chronicles, 1587, *The Description of England,* p. 224, to which Steevens refers, is a sceptical account of this old popular belief: 'it [i.e. the getting a brood of eels from a turf cut beside a fenny river and placed in contact with the water] would seeme a wonder; and yet it is beleeued, with no lesse assurance of some, than that an horse haire laid in a pale full of the like water will in short time stirre and become a liuing creature.' Coleridge, *Shakespeare Notes and Lectures,* says on

the passage in the text: 'This is so far true to appearance, that a horse hair, "laid," as Hollinshead says, "in a pail of water," will become the supporter of seemingly one worm, though probably of an immense number of small slimy water-lice. . . It is a common experiment with schoolboys in Cumberland and Westmoreland. Mr Craig tells me that he recollects being shown, as a child, by his Irish nurse, some horsehairs wriggling about in a tributary of the Bann in Derry, and being informed that they were turning into eels. The thought of a serpent as yet only potentially venomous occurs also in *Mac.,* III. iv. 29–31.'

192–4. *Say . . . from hence*] †The reading of the text is that of F, with the transposititon of the comma from after *us* to after *require.* Most editors follow F2, an interesting example, I think, of the dangers of too readily deserting F. No doubt F's reading would have been an easy 'auditory error', but it gives the right sense, which I suggest F2 does not. Antony does not want *all* his subordinates informed. He is saying, more practically, 'Convey my intention (our immediate departure) to *those of* my subordinates whose positions make it essential for them to be informed.' [R]

[SCENE III.—*The Same.*]

Enter CLEOPATRA, CHARMIAN, ALEXAS, *and* IRAS.

Cleo. Where is he?
Char.   I did not see him since.
Cleo. See where he is, who's with him, what he does:
    I did not send you. If you find him sad,
    Say I am dancing; if in mirth, report
    That I am sudden sick. Quick, and return.   [*Exit Alexas.*
Char. Madam, methinks if you did love him dearly,   6
    You do not hold the method, to enforce
    The like from him.
Cleo.   What should I do, I do not?
Char. In each thing give him way, cross him in nothing.
Cleo. Thou teachest like a fool: the way to lose him.   10
Char. Tempt him not so too far. I wish, forbear;
    In time we hate that which we often fear.

Enter ANTONY.

    But here comes Antony
Cleo.   I am sick, and sullen.
Ant. I am sorry to give breathing to my purpose,—
Cleo. Help me away, dear Charmian, I shall fall.   15
    It cannot be thus long, the sides of nature
    Will not sustain it.
Ant.   Now, my dearest queen,—
Cleo. Pray you stand farther from me.
Ant.   What's the matter?
Cleo. I know by that same eye there's some good news.

Scene III

5. *Exit Alexas*] Capell; not in F.

3. *I did . . . you*] Malone compares similarly elliptical phrasing in *Troil.*, IV. ii. 73: 'I will go meet them: and, my lord Æneas, / We met by chance: you did not find me here.'

sad] probably 'serious' merely, as so commonly.

11. *I wish, forbear*] Prithee, forbear.

Dover Wilson adopts an anonymous conjecture 'iwis' = 'certainly' (*not* 'I wis').

16. *the sides of nature*] Steevens compares *Tw.N.*, II. iv. 95: 'There is no woman's *sides* / Can bide the beating of so strong a passion,' etc. See also on I. ii. 190 *ante*; IV. xiv. 39 *post*.

What, says the married woman you may go?   20
Would she had never given you leave to come!
Let her not say 'tis I that keep you here.
I have no power upon you; hers you are.
Ant. The gods best know—
Cleo.   O, never was there queen
So mightily betray'd! yet at the first   25
I saw the treasons planted.
Ant.   Cleopatra,—
Cleo. Why should I think you can be mine and true
(Though you in swearing shake the throned gods)
Who have been false to Fulvia? Riotous madness,
To be entangled with those mouth-made vows,   30
Which break themselves in swearing!
Ant.   Most sweet queen,—
Cleo. Nay, pray you, seek no colour for your going,
But bid farewell, and go: when you sued staying,
Then was the time for words; no going then;
Eternity was in our lips, and eyes,   35
Bliss in our brows' bent; none our parts so poor,

---

20. What, says . . . go?] What sayes . . . goe? *F;* What says the married woman?
you may go; *Rowe and others.*

20. *What, says . . . go?*] † F's question
mark is probably right, whether we
supply a comma ('What, says the
married woman you may go?') or
another question mark ('What says the
married woman? You may go?'). But
since exclamation and question marks
were frequently confused, and, from
Fulvia, *must* would be more natural
than *may*, perhaps Cleopatra is *assuming* that Fulvia has issued a summons,
and we should read 'What says the
married woman? You may go!' [R]

26. *planted*] either in the gardener's
sense, or = placed (like mines, etc.):
so Braithwaite, *Strappado for the Diuell,*
1615 (1878 repr., p. 92), *The
Wooer:* 'He *plants* his engines deeper,'
etc.

32. *colour*] a very common metaphor
for pretext, specious excuse. See *H8,*
I. i. 178. Lyly plays on the word in

Campaspe, v. iv. 94: 'You lay your
colours grosely; though I could not
paint in your shop, I can spy into your
excuse'; *ibid.* III. i. 14: 'You have bin
so long used to colours, you can doe
nothing but *colour*'; and John Harington in a letter to Sir Antony Standen,
dated from Athlone, 1559: 'On Sun-
day last the Governor marched with
one and twenty companies, or colours
(for indeed some of them were but
mere *colours* of companies, having
sixty for a hundred and fifty) from
Tulske,' etc. See Harington's *Nugæ
Antiquæ,* 1769, i. 51; also the extracts
from North, *post,* pp. 256, 265.

36. *bent*] arch. In Ben Jonson, the
arches of the brow are Love's 'double
bow': see *Underwoods,* Elegy xix: 'By
that fair Stand, your forehead,
whence he bends / His double Bow,
and round his Arrowes sends'; also

But was a race of heaven. They are so still,
Or thou, the greatest soldier of the world,
Art turn'd the greatest liar.

Ant.   How now, lady?

Cleo. I would I had thy inches, thou shouldst know   40
There were a heart in Egypt.

Ant.   Hear me, queen:
The strong necessity of time commands
Our services awhile; but my full heart
Remains in use with you. Our Italy
Shines o'er with civil swords; Sextus Pompeius   45
Makes his approaches to the port of Rome,
Equality of two domestic powers
Breed scrupulous faction: the hated, grown to strength,
Are newly grown to love: the condemn'd Pompey,
Rich in his father's honour, creeps apace   50
Into the hearts of such as have not thriv'd
Upon the present state, whose numbers threaten,

---

ibid., A Celebration of Charis, v: 'Both her *Brows, bent* like my bow.'

37. *race of heaven*] As eternity was in her lips and eyes (cf. Marlowe, *Dr Faustus,* 1330 (sc. 14): 'Sweet Helen, make me immortal with a kiss'), bliss in her brows, so he had found the same or other marks of heaven in her other beauties. *A race of heaven* probably = as Malone thought, 'of heavenly origin' (cf. the use of *race* in *Tp.,* I. ii. 358); but Warburton says *race* is 'smack or flavour of heaven', and Johnson approves, observing that '*the race* of wine is the taste of the soil'; see Massinger, *New Way to Pay Old Debts,* I. iii. 8: 'There came, not six days since, from Hull, a pipe / Of rich Canary. . . / *Greedy.* Is it of the right *race?*'

41. *Egypt*] i.e. Cleopatra, as *post* line 78, and elsewhere.

44. *in use with you*] yours to enjoy, to have the usufruct of; *perhaps* in trust with you, as in *Mer.V.,* IV. i. 384, where, however, the context puts the phrase in strict accord with its counterpart in legal terminology, when a

third party is possessed with land for the express purpose of conveying it to one person after the death of another (*seisitus in usum alicujus*). See in Dyce's *Glossary,* a note by Anon., apud Halliwell, and the aforesaid passage in *Mer.V.,* 'I am content; so he will let me have / The other half *in use,* to render it, / Upon his death, unto the gentleman / That lately stole his daughter.'

45–52. *Sextus Pompeius,* etc.] Cf. I. ii. 182–90 *ante*; I. iv. 36–47 *post.*

46. *port of Rome*] more probably Ostia, the natural objective of a fleet, than = gate of Rome, though *port* = gate in IV. iv. 23 *post.*

48. *Breed . . . faction*] favour the rise of parties which profess a hesitancy in determining where their allegiance is due. Some editors read *breeds* with Pope, to correspond with *Equality:* but the plural is no doubt due to the proximity of *powers.* See Abbott, *Shakespearian Grammar,* §412.

48–9. *the hated . . . to love*] those who were hated are beginning to be loved.

And quietness, grown sick of rest, would purge
By any desperate change. My more particular,
And that which most with you should safe my going,   55
Is Fulvia's death.
Cleo. Though age from folly could not give me freedom,
It does from childishness. Can Fulvia die?
Ant. She's dead, my queen.
Look here, and at thy sovereign leisure read   60
The garboils she awak'd: at the last, best,
See when and where she died.
Cleo.   O most false love!
Where be the sacred vials thou should'st fill

---

53. *sick of . . . purge*] ill through rest, as well as tired of it, would, etc. The diseases of peace and tranquillity similarly suggest purgation (by letting blood) in *2H4*, IV. i. 54–66, e.g. lines 63–6: 'But rather show awhile like fearful war, / To diet rank minds *sick of* happiness / And *purge* the obstructions which begin to stop / Our very veins of life.'

54. *My more particular*] what is more especially my own affair. Cf. IV. ix. 20 *post*, and *Troil.*, II. ii. 9: 'As far as toucheth *my particular*.'

55. *safe my going*] make you feel secure in letting me go. See IV. vi. 26, and note.

58. *It does . . . die*] a mere expression of incredulity, to which it would be needless to draw attention if Steevens and Malone had not shown that it could be mistaken.

61. *garboils*] tumults, commotions, from the old French *garbouil*. Cf. II. ii. 67 *post*. The word occurs fairly often. See Steevens's instances in 1821 Variorum, and Collier's in a note to Barry's *Ram Alley* (Hazlitt's *Dodsley*, x. 287); also *The Weakest Goeth to the Wall*, V. i. 52 (Hazlitt's *Webster*, IV, p. 287): 'these sweating *garbolds*'; *Manningham's Diary*, p. 147 (Camden Society, 1868): 'There was a diligent watch and ward kept . . . to prevent *garboiles*'; Drayton, *The Harmonie of the*

Church (Percy Society, 1843), p. 35: 'They chose them gods; then *garboils* did within their gates abound.' It occurs several times in Drayton's *Barons' Wars*.

at the last, best] Surely this means that the cream of the correspondence is in the part to which her attention is last directed—possibly also the last part of a letter—and consists of convincing intelligence of Fulvia's death. Steevens, however, perceives a 'conjugal tribute to the memory of Fulvia,' comparing *Mac.*, I. iv. 7–8: 'nothing in his life / Became him like the leaving it'; while Boswell interprets: 'her death was the *best* thing I have known of her, as it checked her garboils.'

† The F punctuation, with comma (not semicolon) after 'best', supports Case's interpretation and makes Boswell's almost impossible. [R]

63. *vials*] 'Alluding,' says Johnson, 'to the lachrymatory vials, or bottles of tears, which the Romans sometimes put into the urn of a friend.' That the vials found in tombs were so employed is now considered very doubtful. It has been maintained that they really held unguents. Theobald (and later Steevens) refers to *The Two Noble Kinsmen*, I. v. 4: 'Balms, and gums, and heavy cheers, / Sacred *vials* fill'd with tears.' In Browne's *Britannia's Pastorals*, I. v.

With sorrowful water? Now I see, I see,
In Fulvia's death, how mine receiv'd shall be. 65
Ant. Quarrel no more, but be prepar'd to know
The purposes I bear; which are, or cease,
As you shall give the advice. By the fire
That quickens Nilus' slime, I go from hence
Thy soldier, servant, making peace or war, 70
As thou affects.
Cleo.   Cut my lace, Charmian, come,
But let it be, I am quickly ill, and well,
So Antony loves.
Ant.   My precious queen, forbear,
And give true evidence to his love, which stands
An honourable trial.

71. affects] *F;* affectst *F2 and many edd.*

736, the walls of the house of Repentance are hung with 'crystal *vials* of repentant tears'; and, similarly, Death's cave, 'In bottles tears of friends and Louers vaine,' in Peacham's *Period of Mourning* (1613), Vision iii. See also Angel Day, *The English Secretarie* (1599), pt i, 125: 'I have prepared a golden boxe wherein I mean to consecrate all the teares you shed for that accident, to *Berecynthia* the beldame of the Gods, as a relique of your great kindship and curtesie.'

68. *By the fire*] i.e. the sun. Steevens prefixed *Now* to satisfy his ear, quoting *John*, II. i. 397: 'Now by the sky,' etc. The metrical value of the marked pause (see Abbott, *Shakespearian Grammar*, §508) was not yet appreciated.

71. *affects*] choosest.

Cut my lace] however inappropriate to Cleopatra's unfettered beauty, the first thought, under emotion, real or pretended, of the coarser female character in old plays. See Dekker, *The Honest Whore*, pt 1 (*Works*, Pearson, ii. 30): 'Fie, fie, *cut my lace*, good servant; I shall ha' the mother presently, I'm so vext,' etc.; Webster, *Northward Hoe!* II. i (*Works*, Hazlitt, i. 200): '*Doll.* O, I shall burst, if I *cut not my lace*, I'm so vext!'

72–3. *I . . . So Antony loves*] I am no sooner ill than well again, provided Antony loves. In thus withdrawing the threat of hysterics implied in 'Cut my lace', etc., Cleopatra seems to angle for some convincing evidence of love, which Antony's reply does not afford to her satisfaction. The words are less likely to refer to what precedes, viz. the sworn devotion of lines 68–71; it did not prevent the threat, and probably no admission of its force as a proof of love is involved in the words of withdrawal. Steevens, Capell, and several editors interpret differently, making *so* = thus, and punctuating accordingly, with sense: 'Antony's love is as fluctuating and uncertain as my health.' I have not seen it proposed to make *so* refer wholly to Antony's purpose, disconnecting it altogether from line 72. In that case it would mean: 'This, then, is your love for me.'

74. *give . . . evidence*] bear true witness. The Collier MS corrector substitutes *credence* for *evidence*, and *audience* has been proposed by L. Campbell; but the phrase as it stands has the right ring, and the 'witness' is probably the testimony of being composed and *well*.

Cleo.   So Fulvia told me.   75
I prithee turn aside and weep for her,
Then bid adieu to me, and say the tears
Belong to Egypt. Good now, play one scene
Of excellent dissembling, and let it look
Like perfect honour.
Ant.   You'll heat my blood: no more.
Cleo. You can do better yet; but this is meetly.   81
Ant. Now, by my sword,—
Cleo.   And target. Still he mends.
But this is not the best. Look, prithee, Charmian,
How this Herculean Roman does become
The carriage of his chafe.   85
Ant. I'll leave you, lady.
Cleo.   Courteous lord, one word:
Sir, you and I must part, but that's not it:
Sir, you and I have lov'd, but there's not it;
That you know well, something it is I would,—
O, my oblivion is a very Antony,   90
And I am all forgotten.

---

80. blood: no more.] *Rowe (semicolon);* blood no more? *F.*   82. my] *F2; not in F.*

---

78. *to Egypt*] 'To me, the Queen of Egypt' (Johnson). See line 41 *ante*, and note.

Good now] 'please you,' as in *Ham.*, I. i. 70.

80. *You'll heat . . .*] †Rowe's repunctuation will no doubt serve well enough. It leaves Antony saying 'You'll make me lose my temper. Enough of this.' But the F question mark is obstinately there, and I think it is tempting to transfer the 'no more?', retaining the question mark, to Cleopatra, who thus says, in reply to Antony's 'You'll make me lose my temper,' 'Is that the best you can do by way of retort? You can do better than that, though you've made quite a good start.' [R]

81. *meetly*] reasonably well. Not elsewhere in Shakespeare.

82. *And target*] 'making it a swash-buckler's oath, cf. *1H4*, I. iii. 230' (Dover Wilson).

84. *Herculean*] as descended from Anton, son of Hercules. See extracts from North's *Plutarch, post*, p. 241; and cf. IV. xii. 44 *post.*

84–5. *How . . . chafe*] How he becomes, or lends grace to, his furious bearing. There is still some allusion to playing a part. Staunton is unwarrantably positive that *chafe* is 'a silly blunder of the transcriber or compositor for *chief* [the reading in his text], meaning Hercules, the *head* or *principal* of the house of Antonii.'

90–1. *O, my oblivion . . . forgotten*] my 'oblivious memory' is as faithless as Antony, and, like him, has forgotten my power over it. 'Oblivious memory' is Steevens's phrase, but it is unnecessary to follow him in further, taking here 'I am all forgotten' as = 'I forget

Ant.   But that your royalty
Holds idleness your subject, I should take you
For idleness itself.
Cleo.   'Tis sweating labour,
To bear such idleness so near the heart
As Cleopatra this. But sir, forgive me,   95
Since my becomings kill me, when they do not
Eye well to you. Your honour calls you hence,
Therefore be deaf to my unpitied folly,
And all the gods go with you! Upon your sword
Sit laurel victory, and smooth success   100
Be strew'd before your feet!
Ant.   Let us go. Come;
Our separation so abides and flies,

---

100. laurel] *F* (Lawrell); Lawrell'd *F2 and some edd.*

---

everything,' much like the sense in 'How comes it, Michael, you are thus forgot?' (*Oth.*, II. iii. 190). It seems to mean, not 'I am all forgetful,' but 'I am every way forgotten,' viz. by Antony and my own faculties († surely it means both. [R]). Marston, however, who imitates Shakespeare here and there in *The Insatiate Countess*, has in that play, IV. ii. 67–8: 'Thy intellectual powers oblivion smothers, / That thou art nothing but forgetfulness.'

91–3. *But that . . . itself*] Under the surface meaning—which contains its own rebuke—that Cleopatra can't be both queen and subject, or might be taken for a personification of idleness or trifling, possibly lies the insinuation: Were you not liege lady of trifling, *and able to make her serve* (or: *command her arts for*) your purposes, I should take you, etc. Malone suggests something like this last, and it is substantially the explanation preferred by Clarke and Rolfe. With *idleness*, Steevens compares Webster, *Vittoria Corombona*, IV. i. 114, where Francisco, taking Isabella's ghost to be the product of his imagination, and having asked, 'How cam'st thou by thy death?' continues 'how idle am I / To question mine own

idleness!' His own best interpretation is: 'holds *idleness* in subjection to you, exalting you far above its influence.'

96. *Since my becomings*, etc.] I see here the expression of feelings hurt by Antony's cold answer to the sudden and emotional conversion from mockery to pathos in lines 86–91. Cleopatra says, in effect: 'I have done; even the regrets, the emotion, the fears that become me at such a time, I repress, since it is anguish to me to displease you.' The usual explanation of *becomings* is, however, 'graces.' Steevens suspected in the word an allusion to Antony's phrase in I. i. 49 *ante*.

99–100. *Upon . . . victory*] Cf. *Edward III*, III. iii. 190: 'Be still adorn'd with laurel *victory*,' which confirms the reading, *laurel*, of F, as do similar cases of noun as adjective, e.g. 'the honey of his *music* vows' (*Ham.*, III. i. 165). For the figure cf. *Tryall of Chevalry*, 1605, 'Successful action sit *upon* thy sword' (Bullen's *Old Plays*, iii. 333, where other examples are given); also *Selimus*, 1594 (ed. Grosart, line 2447): 'And white-wing'd *victory* sits on our swords.'

102–4. *Our separation . . . thee*] Their separation is said to *abide* as resulting

That thou, residing here, goes yet with me;
And I, hence fleeting, here remain with thee.
Away!   [*Exeunt.* 105

[SCENE IV.—*Rome. Cæsar's house.*]

Enter OCTAVIUS *reading a letter,* LEPIDUS,
and their Train.

Cæs. You may see, Lepidus, and henceforth know,
It is not Cæsar's natural vice to hate
Our great competitor. From Alexandria
This is the news: he fishes, drinks, and wastes
The lamps of night in revel; is not more manlike   5
Than Cleopatra; nor the queen of Ptolemy
More womanly than he: hardly gave audience, or
Vouchsaf'd to think he had partners. You shall find there
A man who is the abstract of all faults
That all men follow.
Lep.   I must not think there are   10
Evils enow to darken all his goodness:

103. goes] *F;* goest *F2, Rowe;* go'st *Capell and others.*

Scene iv
3. Our] *Singer (Heath and Johnson conj.);* One *F.*   8. Vouchsaf'd] *Johnson;*
vouchsafe *F;* did vouchsafe *F2.*   9. abstract] *F2;* abstracts *F.*

from Cleopatra's *abode* in Egypt, and
to *fly,* as resulting from Antony's fleeting thence. With the conceit in the whole sentence, cf. *Mucedorus,* I. i. 12: "'tis from the realm, not thee: / Though lands part bodies, hearts keep company'; and Donne's famous poem, *A Valediction: Forbidding Mourning.* Steevens quotes Sidney's *Arcadia,* bk i (see lines 169–70 of the poem at its close), as possibly having suggested the thought to Shakespeare: 'She went, they staid; or rightly, for to say, / She staid in them, they went in thought with her.'

Scene iv
3. *competitor*] here, as often, partner, associate. Cf. II. vii. 69 *post,* and *R3,* IV. iv. 505: 'And every hour more *competitors* / Flock to the rebels,' etc. See also

the quotation on I. i. 12, '*triple pillar.*'
4–33. *he fishes, drinks,* etc.] With the charges in these speeches, cf. North, *post,* pp. 248–9, 241, 245.
6. *queen of Ptolemy*] Cleopatra was nominally married by Cæsar to the younger of her two brothers of that name, a mere child, whom she is said to have made away with by poison. Cf. *Egypt's widow,* II. i. 37 *post.*
9–10. *is the abstract . . . follow*] exhibits in himself, and in their highest degree, all the faults of mankind. In respect of faults, he is, like Dryden's Zimri (*Absalom and Achitophel,* i. 546): 'Not one, but all mankind's epitome.' Cf. Jonson, *The Devil is an Ass,* IV. iv. 245: 'The top of woman! all her sex in *abstract*'; Massinger, *The City Madam,* III. iii: 'Heaven's *abstract* or epitome.'

His faults, in him, seem as the spots of heaven,
More fiery by night's blackness; hereditary,
Rather than purchas'd; what he cannot change,
Than what he chooses.   15
Cæs. You are too indulgent. Let's grant it is not
Amiss to tumble on the bed of Ptolemy,
To give a kingdom for a mirth, to sit
And keep the turn of tippling with a slave,
To reel the streets at noon, and stand the buffet   20
With knaves that smells of sweat: say this becomes
    him,—
As his composure must be rare indeed

16. Let's] *F;* Let us *Pope and edd.*   21. smells] *F* (smels) *; smell F2.*

12–13. *His faults . . . blackness*] His
faults are made more conspicuous by
his goodness, as the stars by night's
blackness. The simile aims only at
force of contrast, disregarding correspondence of quality in the things compared, *faults* and *stars*, *goodness* and
blackness. It is otherwise in *Ham.*, v. ii.
266–8, as Malone indicates: 'in mine
ignorance / Your skill shall, like a star
i' the darkest night, / Stick fiery off
indeed.' Quarles, in *The Author's
Dream*, compares his sins to the stars in
brightness: 'My Sins are like the Stars
within the Skies, / In view, in number,
ev'n as bright, as great,' etc. With
spots of heaven, cf. Peele, *Edward I*, sc.
iii, line 74: 'The welkin, spangled
through with golden spots,' etc.

14. *purchas'd*] acquired, as commonly. Cf. Nashe, *The Unfortunate Traveller*,
ii, p. 253, line 2: 'With him we tra-
velled along, having *purchast* his
acquaintance a little before.' The
legal origin of the use is played upon in
the following passage from Shirley's
Love Tricks, iii. v (*Works*, 1833, i, pp.
54–5): '. . . got a great estate of wealth
by gaming and wenching, and so *purchas'd* unhappily this state of damna-
tion you see me in. *Infor.* Came you in
it by *purchase*? then you do not claim it
by your father's interest as an heir:'
etc. See Cowel's *Interpreter* (ed. Man-

ley, 1684, *s.v.*): 'it signifieth the buying
of Lands or Tenements with Money,
or by any other Agreement, and not
the obtaining of it by descent,' etc.

18. *a mirth*] So Beaumont and
Fletcher, *Philaster*, iii. ii. 95: 'made it
[danger] but *a mirth.*'

20. *stand the buffet*] So in *1H4*, iii. ii.
66: 'To laugh at gibing boys and *stand
the push* / Of every beardless vain comparative.' Cf. also the whole passage,
and see Intro., *ante*, p. xxx–xxxi.

21. *smells*] The old Northern plural
(?) in *s* is extremely common, occurring in all kinds of writers, and often,
as here, in F. Cf. line 49 *post*; *Tp.*, iii.
iii. 2, 'bones akes'; *Mer.V.*, iii. ii. 18,
'times Puts,' and quotation in note on
iv. xiv. 76–7 *post.*

22. *As his composure*] Composure =
composition, as in *Troil.*, ii. iii. 254;
Brome, *A Mad Couple*, etc., iv. i
(*Works*, Pearson, p. 63): 'hee is of so
sweete a *Composure*,' etc. For *As* Johnson proposed to read *And*: but the in-
consequence he detected is more
apparent than real, as the inference in
As is from the idea of an untarnishable
Antony involved in 'say this becomes
him.' The whole equals: Grant he is a
prodigy, as prodigy he must be to carry
off such faults. Dr Ingleby's account of
the use of *as* in this and other passages
will be found in ii. ii. 53 *post*, but can,

Whom these things cannot blemish,—yet must Antony
No way excuse his foils, when we do bear
So great weight in his lightness. If he fill'd   25
His vacancy with his voluptuousness,
Full surfeits, and the dryness of his bones
Call on him for't. But to confound such time,
That drums him from his sport, and speaks as loud
As his own state, and ours,—'tis to be chid: 30
As we rate boys, who being mature in knowledge,

24. foils] F (foyles); soils Malone.   30. chid:] F; chid Capell and most edd.;
chid, Hanmer, Johnson.

I think, be dispensed with in the present case at least.

24. foils] The retention of foils in the
text seems inevitably to follow the evidence of OED as to the sense disgrace,
stigma, with mixture of the sense of the
verb foil = to foul, etc. The quotation
there given from Porter, Angry Women
of Abingdon (Percy Soc.), 26, 'It hath
set a foyle upon his fame,' is precisely
apt and unmistakable: 'And it [a
fault] hath set a foil upon thy fame, /
Not as the foil doth grace the diamond'
(Hazlitt's Dodsley, VII. 288). Equally
with Malone's otherwise probable
soils, foils agrees with the defiling pur-
suits just detailed, and no longer
merely depends on Collier's explanation as to the vices 'which foil or defeat'
Antony's virtues, or on Schmidt's citation of Tp., III. i. 46, for the sense
'blemish': or again on the possibility
that Cæsar—who has just granted, for
argument's sake, that Antony's faults
may become him—might refer to
them as the foils of his virtues, as
Lepidus makes the virtues set off his
faults, and as Prince Hal (1H4, I. ii.
234-7) makes his 'fault' the 'foil' to set
off his reformation.

24-5. when . . . lightness] when 'his
trifling levity throws so much burden
upon us' (Johnson).

26. vacancy] similarly used for leisure
by Heywood, ΓΥΝΑΙΚΕΙΟΝ (1624),
p. 318: 'Neither remember I, O king,
. . . that Agamemnon, in all the time

of the tenne yeeres siege of Troy had
such vacancie as thou hast now to prie
into the Boothes of his soulders;' etc.

28. Call on him for 't] insist on a reckoning for it. Cf. Braithwaite, Nature's
Embassie (1621), Satire ii, st. 2, of the
deferred wrath of Nature: 'Though
she delay assure thee she will call, /
And thou must pay both vse and
principall.' OED quotes the passage
under 'To impeach, challenge', adding '1740 Chesterfield Lett. J, clx. 295:
You call upon me for the partiality of
an author to his own works,' and
another late passage.

confound] See on I. i. 45 ante.

31-3. As we rate, etc.] Such conduct
merits the scolding we give boys, who
being old enough to know better,
gratify their present desires against
their judgment. Non-existent difficulties have been found here. Hanmer
read (and Warburton accepted) im-
mature, offended at the idea of maturity
in connection with boys. Daniel conjectures he's to be chid . . . who . . . Pawns
his . . . to his . . . rebels. . . If we are to
press the meaning in Pawn, it is possible to say that experience (which
gives foreknowledge of consequences)
is pledged to pleasure in the sense that
it must be redeemed, or reinforced, by
the undergoing of the foreseen consequences of pleasure; but I doubt if
the thought goes beyond the necessity
of parting with the valuable, the guid-
ance of experience, for the occasion:

Pawn their experience to their present pleasure,
And so rebel to judgment.

Enter a Messenger.

Lep.   Here's more news.
Mess. Thy biddings have been done, and every hour,
Most noble Cæsar, shalt thou have report   35
How 'tis abroad. Pompey is strong at sea,
And it appears he is belov'd of those
That only have fear'd Cæsar: to the ports
The discontents repair, and men's reports
Give him much wrong'd.
Cæs.   I should have known no less;
It hath been taught us from the primal state   41
That he which is was wish'd, until he were;
And the ebb'd man, ne'er lov'd till ne'er worth love,
Comes dear'd, by being lack'd. This common body,
Like to a vagabond flag upon the stream,   45

---

44. dear'd] *Theobald (Warburton)*; fear'd *F*.

---

cf. Braithwaite, *Strappado for the Diuell*, 1615 (1878 repr., p. 291): 'oh why should we, / To get a little sport, *paune* modesty?' †But as to *rate* Mr J. C. Maxwell makes the interesting suggestion that it here means 'estimate'— i.e. 'In the same way that we count as mere boys those men who, being . . .' The F colon after *chid* helps it. [R]

36–47. *Pompey*, etc.] Cf. I. ii. 181–90; I. iii. 45–52 *ante*.

39. *The discontents*] the discontented, or malcontents, as in *1H4*, v. i. 76. Similar instances of the abstract for the the concrete occur in II. ii. 47 *post*: *Lr*, III. i. 24, etc. Cf. *Edward III*, III. iii. 156: 'For what's this Edward but a belly-god, / A tender and lascivious wantonness,' etc.

40. *Give him*] represent him as; as in *Cor.*, I. ix. 55; Shirley, *The Wedding*, v. ii (*Works*, 1833, I. 441): 'my nephew *gives* you valiant,' etc.

41. *from the primal state*] since government began.

42. *That he . . . were*] that the man in power was always the popular candidate for it till, and only till, he obtained it. Cæsar glances at his own loss of popular favour.

43. *ebb'd man*] Copley uses a similar figure in *A Fig for a Fortune*, 1596, p. 6: 'What booteth it to liue . . . A muddie ebbe after a Chrystall flood?'

44. *Comes dear'd*] becomes endeared. Collier (1843) retained *fear'd*, but reads *lov'd* in his second edition, with the Collier MS. Cf. *Cor.*, IV. i. 15: 'I shall be *loved* when I am lack'd.' Knight retains *fear'd* on the ground that the notions of fear and love are almost synonymous in the mind of one who aims at supreme power. But the messenger's distinction between these notions in lines 37–8 confirms the emendation. Cf. I. ii. 183–5 *ante*.

This common body] the common people.

45. *flag*] a common species of iris.

Goes to, and back, lackeying the varying tide,
To rot itself with motion.

Enter a second Messenger.

Mess.　　　　　　　　　　　　Cæsar, I bring thee word,
Menecrates and Menas, famous pirates,
Makes the sea serve them, which they ear and wound
With keels of every kind. Many hot inroads　　　　50
They make in Italy, the borders maritime
Lack blood to think on't, and flush youth revolt:
No vessel can peep forth, but 'tis as soon
Taken as seen; for Pompey's name strikes more
Than could his war resisted.

Cæs.　　　　　　　　　　　　　　Antony,　　　　55

---

46. lackeying] lacquying *Theobald (Anon. MS)*; lacking *F*.　　47. S.D. *Enter* . . .]
Capell; not in F.

---

46. *lackeying*] The servility of popular favour is united with its instability by Theobald's reading. Pope's was *lashing*. For the use of the verb, Steevens quotes, among other passages, Chapman's Homer, *Iliad*, xxiv [ed. Shepherd, 1875, p. 285]: 'I could wish thy grave affairs did need / My guide to Argos, either shipp'd, or *lackeying* by thy side,' etc.

47. Enter . . .] † F has no S.D. and so attributes *Cæsar, I bring* . . . to the messenger who has already come. But I have little doubt that Capell (supported by Steevens) was right in thinking that we must have a second messenger. Quite apart from the expectation of a series of messengers created by 'every hour shalt thou have report' (lines 34–5), the opening 'Cæsar, I bring thee word,' natural in the mouth of a second messenger, is awkward as no more than the introduction to a second item of news from the same messenger who has already addressed Cæsar; and Cæsar's seven lines of philosophic comment are equally awkward if they interrupt the delivery of a piece of news, though natural enough if they follow a report

which has clearly terminated. [R]

48. *Menecrates . . . pirates*] See North, *post*, p. 251.

49. *Makes*] See on line 21 *ante*; *ear*, plough. Cf. 1. ii. 108 *ante*.

52. *flush*] lusty, full of vigour. Cf. *Ham.*, III. iii. 81: 'As *flush* as May.' *OED* gives further examples of a derived sense, 'self-confident,' 'self-conceited,' and it is interesting to note also here another *flush*, of uncertain etymology and dialectal, = fledged.

54–5. *Pompey's name . . . resisted*] † The commentators are mostly silent, but I do not find this so obvious as the silence suggests it should be. If 'war resisted' = 'resistance to his armed forces' (as 'Cæsar interfectus' can mean 'the death of Cæsar'), then the whole means 'His mere name causes you more loss than armed resistance would.' But if we take 'resisted' as conditional, it means 'His mere name is more effective than his armed forces would be, if only you opposed them.' I do not think the two meanings are identical, but perhaps I am merely nosing out difficulty where there is none. [R]

Leave thy lascivious wassails. When thou once
Was beaten from Modena, where thou slew'st
Hirtius and Pansa, consuls, at thy heel
Did famine follow, whom thou fought'st against,
Though daintily brought up, with patience more   60
Than savages could suffer. Thou didst drink
The stale of horses, and the gilded puddle
Which beasts would cough at: thy palate then did deign
The roughest berry, on the rudest hedge;
Yea, like the stag, when snow the pasture sheets,   65
The barks of trees thou browsed. On the Alps
It is reported thou didst eat strange flesh,
Which some did die to look on: and all this—
It wounds thine honour that I speak it now—
Was borne so like a soldier, that thy cheek   70
So much as lank'd not.

---

56. wassails] *Pope;* Vassailes *F, F2;* Vassails *F3;* Vassals *F4.*   57. Was] *F;*
Wast *Steevens (1778) and edd.;* Wert *F2.*   66. browsed] brows'd *F;* browsed'st
F2.

56. *wassails*] Carousals attended
with lust are naturally contrasted with
the scant and repulsive diet, and
severe hardships stoically endured,
which the next lines describe. Some,
however, prefer the old reading *vassals*,
to which alone, and not to 'drunken
revelry' (*wassails*), Knight unaccountably considers the epithet *lascivious*
appropriate.

57. *Modena*] accented on second syl-
lable (as also by the Countess of Pem-
broke in *Antonie*, Act III), whereas
Italian, 'Módena', Latin, 'Mútina'.
For the whole passage, to line 71, see
North, *post*, p. 243.

59. *whom*] Abbott (*Shakespearian
Grammar*, §264) shows that *who* stands
for irrational antecedents where there
is any approach to personification; but
adds that *whom* is rare, comparing *Tp.*,
III. iii. 62: 'the elements/Of *whom*,' etc.

61. *Than . . . suffer*] explicable, I
think, as a case of cognate accusative,
and = 'Than that which savages
could suffer.' For the thought, cf.
D'Avenant, *Gondibert*, II. ii. 25: 'Still I

have fought, as if in Beauty's sight, /
Outsuffer'd patience, bred in Captives
Breasts;' etc. It is usually taken as an
instance of omission to repeat the preposition in relative sentences (see
Abbott, *Shakespearian Grammar*, §394)
and = 'Than savages could suffer
with,' or 'Than that with which,' etc.

62. *gilded*] overspread with iride-
scent scum; 'filthy-mantled', as in
Tp., IV. i. 182.

63. *deign*] not disdain.

66. *The barks . . . brows'd*] So Nashe,
in *Christ's Tears*, II, p. 70, line 2: 'All
the bushes and boughes, within or
rounde about Ierusalem, were hewd
down and feld, for men (like brute
beasts) to *brouse* on'; Browne, *Britannia's Pastorals*, bk ii (1616), Song i.
663–7: 'As in a forest well complete
with deer / We see the hollies, ashes,
everywhere / Robb'd of their clothing
by the browsing game: / So near the
rock all trees where'er you [i.e. Limos
or Famine] came, / To cold Decem-
ber's wrath stood void of bark.'

71. *lank'd*] grew thin.

Lep.   'Tis pity of him.
Cæs. Let his shames quickly
      Drive him to Rome, 'tis time we twain
      Did show ourselves i' the field, and to that end
      Assemble we immediate council; Pompey   75
      Thrives in our idleness.
Lep.   To-morrow, Cæsar,
      I shall be furnish'd to inform you rightly
      Both what by sea and land I can be able
      To front this present time.
Cæs.   Till which encounter,
      It is my business too. Farewell.   80
Lep. Farewell, my lord; what you shall know meantime
      Of stirs abroad, I shall beseech you, sir,
      To let me be partaker.
Cæs.   Doubt not, sir,
      I know it for my bond.   [*Exeunt.*

[SCENE V.—*Alexandria. Cleopatra's palace.*]

Enter CLEOPATRA, CHARMIAN, IRAS, *and* MARDIAN.

Cleo. Charmian!
Char. Madam?
Cleo. Ha, ha!
      Give me to drink mandragora.

75. we] *F2;* me *F.*   84. know] *Walker;* knew *F.*

75. *Assemble we*] *we*, the reading of F2, sorts with *we twain*, line 73, and *our*, line 76, as well as with the fact that, as Malone says, Cæsar is addressing an equal. *Me* is retained by one or two editors, among whom Knight thinks 'the commentators forget Cæsar's contempt for Lepidus and the crouching humility of Lepidus himself.' Neither of these ascribed qualities appears in this scene.

78. *what . . . I can be able*] what my powers can be.

79. *front*] face, confront. Cf. *2H4,* IV. i. 25: 'What well-appointed leader

fronts us here?' See also II. ii. 61 *post.*

84. *I know . . . bond*] † I recognize it as part of my engagements. F's *knew* is no doubt possible, in the sense '1 knew what my commitments were when we came to our original agreement (and have not forgotten them since)' but the emendation is graphically easy, and attractive. [R]

Scene v

3. *Ha, ha!*] 'A yawn of ennui' (Kittredge).

4. *mandragora*] the juice of mandragora or mandrake, a plant with strong

Char.   Why, madam?
Cleo. That I might sleep out this great gap of time   5
      My Antony is away.
Char.   You think of him too much.
Cleo. O, 'tis treason!
Char.   Madam, I trust not so.
Cleo. Thou, eunuch Mardian!
Mar.   What's your highness' pleasure?
Cleo. Not now to hear thee sing. I take no pleasure
      In aught an eunuch has: 'tis well for thee   10
      That, being unseminar'd, thy freer thoughts
      May not fly forth of Egypt. Hast thou affections?
Mar. Yes, gracious madam.
Cleo. Indeed?
Mar. Not in deed, madam, for I can do nothing   15
      But what indeed is honest to be done:
      Yet have I fierce affections, and think
      What Venus did with Mars.
Cleo.   O Charmian!
      Where think'st thou he is now? Stands he, or sits he?
      Or does he walk? or is he on his horse?   20
      O happy horse to bear the weight of Antony!

---

5. time] *Rowe* (time,); time: *F.*   8. Thou, eunuch] *F;* Thou eunuch, *Pope.*

narcotic qualities. 'The juice thereof with woman's milk laid to the temples maketh to sleep, yea though it were in the most hot ague' (*Bartholomew* [Berthelet], bk xvii, §104). Cf. *Oth.*, III. iii. 330: 'Not poppy, nor mandragora, / Nor all the drowsy syrups of the world, / Shall ever medicine thee to that sweet sleep / Which thou ow'dst yesterday.' *How a Man may Choose a Good Wife*, etc., III. ii (Hazlitt's *Dodsley*, ix. 48): 'in this paper is / The juice of mandrake, by a doctor made / To cast a man, whose leg should be cut off, / Into a deep, a cold, and senseless sleep; / Of such approved operation / That whoso takes it, is for twice twelve hours, / Breathless, and to all men's judgments past all sense'; etc.

9–12. *Not now . . . affections?*] † Mardian is the official singer; cf. II.

v. 2 S.D. '*Tis well for thee that* means, I think, not 'it's just as well for you that . . .' (i.e. 'you escape blame because . . . ,' Cleopatra-like remark though that would be), but 'you are happy in that . . .' Cleopatra is, or pretends to be, congratulating him on his sexless immunity from desire, when her own 'freer', and far from unsexed, thoughts are flying with passionate longing to Rome (cf. line 21, *to bear the weight*, a characteristic, purely physical, touch). *Affections* is nearer to 'passions' or 'desires' than our modern sense. [R]

16. *honest*] in the restricted sense of 'chaste'; cf. *Wiv.*, IV. ii. 110, 'Wives may be merry, and yet *honest* too.'

18. *What Venus . . .*] Venus, wife of Vulcan, was Mars' paramour, and Vulcan trapped them in the act.

Do bravely, horse, for wot'st thou whom thou mov'st,
The demi-Atlas of this earth, the arm
And burgonet of men. He's speaking now,
Or murmuring, 'Where's my serpent of old Nile?'   25
For so he calls me. Now I feed myself
With most delicious poison. Think on me,
That am with Phœbus' amorous pinches black,
And wrinkled deep in time. Broad-fronted Cæsar,
When thou wast here above the ground, I was   30
A morsel for a monarch: and great Pompey
Would stand and make his eyes grow in my brow,
There would he anchor his aspect, and die
With looking on his life.

Enter ALEXAS *from Antony.*

Alex.   Sovereign of Egypt, hail!
Cleo. How much unlike art thou Mark Antony!   35

29. time.] *F;* time? *Capell.*   34. S.D. *from Antony*] *Collier MS; from Cæsar*
F.

23–4. *arm And burgonet*] † I suppose
we must be content, as most commentators seem to be, to take this as meaning simply 'the complete soldier',
equipped both for offence with his
own strong arm, and for defence with
the most efficient helmet yet devised.
But it seems something of an anticlimax after 'the demi-Atlas', and it
is difficult to feel happy about it.
[R]

24. *burgonet*] a helmet of Burgundian
invention, whence its name. 'It was so
fitted to the gorget that the head
moved freely, without producing a
chink through which an enemy might
pierce the neck.' So Morley, on stanza
82, canto vi of Drayton's *Barons' War*
(1887 ed.).

27–9. *Think . . . time*] † Capell's
question mark (adopted by both Case
and Dover Wilson) is not wholly convincing. It makes Antony, rather awkwardly, the subject of *think.* F makes
Cleopatra address Charmian, 'it's me
that he loves, in spite of my wrinkles,'

and then she goes on, characteristically, to say that it is not so surprising
after all, considering her other conquests. But it is true that *think on* often
means 'to think kindly of,' as in *Cor.*,
II. iii. 61 and 196. [R]

28. *amorous pinches*] † Cf. v. ii. 294,
'The stroke of death is as a lover's
pinch.' She includes both the sun and
death among her lovers. [R]

29. *Broad-fronted*] obviously, 'with a
broad forehead'. Henley and Singer
fancy there is an allusion to Cæsar's
baldness, and Seward proposed *bald-
fronted Cæsar*. See on II. vi. 68–70 *post*,
and North, *post*, p. 246, for his intrigue
with Cleopatra.

31. *great Pompey*] Cneius, son of
Pompey the Great, as in III. xiii. 118
post, *q.v.*, and North, *post*, p. 246. The
epithet is misleading.

33. *anchor his aspect*] Cf. *Sonn.* cxxxvii.
6: 'If eyes corrupt by over partial
looks / Be *anchored* in the bay where
all men ride,' etc.; and *Meas.*, II.
iv. 4.

Yet coming from him, that great med'cine hath
With his tinct gilded thee.
How goes it with my brave Mark Antony?
Alex. Last thing he did, dear queen,
He kiss'd—the last of many doubled kisses—   40
This orient pearl. His speech sticks in my heart.
Cleo. Mine ear must pluck it thence.
Alex.   'Good friend,' quoth he,
'Say the firm Roman to great Egypt sends
This treasure of an oyster; at whose foot
To mend the petty present, I will piece   45

40. kiss'd—the . . . kisses—] *Theobald (substantially)*; kist the . . . kisses *F*.

36–7. *great med'cine . . . thee*] The terms the medicine or great medicine, tinct or tincture, were applied by the alchemists to the supreme result of their labours, regarded rather as the agent for transmuting metals than the elixir to renew youth. See *All's W.*, v. iii. 102: 'That knows the tinct and multiplying *medicine*'; Donne, *Resurrection* (Nonesuch *Donne*, ed. Hayward, p. 290): 'He was all gold when he lay down, but rose / All tincture, and doth not alone dispose / Leaden and iron wills to good,' etc.; Jonson, *The Alchemist, passim,* but especially ii. i. 37 *et seq.*, 'But when you see th' effects of the *great med'cine*,' etc. In the text, as in *Tp.*, v. i. 280, where a similar allusion underlies the expressed cause and effect of drunkenness: 'where should they / Find this grand liquor that hath gilded them?' the effect is but external. *Tincture* is often used for a mere surface deposit; so Lord Brooke, 'An Inqvisition vpon Fame and Honovr', 10 (*Works*, ed. Grosart, ii. 70): 'Goodnesse puts only *tincture* on our gall'; on which the editor observes: 'Tincture was supposed to turn the basest metal into gold. *Supra*, it means a golden covering as of a pill in medicine.' Walker (*Critical Examination of the Text of Shakespeare*, 1860) suggests *medicine* possibly = physician, as it may possibly in *All's W.*, ii. i. 75.

41. *orient*] bright, lustrous. *Pearl* and

this epithet were almost inseparable. Cf. 'What a sight would it be to embrace one whose haire were as *orient* as the pearle!' (Lyly, *Endimion*, v. ii. 95: 'to make a pearl more pure / We give it to a dove, in whose womb pent / Some time, we have it forth most *orient*.' (Wm Browne, *An Elegy on Sir Thomas Overbury*, etc., lines 26–8). *OED* says the epithet is applied to pearls 'as coming anciently from the East,' and cites 1555 Eden *Decades* 39: 'Many of these perles were as bygge as hasell nuttes, and *oriente* (as we caule it), that is, lyke unto them of the Easte partes.' *Pearl of Orient* = orient pearl, oriental pearl (*OED*) also supports this, but a quotation supplied by Mr Craig shows that another derivation was current: Harrison, *Description of England*, bk iii, chap. i (New Shakes. Soc., ed. Furnivall, pt i, p. 80): 'They [pearls] are called *orient* because of the cleerenesse which resembleth the colour of the cleere air before the rising of the sun.'

43. *firm*] constant.

45. *piece*] *To piece* can mean to make additions to as well as simply to mend. See Earle's *Microcosmographie*, 1628, *A young rawe Preacher*: 'He has more tricks with a sermon, than a Tailer with an old cloak, to turne it, and *piece* it,' etc.; Lyly's *Campaspe*, iv. i. 12: 'He hath found *Dedalus* old waxen wings, and hath beene *peecing* them this moneth, he is so broade in the

    Her opulent throne with kingdoms. All the east,
    (Say thou) shall call her mistress.' So he nodded
    And soberly did mount an arm-gaunt steed,
    Who neigh'd so high, that what I would have spoke
    Was beastly dumb'd by him.
Cleo.   What, was he sad, or merry?
Alex. Like to the time o' the year between the extremes   51
    Of hot and cold, he was nor sad nor merry.
Cleo. O well-divided disposition! Note him,
    Note him, good Charmian, 'tis the man; but note him.
    He was not sad, for he would shine on those   55
    That make their looks by his; he was not merry,
    Which seem'd to tell them, his remembrance lay
    In Egypt with his joy; but between both.
    O heavenly mingle! Be'st thou sad, or merry,
    The violence of either thee becomes,   60
    So does it no man else. Met'st thou my posts?

---

48. an arm-gaunt] an Arme-gaunt *F.*   50. dumb'd] *Theobald;* dumbe *F.*
What . . . merry] What was he sad, or merry *F;* What was he, sad or merry
Furness conj.   61. man] *F2;* mans *F.*

shoulders'; Kyd, *1 Ieronimo,* III. iv. 10:
'My armes / Are of the shortest; let
your loues *peece* them out.' Antony will
lay his conquests at Cleopatra's feet to
extend her dominion.

    48. *arm-gaunt*] See App. I.

    50. *beastly dumb'd*] 'Deep clerks she
dumbs' (*Per.,* v, prol. 5), quoted by
Steevens, supports this reading. See
also Sylvester's *Du Bartas,* 1621 ed.,
p. 910 (*Job Triumphant*): 'He dulls the
Learned, *dumbs* the Eloquent,' etc.
Shakespeare uses *beastly* as an adverb
in *Cym.,* v. iii. 27, and elsewhere.

    What . . . merry?] † Furness's punc-
tuation is undeniably attractive, and
Dover Wilson promotes it to the text.
But I do not feel very happy about it.
I fancy that the most natural Elizabethan for what it makes Cleopatra
say would have been '*Whether* was he
sad or merry?', and the *What* followed
by comma of most editors (precisely
the oratorical Latin 'Quid?' = 'now
for the next point') is common Elizabethan. [R]

    54. *but*] just, only (not adversative).

    56. *That make . . . his*] Cf. *John,*
v. i. 50: 'inferior eyes / That borrow
their behaviours from the great,' etc.

    59. *mingle*] as a noun, not elsewhere
in Shakespeare save IV. viii. 37 *post.* Cf.
Poems on Several Occasions, Sir R.
Howard, 1696, *To the Reader,* sig. A4:
'the *Mingle* it has with my private
Papers, was the greatest cause, that it
received its share in the publick
Impression.'

    60. *The violence . . . becomes*] the com-
pliment of I. i. 49 *ante,* returned.

    † But *violence* is an odd word to use of
either sadness (even if here probably
nearer to the modern use than the frequent Elizabethan meaning of 'sober-
ness') or merriment, and even odder
when both Alexas and Cleopatra have
been stressing that Antony's behaviour
has been the happy mean *between* two
extremes. I suppose that Cleopatra
must be taken to mean '*Even if* he had
to run to either extreme it would still
have become him.' [R]

Alex. Ay, madam, twenty several messengers:
          Why do you send so thick?
Cleo.   Who's born that day
          When I forget to send to Antony,
          Shall die a beggar. Ink and paper, Charmian.   65
          Welcome, my good Alexas. Did I, Charmian,
          Ever love Cæsar so?
Char.   O that brave Cæsar!
Cleo. Be chok'd with such another emphasis,
          Say the brave Antony.
Char.   The valiant Cæsar!
Cleo. By Isis, I will give thee bloody teeth,   70
          If thou with Cæsar paragon again
          My man of men.
Char.   By your most gracious pardon,
          I sing but after you.
Cleo.   My salad days,
          When I was green in judgment, cold in blood,
          To say as I said then. But come, away,   75
          Get me ink and paper,
          He shall have every day a several greeting,
          Or I'll unpeople Egypt.   [*Exeunt.*

65. *Shall die a beggar*] According to
Deighton, she implies that the day will
be so ill-fated as to carry with it such
consequences. Perhaps, however, there
is nothing more than a quaint way of
expressing the certainty of a daily
despatch.

71. *paragon*] match *or* compare. See
note on the word in *Oth.*, II. i. 62
(Arden Shakespeare).

74-5. *green . . . then*] I have restored
the pointing of F. The reading generally adopted, *green in judgment; cold in
blood, To . . . then!* is Warburton's, who
says: '*Cold in blood* is an upbraiding ex-
postulation to her maid. "Those (says
she) were my sallad days, when I was

green in judgment; but your blood is
as cold as my judgment, if you have the
same opinion of things now as I had
then."' Boswell justly objected that
cold as well as *green* seems 'to be suggested by the metaphor *sallad* days';
but besides this, it is more probable
that Cleopatra should strengthen her
contention with regard to *herself*, and
further, do so by adding the physical
sensation to the mental attitude, than
that she should break off to reproach
her maid, whose judgment might be in
question, but whose blood was not
supposed to take its temperature from
Antony. Judgment and beauty only
are touched on in North, see pp. 246-7.

ACT II

[SCENE I.—*Messina. Pompey's house.*]

Enter POMPEY, MENECRATES, *and* MENAS, *in warlike manner.*

Pom. If the great gods be just, they shall assist
    The deeds of justest men.
Mene.   Know, worthy Pompey,
    That what they do delay, they not deny.
Pom. Whiles we are suitors to their throne, decays
    The thing we sue for.
Mene.   We, ignorant of ourselves,   5
    Beg often our own harms, which the wise powers
    Deny us for our good; so find we profit
    By losing of our prayers.
Pom.   I shall do well:
    The people love me, and the sea is mine;
    My powers are crescent, and my auguring hope   10
    Says it will come to the full. Mark Antony
    In Egypt sits at dinner, and will make
    No wars without doors. Cæsar gets money where

ACT II

Scene I

3. what] *F;* which *F2.*

4–5. *Whiles . . . sue for*] Cf. Cassio in *Oth.,* III. ii. 13–18.

5–8. *We . . . prayers*] Mr Churton Collins (*Studies in Shakespeare,* 1904, p. 29) quotes these lines as a 'terse translation of Juvenal, *Satire* x. 346–52, not attributable to mere coincidence. But it would be surprising if the reflection could be proved to have been any less common in Shakespeare's time than it is today.

10. *My powers are crescent*] Cf. *Ham.,* I. iii. 11: 'For nature, *crescent,* does not

grow alone,' etc. Theobald obtained concord with the following *it* by reading *My pow'r 's a crescent.* Cf. *MND.,* v. i. 248: 'He is no *crescent*'; but the metaphor from the waxing moon, which accounts for *it,* was probably a second thought, and usage did not forbid *it* to relate to a plural noun. So in *Tim.,* III. vi. 102: 'Who, stuck and spangled with your flatteries, / Washes *it* off,' etc.

13. *No wars . . . doors*] an allusion to a commonplace of love poetry: 'Love

43

He loses hearts: Lepidus flatters both,
Of both is flatter'd: but he neither loves,   15
Nor either cares for him.
Men.   Cæsar and Lepidus
Are in the field, a mighty strength they carry.
Pom. Where have you this? 'tis false.
Men.   From Silvius, sir.
Pom. He dreams: I know they are in Rome together
Looking for Antony: but all the charms of love,   20
Salt Cleopatra, soften thy wan'd lip!
Let witchcraft join with beauty, lust with both,
Tie up the libertine in a field of feasts,

16, 18, 38. Men.] *Malone; Mene. F.*
wand *F;* wan *Pope.*

21. wan'd] *Steevens, 1793 (Percy conj.);*

calls to war; / Sighs his alarms, / Lips his swords are, / The field his arms.' So Chapman, *Epithal. Teratos* in *Hero and Leander,* 5th Sestiad.

15. *neither*] object of *loves* (not correlative to the following *nor*).

16. Men.] Malone altered *Mene.* (Menecrates) to *Men.* for Menas both here and in line 18 conjecturally, as well as in line 38, where the context demands the change. As he says: 'It is a matter of little consequence.' Johnson gave all to Menas, observing: 'I know not why Menecrates appears; Menas can do all without him.'

20. *Looking for*] waiting for.

21. *Salt*] lustful; as in *Meas.,* v. i. 402. So D'Avenant, *Albovine,* iv *(Dramatists of Restoration,* i. 81): 'Let 'em revel / With their *salt* lips. Th' other sport is fulsome.'

wan'd] In reading *wan'd* Steevens does not decide between the sense '*waned,* declined, gone off from its perfection; comparing Cleopatra's beauty to the moon past the full' (Percy), and that of *wanned* or *made wan,* for which he quotes *Ham.,* ii. ii. 588, where F has *warm'd* but Q *wand:* 'That from her [i.e. his soul's] working all his visage *wann'd.*' With *waned,* the more natural and usually accepted epithet, compare *wither'd* in Webster, *The White Devil,*

II. i. 168: 'You have oft, for these two lips, / Neglected cassia or the natural sweets / Of the spring-violet; they are not yet much *wither'd.*' *Waned* frequently occurs in conjunction with cheek, but not with lip. Steevens quotes (anent *wan* or *wanned*) Beaumont and Fletcher, *Queen of Corinth* [IV. i; (Camb. vi. 51)]: 'Now you look *wan* and pale, lips, ghosts ye are.' Collier (1843) reading *wand,* suggests *wand-lip* = lip potent as a wand, i.e. similarly commanding enchantment, and saw confirmation of his view in *witchcraft,* next line; but Z. Jackson had urged all this in 1819. Collier (1858) reads *wan'd.*

22. *join*] † F reads *ioyne;* is this perhaps the common *e:d* error for *ioynd?* [R]

23. *Tie . . . field of feasts*] Mr Craig supplies me with the following from *A Glossary of Words in the County of Chester* by Robert Holland (Eng. Dial. Soc., 1886, pt ii): '*Tied by the tooth,* idiom., a curious expression, explaining why sheep and cattle do not break through fences, though they are bad, because the pasture is good, which prevents rambling. L.' The source (L) is Col. Egerton Leigh's *Glossary,* etc., 1877. Perhaps, as Mr Craig further suggests, though Antony would be like

Keep his brain fuming; Epicurean cooks
Sharpen with cloyless sauce his appetite,   25
That sleep and feeding may prorogue his honour,
Even till a Lethe'd dulness—

Enter VARRIUS.

How now, Varrius?
Var. This is most certain, that I shall deliver:
    Mark Antony is every hour in Rome
    Expected: since he went from Egypt, 'tis   30
    A space for farther travel.
Pom.   I could have given less matter
    A better ear. Menas, I did not think
    This amorous surfeiter would have donn'd his helm
    For such a petty war: his soldiership
    Is twice the other twain: but let us rear   35
    The higher our opinion, that our stirring
    Can from the lap of Egypt's widow pluck
    The ne'er-lust-wearied Antony.
Men.   I cannot hope

an animal in such a fat pasture, the reference (if any) is merely to the large pasture fields of Shakespeare's day, in which the severally owned portions were not enclosed. The following passages from Elton's *Wm Shakespeare, his Family and Friends* (1904), are relevant: 'The rights incidental to Shakespeare's "yard-lands" comprised privileges on other people's fallows, called "hades, leys, and tyings"' (p. 142); 'The word "tyings" meant the right of tethering a horse, hobbled with a "tye" or chain, so as to graze on the neighbour's herbage' (p. 144). Deighton sees, apparently, an implied contrast in 'field of feasts', as he explains: 'where he may . . . forget all thoughts of the field of battle.'

25. *cloyless*] apparently only used here and in Hogg's *Queen's Wake* (1813), p. 251: '*Cloyless* song, the gift of heaven,' quoted by *OED*.

26–7. *prorogue . . . Lethe'd dulness*] suspend the operation of his honour

till it becomes too insensible to prompt. For *prorogue* = put off, see *Rom.*, II. ii. 78, IV. i. 48. Nashe also uses the word in this sense in *The Unfortunate Traveller*, II, p. 220, line 16, and p. 325, line 1113 in the sense 'prolonged'. 'No paines I will refuse how euer *prorogued*, to have a little respite to purifie my spirit.'

30–1. *since he went . . . travel*] There has been time enough, since he left Egypt, for him to have got further than Rome. For *space* meaning 'space of time' cf. *Lr*, V. iii. 54, 'To-morrow, or at further *space*.'

35–6. *rear . . . opinion*] think more highly of ourselves.

37. *Egypt's widow*] See on I. iv. 6 *ante*.

38. *hope*] expect; as, e.g., in *H5*, III. vii. 82, and Rowley, *A Woman Never Vexed*, II (Hazlitt's *Dodsley*, xii. 132): 'I *hope* thou'lt vex me.' Boswell cites Puttenham (*The Arte of English Poesie*, 1589, lib. iii, p. 263 in Arber's ed.) for ridicule of the word's use in this sense:

Cæsar and Antony shall well gree together:
His wife that's dead did trespasses to Cæsar,   40
His brother warr'd upon him, although I think
Not mov'd by Antony.
Pom.   I know not, Menas,
How lesser enmities may give way to greater.
Were't not that we stand up against them all,
'Twere pregnant they should square between
    themselves,   45
For they have entertained cause enough
To draw their swords: but how the fear of us
May cement their divisions, and bind up
The petty difference, we yet not know.
Be't as our gods will have't! It only stands   50
Our lives upon to use our strongest hands.
Come, Menas.   [*Exeunt.*

---

39. gree] *Furness conj.;* greet *F.*   41. warr'd] *F2;* wan'd *F.*   43–4. greater.
Were't . . . all,] *Rowe's pointing;* greater, Were't . . . all; *F.*

'Such manner of vncouth speech did
the Tanner of Tamworth vse to king
Edward the fourth, which Tanner
hauing a great while mistaken him,
and vsed very broad talke with him, at
length perceiuing by his traine that it
was the king, was afraide he should be
punished for it, said thus with a certain
rude repentance: *I hope I shall be hanged
to-morrow.* For [*I feare me*] *I shall be
hanged,* whereat the king laughed a
good, not only to see the Tanners
vaine feare, but also to heare his ill
shapen terme,' etc.

39. *gree*] † Furness's suggestion
seems to me almost certain. 'Greet
together' is an awkward phrase
(apparently unknown except in this
passage); and a doubling of a letter is
an easy error. For *gree* = *agree* (a
common form) see, e.g., II. vi. 37. [R]

45. *pregnant*] extremely probable,
big with the consequence; one of many
figurative uses of the word. Cf. *Oth.*, II.
i. 240: 'Now, sir, this granted, as it is a

most *pregnant* and unforced position,'
etc.

square] quarrel; as in *MND.*, II. i. 30,
where Mr Cuningham cites Cotgrave,
'*Se quarrer;* to strout, or square it, looke
big on't, carrie his armes a-kemboll
braggadochio-like,' which shows how
this sense became attached to the
word. Cf. H. Gifford, *A Posie of Gillo-
flowers,* 1580 (p. 103, Grosart's repr.):
'When men doe *square* for every fly, /
To make them friends the women
runne,' etc.

48. *cement*] accented as commonly
(*cément*). Cf. Massinger, *The Unnatural
Combat,* I. i: 'Being made up again and
cemented / With a son's blood' and
Donne, *The Extasie,* lines 5–6: 'Our
hands were firmly cimented / With a
fast balme, which thence did spring.'

50–1. *stands Our lives upon*] is a matter
of life and death; cf. *Err.*, IV. i. 68,
'Consider how it stands upon my
credit.' The more usual sense is *be
incumbent on,* as in *Ham.*, V. ii. 63.

[SCENE II.—*Rome. The house of Lepidus.*]

Enter ENOBARBUS *and* LEPIDUS.

Lep. Good Enobarbus, 'tis a worthy deed,
    And shall become you well, to entreat your captain
    To soft and gentle speech.
Eno.   I shall entreat him
    To answer like himself: if Cæsar move him,
    Let Antony look over Cæsar's head,   5
    And speak as loud as Mars. By Jupiter,
    Were I the wearer of Antonius' beard,
    I would not shave't to-day.
Lep.   'Tis not a time
    For private stomaching.
Eno.   Every time
    Serves for the matter that is then born in't.   10
Lep. But small to greater matters must give way.
Eno. Not if the small come first.
Lep.   Your speech is passion:
    But, pray you, stir no embers up. Here comes
    The noble Antony.

Enter ANTONY *and* VENTIDIUS.

Eno.   And yonder, Cæsar.

Enter CÆSAR, MÆCENAS, *and* AGRIPPA.

Ant. If we compose well here, to Parthia: 15

Scene II

7. Antonius'] *Steevens (1773); Anthonio's* F.

8. *I . . . shave't*] i.e. I would not
remove the temptation to pluck or
shake it, if he dare. Cf. *Lr*, III. vii. 76–
7: 'If you did wear a beard upon your
chin, / I'd *shake* it in this quarrel';
Ham., IV. vii. 32, etc. My interpretation conflicts with the accepted one
(Johnson's), which imports that the
speaker would not show even Cæsar
the respect of a shorn chin. This is too
tame for what precedes.
    9. *private stomaching*] indulgence of
personal resentments or dislikes. See

on III. iv. 12 *post*, and cf. the verb in
Ralph Roister Doister, IV. iii. 34: 'And
where ye halfe *stomaked* this gentleman
afore, / For this same letter, ye wyll
love hym now therefore,' etc.
    12. *Your speech is passion*] You are
letting your feelings run away with
you.
    14–17.] As Antony and Cæsar come
in, by different doors, each is in brisk
conversation with his own friends till
interrupted by Lepidus.
    15. *compose*] come to an agreement;

Hark, Ventidius.

Cæs.   I do not know,
Mæcenas: ask Agrippa.

Lep.   Noble friends,
That which combin'd us was most great, and let not
A leaner action rend us. What's amiss,
May it be gently heard. When we debate   20
Our trivial difference loud, we do commit
Murther in healing wounds. Then, noble partners,
The rather for I earnestly beseech,
Touch you the sourest points with sweetest terms,
Nor curstness grow to the matter.

Ant.   'Tis spoken well.   25
Were we before our armies, and to fight,
I should do thus.   [*Flourish.*

Cæs. Welcome to Rome.

Ant.   Thank you.

Cæs.   Sit.

Ant.   Sit, sir.

Cæs.   Nay, then.

Ant. I learn, you take things ill which are not so:
Or being, concern you not.

Cæs.   I must be laugh'd at,   30
If or for nothing, or a little, I

cf. *composition*, II. vi. 58 *post*, and Johnson, *The New Inn*, IV. iv. 86: '*Compose* with them, and be not angry valiant.'

17–25. *Noble friends*, etc.] 'the frendes of both parties would not suffer them to unrippe any old matters,' etc. See North, *post*, p. 250.

21–2. *commit . . . wounds*] A surgeon may handle trifling wounds—which would heal themselves if left alone—so clumsily as to cause death.

25. *Nor curstness . . . matter*] 'Let not *ill-humour* be added to the real *subject* of our difference' (Johnson). Cf. Puttenham, *Arte of English Poesie*, 1589, III. xix (Arber's repr., p. 209 [cited in *OED*]): 'With spitefull speach, *curstnesse* and crueltie'; Mabbe's *Celestina*, 1631, ix (Tudor Trans., p. 168):

'There is . . . not any that can indure their tartnesse and *curstnesse*,' etc. Ladies who have maid-servants are here the offenders.

27. *I . . . thus*] Some welcoming action or embrace must be understood here, unless Antony is merely asserting that his words would be temperate in any event.

28. *Sit . . . Nay, then*] † Steevens and Johnson both detected in this interchange a resentment on Antony's part at Cæsar's arrogating to himself the right to give Antony his gracious permission to be seated. But surely Malone was right in seeing in it no more than an exchange of 'After you' courtesies, which Cæsar, anxious to get on with business, terminates by yielding. [R]

Should say myself offended, and with you
Chiefly i' the world: more laugh'd at, that I should
Once name you derogately, when to sound
Your name it not concern'd me.

Ant.   My being in Egypt,   35
Cæsar, what was't to you?

Cæs. No more than my residing here at Rome
Might be to you in Egypt: yet if you there
Did practise on my state, your being in Egypt
Might be my question.

Ant.   How intend you, practis'd?   40

Cæs. You may be pleas'd to catch at mine intent
By what did here befall me. Your wife and brother
Made wars upon me, and their contestation
Was theme for you, you were the word of war.

Ant. You do mistake your business, my brother never   45

---

44. theme] *F3;* theame *F;* theam'd *Warburton;* then (thenne) *Deighton* ('*Old Dramatists*', *1898*).

---

34. *derogately*] in a detracting manner, with disparagement. The sole instance of the word in *OED.*

39. *practise on*] plot or intrigue against, as in *Lr*, III. ii. 57. Common in this and the sense 'craftily play upon,' as in *Ado*, II. i. 401.

40. *my question*] 'my business,' 'a matter that I should particularly enquire into' (Beckett).

42-3. *Your wife . . . me*] See North, *post*, p. 250.

44. *Was theme for you*] The sense accepted as *intended* by Shakespeare is that conveyed in Staunton's conjecture, *Had you for theme*, i.e. was about *you*: and is also implied in Johnson's *Had theme for you* or *You were theme for*, Malone's *Was them'd from you*, and in other conjectures. Malone argues the necessity of this meaning, and consequent existence of corruption, from what immediately follows. If, however, we are to stand by the text, it is possible to connect *Was theme for you* with *practise* instead, making the words *You were the word of war* confirmatory or

evidential rather than explanatory, and punctuating accordingly. (F has a comma after *for you*.) In this event, Cæsar says: 'By "practised" I mean that their quarrel with me supplied you with a theme to work upon, a ground for your intrigues, *witness as proof* the use of your name in the war.' Antony deals at once and solely with the *proof* of practice (which my supposition would confine to these last words) without troubling himself to deny the *charge* of practice which depends on it. Steevens quotes *Cor.*, I. i. 226: 'throw forth greater *themes* / For insurrection's arguing,' and perhaps was not far wrong in explaining our text: 'Was proposed as an example for you to follow on a yet more extensive plan, as *themes* are given for a writer to dilate upon.'

† After all which, is there not much to be said for Deighton's straightforward emendation? [R]

word of war] Cf. III. i. 31 *post*, and *R3*, v. iii. 350: 'Our ancient word of courage, fair Saint George,' etc.

Did urge me in his act: I did inquire it,
And have my learning from some true reports
That drew their swords with you. Did he not rather
Discredit my authority with yours,
And make the wars alike against my stomach,   50
Having alike your cause? Of this, my letters
Before did satisfy you. If you'll patch a quarrel,
As matter whole you have to make it with,

---

53. you have to make] *F;* you have to take *F2;* you have not to make *Rowe*
(you've) *and most edd.*

46. *Did urge . . . act*] represented his
wars as waged in my cause, made
capital of my name in the war. Cf.
The Weakest Goeth to the Wall, II. ii.
55 (Hazlitt's *Webster*, IV. 245): 'I
trust you will not *urge me* in the matter,'
where the speaker deprecates being
cited as the source of certain information.

47. *reports*] reporters. See on *discontents*, I. iv. 39 *ante.*

49. *Discredit*] i.e. bring into discredit, as in *Meas.*, IV. ii. 30.

with] along with.

50. *stomach*] inclination. Cf. *Tp.*, II.
i. 113: 'You cram these words into
mine ears against / The *stomach* of my
sense.'

51. *Having . . . cause*] since I had as
much cause to resent them as you. So
I understand the words, but the usual
explanation (Steevens's and Malone's)
is = since I was engaged in the same
cause with you.

53. *As matter whole you have*] † Rowe
emended *you have* to *you've not* and
Capell to *you have not*, and almost all
editors since have accepted this insertion of the negative, including Case
(though in a balanced note he gave a
selection of argument on the other
side), and Dover Wilson (surprisingly,
since in his glossary he gives a sense for
as which seems to make needless, if not
to preclude, the insertion).

The case for the retention of *F*'s
reading is, I think, much simpler than
one would suppose from the tortuous

ingenuity of many of the arguments
used to support it. There are two crucial points, the first purely linguistic,
namely, what does *as* mean in this
context, the second more general,
namely, what sense is demanded by
the general drift of the whole passage,
lines 29–98? As to *as*, there is a section
in *OED sub voc.* B. II. 8d, which is
exactly apposite (more exactly, I
think, than that cited by Dover Wilson, which is B. I. 3b): 'In antitheti-
cal or parallel clauses, introducing a
known circumstance with which a
hypothesis is contrasted; . . . whereas.
Hamlet, v. ii. 347, Had I but time (as
this fell sergeant death is strick'd in his
Arrest).' The *Hamlet* parallel seems to
me wholly convincing. As to the more
general point, Antony, if we accept
this meaning of *as*, is saying in effect:
'If you will insist on patching a quarrel,
even when you have whole cloth to cut
it from, this particular patch will not
serve your turn.' And that seems to me
exactly in line with Antony's general
tactics in the scene, which are worth
watching, and have not always been
watched. He knows from the start that
on one point, and one only,—the
'arms and aid' of line 88—Cæsar has
an irrefutable case, and on that point
he is prepared to 'play the penitent'.
But he would prefer to come to this
main point at once, and not waste time
over accusations which he can either
flatly deny, or deal with by a plea of
ignorance, or dismiss as trivial. It is

It must not be with this.

Cæs.   You praise yourself,
By laying defects of judgment to me; but   55
You patch'd up your excuses.

Ant.   Not so, not so;
I know you could not lack, I am certain on't,
Very necessity of this thought, that I,
Your partner in the cause 'gainst which he fought,
Could not with graceful eyes attend those wars   60
Which fronted mine own peace. As for my wife,
I would you had her spirit in such another;
The third o' the world is yours, which with a snaffle
You may pace easy, but not such a wife.

Eno. Would we had all such wives, that the men might   65
go to wars with the women!

Ant. So much uncurbable, her garboils, Cæsar,
Made out of her impatience, which not wanted
Shrewdness of policy too, I grieving grant
Did you too much disquiet: for that you must   70
But say, I could not help it.

Cæs.   I wrote to you,
When rioting in Alexandria you

---

60. graceful] *F;* grateful *Pope.*

just worth notice that when Cæsar does
come to the main point, the 'article of
the oath,' Antony is impatient of interruption. [R]

55. *laying . . . but*] † As the line stands
it is impossible to throw the apparently
required emphasis on to *me*. Capell
therefore printed the line as *By laying
to me defects of judgment; but.* It is to be
noticed that F, giving what precedes
and follows as verse, prints this speech
alone as prose, which perhaps suggests
some confusion in the manuscript. [R]

60. *with graceful . . . attend*] favourably regard. The only instance of
graceful in this sense in *OED.*

† And *c : t* with Elizabethan script is
an easy error, so that Pope was very
probably right. [R]

61. *fronted*] opposed. Cf. I. iv. 79
ante.

62. *her spirit*] See North, *post,* pp.
242, 250.

63. *snaffle*] Flecknoe, *Heroick Portraits* (1660), sig. H *verso,* uses this
figure from horsemanship in speaking
of the subjects of Charles I as 'onely
rid with a *snaffle,* and gentle hand.'

64. *pace*] train; cf. *Per.,* IV. vi. 68–70,
'My lord, she's not paced yet; you
must take some pains to work her to
your manage.'

65–6. *that the men . . . women*] probably purposely ambiguous. The lines
have always been printed as prose.

67. *garboils*] See on I. iii. 61 *ante.*

71–2. *I . . . you*] The punctuation
(Lloyd conj.) is substantially that of
the folio. I agree with Mr Thiselton
in thinking it no improvement to read
with modern editors: 'I wrote to you /
When rioting in Alexandria; you'.

Did pocket up my letters; and with taunts
Did gibe my missive out of audience.
Ant.   Sir,
He fell upon me, ere admitted, then: 75
Three kings I had newly feasted, and did want
Of what I was i' the morning; but next day
I told him of myself, which was as much
As to have ask'd him pardon. Let this fellow
Be nothing of our strife; if we contend,   80
Out of our question wipe him.
Cæs.   You have broken
The article of your oath, which you shall never
Have tongue to charge me with.
Lep.   Soft, Cæsar!
Ant. No, Lepidus, let him speak;
The honour is sacred which he talks on now,   85
Supposing that I lack'd it. But on, Cæsar,
The article of my oath.
Cæs. To lend me arms and aid when I requir'd them,
The which you both denied.
Ant.   Neglected, rather;
And then when poisoned hours had bound me up   90
From mine own knowledge; as nearly as I may,
I'll play the penitent to you. But mine honesty
Shall not make poor my greatness, nor my power

75. admitted, then:] *F;* admitted: then *Rowe.*

74. *missive*] messenger. So in *Mac.,*
I. v. 7, Macbeth's letter speaks of Ross
and Angus as *'missives* from the king.'
For Antony's action, see note on I. i. 52.

75. *admitted then:*] †Rowe's emendation is an example of needless
tinkering with F's punctuation. 'Transposed pointing' is always possible, but
why assume it here? Antony's *then* is
contrasted with *next day,* when the
messenger was admitted in proper
form. [R]

80. *Be nothing of*] have no place in.

82. *article*] precise terms.

85–6. *The honour . . . it*] Malone is
probably right in his view of 'Supposing', etc. which governs his (the

usual) interpretation of the passage:
'The theme of honour which he now
speaks of, namely, the religion of an
oath, for which he supposes me not to
have a due regard, is sacred; it is a
tender point, and touches my character nearly. Let him therefore urge
his charge, that I may vindicate myself.' Yet in what follows, Antony practically admits that his honour slept
in poisoned hours, and the following
sense seems not impossible: 'He is
speaking of an undeniable point of
honour, even supposing mine failed
me.'

90–1. *bound . . . knowledge*] drugged
me so that I was not myself.

Work without it. Truth is, that Fulvia,
To have me out of Egypt, made wars here,   95
For which myself, the ignorant motive, do
So far ask pardon, as befits mine honour
To stoop in such a case.

Lep.   'Tis noble spoken.

Mæc. If it might please you, to enforce no further
The griefs between ye: to forget them quite   100
Were to remember that the present need
Speaks to atone you.

Lep.   Worthily spoken, Mæcenas.

Eno. Or if you borrow one another's love for the instant,
you may, when you hear no more words of Pompey,
return it again: you shall have time to wrangle in,   105
when you have nothing else to do.

Ant. Thou art a soldier only, speak no more.

Eno. That truth should be silent, I had almost forgot.

Ant. You wrong this presence, therefore speak no more.

Eno. Go to, then: your considerate stone.   110

---

98. noble] *F;* nobly *F2.*   102. Worthily] *F;* Worthy *F2.*   107. soldier only,]
soldier only; *Theobald;* Souldier, onely *F.*

---

94. *without it*] 'without mine honesty.' So Malone, on whose side is, perhaps, the accentuation of *it.* It may be a question, however, whether he and others do not too readily identify *power* with *greatness.* Perhaps *it* refers to greatness, and Antony declines to exert his *power*, except his *greatness* in no respect suffer diminution, either by his stooping too far or by the way in which his admissions are taken.

95. *To have . . . here*] See North, *post,* p. 250.

98. *noble*] adjective as adverb. Very common. Cf. *Cæs.,* v. i. 60.

100. *griefs*] grievances; a frequent sense. Cf. *Cæs.,* i. iii. 118.

102. *atone*] make at one, reconcile, as in *Cym.,* i. iv. 44. So Jonson, *The Silent Woman,* iv. v. 165: 'Nay, if he had been cool enough to tell us that, there had been some hope to *atone* you.'

108. *That truth,* etc.] Cf. *Lr,* i. iv. 124: '*Truth's* a dog must to kennel.'

Grey quotes Ray's *Proverbs:* 'All *truth* must not be told at all times.'

109. *presence*] august company; as often in Shakespeare. Cf. *Ancient Popular and Romance Poetry of Scotland* (ed. Laing and Small, 1885), xvii. 18: 'The God of most magnificence, / Conserf this high *presens*,' etc.

110. *your considerate stone*] Much needless tinkering here began with Johnson's *You considerate ones.* With the metaphor, compare Steevens's excellent examples (1821 Variorum), e.g. *Tit.,* iii. i. 46: 'A *stone* is silent, and offendeth not'; *Jacob and Esau* [1568, iv. vi. 18–23, Hazlitt's *Dodsley,* ii. 237]: 'Bring thou in thine, Mido, and see thou be a *stone. Mido.* A *stone?* how should that be, mistress? . . . *Rebecca.* I meant thou shouldest nothing say'; or a new one from Beaumont and Fletcher, *The Captain,* iv. iv (Camb. v. 297): 'Think she is a *stone.* / She is a kind of bawdy confessor, / And will not

Cæs. I do not much dislike the matter, but
  The manner of his speech; for't cannot be
  We shall remain in friendship, our conditions
  So differing in their acts. Yet, if I knew   114
  What hoop should hold us staunch from edge to edge
  O' the world, I would pursue it.
Agr.   Give me leave, Cæsar.
Cæs. Speak, Agrippa.
Agr. Thou hast a sister by the mother's side,
  Admir'd Octavia? Great Mark Antony
  Is now a widower.
Cæs.   Say not so, Agrippa: 120
  If Cleopatra heard you, your reproof

115–16. staunch from . . . world,] *F*; staunch, from . . . world *Pope*. 120. not so,] *Rowe*; not, say *F*. 121. reproof] *Hanmer* (*Warburton conj.*); proofe *F*; approof *Theobald*.

utter secrets.' *Considerate* is here = considering, reflective, as in *R3*, IV. ii. 30: 'none are for me / That look into me with *considerate* eyes'; D'Avenant, *Gondibert* (1651), II. ii. 10: 'on whose *considerate* brow, Sixtie experienc'd summers he discern'd.' Enobarbus obviously means: Very well; have me dumb, but reflective, i.e. none the less aware that your friendship will be hollow. *Consideration* occurs in IV. ii. 45 *post*.

113. *conditions*] dispositions, as often. Cf. *Lr*, IV. iii. 35.

115. *What hoop . . . staunch*] Steevens quotes *2H4*, IV. iv. 43: 'A *hoop* of gold to bind thy brothers in.' See also *Ham.*, I. iii. 63.

118. *Thou hast*, etc.] For hence to line 170, see North, *post*, p. 251.

sister by . . . side] Octavia was the emperor's own sister, daughter of C. Octavius and his second wife, Atia. An elder sister, daughter of Ancharia, and also named Octavia, is given to Antony by Plutarch (see *post*, p. 251), but this does not account for Shakespeare's 'sister by the mother's side' as some appear to fancy.

119. *Octavia?*] † I think that F's question mark may well be retained,

though it has been almost universally changed to exclamation mark or semicolon. Agrippa's is a half-rhetorical question—'you can't have forgotten that . . .' [R]

121–2. *your reproof . . . rashness*] Abbott (*Shakespearian Grammar*, §423) thinks we have here a case of the pronominal adjective being placed before the first of two nouns connected by *of*, and that, therefore, *your reproof* connected with *of rashness* is used 'where we should say, "the reproof of your rashness" (unless "of" here means "about," "for").' The latter alternative, or that *of* = by *or* as a consequence of, seems far more likely in view of the position of the nouns. Cf. II. iii. 26 *post*.

your reproof] † It is tempting to guess that what the compositor found in front of him was *yourreproofe*, which he read as *youre proofe*, and regularized the *youre* to *your*, which is the normal F spelling. But the temptation must, I think, be resisted, however easy it makes the emendation. There is no evidence, so far as I know, that Shakespeare normally wrote *youre*, and some that he did not. Writers of an earlier generation, like More, naturally wrote the word with the final *e*, but by

Were well deserv'd of rashness.

Ant. I am not married, Cæsar: let me hear
Agrippa further speak.

Agr. To hold you in perpetual amity,   125
To make you brothers, and to knit your hearts
With an unslipping knot, take Antony
Octavia to his wife; whose beauty claims
No worse a husband than the best of men;
Whose virtue, and whose general graces, speak   130
That which none else can utter. By this marriage,
All little jealousies which now seem great,
And all great fears, which now import their dangers,
Would then be nothing: truths would be tales,
Where now half tales be truths: her love to both   135
Would each to other and all loves to both
Draw after her. Pardon what I have spoke,
For 'tis a studied, not a present thought,
By duty ruminated.

Ant.   Will Cæsar speak?

Cæs. Not till he hears how Antony is touch'd,   140
With what is spoke already.

Ant.   What power is in Agrippa,
If I would say, 'Agrippa, be it so,'
To make this good?

Cæs.   The power of Cæsar, and
His power unto Octavia.

134, 135. truths] *F3;* truth's *F.*

Shakespeare's time this spelling was
fading out (and for what it is worth the
spelling in the 'three pages' of *Sir
Thomas More* is not even *your* but *yor*).
The compositor, therefore, accustomed
to *your* or *yor* would naturally break
the hypothetically run-together words
after *your* and not after *yourre.* Possibly
it was an auditory error. [R]

133. *import*] carry with them, in-
volve. Cf. *Lr,* IV. iii. 5: 'which *imports*
to the kingdom so much fear and
danger.'

134. *truths . . . tales*] Cf. Yarington,
Two Lamentable Tragedies, 1601 (Bullen's *Old Plays,* iv, p. 9): 'Would Truth
were false, so this were but a tale!'
Pope read *but tales,* and various other
insertions before *tales* have been proposed, for want of appreciating the
metrical force of the pause. The sense
is that whereas, under present circumstances, reports only partially true are
credited [and cause distrust], this marriage would make even true ones [of a
disturbing nature] disbelieved, *or* deprive even true ones of significance.

135. *both*] † ? *each.* [R]

138. *present*] on the spur of the
moment.

Ant.   May I never
To this good purpose, that so fairly shows,   145
Dream of impediment! Let me have thy hand
Further this act of grace: and from this hour,
The heart of brothers govern in our loves,
And sway our great designs!
Cæs.   There's my hand.
A sister I bequeath you, whom no brother   150
Did ever love so dearly. Let her live
To join our kingdoms, and our hearts, and never
Fly off our loves again!
Lep.   Happily, amen!
Ant. I did not think to draw my sword 'gainst Pompey,
For he hath laid strange courtesies and great   155
Of late upon me: I must thank him only,
Lest my remembrance suffer ill report;
At heel of that, defy him.
Lep.   Time calls upon's,
Of us must Pompey presently be sought,
Or else he seeks out us.
Ant.   Where lies he?   160
Cæs. About the Mount Misena.
Ant.   What is his strength?
Cæs. By land, great, and increasing: but by sea

146-7. hand Further] *F;* hand; Further *Theobald and most edd. See note.*   149.
There's] *F;* There is *Theobald.*   162. *Cæs.* By land] *Hanmer. See note.*

144-6. *May . . . impediment*] Cf.
Sonn. cxvi: 'Let me not to the marriage
of true minds / Admit *impediments.*'

146-7. *hand Further*] †a good example of a tinkering with F's punctuation which destroys the intended sense.
Antony means 'I hope your hand-
clasp will ratify this act of grace.' For
this use of 'have' cf. *Oth.*, v. ii. 87: 'I
would not have thee linger in thy
pain.' [R]

153. *Fly off*] Cf. *Lr*, II. iv. 91: 'The
images of revolt and *flying off*'; R.
Flecknoe, *Heroick Portraits* (1660), sig.
F2: 'and if you deceive them when it
comes to the push indeed, and *fly off*,
shrink, frown,' etc.

157. *remembrance*] memory for favours.

159. *presently*] immediately, as commonly. Cf. Pepys's *Diary*, 7 May 1660:
'This morning Captain Cuttance sent
me 12 bottles of Margate ale. Three of
them I drank *presently* with some
friends,' etc.; also North, *post*, p.
250.

161. *Mount Misena*] As North (see
post, p. 251) has 'the Mount of Misena,'
Shakespeare certainly did not write
'Misenum,' as corrected by Rowe and
successive editors.

162.] † The Hanmer emendation
seems to me almost as certain as such
things can be, though it has had few

He is an absolute master.

Ant.   So is the fame.
Would we had spoke together! Haste we for it,
Yet ere we put ourselves in arms, despatch we   165
The business we have talk'd of.

Cæs.   With most gladness,
And do invite you to my sister's view,
Whither straight I'll lead you.

Ant.   Let us, Lepidus,
Not lack your company.

Lep.   Noble Antony,
Not sickness should detain me.   170
        [*Flourish. Exeunt all but Enobarbus, Agrippa, and Mæcenas.*

Mæc. Welcome from Egypt, sir.

Eno. Half the heart of Cæsar, worthy Mæcenas! My
    honourable friend Agrippa!

Agr. Good Enobarbus!

Mæc. We have cause to be glad, that matters are so well   175
    disgested. You stay'd well by 't in Egypt.

Eno. Ay, sir, we did sleep day out of countenance; and
    made the night light with drinking.

---

170. S.D. *Exeunt . . .*] *Capell; Exit omnes. Manet Enobarbus, Agrippa, Mecenas. F.*

followers. F reads '*Anth.* What is his
strength by land? *Cæsar.* Great, and
increasing. . .' But Antony was not
likely to narrow the scope of his question to the enemy's land forces, whereas the two abrupt questions from him,
with Cæsar's itemized reply to the
second, seem to me much more effective and more in character. [R]

164. *spoke together*] joined battle. Cf.
II. vi. 25 *post*, and *Cor.*, I. iv. 4. †But
I think Dover Wilson undoubtedly
right that Antony's *we* means not himself and Pompey, but himself and
Cæsar. 'If only we had had a chance of
consultation, this danger from Pompey
would never have arisen.' [R]

166. *most*] the greatest, as in *1H6*,
IV. i. 38: 'But always resolute in *most*
extremes'; Googe, *Eglogs*, 1563 (Arber's repr., p. 126): 'Syth that the
most misfortune nowe,' etc.

167. *do*] I do. So in *Lr*, v. i. 68,
shall = they shall.

172. *Half . . . Cæsar*] beloved of
Cæsar. Deighton: 'the translation of a
Latin poetical phrase used by Horace
of Vergil, *Odes*, I. iii. 8: *animæ dimidium
meæ.*'

176. *stay'd well by't*] †not, I think, so
obvious as the silence of most commentators suggests that it is. Dover
Wilson's reference to *Cor.*, II. ii. 176 is
not very helpful, since 'stay'd by him'
there need mean no more than 'continued to fight him.' Onions gives
'kept things going.' I think it means
'you stuck well to your guns' or, almost with the racing sense of *stay*, 'your
stamina must have been pretty good.'
[R]

177–8.] Day was disconcerted by
being treated as night, and night made
light in a two-fold sense, i.e. bright,

Mæc. Eight wild-boars roasted whole at a breakfast, and
    but twelve persons there; is this true?   180

Eno. This was but as a fly by an eagle: we had much
    more monstrous matter of feast, which worthily
    deserved noting.

Mæc. She's a most triumphant lady, if report be square
    to her.   185

Eno. When she first met Mark Antony, she purs'd up his
    heart upon the river of Cydnus.

Agr. There she appear'd indeed; or my reporter devis'd
    well for her.

Eno. I will tell you.   190
    The barge she sat in, like a burnish'd throne
    Burn'd on the water: the poop was beaten gold;
    Purple the sails, and so perfumed that
    The winds were love-sick with them; the oars were
        silver,
    Which to the tune of flutes kept stroke, and made   195
    The water which they beat to follow faster,
    As amorous of their strokes. For her own person,
    It beggar'd all description: she did lie

---

187. Cydnus] *F2;* Sidnis *F.*   194. love-sick with them; the] *Pope's pointing;*
love-sicke. With them the *F.*

---

and either of light behaviour or light-
headed.

  179. *Eight wild-boars*] See North,
post, p. 248.

  181. *by*] compared with.

  184. *square*] just; cf. *Tim.,* v. iv. 36.

  187. *Cydnus*] The river of Cilicia on
which Tarsus is situated. For the rest
of the scene, see North, *post,* pp. 246-7.
Mason thinks it due to negligence that
Antony is represented as captivated by
Cleopatra on *Cydnus,* he being all the
time in the market-place (line 215),
nay, we may add, being made to yield
up his heart later at supper (line 225).
But in the mind of Enobarbus, 'the
quick forge' already glowing with the
task before it, I think Antony was
already won on *Cydnus:* and, undoubtedly, knowing Antony as he did,

he must have reckoned him as good as
won when he saw what he reports.
Indeed, the emotions of Antony—left
in the magically dispeopled city—
would carry him far on the road to
love.

  188. *There . . . indeed*] Dover Wilson,
very reasonably, 'suspects an omission,
perhaps of "triumphantly" or "in
triumph."'

  devis'd] invented; '*devis'd* well for
her' may contain the sense, invented a
fine description of her.

  191-2. *The barge . . . Burn'd*] Cf.
Fairfax's Tasso, *Godfrey of Bulloigne*
(1600), xvi. iv, of a representation of
the battle of Actium: 'The waters
burnt about their vessels good, / Such
flames the gold therein enchased
threw,' etc.

In her pavilion—cloth of gold, of tissue—
O'er-picturing that Venus where we see   200
The fancy outwork nature. On each side her,
Stood pretty dimpled boys, like smiling Cupids,
With divers-colour'd fans, whose wind did seem

199. *cloth of gold, of tissue*] One of the two current explanations, viz., 'cloth of gold in tissue or texture,' may, I think, be dismissed; for, like 'of Damaske' in 'his grace was apparelled in a garment of Clothe of Silver, of Damaske, ribbed with Cloth of Golde, so thicke as might bee' (Hall's *Chronicle*, 1548, Henry VIII, xii. yere, f. lxxvi), '*of tissue*' added to the otherwise sufficient '*cloth of gold*' must denote something, in view of the independent existence of *tissue* and *cloth of tissue*: whether the inter-mixture of coloured silks, or else quality, depending on the number of threads in the warp. Cf. 'Which sat behynde a traues of sylke fyne / Of golde of tessew, the fynest that might be' (Skelton, *Bouge of Court*, prologue, st. 9), and the following definitions: '*Tissu* of the French *Tissu*, i.e. woven cloth of Tissu, with us cloth of silke and silver, or of silver and gold woven together' (Minshew, *Guide to the Tongues*, 1617); '*Tissue*, made of three threads of divers colours of Tissue' (*ibid.*); 'to weave cloth *of tissue* with twisted threads both in woofe and warp, and the same in sundry colours was the invention of Alexandria,' etc. (Mr Craig from Holland's *Pliny*, bk VIII, chap. xlviii, pt i, p. 228, ed. 1634).

The other explanation current is Staunton's, '*cloth of gold* on a ground *of tissue*,' which suggests no objection save that the reversal of the positions of *gold* and *tissue* is possible, indeed probable, judging by the frequency of examples. Cf. 'in a coate of rich *tyssue* cut on cloth of silver' (Hall's *Chronicle*, 1548, Henry VIII, yere ix. f. lxv); 'This gold-ground *Tissue*' (Sylvester's *Du Bartas*, ed. 1621, p. 442, week 2, day 4, bk ii, line 22); 'With gold-

ground Velvets, and with silver *Tissue*' (*ibid.*, p. 71, week 1, day 3, line 1181). Shakespeare had the phrase from North (see *post*, p. 246), now first supported by other instances: 'The Kyng of Englande mounted on a freshe courser, the trapper of *clothe of golde, of Tissue*' (Hall, as before, xii. yere, f. lxxviii; I owe this reference to Mr Craig); 'The aultars of the Chapell were hanged with riche revesture of *clothe of golde, of Tissue*, Embroidered with pearles' (*ibid.*, f. lxxiii). The Collier MS correction, '*cloth of gold, and tissue*,' was therefore needless, though the phrase apparently occurs. See Nichols, *Progresses of James I* (1828), ii. 550.

200–1. *O'er-picturing . . . nature*] surpassing the picture of Venus in which artistic imagination has outdone nature. Warburton (whose suggestion is still frequently quoted) has: 'Meaning the Venus of Protogenes, mentioned by Pliny, l. xxxv, c. x'; but as Pliny records no Venus by Protogenes we must surely substitute that of Apelles (Pliny, *Nat. Hist.*, lib. xxxv. 36 [x]), whose famous Venus Anadyomene was inferentially said to outdo nature in the poetical assertion that Juno and Pallas would contend no further for the prize of beauty if they saw her. Sylvester says that certain works of art, including Apelles' Venus, 'Are proofs enow that learned Painting can, [*sic*] Can (Goddess-like) another Nature frame' (*Du Bartas*, week 1, day 6, 1621 ed., p. 133). North has merely: 'apparelled and attired like the goddesse Venus, commonly drawen in picture'. Theobald had correctly referred to Apelles' Venus.

203–5. *fans . . . undid did*] According

To glow the delicate cheeks which they did cool,
And what they undid did.

Agr.   O, rare for Antony!   205
Eno. Her gentlewomen, like the Nereides,
So many mermaids, tended her i' the eyes,
And made their bends adornings. At the helm
A seeming mermaid steers: the silken tackle
Swell with the touches of those flower-soft hands,   210
That yarely frame the office. From the barge
A strange invisible perfume hits the sense
Of the adjacent wharfs. The city cast
Her people out upon her; and Antony,

204. glow] *Rowe;* gloue *F;* glove *F2.*   205. undid did] *F;* did, undid *Johnson conj.;* undy'd, dy'd *Staunton.*   209. tackle] *F;* tackles *F2.*

to the syntax the *fans* cooled or 'undid' heat, their *wind* seemed to produce it, or 'did' the reverse of the action; but the imagination readily identifies the fans with the wind and makes it equally unnecessary to read *winds* or refer *they* to *boys* (line 202). Helen, in Venus' Show (Peele, *The Arraignment of Paris,* II. i. 79), has 'four Cupids attending on her, each having his *fan* in his hand to fan fresh air in her face.'

206–7. *Nereides . . . mermaids*] As Steevens observed, the fifty daughters of Nereus and Doris, divinities of the Ægean Sea, were unlike mermaids in having complete human shapes.

207. *tended her i' the eyes*] waited in her sight, i.e. were not just a group of attendants in the background. The following new example seems especially to favour this common interpretation: Chapman translates 'Flos Asiae ante ipsum' (Juvenal, *Sat.* v, line 56) by '*In his eye* waits the flower of Asia,' where the intention is to contrast a rich host's personal attendant with the rude slaves who minister to his guests. Steevens quotes *Ham.,* IV. iv. 6: 'We shall express our duty *in his eye.*' See also *MND.,* III. i. 172: 'Hop in his walks and gambol *in his eyes.*'

208. *made . . . bends adornings*] † There are five close-packed pages of selected comments on this and the preceding line in the Furness Variorum, from which we learn, amongst many other things, that the *bends* are Cleopatra's eyebrows, which the attendants are 'adjusting', or, alternatively, the thickest outer planks of the ship's side; while the *eyes* are either the hawse-holes or 'dead-eyes'. I am not clear what all the pother is about, and one quotation from Drayton, given by Case, seems to me almost decisive in favour of the obvious meaning: *Mortimeriados* (slightly varied in *The Barons' Wars,* vi): 'The naked nymphs, some up, some downe descending, / Small scattering flowres one at another flung, / With pretty turns their lymber bodies bending.' Cleopatra's attendants, as they wait on her, fall into such graceful postures that they compose a lovely frame for the central figure. [R]

209. *tackle*] collective; sails, ropes, etc.

211. *yarely*] readily, nimbly. So in *Tp.,* I. i. 3: 'fall to't, *yarely,* or we run ourselves aground.'

frame] perform, manage. See *Lr,* I. ii. 109; Basse, *Works* (ed. Bond), p. 232: 'wish'd to *frame* these rites to you,' etc.

213. *wharfs*] banks. So in *Ham.,* I. v. 33: 'on Lethe *wharf.*'

   Enthron'd i' the market-place, did sit alone,   215
   Whistling to the air; which, but for vacancy,
   Had gone to gaze on Cleopatra too,
   And made a gap in nature.
Agr.   Rare Egyptian!
Eno. Upon her landing, Antony sent to her,
   Invited her to supper: she replied,   220
   It should be better he became her guest,
   Which she entreated: our courteous Antony,
   Whom ne'er the word of 'No' woman heard speak,
   Being barber'd ten times o'er, goes to the feast;
   And for his ordinary, pays his heart,   225
   For what his eyes eat only.
Agr.   Royal wench!
   She made great Cæsar lay his sword to bed;
   He plough'd her, and she cropp'd.
Eno.   I saw her once
   Hop forty paces through the public street,
   And having lost her breath, she spoke, and panted, 230
   That she did make defect perfection,
   And, breathless, power breathe forth.

232. breathless, power breathe] *Pope;* breathless power breathe *F3,4;* breath-lesse powre breath *F;* breathlesse power breath *F2.*

216. *but for vacancy*] except that it would have created a vacuum. 'Allud-ing to an axiom in the peripatetic philosophy then in vogue, that *Nature abhors a vacuum*' (Warburton). Cf. Sylvester's *Du Bartas*, p. 9, in ed. 1621: 'To all, so odious is *Vacuitie*.'

225. *ordinary*] supper. The ordinary, or regular public dinner, was a very flourishing institution in Shakespeare's time, and a convenient centre for news-gathering, discussion, dicing, etc. For its humours, see Dekker, *The Gull's Hornbook*, 1609, chap. v, *How a yong Gallant should behaue himselfe in an Ordinary.* His instructions begin thus: 'First, hauing diligently enquired out an Ordinary of the largest reckoning, whither most of your Courtly Gallants do resort, let it be your vse to repaire thither some halfe houre after eleuen;

for then you shall find most of your fashion-mongers planted in the roome waiting for meate.'

227. *Cæsar*] See on II. vi. 68–70 *post.*

228. *cropp'd*] bore fruit. See North, *post*, p. 258, and North's *Julius Cæsar* (Tud. Trans. v. 52): 'Thereuppon Cæsar made Cleopatra his [the king's] sister Queene of Ægypt, who being great with childe by him, was shortly brought to bedde of a sonne, whom the Alexandrians named Cæsarion'; and *ibid.* in margin: 'Cæsarion, Cæsars sonne, begotten of Cleopatra.' Mar-ston uses the word in a similar con-nection, but transitively, see *2 Antonio and Mellida*, I. i. 26: 'He wan the ladie to my honours death, / And from her sweetes *cropt* this Antonio.'

232. *power . . . forth*] did breathe forth charm, i.e. made her want of

Mæc. Now Antony must leave her utterly.
Eno. Never; he will not:

> Age cannot wither her, nor custom stale   235
> Her infinite variety: other women cloy
> The appetites they feed, but she makes hungry,
> Where most she satisfies. For vilest things
> Become themselves in her, that the holy priests
> Bless her, when she is riggish.   240

Mæc. If beauty, wisdom, modesty, can settle
> The heart of Antony, Octavia is
> A blessed lottery to him.
Agr.   Let us go.
> Good Enobarbus, make yourself my guest,
> Whilst you abide here.
Eno.   Humbly, sir, I thank you.   245

[*Exeunt.*

[SCENE III.—*The same. Cæsar's house.*]

Enter ANTONY, CÆSAR, OCTAVIA *between them.*

Ant. The world, and my great office, will sometimes
> Divide me from your bosom.
Octa.   All which time

238. vilest] *F4 and edd.;* vildest *F.*

breath a source of fascination. F text yields rather Daniel's *pour breath forth,* and might forbid change, were the clause co-ordinate with *spoke, and panted.* But as a consequence of speaking and panting it is lame, and if = *sing* (Staunton, *Athenæum,* 1873, Apl. 12) becomes lamer.

234. *Never; he will not*] † I have retained the accepted punctuation. But 'he will not' is something of an anticlimax after the emphatic 'never', and I suspect that F's unpunctuated reading, 'Never he will not', with double negative, is right; or perhaps even more probably that 'Never' and 'he will not' were alternatives, neither of which was clearly marked for omission. [R]

238–9. *For vilest . . . her*] Cf. 1. iv. 21 *ante.*

240. *riggish*] wanton. So in Lane's *Tom Tel-Troth's Message,* etc., 1600 (New Shakespeare Soc. 1876), stanza 52: 'Their *riggish* heads must be adorned with tires,' etc. The substantive *rig* = strumpet is common; the verb (= to gad) occurs in Lyly's *Midas,* 1. ii. 90.

243. *lottery*] allotment, prize. Similarly *lotteth* = allotteth: 'Thee towns neglecting, that to hym set destenye lotteth' (Stanyhurst's *Virgil,* iv [ed. Arber], p. 102); *lotted* = allotted: 'thou didst spend thy lotted days' (*A Collection of Seventy-nine Black-letter Ballads,* etc., p. 264, Lilly, 1867).

Before the gods my knee shall bow my prayers
To them for you.

Ant.   Good night, sir. My Octavia,
Read not my blemishes in the world's report: 5
I have not kept my square, but that to come
Shall all be done by the rule. Good night, dear lady.

Octa. Good night, sir.

Cæs. Good night.   [*Exeunt Cæsar and Octavia.*

Enter Soothsayer.

Ant. Now, sirrah; you do wish yourself in Egypt?   10

Sooth. Would I had never come from thence, nor you
Thither!

Ant.   If you can, your reason?

Sooth.   I see it in
My motion, have it not in my tongue: but yet

---

8. Good night, sir] *See note.*   9. *Exeunt Cæsar and Octavia*] *Rowe; Exit. F.*

---

6. *kept my square*] †not, I think, 'kept within due bounds,' as it is sometimes explained, but 'kept to the straight line'. The metaphor is from a carpenter's set square, by which a line can be ruled not only straight but in the right relation to another. Cf. *squier* (a common Elizabethan form of *square*) meaning a footrule, as in *1H4*, II. ii. 14, 'four foot by the squire'. [R]

7–8. *Good night, dear lady. Good night, sir*] † F gives both sentences to Antony, so that Octavia has no farewell speech. F2, almost certainly rightly, gives *Good night, sir* to Octavia. Antony has already said good night to Cæsar in line 4. He now says good night to Octavia, and both Octavia and Cæsar reply. [R]

10.] For remainder of scene, see North, *post*, pp. 252–3.

12. *Thither*] † Mason boldly proposed to read 'Hither', and F's reading is undeniably awkward. It makes the soothsayer regret (*a*) that he ever left his own country, and (*b*) that Antony had ever gone to it. But the second regret, implying that it is Antony's visit to Egypt which has caused all the later trouble, is not only quite irrelevant to his line of argument, but contrary to it. Antony's 'demon' would have been just as much subdued by Cæsar's if he had stayed in Rome, and the only hope for him is to get back to Egypt as soon as may be. It would be just possible to retain F's words, but repunctuate: 'Would I had never come from thence, nor you. / Thither!' making 'Thither' a command. But though 'Thither again' would serve well enough, and be picked up by 'Hie you to Egypt again,' 'Thither' by itself is a weak word to take the necessary stress. [R]

12–13. *in My motion*] in the involuntary movement of my brain, i.e. intuitively, 'by self-unable motion' (*All's W.*, III. i. 13). Cf. Lord Herbert, *Occasional Verses* (1665), in preface: 'belief ... that their Poets, as Orpheus, Linus, and Musæus, were descended of the Gods, and divinely inspired, from the extraordinary *Motions* of their Minds,' etc.; F. Spence's *Lucian* (1684), *The Epistle Dedicatory*, sig. B7: 'In his Works he has couch't . . . a perfect *Anatomy* of the Passions and *inward*

Hie you to Egypt again.
Ant.   Say to me,
Whose fortunes shall rise higher, Cæsar's or mine?   15
Sooth. Cæsar's.
Therefore, O Antony, stay not by his side:
Thy demon, that thy spirit which keeps thee, is
Noble, courageous, high, unmatchable,
Where Cæsar's is not. But near him, thy angel   20
Becomes afeard; as being o'erpower'd, therefore
Make space enough between you.
Ant.   Speak this no more.
Sooth. To none but thee; no more but when to thee.
If thou dost play with him at any game,
Thou art sure to lose; and of that natural luck,   · 25
He beats thee 'gainst the odds. Thy lustre thickens,
When he shines by: I say again, thy spirit
Is all afraid to govern thee near him;
But he away, 'tis noble.
Ant.   Get thee gone:
Say to Ventidius I would speak with him.   30
                                              [*Exit Soothsayer.*

18. that thy] *F*; that's thy *F2*.   19. high, unmatchable] *F3*; high unmatchable
F, *F2*; high-unmatchable *anon. conj.*   21. afeard;] afeard, *Thirlby*; a feare; *F*.
23. To . . . to thee] *Theobald's pointing*; To none but thee no more but: when to
thee, *F*.   29. he away, 'tis] *Pope*; he alway 'tis *F*.   30, 39. Ventidius] *F2*;
Ventigius F.   30. S.D. *Exit Soothsayer*] *Exit. F*.

Motions of Man,' etc. Shakespeare
seems to use the singular variously for
the operation of the mind and the
natural impulses. Cf. *Oth.*, I. ii. 75; I.
iii. 95. On the Soothsayer, see notes on
I. ii *ante*.
    18. *that thy*] Some editors read
that 's with F2–4, comparing North,
q.v., p. 253 *post*. In support of the text
Rolfe refers to III. v. 18; IV. xiv. 79
post; *Mac.*, I. vii. 53, etc.
    18–21.] See North, *post*, p. 253, for
this allusion to the ancient belief that a
guardian spirit attends each of us from
birth to guide and admonish; and cf.
Mac., III. i. 54–7: 'There is none but
he / Whose being I do fear: and under
him, / My Genius is rebuk'd, as it

is said / Mark Antony's was by
Cæsar.'
    21. *afeard*] †The *e:d* confusion is
so usual, and the consequent emendations such common form, that there is
little to guide us in choosing between
F and Thirlby except 'suitability'.
Afeard has been scorned, and *a fear*
praised as 'characteristically Shakespearean'; which no doubt it is, but is
it characteristic of the soothsayer? In
lines 28–9 he makes precisely the same
distinction between *afraid* and *noble*;
and see North, p. 253 *post*. [R]
    25. *of*] in consequence of.
    26. *thickens*] grows dim, is no longer
clear and bright. So in *Mac.*, III. ii. 50,
'Light *thickens*'.

He shall to Parthia. Be it art or hap,
He hath spoken true. The very dice obey him,
And in our sports my better cunning faints
Under his chance: if we draw lots, he speeds,
His cocks do win the battle still of mine   35
When it is all to nought; and his quails ever
Beat mine, inhoop'd, at odds. I will to Egypt:
And though I make this marriage for my peace,
I' the east my pleasure lies. O, come, Ventidius.

Enter VENTIDIUS.

You must to Parthia, your commission's ready;   40
Follow me, and receive 't.   [*Exeunt.*

[SCENE IV.—*The same. A street.*]

Enter LEPIDUS, MÆCENAS, *and* AGRIPPA.

Lep. Trouble yourselves no further: pray you hasten
Your generals after.
Agr.   Sir, Mark Antony

36. *all to nought*] even when the odds are infinite in my favour.

37. *inhoop'd, at odds*] If confined within a hoop the birds could not avoid fighting. Farmer quotes the first two lines of one of John Davies of Hereford's Epigrams [*Vpon English Proverbes* No. 287; *Scourge of Folly*, p. 47 (*Works*, ed. Grosart, vol. ii)]: "'Hee sets cocke on the hoope'' as you wou'd say: / For cocking in hoopes is now all the play, / And therefore no maruell mens stockes often droope, / That still vse the cocke-pit to set cocke *in hoope.*' The first line is in the original incorrectly, "'Hee sets cocke on the hoope in,"'' etc.; the sense of the phrase in the last is illustrated by a reference of Mr Craig's to Horman's *Vulgaria*: 'He setteth all things at cock in the *hope*; omnia in fortunae casibus ponit.' This epigram makes it clear that Shakespeare em-

bellished what he took here from North, by an allusion to the practice of his own time in cock-fighting; and disposes of Capell's reading (Seward's conjecture), *in whoop'd-at odds*, i.e. odds so much in Antony's favour as to excite the cries of the onlookers), notwithstanding frequent spellings like *Hoop'd* for *Whoop'd* in *Cor.*, IV. v. 84. Douce (*Illustrations of Shakespeare*, 1807, ii, p. 867) says: 'Quail combats were well known among the ancients, and especially at Athens. Julius Pollux relates that a circle was made in which the birds were placed, and he whose quail was driven out of this circle lost the stake,' etc. He also gives an illustration of the sport among the Chinese, copied from a Chinese miniature painting, in which the quails are actually placed within a hoop, a small, low circular enclosure, set on a table.

Will e'en but kiss Octavia, and we'll follow.
Lep. Till I shall see you in your soldiers' dress,
     Which will become you both, farewell.
Mæc.   We shall,   5
     As I conceive the journey, be at the Mount
     Before you, Lepidus.
Lep.   Your way is shorter,
     My purposes do draw me much about,
     You'll win two days upon me.
Both.   Sir, good success!
Lep. Farewell.   [*Exeunt.*   10

[SCENE V.—*Alexandria. Cleopatra's palace.*]

Enter CLEOPATRA, CHARMIAN, IRAS, *and* ALEXAS.

Cleo. Give me some music; music, moody food
     Of us that trade in love.
All.   The music, ho!

Enter MARDIAN *the Eunuch.*

Cleo. Let it alone, let's to billiards: come, Charmian.

6. at the] *F2;* at *F.*

3. billiards] *F2;* billards *F.*

6. *Mount*] Mount Misenum. See II.
ii. 161 *ante*, and North, *post*, p. 251.
9. *win . . . upon me*] Cf. Jonson, *The
New Inn*, II. ii. 25: 'You will *win upon
me* in compliment.'
     good success] So in *Lr*, v. iii. 196: 'this
good success.' The word was used for
result, good or bad. Cf. Daniel,
Hymen's Triumph, III. ii (line 1133)
(*Works*, ed. Grosart, iii. 372): 'That
learns his errours but by their *successe*, /
And when there is no remedie.' See
also III. v. 5 *post*.

Scene v

1. *moody food*] Cf. *Twelfth Night*, I. i.
1: 'If music be the *food* of love, play
on.' Moody = melancholy: Quarles
uses it nobly of the passing bell: 'This

moody musick of impartial *death*.' See
his 'Pentelogia', *Mors Tua*, i. 9.
2. *trade in*] probably much as now,
'have dealings in', etc.; but the word
(verb and noun) retained senses nearer
that of its source, *tread*. Cf. Sylvester's
Du Bartas, week II, day II, pt iii,
p. 282, ed. 1621: 'Ships . . . To *trade* the
seas', Cartwright, *Poems*, 1651, p. 312:
'Thine equall skill thus wresting nothing, made / Thy Pen seem not so
much to write, as *Trade*.' Turbervile,
The Speech of Reason against Love (repr.
in *The Muses Library*, 1741, p. 192),
uses the noun of lustful intercourse:
'They spent their youthfull Yeares /
In foule, and filthie *Trade*,' etc.
3. *billiards*] In a citation by Dr Furness from A. A. Adee in *Lit. World*,

Char. My arm is sore, best play with Mardian.

Cleo. As well a woman with an eunuch play'd,   5
    As with a woman. Come, you'll play with me, sir?

Mar. As well as I can, madam.

Cleo. And when good will is show'd, though 't come too short,
    The actor may plead pardon. I'll none now,
    Give me mine angle, we'll to the river there,   10
    My music playing far off. I will betray
    Tawny-finn'd fishes, my bended hook shall pierce
    Their slimy jaws; and as I draw them up,
    I'll think them every one an Antony,
    And say 'Ah, ha! y'are caught.'

Char.   'Twas merry when   15
    You wager'd on your angling, when your diver
    Did hang a salt-fish on his hook which he
    With fervency drew up.

Cleo.   That time? O times!
    I laugh'd him out of patience; and that night
    I laugh'd him into patience, and next morn,   20
    Ere the ninth hour, I drunk him to his bed;
    Then put my tires and mantles on him, whilst

---

12. Tawny-finn'd] *Theobald;* Tawny fine *F.*   18. time? O times!] time? oh times: *F.*

---

21 April 1883, Boston, it is urged that 'Shakespeare got the idea that billiards was an Egyptian game, and a favourite pastime of women' from Chapman, *The Blind Beggar of Alexandria,* iv. 11: 'go, Aspasia, / Send for some ladies to go play with you, / At chess, at billiards and at other game.'

    10. *angle*] fishing tackle.

    15–18. *'Twas merry,* etc.] See North, *post,* p. 250. Nashe, *Lenten Stuffe,* III, p. 212, lines 11–28, has a story of a scholar in Cambridge who amused the 'gaping rural fools' by drawing up a red herring, with which he had secretly baited his hook, at the town-bridge there. There is also a story quoted by Dr Grey (*Critical, etc., Notes on Shakespeare,* 1754, ii. 198) from *Memoirs of the English Court,* 1707, pp. 489–90, that Nell Gwynn similarly caused

Charles II to draw up a dozen fried smelts, and the Prince of Newburg a purse containing 'the picture of my Lady ——' set in gold and jewelled. 'Cleopatra,' said the king, 'caused a *sardian* to be tied to *Mark Anthony's* hook, but you exceed her in your contrivance; for you bestow pictures, which are much more acceptable.'

    21. *ninth hour*] probably 9 a.m. rather than 3 p.m. Cf. *Cæs.,* II. iv. 23.

    22. *tires*] usually understood here as = head-dresses. Cf. *Wiv.,* III. iii. 60; Chapman, *A Justification of a Strange Action of Nero,* 1629: 'it shall no more be tortured with curling bodkins, tied up each night in knots, wearied with *tires,*' etc. In sense *attire,* the word is also common. Cf. Heywood, *The Brazen Age* (*Works,* Pearson, iii. 245): 'Hence with these womanish *tyres,*'

I wore his sword Philippan. O, from Italy!

Enter a Messenger.

Ram thou thy fruitful tidings in mine ears,
That long time have been barren.
Mess.   Madam, madam,—
Cleo. Antonius dead!—If thou say so, villain,   26
Thou kill'st thy mistress: but well and free,
If thou so yield him, there is gold, and here
My bluest veins to kiss; a hand that kings
Have lipp'd, and trembled kissing.   30
Mess. First, madam, he is well.

24. Ram] *F;* Rain *Hanmer.*   25. been] bin *F (and often elsewhere).*   26.
Antonius] *Delius; Anthonyo's F; Anthonys F2.*   28. him, there] *Pope (ed. 2);*
him. There] *F.*

said by Hercules, Antony's supposed
ancestor, with whose treatment by
Omphale in this point there is a resemblance here, intentional or otherwise, as has been observed. Cf. also
Rowlands, *The Knave of Hearts,* 1613
(Percy Society, No. xxxiv, p. 74):
'Reach me my stockings, and my
other *tire.*'

23. *Philippan*] The contrast is
heightened by selecting the sword
which triumphed in the overthrow
of Brutus and Cassius at Philippi.
Philippan is doubtless noun, not adjective, though, as Theobald points out,
we have no warrant for supposing
swords to have received names till
very much later times.

24. *Ram*] Some read *Rain* with Hanmer, but *Ram* is thoroughly characteristic, and is supported by Malone's
references to *Cæs.,* v. iii. 74: 'thrusting
this report / Into his ears,' and *Tp.,* II.i.
113: 'You cram these words into my
ears,' etc. Cf. also Jonson's use of
rammed; 'And for his poesy, 'tis so
ramm'd with life' (*The Poetaster,* v. i.
136).

26. *Antonius*] † Dover Wilson takes
F's spelling to 'suggest intimacy,
natural to the context'; over-subtle, I
think. And what about II. ii. 7 ? [R]

27. *mistress*] The word may be tri-
syllabic here, like *frustrate,* v. i. 2 *post,*
and according to a very common practice of syllabifying *r.* Cf. *Rom.,* II. iv.
207, and Sylvester's *Du Bartas,* week I,
day 3, p. 67, in 1621 ed.: 'Wherewith
he wooes his *Iron Misteriss,* / And never
leaues her till he get a kiss,' etc. But the
pause after *mistress* is sufficient for
metre, and the quicker enunciation
more in agreement with the speaker's
mood.

31–2. *First, madam . . . we use*] †F
lineates thus:
Mess. First Madam, he is well.
Cleo. Why there's more Gold.
        But sirrah marke, we use
        To say, . . .
That is, we have three incomplete
lines, of which either the first and
second, or the second and third, taken
together make a regular complete line.
The narrowness of the Folio column is
probably here, as in some other places,
the cause of F's lineation, since the first
and second half-lines will not go into
the column at all, and the second and
third, though in fact they just will,
would have been so tight a squeeze
that a compositor might very naturally, looking at them in manuscript,
conclude that he could not get them in,

Cleo.　　　　　　　　　　Why, there's more gold.
　　But, sirrah, mark, we use
　　To say, the dead are well: bring it to that,
　　The gold I give thee will I melt and pour
　　Down thy ill-uttering throat.　　　　　　　　　35
Mess. Good madam, hear me.
Cleo.　　　　　　　　　　Well, go to, I will;
　　But there's no goodness in thy face, if Antony
　　Be free and healthful,—so tart a favour
　　To trumpet such good tidings! If not well,
　　Thou shouldst come like a Fury crown'd with snakes,　40
　　Not like a formal man.

37. face, if] face if *F;* face: if *F2.*　　38. so] *F;* why so *Rowe.*

and so start a new line without wasting time on an experiment. We are therefore entitled to re-lineate. But there are two ways of doing it, and they are worth a moment's examination, since something like the same problem with two or more solutions is presented in other places where re-lineation is called for. Which of the two ways one prefers depends on where one prefers to retain the incomplete line which we cannot avoid somewhere. Dr Brooks prefers the following:

　　Mes. First, madam, he is well.
　　Cleo. Why, there's more gold. But, sirrah, mark, we use
　　To say, . . .

That is, clearly, perfectly possible, and there is a certain effectiveness in leaving the messenger's brief announcement standing by itself. I prefer the arrangement of the text, for these reasons: Cleopatra's impulsive offer of more gold comes, I think, the moment his words are out of the messenger's mouth; but she then has a second, and alarming, thought, and makes a new start with it. And it will be observed that Cleopatra's second incomplete line may be regarded rhythmically not as unfinished but as 'un-begun', the gap at the beginning being occupied by the giving of the gold. This would be made plainer in a modern text,

more lavish of stage-directions for business even when the business is clearly implied, thus:

　　Why, there's more gold.
　　(*gives him gold*) But sirrah, mark,
　　we use
　　To say, . . . [R]

33. *the dead are well*] Cf. 2 Kings, iv. 26. The same thought occurs in *Mac.,* IV. iii. 176–7: '*Macd.* How does my wife? *Ross.* Why, well. *Macd.* And all my children? *Ross.* Well too'; *2H4,* v. ii. 3; *Rom.,* IV. v. 76, etc. Mr Churton Collins (*Studies in Shakespeare,* 1904, p. 54) notes the parallel with Euripides, *Troades,* 268: εὐδαιμόνιζε παῖδα σήν· ἔχει καλῶς.

34–5. *The gold . . . throat*] perhaps suggested by the treatment of Crassus' body by Orodes. See on III. i. 2 *post.*

38–9. *so tart . . . tidings*] so sour an aspect, etc. Cf. *Rom.,* II. v. 23–4: 'If good, thou sham'st the music of sweet news / By playing it to me with *so sour a face.*' Also *Cym.,* III. iv. 11–14. *Favour* is very common for 'face,' 'appearance,' etc.; so in *Oth.,* I. iii. 346.

41. *a formal man*] Here merely, I think, with Malone, a man in shape or form, though in *Err.,* v. i. 105, the phrase means a man in his normal condition of mind; as also elsewhere. Chester, *Love's Martyr* (ed. Grosart, New Shakespeare Soc., p. 108),

Mess.   Will't please you hear me?
Cleo. I have a mind to strike thee ere thou speak'st:
          Yet if thou say Antony lives, is well,
          Or friends with Cæsar, or not captive to him,
          I'll set thee in a shower of gold, and hail   45
          Rich pearls upon thee.
Mess.   Madam, he's well.
Cleo.   Well said.
Mess. And friends with Cæsar.
Cleo.   Th'art an honest man.
Mess. Cæsar, and he, are greater friends than ever.
Cleo. Make thee a fortune from me.
Mess.   But yet, madam,—
Cleo. I do not like 'But yet,' it does allay   50
          The good precedence, fie upon 'But yet,'
          'But yet' is as a gaoler to bring forth
          Some monstrous malefactor. Prithee, friend,
          Pour out the pack of matter to mine ear,
          The good and bad together: he's friends with Cæsar, 55
          In state of health, thou say'st, and thou say'st, free.
Mess. Free, madam, no; I made no such report,
          He's bound unto Octavia.

---

43. is] *Capell* (*Tyrwhitt conj.*) ; 'tis *F*.

speaks of the bear bringing forth: 'A lump of flesh without all fashion, / Which she by often licking brings to rest, / Making a *formal* body good and sound,' etc. 'A mere *formall man*' in Earle's *Micro-cosmographie* (1628) is one that is mere outside, all he does or says being pure imitation: 'When you have seen him *outside*, you have lookt through him, and need imploy your discouery no further.'

45–6. *I'll . . . thee*] Warburton is, doubtless, too specific in making this = 'I will give thee a kingdom', because of an Eastern coronation ceremony alluded to by Milton, *Paradise Lost*, II. 4: 'Or where the gorgeous East with richest hand / Showrs on her Kings *Barbaric* Pearl & Gold.' Cleopatra, however, proffers a province in line 68 *post*.

50–1. *does allay . . . precedence*] qualifies the good [news] that preceded it. Cf. for *precedence*, *LLL*., III. i. 83. Daniel, in *Hymen's Triumph* (1615), II. iv (line 901 in Grosart's *Daniel*) imitates with: 'But—*Clo*. Ah now comes that bitter vvord of But / Which makes all nothing, that vvas said before.' There are several verbs *allay* (whence confusion, see *OED*), and the word here is not *allay* = alleviate, but belongs to *allay* = put down, abate, confused with *allay* = alloy; whence comes: temper or qualify by admixture of something undesirable, as here; cf. *Cor*., II. i. 53: 'a cup of hot wine with not a drop of allaying Tiber in't.'

54. *pack*] Cleopatra thinks of the messenger with his news as like a pedlar with his pack, and elaborates the image later, in lines 104–6.

Cleo.   For what good turn?

Mess. For the best turn i' the bed.

Cleo.   I am pale, Charmian.

Mess. Madam, he's married to Octavia.   60

Cleo. The most infectious pestilence upon thee!

                                        [*Strikes him down.*

Mess. Good madam, patience.

Cleo.   What say you? Hence,

                                        [*Strikes him.*

Horrible villain, or I'll spurn thine eyes
Like balls before me; I'll unhair thy head,

                        [*She hales him up and down.*

Thou shalt be whipp'd with wire, and stew'd in brine,
Smarting in lingering pickle.

Mess.   Gracious madam,   66
I that do bring the news made not the match.

Cleo. Say 'tis not so, a province I will give thee,
And make thy fortunes proud: the blow thou hadst
Shall make thy peace for moving me to rage,   70
And I will boot thee with what gift beside
Thy modesty can beg.

Mess.   He's married, madam.

Cleo. Rogue, thou hast liv'd too long.   [*Draw a knife.*

Mess.   Nay, then I'll run.
What mean you, madam? I have made no fault.   [*Exit.*

Char. Good madam, keep yourself within yourself,   75
The man is innocent.

Cleo. Some innocents 'scape not the thunderbolt:
Melt Egypt into Nile! and kindly creatures

---

58. *turn*] purpose (but the messenger takes the straightforward sense).

65. *whipp'd with wire*] So in Nashe, *The Unfortunate Traveller*, II, p. 315, line 34: 'Then did they scourge hys backe parts so blistered and basted, with burning whips of red hot *wire*'; Sylvester's *Du Bartas, The Decay*, p. 503, in ed. 1621: 'With *wyery* Rods, thou shalt to death bee *whipt*.'

66. *lingering pickle*] *either* long-continuing pickle, *or* pickle whose effects will be so.

71. *boot thee with*] give thee into the bargain, *or merely* benefit thee with; *OED* 'benefit, increase, enrich,' giving this passage only for this sense. The noun (= something over and above, advantage) occurs in IV. i. 9 *post*.

73. Draw a knife] the not infrequent 'imperatival' S.D.

75. *keep . . . yourself*] control yourself.

77. *innocents*] This is perhaps a play on the sense fools, naturals, occurring, e.g., in *Lr*, III. vi. 9.

78. *Melt . . . Nile*] Cf. I. i. 33 *ante*.

Turn all to serpents! Call the slave again,
Though I am mad, I will not bite him: call!   80
Char. He is afeard to come.
Cleo.   I will not hurt him.
These hands do lack nobility, that they strike
A meaner than myself; since I myself
Have given myself the cause.

Enter the Messenger again.

                    Come hither, sir.
Though it be honest, it is never good   85
To bring bad news: give to a gracious message
An host of tongues, but let ill tidings tell
Themselves, when they be felt.
Mess.   I have done my duty.
Cleo. Is he married?
I cannot hate thee worser than I do,   90
If thou again say 'Yes'.
Mess.   He's married, madam.
Cleo. The gods confound thee, dost thou hold there still?
Mess. Should I lie, madam?
Cleo.   O, I would thou didst,
So half my Egypt were submerg'd and made
A cistern for scal'd snakes! Go get thee hence,   95
Hadst thou Narcissus in thy face, to me

81–5. S.D.s] † I have kept the single
S.D. of F. Dyce, followed by others,
inserted an *Exit Charmian* after *I will
not hurt him*, and read *Re-enter Charmian
and Messenger* just before *Come hither,
sir*. But this misses the stage business.
Charmian does not leave the stage, but
goes to the door to call the messenger,
whom she finds trembling outside, and
reports accordingly. Then Cleopatra
sees him in the doorway and encourages him with *Come hither, sir*, and he
enters. [R]

82–3. *These hands . . . myself*] Steevens
saw an allusion here to the laws of
chivalry, which 'forbade a knight to
engage with his inferior'; but chastise-
ment has nothing to do with combat
on equal terms. There is another dif-

ficulty: are there two reasons for lack
of nobility? (1) the blow to an inferior, (2) the wrong assignment of
blame; or, as I am half inclined to
think, only one, the latter, thus: My
hands act ignobly in bestowing blows
on any less person than myself, for I
myself am the real offender (by my
infatuation for Antony) who has
deserved them. Malone (see also iii. iii.
14) sees a probable hit at Queen
Elizabeth's temper, after her death,
when it '*might be safely hazarded!*' The
italics are mine.

95–7. *Go . . . ugly*] Steevens quotes
John, iii. i. 36–7: 'Fellow, be gone! I
cannot brook thy sight: / This news
hath made thee a most *ugly* man.'

96. *Narcissus*] See Golding's Ovid's

   Thou wouldst appear most ugly. He is married?
Mess. I crave your highness' pardon.
Cleo.   He is married?
Mess. Take no offence that I would not offend you:
   To punish me for what you make me do   100
   Seems much unequal: he's married to Octavia.
Cleo. O that his fault should make a knave of thee,
   That art not what th'art sure of. Get thee hence,
   The merchandise which thou hast brought from Rome
   Are all too dear for me: 105
   Lie they upon thy hand, and be undone by 'em!
                                   [*Exit Messenger.*
Char. Good your highness, patience.
Cleo. In praising Antony, I have disprais'd Cæsar.
Char. Many times, madam.

103. That . . . th' art sure of.] *F;* That say'st but what thou'rt sure of! *Hanmer;*
That art not!—what? thou'rt sure of't!— *Mason conj., adopted by Steevens and others;*
That art but . . . *Grant White;* That art in . . . *Hudson.*   106. S.D. *Exit Messenger*]
Rowe; not in F.

Metam., bk III, line 428 *et seq.*: '. . .
freckled Lyriop, whome sometime
surprised in his streame, / The floud
Cephisus did inforce. This lady bare a
sonne, / Whose beauty at his very birth
might justly love have wonne. /
Narcissus did she call his name,' etc.

   99. *Take . . . you*] Don't be angry at
my reluctance to give a reply which I
know will anger you.

   101. *unequal*] unjust. So *2H4*, IV. i.
102; Jonson, *Volpone*, III. ii. 14: 'You
are *unequal* to me,' etc.; Lord Brooke,
Life of Sidney (Works, Grosart, iv. 8):
'Witnes his sound establishments both
in Wales and Ireland, where his memory is worthily grateful unto this day:
how *unequall* and bitter soever the
censure of provincialls is usually
against sincere monarchall gover-
nours,' etc.

   102–3. *O . . . sure of*] The first of
these two lines seems to me to require
some stress on *his,* and to be suggested
by the messenger's complaint in line
100. He says, in effect: 'You are unjust: *you make* me commit the fault you
punish me for'; she replies: 'O that it

should be *his* fault that makes you a
subject for punishment.' What follows: 'That art not what thou'rt *sure
of,*' seems to imply Cleopatra's recog-
nition that the messenger's offence to
her lies in the obstinate persistence
that his news is authentic, out of which
he can neither be beaten nor cajoled.
(This is precisely the offence in Marston's imitation in *The Insatiate Countess,* IV. ii.) In this view the sense of the
whole will be: 'O that it should be *his*
fault that makes thee a subject for
punishment, that art not thyself the
thing of which thou art so hatefully
positive.'

   † Case is, I think, right about the
first line, but doubtfully so about the
second. It is one of those Shakespearean phrases, common in his later
work, of which the sense has to be 'felt'
and not arrived at by syntactical
analysis. Cleopatra 'means' 'It is the
fact of which you are so positive that
deserves my anger, and not *you,* the
bringer of the news.' [R]

   105–11. †*Are all . . . no matter.*] an
admirable example of the lineation

Cleo. I am paid for't now. Lead me from hence; I faint, 110
    O Iras, Charmian! 'tis no matter.
    Go to the fellow, good Alexas, bid him
    Report the feature of Octavia; her years,
    Her inclination, let him not leave out

problem, 'admitting a wide solution'.
F has this:

    Are all too deere for me:
    Lye they vpon thy hand, and be
      undone by em.
    Char. Good your Highnesse
      patience.
    Cleo. In praysing *Anthony*, I haue
      disprais'd *Cæsar*.
    Char. Many times, Madam.
    Cleo. I am paid for't now: lead
      me from hence,
    I faint, oh *Iras, Charmian*: 'tis no
      matter.

I first adopted, without much conviction, the usual relineation (which
derives from Capell), thus:

    Are all too dear for me: lie they
      upon thy hand,
    And be undone by 'em!
    Char.   Good
      your Highness, patience.
    Cleo. In praising Antony, I have
      disprais'd Cæsar.
    Char. Many times, madam.
    Cleo.   I am paid for't now.
    Lead me from hence;
    I faint, O Iras, Charmian! 'tis
      no matter.

Well, that bed of Procrustes no doubt
produces something more regular
than F, but at the cost of an awkwardly
hypermetrical line to start with, which
can only be regularized by a slurring
which destroys the emphasis, and of a
suspicious half-line for Cleopatra. The
following was then suggested to me,
with the comment 'Is this too fanciful?':

    Are all too dear for me: lie they
      upon
    Thy hand, and be undone by
      'em.
    Char.   Good your highness
      Patience.

    Cleo.   In praising Antony,
    I have
    Disprais'd Cæsar.
    Char.   Many times,
      Madam.
    Cleo.   I
    Am paid for't now.—Lead me
      from hence,
    I faint, O Iras, Charmian! 'tis
      no matter.

That seems to me not too fanciful, but
too jerky. And if one looks again at F,
is there really much the matter with
it? In the first two lines it retains the
contrasted emphasis on *me* and *thy*. At
for me Cleopatra has said all she has to
say, and pauses, and then spits out her
vituperative dismissal; and though the
second line is, by count of syllables,
hypermetric, the last three syllables
(-*done by* '*em*) amount in naturally
rapid delivery to no more than a feminine ending. Half-lines like Charmian's are not uncommon (cf. e.g.
Mardian's line 7 in this scene). But
what is suspicious is Cleopatra's awkwardly incomplete line starting eleven
lines of continuous verse. But a glance
at the Folio shows that after *hence*,
there is room for only at most six
letters (less, that is, than *I faint*, by a
space and a comma) and suggests as
a reasonable conjecture that Shakespeare wrote the complete line as in the
text above, and intended a pause in the
next line between *Charmian* and '*tis no
matter*, while Cleopatra recovers herself. [R]

113. *feature*] applies most commonly
to the shape of the whole body, as in
R3, i. i. 19; sometimes to facial characteristics more especially, as in *John*,
iv. ii. 264.

114. *inclination*] temperament; to
which Henley (1821 Variorum)

The colour of her hair; bring me word quickly.   115
                                              [*Exit Alexas.*
Let him for ever go, let him not—Charmian,
Though he be painted one way like a Gorgon,
The other way's a Mars. Bid you Alexas
[*To Mardian*] Bring me word how tall she is. Pity me,
   Charmian,
But do not speak to me. Lead me to my chamber.   120
                                              [*Exeunt.*

[SCENE VI.—*Near Misenum.*]

Flourish. Enter POMPEY *at one door, with drum and trumpet; at another* CÆSAR, LEPIDUS, ANTONY, ENOBARBUS, MÆCENAS, AGRIPPA, MENAS *with Soldiers marching.*

Pom. Your hostages I have, so have you mine;
   And we shall talk before we fight.

---

115. S.D. *Exit Alexas*] *Capell; not in F.*   118. *To Mardian*] *Capell; not in F.*

thought Cleopatra expected to find an index in the colour of Octavia's hair.
   116. *him*] i.e. Antony.
   117–18. *Though . . . Mars*] alluding, as Staunton pointed out, to the pictures formerly called perspectives (cf. *Tw.N.*, v. i. 227; *H5*, v. ii. 347) and still to be seen. Different objects are painted on the opposite surfaces of any suitable material (care being taken to paint one in the reverse direction), which is then cut into regular strips and attached to a third painted surface at small equal intervals, and at right angles to it. An example sometimes seen in village inns shows Lord Beaconsfield from one side, Mr Gladstone from the other, and a basket of flowers if the observer faces it. In [Sir George Mackenzie's] *Religio Stoici* (1665), sig. A7, occurs: 'Thus we see, that one may account that a miracle which another looks upon as a folly; and yet, none but Gods Spirit can decide the controversie. Matters of Religion and Faith, resembling some curious Pictures,

and Optick Prismes, which seems to change shape and colours, according to the several stances from which the aspicient views them.'
   Gorgon] presumably the particular Gorgon, Medusa, the sight of whose face turned men to stone.
   118. *way's*] surely 'The other way' = the other way of the picture. But Hanmer and others print *way he's*, and *way's* is so explained by recent editors.

Scene VI

[See North, *post*, p. 252.]
   S.D.] † I have, with hesitation, retained F's S.D., since, though odd, it is not impossible. The usual practice has been to bring in Menas with Pompey, and then excise Agrippa altogether, both somewhat drastic changes. But the S.D. is interpretable as it stands. There enter first, by their respective doors, Pompey, the triumvirs, Enobarbus, and Maecenas; they are followed by Agrippa (who does not talk at all) and Menas (who does not talk till all

Cæs.   Most meet
That first we come to words, and therefore have we
Our written purposes before us sent,
Which if thou hast considered, let us know   5
If 'twill tie up thy discontented sword,
And carry back to Sicily much tall youth,
That else must perish here.
Pom.   To you all three,
The senators alone of this great world,
Chief factors for the gods: I do not know   10
Wherefore my father should revengers want,
Having a son and friends, since Julius Cæsar,
Who at Philippi the good Brutus ghosted,
There saw you labouring for him. What was 't
That mov'd pale Cassius to conspire? And what   15
Made the all-honour'd, honest Roman, Brutus,
With the arm'd rest, courtiers of beauteous freedom,
To drench the Capitol, but that they would
Have one man but a man? And that is it
Hath made me rig my navy: at whose burthen   20
The anger'd ocean foams, with which I meant
To scourge the ingratitude that despiteful Rome
Cast on my noble father.
Cæs.   Take your time.

10. gods: I] gods. I *F*; gods, I *most edd.*   16. the] *F2; not in F.*   honest Roman,
Brutus,] *most modern edd.;* honest, Roman Brutus, *F and Delius.*

but he and Enobarbus have left), each
as leader of a group of soldiers, and
they stand in the background. ('Door'
is the usual terminology of the Elizabethan playhouse, in which all entries
to the main stage, whether the scene
represented was indoors or not, were
by 'doors'). [R]

7. *tall*] stout, bold; as often in Shakespeare. Also used sportively, in other
connections than plain valour, as e.g.
by Massinger, *The Unnatural Combat*,
III. i. 23: 'As *tall* a trencherman, that is
most certain, / As e'er demolish'd pye-
fortification,' etc. See also *Wiv.*, I. iv.
26, for '*tall* . . . of his hands,' i.e. formidable in combat.

10. *gods: I*] † The heavy punctuation
of F is surely right. Pompey starts with
a formal address, and then states his
case; and *To you I do not know* is almost
impossibly awkward. [R]

10–14. *I do . . . for him*] This appears
to mean, in brief: Julius Cæsar found
active avengers in you; I do not see
why my father, who has a son alive,
and friends likewise, should go without revenge.

13. *ghosted*] haunted. See *Cæs.*, IV.
iii. 275–87; v. iii. 94–6; v. v. 17–19.
Steevens quotes Burton, *Anatomy of
Melancholy*, 1632 ed., preface, p. 22:
'What madnesse *ghosts* this old man?
but what madnesse ghosts us all?'

Ant. Thou canst not fear us, Pompey, with thy sails.
We'll speak with thee at sea. At land thou know'st   25
How much we do o'er-count thee.

Pom.   At land, indeed,
Thou dost o'er-count me of my father's house:
But since the cuckoo builds not for himself,
Remain in't as thou may'st.

Lep.   Be pleas'd to tell us—
For this is from the present—how you take   30
The offers we have sent you.

Cæs.   There's the point.

Ant. Which do not be entreated to, but weigh
What it is worth embrac'd.

Cæs.   And what may follow,
To try a larger fortune.

Pom.   You have made me offer
Of Sicily, Sardinia; and I must   35
Rid all the sea of pirates. Then, to send

24. *fear*] frighten; as often. Cf. Jonson, *Bartholomew Fair*, III. ii. 129: 'Well said, brave Whit! in, and *fear* the ale out o' the bottles into the bellies of the brethren,' etc.

25. *speak with thee*] encounter thee. Cf. II. ii. 164 *ante*.

27. *o'er-count . . . house*] Plutarch relates that Antony, having bought the elder Pompey's house at auction, afterwards refused to pay for it. See North, pp. 241, 244, 252. Hence, as Malone observes, the phrase is equivocal; *outnumber* me by your possessing my father's house, and *cheat* me out of it by your sharp practice.

28. *But since the cuckoo*, etc.] 'Since, like the cuckoo, that seizes the nests of other birds, you have invaded a house which you could not build, keep it while you can' (Johnson). A sharp taunt, emphasizing the insinuation of cheating. Cf. R. Chester, *Love's Martyr*, 1601 (New Shakespeare Soc., 1878, p. 118): 'She scornes to labour or make vp a nest, / But creeps by stealth into some others roome, / And with the *Larkes* deare yong, her yong

ones rest, / Beeing by subtle dealing ouercome,' etc. The cuckoo's usual victim is the hedge-sparrow. See *1H4*, V. i. 60; *Lucr.*, 849.

30. *this . . . present*] This (the matter of the house) is beside the present point.

32–3. *Which do not . . . embrac'd*] Do not regard this as a plea; simply consider your own interests.

33–4. *And . . . fortune*] understood as a veiled menace in case his ambition rejects all offers and resorts to arms. It may, however, be meant for encouragement (as implied in Schlegel and Tieck's translation), and signify: 'And what it may lead to, if you take the chance of developments in this alliance.' *To try*, the infinitive used indefinitely, as often. Cf. *Wint.*, II. ii. 57: 'I know not what I shall incur to pass it, / Having no warrant.'

36. *to send*] The insertion of *to* before a second infinitive depending on an auxiliary verb is frequent in Shakespeare and elsewhere. Cf. *The Parliament of Criticks*, 1702, p. 79: 'Let the *Keeper of Bedlam* take such distracted

Measures of wheat to Rome; this 'greed upon,
To part with unhack'd edges, and bear back
Our targes undinted.

Cæs. Ant. Lep.   That's our offer.

Pom.   Know, then,
I came before you here a man prepar'd   40
To take this offer. But Mark Antony
Put me to some impatience: though I lose
The praise of it by telling, you must know,
When Cæsar and your brother were at blows,
Your mother came to Sicily, and did find   45
Her welcome friendly.

Ant.   I have heard it, Pompey,
And am well studied for a liberal thanks
Which I do owe you.

Pom.   Let me have your hand:
I did not think, sir, to have met you here.

Ant. The beds i' the east are soft, and thanks to you,   50
That call'd me timelier than my purpose hither;
For I have gain'd by 't.

Cæs.   Since I saw you last,
There is a change upon you.

Pom.   Well, I know not

---

39. *Cæs. Ant. Lep.*] Capell; Omnes. F.   45. Sicily] Cicelie F.   53. There is] Rowe;
Ther's F.

---

gentlemen as those into his Care, and consider whether their *Madness* be in the *Brain* or the *Blood*, and to report to the above-mentioned censors,' etc.

39. *targes*] said to be monosyllabic here (*targs*), and in *Cym.*, v. v. 5.

45. *Sicily*] † F's *Cicelie* is a real oddity. One can see Shakespeare mis-spelling some of the less familiar proper names, but hardly so common a geographical name as this (with which elsewhere, by the way, as in *Wint.*, he had apparently no difficulty). But it is an easy 'auditory' error, and I wonder whether in the light of it one should not examine with a more suspicious eye the easy writing-off of other similar errors as

'Shakespeare's mis-spellings.' Apart from *Ventigius - Ventidius*, elsewhere commented on, what about *Sidnis* for *Cydnus*? As a 'mis-spelling' it is surely extravagantly 'far wide.' But as a mis-hearing it is easy enough. [R]

47. *am well studied*, etc.] See II. ii. 154–6 *ante*. I am well equipped for amply thanking you, by much thought of my debt. Cf. II. ii. 138 *ante*; *Mer. V.*, II. ii. 211: 'Like one *well studied* in a sad ostent, / To please his grandam,' etc.; Dekker, *The Bel-man of London*, 1608 (Temple Classics, p. 133): 'so *well studied* that he hath the principles of the *Black-Art*, and can pick a lock if it be not too much cross warded,' etc.

What counts harsh fortune casts upon my face,
But in my bosom shall she never come,   55
      To make my heart her vassal.
Lep.   Well met here.
Pom. I hope so, Lepidus, thus we are agreed:
      I crave our composition may be written
      And seal'd between us.
Cæs.   That's the next to do.
Pom. We'll feast each other, ere we part, and let's   60
      Draw lots who shall begin.
Ant.   That will I, Pompey.
Pom. No, Antony, take the lot: but, first or last,
      Your fine Egyptian cookery shall have
      The fame. I have heard that Julius Cæsar
      Grew fat with feasting there.
Ant.   You have heard much.   65
Pom. I have fair meanings, sir.
Ant.   And fair words to them.
Pom. Then so much have I heard,
      And I have heard Apollodorus carried—

---

54. casts] cast's *F*.   57. Lepidus, thus] *F;* Lepidus. Thus *most edd.*   66. meanings] *Malone (Heath conj.) ;* meaning *F.*

54. *counts*] reckonings. So George Herbert, *The Discharge,* line 6: 'Hast thou not made thy *counts,* and summ'd up all?' In his careless answer, Pompey makes Fortune *score* on his face the record of her cruelties to him. Cf. *Edward III* (1596), ed. Moore Smith, IV. iv. 128-9: 'And stratagems forepast with iron pens / Are texted in thine honourable face.'

casts] used, of course, in the technical sense: 'Dost thou not know numbers? Canst thou not *cast*?' (*The Puritan,* 1607, III. i. 42.)

† Should we perhaps read *fortune's cast* (i.e. *has cast*), which might account for F's odd apostrophe? [R]

57.] † I think F's punctuation makes Pompey more deliberately courteous to the unimportant member of the triumvirate. *Thus* then = 'if you also are content.' [R]

58. *composition*] agreement. Cf. the use of *compose,* II. ii. 15 *ante.*

64-5. *Cæsar . . . feasting there*] 'Cæsar beganne thenceforth to spend all the night long in *feasting* and bancketing' (North's Plutarch, 1579, *Julius Cæsar,* Tudor Trans., v. 50).

68-70. *Apollodorus . . . mattress*] '[Cæsar] secretly sent for Cleopatra which was in the contry to come unto him. She onely taking Apollodorus Sicilian of all her friendes, tooke a litle bote and went away with him in it in the night, and came and landed hard by the foote of the castell. Then having no other meane to come in to the court, without being knowen, she laid her selfe downe upon a mattresse or flock-bed, which Apollodorus her frend tied and bound up together like a bundle with a great leather thong, and so tooke her up on his backe, and brought

Eno. No more of that: he did so.

Pom.   What, I pray you?

Eno. A certain queen to Cæsar in a mattress.   70

Pom. I know thee now: how far'st thou, soldier?

Eno.   Well,
And well am like to do, for I perceive
Four feasts are toward.

Pom.   Let me shake thy hand,
I never hated thee: I have seen thee fight,
When I have envied thy behaviour.

Eno.   Sir,   75
I never lov'd you much, but I ha' prais'd ye,
When you have well deserv'd ten times as much
As I have said you did.

Pom.   Enjoy thy plainness,
It nothing ill becomes thee.
Aboard my galley, I invite you all: 80
Will you lead, lords?

Cæs. Ant. Lep.   Show's the way, sir.

Pom.   Come.

[*Exeunt all but Menas and Enobarbus.*

Men. [*Aside*] Thy father, Pompey, would ne'er have
made this treaty.—You and I have known, sir.

Eno. At sea, I think.

Men. We have, sir.   85

---

69. more of that] *F3;* more that *F.*   81. Show's] *F* (Shew's); Shew us
Hanmer.   S.D. *Exeunt . . .*] Exeunt. Manet Enob. and Menas. *F.*   82. *Aside*]
Johnson.

her thus hamperd in this fardell unto
Cæsar, in at the castell gate. This was
the first occasion, (as it is reported)
that made Cæsar to love her: but afterwards, when he sawe her sweete conversation and pleasaunt entertainment, he fell then in further liking with
her, and did reconcile her againe unto
her brother the king, with condition,
that they two joyntly should raigne
together' (*ibid.* Tudor Trans., pp.
50–1).

73. *toward*] impending; as in *Ham.,*
v. ii. 378: 'O proud Death! / What
feast is *toward* in thine eternal cell,'

etc. Jonson, *E.M.I.,* i. i. 1 (F): 'A
goodly day toward! and a fresh
morning!'

78. *Enjoy thy plainness*] Cf. Brome,
The Damoiselle, i. ii (Pearson's *Brome,* i.
391): 'Youle give me leave to use my
plainnesse[?]', i.e. to speak plainly.

Enjoy] give rein to, 'indulge.'

83. *known*] been acquainted. So in
Cym., i. iv. 38: 'Sir, we have *known* together in Orleans,' on which Professor
Dowden quotes Jonson, *Cynthia's
Revels* iv. iii. 76: 'he salutes me as
familiarly as if we had *known* together
since the Deluge,' etc.

Eno. You have done well by water.

Men. And you by land.

Eno. I will praise any man that will praise me, though it
cannot be denied what I have done by land.

Men. Nor what I have done by water.   90

Eno. Yes, something you can deny for your own safety:
you have been a great thief by sea.

Men. And you by land.

Eno. There I deny my land service. But give me your
hand, Menas: if our eyes had authority, here they   95
might take two thieves kissing.

Men. All men's faces are true, whatsome'er their hands
are.

Eno. But there is never a fair woman has a true face.

Men. No slander, they steal hearts.   100

Eno. We came hither to fight with you.

Men. For my part, I am sorry it is turned to a drinking.
Pompey doth this day laugh away his fortune.

Eno. If he do, sure he cannot weep't back again.

Men. Y'have said, sir. We look not for Mark Antony   105
here: pray you, is he married to Cleopatra?

Eno. Cæsar's sister is called Octavia.

Men. True, sir, she was the wife of Caius Marcellus.

Eno. But she is now the wife of Marcus Antonius.

Men. Pray ye, sir?   110

Eno. 'Tis true.

Men. Then is Cæsar and he for ever knit together.

---

95. *authority*] i.e. as constables.

96. *two thieves kissing*] i.e. fraterniz-
ing, in a general sense, if the speakers
are the 'two thieves,' as lines 92–3
indicate; but line 97 points rather to
their hands, which the word *kissing*
would suit very well. Cf. *Rom.*, I. v.
103–4: 'For saints have hands that
pilgrims' hands do touch. / And palm
to palm is holy Palmer's *kiss*:' and
Ham., III. ii. 355, 'by these pickers and
stealers.'

97. *true*] honest, as in *1H4*, II. ii. 25.
S. Rowlands, *The Four Knaves* (Percy
Society, 1843, p. 89), versifies on the

proverb: 'When theeves fall out *true*
men come by their goods.' In the next
line there appears to be a play on the
word as meaning unsophisticated as
well as honest. Mr Craig suggests that
in 'All men's faces are true,' *true* means
(as well as 'honest') 'true indices of
character, of their thoughts', and that
Enobarbus, as he thinks of the in-
scrutable eyes of Cleopatra, objects
that women's faces, or at any rate fair
women's faces, are far from true
indices.

103–4. *laugh away...weep't back*] proverbial, perhaps, but I fail to trace it.

Eno. If I were bound to divine of this unity, I would not
    prophesy so.

Men. I think the policy of that purpose made more in   115
    the marriage than the love of the parties.

Eno. I think so too. But you shall find the band that
    seems to tie their friendship together will be the
    very strangler of their amity: Octavia is of a holy,
    cold, and still conversation.   120

Men. Who would not have his wife so?

Eno. Not he that himself is not so; which is Mark
    Antony. He will to his Egyptian dish again: then
    shall the sighs of Octavia blow the fire up in Cæsar;
    and (as I said before) that which is the strength of   125
    their amity shall prove the immediate author of
    their variance. Antony will use his affection where
    it is. He married but his occasion here.

Men. And thus it may be. Come sir, will you aboard? I
    have a health for you.   130

Eno. I shall take it, sir: we have us'd our throats in
    Egypt.

Men. Come, let's away.   [*Exeunt.*

---

119. strangler] *F;* stranger *F2–4;* estranger *Rowe.*

115. *made*] counted.

119. *strangler*] † Rowe's reading is an
excellent example of the dangers of
paying attention to the later Folios,
since what he was doing was emending
them (not the first, which needed no
emendation) and so moving steadily
further from the first. [R]

120. *conversation*] behaviour, system
of life. So in *Per.,* II, Gower, 9: 'The
good in *conversation*'; Rosse, *Mel Heli-
conium* (1640), p. 8: 'Before Christ

came, the *Gentiles* were but Ants, men
of Earthly *conversation,*' etc.; *Life and
Death of Sir Henry Vane* (1662), p. 23:
'men of debauched consciences and
bruitish *conversations.*'

127. *affection*] passion.

128. *but his occasion*] i.e. merely with
an eye to expedience.

131. *us'd*] Whether we take this as =
made use of *or* accustomed, the inference of practised pledging is the
same.

[SCENE VII.—*Aboard Pompey's galley, off Misenum.*]

Music plays. Enter two or three Servants with a banquet.

First Serv. Here they'll be, man. Some o' their plants are
   ill-rooted already, the least wind i' the world will
   blow them down.
Sec. Serv. Lepidus is high-coloured.
First Serv. They have made him drink alms-drink.   5
Sec. Serv. As they pinch one another by the disposition, he

Scene VII

1, 4, etc. *First* (*Sec.*) *Serv.*] *1.* (*2.*) *Ser. Rowe; 1. 2. F.*   4. high-coloured] *F2;*
high Conlord *F.*

S.D. a banquet] i.e. as often, a des-
sert with wine. Malone quotes *The Life
and Death of Thomas, Lord Cromwell,*
1602 [III. iii, *Supplement to Shakespeare,*
ii. 411]: '"Tis strange, how that we and
the Spaniard differ; / Their dinner is
our *banquet* after dinner,' etc. See also
Osborne, *Historical Memoires,* etc. 1658
(James I, pt i, §39): 'And after such
suppers huge *banquets* no lesse profuse,
a waiter returning his servant home
with a cloak-bag full of dried sweet-
meats and confects, valued to his lordship at more than ten shillings the
pound.'

1. *plants*] a play, as Johnson noted,
on the two senses of *plants*. For *plants*, a
common Latinism for the soles of the
feet and the feet themselves, cf. Jonson,
Oberon, line 403: 'Knotty legs, and
plants of clay'; Nashe, *Christ's Tears,* II.
63, line 7: '. . . you Pilgrims, that . . .
weare the *plants* of your feete to the
likenesse of withered rootes, by bare-
legd processioning (from a farre) to the
Sepulcher,' etc.

5. *alms-drink*] ordinarily 'the remains of liquor reserved for alms-
people' (*OED*); hence, perhaps, 'leavings' here, possibly mixed leavings, not
likely to agree with the recipient.
Beaumont (Letter to Ben Jonson)
speaks of water and claret lees as
drink: 'So mixt that given to the
thirstiest one / 'Twill not prove *alms*
unless he have the stone.' Warburton
is apparently the sole authority for

'almsdrink' 's being 'a phrase among
good fellows to signify that liquor of
another's share which his companion
drinks to ease him.' Can it here =
drink taken as a work of charity, i.e. to
further the reconciliation? See next
speech. *Almsdrink* supplies a bitter reflection in Churchyard's *Tragicall Discourse of the Vnhappy Man's Life,* stanza
70 (reprinted in *Bibliographical Miscellanies,* Oxford, 1813, p. 31): 'I see
some bring from doells an empty cup /
Yet craues an *almes,* and shoes a needye
hand'; etc.

6. *pinch . . . disposition*] Some later
editors decline to accept the natural
explanation that the differing dispositions of the newly reconciled three
occasionally clashed. Mr Deighton
says: 'we have no reason for thinking
they were quarrelsome in their cups':
but the probability of some friction
was great, and the next speech has far
more point if it signifies that the means
(more drink) whereby Lepidus *healed
strife between the others,* increased that
between himself and his discretion.
That *pinch . . . disposition* should mean:
'as they ply each other hard with the
mischievous desire of seeing one another under the table' (Deighton), *or*
= stint themselves by the disposal of
alms (i.e. an extra share) to Lepidus,
which is according to Mr A. E. Thiselton, or that it refers to 'the sign they
give each other regarding "the disposition" of Lepidus to drink' (Col-

cries out 'No more'; reconciles them to his entreaty,
and himself to the drink.

First Serv. But it raises the greater war between him and
his discretion.   10

Sec. Serv. Why, this it is to have a name in great men's
fellowship: I had as lief have a reed that will do me
no service, as a partisan I could not heave.

First Serv. To be called into a huge sphere, and not to be
seen to move in't, are the holes where eyes should be,   15
which pitifully disaster the cheeks.

A sennet sounded. Enter CÆSAR, ANTONY, POMPEY, LEPIDUS,
AGRIPPA, MÆCENAS, ENOBARBUS, MENAS, *with other
captains.*

12. lief] *Capell;* liue *F;* lieve *F3.*

lier), is surely unlikely; as also the
consequence that *No more* = no more
drink, instead of being an exclamation
like 'Soft, Cæsar!' (II. ii. 83 *ante*), and
that 'reconciles them to his entreaty,'
etc. = obtains their assent to his taking
no more and yet persuades himself to
take it.

12–13. *a reed that will do me no service*]
†not, I think, 'a reed which will not
serve me well *qua* reed,' but 'a reed,
which (in the nature of the case) is no
use as a weapon.' [R]

13. *partisan*] 'a sharp two-edged
sword placed on the summit of a staff
for the defence of foot soldiers against
cavalry' (Fairholt).

14–16. *To . . . cheeks*] According to
the construction, two circumstances,
the call to occupy a high position and
the failure to make a figure in it, are
compared to eyeless sockets. *Spheres*
has been regarded as an allusion to
the Ptolemaic system of astronomy,
and the hollow concentric spheres,
each of the first seven with its planet,
with which that system surrounds the
earth. The servant's elliptical speech
seems to compare (1) such spheres,
supposing their planets were *unseen*, to
disfiguring eyeless sockets; (2) great
positions in life, meanly tenanted, to

spheres in such a case; and, finally,
Lepidus, the man of no account, to the
hypothetically non-luminous planets.
Malone quotes for Shakespeare's use
of *sphere* in connection with *eyes*, *Sonn.*
cxix. 7, and *Ham.*, I. v. 17. The spheres
aforesaid are those of the Moon, Mercury, Venus, the Sun, Mars, Jupiter,
Saturn; after them is that of the fixed
stars, and, finally, enfolding all, the
Primum Mobile, which was the first
moved and communicated its motion
to the inner spheres. See also on IV. xv.
10–11 *post*.

16. *disaster*] a word of astrological
origin, and so probably suggested here,
as Rolfe notes, by the preceding figure.
An adjective *disastered* (cf. 'ill-starred')
occurs thrice in the Countess of Pembroke's *Antonie* (1595), e.g. in Act II:
'us *disastered* men,' 'this *disastered*
woe.'

16. S.D. A sennet] a particular set
of notes (not now known) on the trumpet, differing from a flourish. Cf.
Satiromastix (Pearson's *Dekker*, i. 222):
'Trumpets sound a florish, and then *a
sennate*.' See the derivation discussed in
Naylor's *Shakespeare and Music* (1896),
p. 178. The forms *sonet*, *sonnet*, have
suggested *sonare*,—*synnet*, *signet*, etc.,
signum, as the source.

Ant. [*To Cæsar*] Thus do they, sir: they take the flow o'
    the Nile
    By certain scales i' the pyramid; they know,
    By the height, the lowness, or the mean, if dearth
    Or foison follow. The higher Nilus swells,   20
    The more it promises: as it ebbs, the seedsman
    Upon the slime and ooze scatters his grain,
    And shortly comes to harvest.
Lep. Y'have strange serpents there?
Ant. Ay, Lepidus.   25
Lep. Your serpent of Egypt is bred now of your mud by
    the operation of your sun: so is your crocodile.

17. *To Cæsar*] Capell.

18. *By certain scales*, etc.] Cf. Lyly, *Campaspe*, The prologue at the Blacke Friers: 'It was a signe of famine to Ægypt, when Nylus flowed lesse than twelve cubites, or more than eighteene.' Malone thinks Shakespeare got his information from Pory's translation of Leo's *History of Africa* (1600): 'Upon another side of the island standeth an house alone by itselfe, in the midst whereof there is a foure-square cesterne or channel of eighteen cubits deep, whereinto the water of Nilus is conveyed by a certaine sluice under ground. And in the midst of the cisterne there is erected a certaine *piller*, which is *marked and divided into so many cubits as the cisterne containeth in depth.* . . If the water reacheth only to the fifteenth cubit of the said *piller*, they hope for a fruitful yeere following; but if [it] stayeth between the twelfth cubit and the fifteenth, then the increase of the yeere will prove but mean: if it resteth between the tenth and twelfth cubits, then it is a sign that corne will be solde ten ducates the bushel.' Reed quotes Holland's *Pliny* (1601), bk v, chap. ix, but the resemblance there is more distant.

20. *foison*] profusion, plenty. Cf. *Tp.*, II. i. 170; IV. i. 110, etc.

26. *Your*] a common colloquialism.

So in *Ham.*, IV. iii. 22: '*Your* worm is *your* only emperor for diet,' etc. On its occurrence in the text, Abbott (*Shakespearian Grammar*, §221) observes: 'Though in this instance the *your* may seem literally justified, the repetition of it indicates a colloquial vulgarity which suits the character of Lepidus.' It may or may not suit his character, but it certainly sets off his temporary condition.

bred . . . mud] The doctrine (abiogenesis or equivocal generation) was current in Shakespeare's day, that living matter can be produced from matter without life. So Jonson, *The Alchemist*, II. i. 171: 'Beside, who doth not see, in daily practice, / Art can beget bees, hornets, beetles, wasps, / Out of the carcasses, and dung of creatures; / Yea, scorpions of an herb, being rightly placed?' Cf. also Shirley, *The Traitor*, IV. ii (Mermaid ed., p. 137): 'oh that my voice / Could call a serpent from corrupted Nile,' etc.; and Sylvester's *Du Bartas*, week 1, day 2, p. 31 in 1621 ed.: 'As on the edges of som standing Lake . . . / The foamy slime itselfe transformeth oft / To green half-Tadpoles, . . . / Half dead, half-living; half a frog, *half-mud.*' At the present time the question has been re-opened owing to the results of certain experiments.

Ant. They are so.

Pom. Sit,—and some wine! A health to Lepidus!

Lep. I am not so well as I should be: but I'll ne'er out. 30

Eno. Not till you have slept; I fear me you'll be in till then.

Lep. Nay, certainly, I have heard the Ptolemies' pyramises are very goodly things; without contradiction I have heard that. 35

Men. [*Aside to Pom.*] Pompey, a word.

Pom. [*Aside to Men.*]   Say in mine ear, what is't?

Men. [*Aside to Pom.*] Forsake thy seat, I do beseech thee, captain,

And hear me speak a word.

Pom. [*Aside to Men.*]   Forbear me till anon.—

This wine for Lepidus!

Lep. What manner o' thing is your crocodile? 40

Ant. It is shap'd, sir, like itself, and it is as broad as it hath breadth: it is just so high as it is, and moves with it own organs. It lives by that which nourisheth it, and the elements once out of it, it transmigrates.

Lep. What colour is it of? 45

36–8.] *As asides first by Rowe.*   38. anon.—] anon. *Whispers in 's Eare. F.*

---

30. *I'll ne'er out*] I'll never refuse a pledge, never stand out. See *2H4*, v. iii. 68 (of drinking): 'A' will not out; he is true bred'; Massinger, *The Parliament of Love*, II. i, at end: '*I'll not out* for a second,' where it is said by the second person to take up a bet; F. Spence's *Lucian* (1684), *The Epistle Dedicatory*, sig. C2: 'Yet *Custom* so requiring, I have very slavishly imitated *Others*, and fancy myself like those *Sparks*, who will ever be in the *Fashion*, Let it never be so damn'd Foppish, silly and Troublesome: Nay, rather than be *out*, we'll go upon *Trust for Ridiculousness* and *Mortification*,' etc.

31. *in*] a play on the opposite phrase to 'be out' (so Felltham, *Lusoria*, 1661, xxxv, p. 33: 'being *in*, I must go on') and the sense '*in* drink.'

33–4. *pyramises*] a plural peculiar to the bibulous Lepidus, but corresponding with the Latin singular *pyramis*, the common form in Shakespeare's time. For the usual plural *pyramides*, cf. v. ii. 61 *post*.

42, 46. *it*] its. A common flexionless form, transitional between the usual neuter possessive *his* and the later *its*. Cf. *Lr*, I. iv. 238–9: 'The hedge-sparrow fed the cuckoo so long, That it had it head bit off by it young.'

44. *elements . . . transmigrates*] Here 'elements' apparently = the vital elements, life, not the complete group of four which compose everything (see on v. ii. 288 *post*). In 'transmigrates' is probably, as Delius says, a facetious allusion to the Pythagorean doctrine of the transmigration of souls, as in *AYL.*, III. ii. 188, and *Tw.N.*, IV. ii. 55–66; unless the word be merely 'rots,' 'passes into other forms of matter,' in a quaint disguise.

Ant. Of it own colour too.

Lep. 'Tis a strange serpent.

Ant. 'Tis so, and the tears of it are wet.

Cæs. Will this description satisfy him?

Ant. With the health that Pompey gives him, else he is a   50
very epicure.

Pom. [*Aside to Men.*] Go hang, sir, hang! Tell me of that?
away!
Do as I bid you.—Where's this cup I call'd for?

Men. [*Aside to Pom.*] If for the sake of merit thou wilt hear
me,
Rise from thy stool.

Pom. [*Aside to Men.*]   I think th'art mad. The matter?   55
[*Rises and walks aside.*

Men. I have ever held my cap off to thy fortunes.

Pom. Thou hast serv'd me with much faith: what's else to
say?
Be jolly, lords.

Ant.   These quick-sands, Lepidus,
Keep off them, for you sink.   59

Men. Wilt thou be lord of all the world?

52–5.] *As asides first by Johnson.*   55. S.D. *Rises . . .*] *Johnson; not in F.*   59. for]
F; 'fore *Theobald; or Dyce, ed. 2 (S. Walker conj.).*

48. *tears*] a by-allusion to the popular belief which furnishes a figure in
Oth., IV. i. 257; *2H6,* III. i. 226. 'If the
Crocodile findeth a man by the brim
of the water, or by the cliff, he slayeth
him if he may, and then he weepeth
upon him, and swalloweth him at the
last. . .' (*Bartholomew* [Berthelet], bk
xviii, §33.)

56. *held my cap off to*] been a servant
to, followed. The phrase here seems
rather to derive from the etiquette of
service at a time when head-coverings
were more constantly worn than now,
than from occasional acts of deference
or courtesy, such as '*Off-capp'd* to him'
in *Oth.,* I. i. 10 (F). Cf. Beaumont and
Fletcher, *The Honest Man's Fortune,* I. i
(Camb., x. 213): '*Long.* Counsel's the
office of a servant, . . . | *Mont.* Stay, sir,
what one example since the time /
That first you put your *hat off* to me,

have / You noted in me to encourage
you / To this presumption?' In some
notes on England quoted by Sir W.
Besant (*London in the Time of the Tudors,*
1904, p. 191) as written in 1558, and
translated for and published in *The
Antiquarian Repertory,* vol. iv, occurs:
'The servants wait on the master bare-
headed, and leave their *caps* on the
buffet.'

58–9. *These quick-sands . . . sink*] Perhaps Lepidus collapses here. Pompey's
health (see line 84 *post*) is too late.
There is a drinking scene in Heywood's
Iron Age, I (Pearson's *Heywood,* iii. 281)
in which Paris is similarly overcome,
but feignedly, as afterwards appears,
while Thersites has something of the
mocking spirit of Enobarbus and the
temperance of Cæsar.

60–79.] For this dialogue, see
North, *post,* p. 252.

Pom.   What say'st thou?
Men. Wilt thou be lord of the whole world? That's twice.
Pom. How should that be?
Men.   But entertain it,
  And though thou think me poor, I am the man
  Will give thee all the world.
Pom.   Hast thou drunk well?
Men. No, Pompey, I have kept me from the cup.   65
  Thou art, if thou dar'st be, the earthly Jove:
  Whate'er the ocean pales, or sky inclips,
  Is thine, if thou wilt ha't.
Pom.   Show me which way.
Men. These three world-sharers, these competitors,
  Are in thy vessel. Let me cut the cable,   70
  And when we are put off, fall to their throats:
  All there is thine.
Pom.   Ah, this thou shouldst have done,
  And not have spoke on't! In me 'tis villainy,
  In thee, 't had been good service. Thou must know,
  'Tis not my profit that does lead mine honour;   75
  Mine honour, it. Repent that e'er thy tongue
  Hath so betray'd thine act. Being done unknown,
  I should have found it afterwards well done,
  But must condemn it now. Desist, and drink.
Men. [*Aside*] For this,   80
  I'll never follow thy pall'd fortunes more.
  Who seeks and will not take, when once 'tis offer'd,

72. there] *F; then* Pope, *and Southern MS notes in F4;* theirs *Steevens conj.*   80.
Aside] *Capell.*

67. *pales . . . inclips*] fences in, as with
pales . . . embraces. Cf. *clip*, IV. viii. 8.
69. *competitors*] confederates. See on
I. iv. 3 *ante.*
72. *All there is thine*] † Pope's *then* is
attractive, and makes easy sense. But
we can retain F, I think, so long as we
do not take *there* as a demonstrative,
and do, in thought if not in type. insert
a comma: *All there is, thine,* i.e. 'then all
the world is yours.' This is almost
Furness's conjecture (*All there is, is
thine*) but his second *is* is needless. [R]

81. *pall'd*] decayed, dwindled. Compare *Ham.*, v. ii. 9: 'When our deep
plots do *pall*'; Kyd, *1 Ieronimo*, II. iv.
54: 'Which strooke amazement to
their *pauled* speeche,' etc. *Pall* is said to
be an abbreviated form of *appal*, both
originally meaning to become *or* be
made pale. So of wine when it loses
colour and becomes vapid by standing.
Compare Spence's *Lucian*, 1684, ii. 78:
'swallow delitious Wine, whilst you
must only drink such as is *pall'd* and
Taplash.'

Shall never find it more.

Pom.   This health to Lepidus!

Ant. Bear him ashore, I'll pledge it for him, Pompey.

Eno. Here's to thee, Menas!

Men.   Enobarbus, welcome!   85

Pom. Fill till the cup be hid.

Eno. There's a strong fellow, Menas.

> [*Pointing to the Attendant who carries off Lepidus.*

Men. Why?

Eno. 'A bears the third part of the world, man; see'st not?

Men. The third part, then, is drunk: would it were all,   90
That it might go on wheels!

Eno. Drink thou; increase the reels.

Men. Come.

Pom. This is not yet an Alexandrian feast.

Ant. It ripens towards it; strike the vessels, ho!   95

---

87. S.D. *Pointing . . .*] *Steevens; Pointing to Lepidus. Rowe; not in F.*   90. part, then, is] part, then he is *F*; part, then is *Rowe*.

91. *go on wheels*] proverbial for 'go fast,' and especially of the world. Cf. *Gent.*, III. i. 320; B. Rich, *The Honestie of this Age*, 1614 (Percy Society, 1844, p. 30): 'They were wont to say, the world did runne on *wheeles*: and it may well bee it hath done so in times past, but I say now it goes on crouches, for it is waxen old,' etc.; A. Wilson, *The Inconstant Ladie*, I. i. 11: 'I am angrie / To see the guiddie world run thus o' *wheeles* / In such untoward tracks,' etc.; Mabbe's *Celestina*, 1631, ix (Tudor Trans., p. 169): 'But such is this world, it comes and goes upon *wheeles*.'

92. *increase the reels*] Cf. line 115 *post*, and example in note on line 123; *Cor.*, II. i. 123; also *Histriomastrix*, iv. i. 28 (Simpson's *School of Shakspere*, ii. 57): 'Why should this *reeling* world (drunke with the juice / Of *Plenties*' bounty),' etc.; Heywood, *Rape of Lucrece* (Pearson's repr., v. 168): 'heres a giddy and drunken world, it *Reeles*, it hath got the staggers,' etc. Douce conjectured *revels* for *reels*, and there is another word *rule*, signifying revel, bustle, rowdy behaviour: cf. *Tw.N.*, II. iii.

133; Middleton, *A Chaste Maid*, etc., I. i. 208: 'Come now, we'll see how the *rules* go within': but there seems no need of change. Steevens cleverly conjectured 'and grease the wheels.'

95. *strike the vessels*] ? tap the casks. So Weber, the editor of Beaumont and Fletcher's works, which supply: 'Home, Launce, and *strike* a fresh piece of wine,' etc. (*Monsieur Thomas*, v. x. 42); '*Strike* me the oldest Sack,' etc. (*Love's Pilgrimage*, II. iv (Camb. vi, p. 272). Dyce adds from Prior's *Alma*, chap. iii. 524: '*Strikes* not the present tun, for fear / The vintage should be bad next year,' etc. The demand comes rather late in the feast, but its giver had had to call thrice for wine, lines 29, 39, 53 *ante*. On the other hand, I suspect that a sense 'fill the vessels (i.e. the cups) full' may some day find at least excuse. A 'strike' was 'an instrument with a straight edge for levelling (striking off) a measure of grain' (Skeat, *Etymol. Dict.*, §v), whence came 'strike,' a measure of varying amount, and a verb meaning to level corn to the top of the measure with a 'strike'; and

Here's to Cæsar!

Cæs.   I could well forbear't.
It's monstrous labour when I wash my brain
And it grow fouler.

Ant.   Be a child o' the time.

Cæs. Possess it, I'll make answer:

98. And it grow] *F;* . . . grows *F2.*

further (see Wright, *Eng. Dial. Dict.*),
the adverb *strike* = full to the top.
Again, the sense 'fill' might conceivably be reached from that of 'to lade
a fluid from one vessel into another,'
as cane juice into a cooler in sugar-
making. This is clearly the sense in
Harrison's directions for brewing
(Holinshed's Chronicle, 1587, *Description of England*, bk ii, chap. vi, p. 170):
'and when it hath sodden, . . . she
striketh it also, and reserveth it vnto
mixture with the rest when time dooth
serue therefore.' Just before (p. 169)
we have 'where it is *stricken* ouer, or
from whence it is taken againe,' etc.
The suggestion of Holt White again,
that the vessels were kettledrums,
though entirely neglected, is backed
up by the likelihood of a call for a *noisy*
toast in response to Pompey's request
for Alexandrian riot. He quotes *Ham.*,
v. ii. 284, and Enobarbus, line 108 *post.*
The idea of healths to music was familiar apart from Danish customs. Cf.
Beaumont and Fletcher, *The Scornful
Lady*, I. i. 6: 'at a gulp, without trumpets'; D'Avenant, *Albovine*, 1629, II
(*Dram. Works*, 1872, i, p. 36), where, if
he had this scene in view, he is a valuable witness for Holt White: '*Cuny.*
Sound high! / *Alb.* More wine and
noise! Now boy, I celebrate / Val-
daura's health— / *Cuny.* Bid their
instruments speak louder.'
Cf. also Shadwell, *The Miser*, III. ii
(*Works*, 1720, iii. 52): 'Come on,
Musicianers, strike up, hey: Here Forsooth, here's your Health; . . . [*He
drinks, they flourish.*] Ha, Ha; this is the
prettiest way of drinking, I vow; it
encourages us, as Drums and Trum-

pets do, when we let off our Guns at a
Muster'; *ibid.* (IV. i), p. 71: 'Oh, if I
had but Fiddles to play a Health
now!' Steevens's view that 'strike the
vessels' may be compared with 'chink
glasses,' found a supporter in Cowden
Clarke among modern editors.
97. *wash my brain*] Mr Craig compares Nashe, *Anatomie of Absurditie*,
1589 (ed. McKerrow, p. 41, line 3):
'Euery one knowes that he that
washeth his braines with diuers kinds
of wines, is the next doore to a drunken
man,' etc.
98. *And it grow*] Editors (save Singer,
ed. 2, '*An it grow*') read with F2. But
and = if (whence the usual *an*) is used
by Shakespeare. Cf. *Tp.*, II. i. 187:
'*Ant.* What a blow vvas there giuen? /
Seb. And it had not falne flat-long.'
† I think that *and* is more probably
the ordinary copula, and *grow* a sub-
junctive, caused by the feeling that
when is in effect a conditional, not
temporal, conjunction. [R]
99. *Possess it*] have your way, enjoy
your wish to pledge me; a somewhat
freer, but quite intelligible, use of
possess than e.g. in Jonson's *Volpone*,
v. iv. 15: 'He says, sir, he has weighty
affairs of state, / That now require him
whole, some other time / You may
possess him.' Indeed we might boldly
explain 'take it.' Cf. *Tp.*, III. ii. 102:
'Remember / First to *possess* his books;'
etc. Among unnecessary conjectures
are *Profess it* (Collier MS and ed. 2),
Propose it (Staunton).
† An anonymous explanation, quoted by Furness, is 'Rather be its master,
say I,' which would be wholly convincing if it were not for the 'But' at the

But I had rather fast from all, four days,   100
Than drink so much in one.

Eno. [*To Antony*]   Ha, my brave emperor,
Shall we dance now the Egyptian Bacchanals,
And celebrate our drink?

Pom.   Let's ha 't, good soldier.

Ant. Come, let's all take hands,
Till that the conquering wine hath steep'd our sense 105
In soft and delicate Lethe.

Eno.   All take hands.
Make battery to our ears with the loud music:
The while, I'll place you, then the boy shall sing.
The holding every man shall bear as loud
As his strong sides can volley.   110

[*Music plays. Enobarbus places them hand in hand.*

THE SONG.

Come, thou monarch of the vine,
Plumpy Bacchus with pink eyne!

101. *To Antony*] *added by Capell.*   109. bear] *Theobald;* beate *F.*

opening of the next line, where we should rather expect 'Nay,' or 'Indeed.' Even so, I prefer it to any of the others. [R]

105–6. *steep'd . . . Lethe*] Cf. *Tw.N.*, IV. i. 66: 'Let fancy still my sense in *Lethe steep*'; and Armin, *Two Maids of Moreclacke* (1609), Grosart's *Occas. Issues*, vol. xiii, p. 99: 'What is thy haste in *leathe steep't*? speak,' etc.

109. *holding*] Malone quotes a pamphlet, *The Servingman's Comfort* (1598): 'A song is to be song, the undersong or holding whereof is, It is merrie in Haul, when Beardes wagges all.' This suggests the same meaning as the Somonour's 'stif burdoun' in Chaucer (*Prol.*, line 673), a bass part or 'ground melody.' But the meaning here must be rather 'refrain', since if Enobarbus' directions were followed the boy's song would be drowned by an 'undersong.'

112. *pink eyne*] 'small, winking, halfshut eyes.' Steevens quotes Holland's *Pliny*, bk xi [cxxxvii, p. 335 E in vol. i,

1601 ed.]: 'also them that were *pinkeyed* and had verie small eies they termed *ocellae.*' Dyce cites Cotgrave, *Fr. and Eng. Dict.*: '*Oeil de rat*, a small eye, *pinke-eye*, little sight.' Cf. also Minshew, *Guide to the Tongues* (1617): 'to Pinke, or *winke in slumbering, pinckeyd, somniculosus*'; Lyly's *Euphues* (W. Bond, I, p. 254, line 25): 'if she be gagge toothed, tell hir some merry ieste, to make hir laughe, if *pinke eyed*, some dolefull Historye, to cause hir weepe, in the one hir grinning will shewe hir deformed, in the other hir whininge, lyke a Pigge halfe rosted'; Kyd, *Soliman and Perseda* (V. iii. 7 in *Works*, ed. Boas, who prints *pinky-ey'd*): 'The mightie *pinckanyed* brand-bearing God'; *Laneham's Letter* (*Captain Cox*, etc., Ballad Society, 1871, p. 17): 'the bear with his *pink nyez* leering after his enmiez approch'; Harrison's *Description of England* (Holinshed's *Chronicle*, 1587, bk ii, chap. vi, p. 170): 'and either fall quite vnder the boord, or else not daring to stirre from their

In thy fats our cares be drown'd,
With thy grapes our hairs be crown'd:
  Cup us till the world go round,   115
  Cup us till the world go round!

Cæs. What would you more? Pompey, good-night. Good
    brother,
Let me request you off: our graver business
Frowns at this levity. Gentle lords, let's part,
You see we have burnt our cheeks. Strong Enobarb   120
Is weaker than the wine, and mine own tongue
Splits what it speaks: the wild disguise hath almost
Antick'd us all. What needs more words? Good night.
Good Antony, your hand.
Pom.   I'll try you on the shore.
Ant. And shall, sir; give's your hand.

---

118. you off: our] *Rowe (semicolon)*; you of our *F.*   122. Splits] *F4*; Spleet's
F.

---

stooles, sit still *pinking* with their narrow *eies* as halfe sleeping, till the fume
of their aduersarie be digested that he
may go to it afresh'; D'Avenant, *The
Platonic Lovers*, II. i (*Dramatic Works*,
1872, ed. ii, 26): 'O Sir, she hath the
prettiest *pinking eyes*: / The holes are no
bigger than a pistol bore.' Even the
indefinite among these examples and
others point rather to smallness than
redness, a sense some think may be
also referred to. In two or three allusions to the colour of Bacchus' eyes
which I have come upon the word *red*
is used. Compare S. Rowlands, *More
Knaves Yet?* etc. (Percy Society, xxxiv,
1843, p. 100): 'What rhume's in
Bacchus's eyes? how *red* they looke:'
etc.

113. *fats*] vats, which is the Southern
form of the word. Cf. Browne, *Britannia's Pastorals*, II. i. 373: 'Within a
tanner's *fat* I oft have eyed . . . a large
ox-hide / In liquor mix'd', etc.

122. *Splits what it speaks*] a perilously
fissile combination of sounds.

disguise] *OED* cites Jonson, *Masque
of Augurs*, line 46: '*Disguise!* what

mean you by that? do you think that
his majesty sits here to expect drunk-
ards?' See also Shirley, *The Wedding*,
v. ii (*Works*, 1833, i. 448): '*Raw.* I am
not drunk. *Lod.* No, but thou art *dis-
guis'd* shrewdly.'

123. *Antick'd us*] made antics or gro-
tesques of us. Cf. Dekker, *The Bel-man
of London*, pt i, 1608 (Temple Classics
ed., p. 86): 'At the length, drunken
healths reeled up and downe the table.
. . . The whole *Roome* showed a farre off
(but that there was heard such a noyse)
like a Dutch peece of *Drollery*: for they
sat at table as if they had beene so
many *Anticks*;' etc.

124. *I'll try . . . shore*] This may mean
'I'll test your hospitality ashore,' with
time of so doing undefined; but more
probably Pompey, fired by the 'Alexandrian feast,' wants to continue the
debauch, offers to vie drinking powers
on shore then, and actually accom-
panies the other 'great fellows.' This
suits Antony's reply and his own:
'Come down into the boat' (line 127),
which is otherwise rather abrupt to a
departing guest.

Pom.   O Antony,   125

    You have my father's house. But what, we are friends?
    Come down into the boat.

Eno.   Take heed you fall not.

                        [*Exeunt all but Enobarbus and Menas.*

    Menas, I'll not on shore.

Men.   No, to my cabin.

    These drums, these trumpets, flutes! what!
    Let Neptune hear we bid a loud farewell   130
    To these great fellows: sound and be hang'd,
            sound out!   [*Sound a flourish, with drums.*

Eno. Hoo! says 'a. There's my cap.

Men. Hoo! Noble captain, come.   [*Exeunt.*

127–8. fall not. Menas,] fall not *Menas; F.*   127 S.D. *Exeunt . . .] Camb. edd.;*
not in *F.*   128. *Men.] Capell; not in F. See note.*   130. a loud] *Rowe, ed. 3;*
aloud *F.*

126. *my father's house*] See on II. vi. 27
ante.

127–8. †I have given the usually
accepted reading, but it is not, I think,
satisfactory.   Enobarbus'   warning
would be more naturally addressed (in
spite of his 'plainness') to his equal,
Menas, than to the triumvirs and
Pompey; 'Menas' is a rather awkwardly formal opening to 'I'll not on
shore'; and would even Enobarbus
thus force his continued company on
Menas? F reads as follows:

    Eno. Take heed you fall not *Menas:*
            Ile not on shore,
            No to my cabin: . . .

thus giving the whole speech to Enobarbus, which is clearly wrong, since

the cabin is Menas'. I suggest that the
MS had *Menas* twice, once as vocative,
and once as speech heading, and that
we should read:

    Eno. Take heed you fall not, Menas.
    Men. I'll not on shore. No, to my
            cabin.

Menas is then saying, in effect, 'No
need for your kindly warning; I'm not
going ashore; no, we're both going to
my cabin, but let's give the great fellows a good send-off.' [R]

132. *says 'a*] †Again I retain the
usual reading (F *Hoo saies a*), but with
even more doubt, and suggest *Hoo!*
Sessa! (an easy 'auditory error'); cf.
Shr., Ind. i. 5–6, 'Let the world slide.
Sessa!' [R]

ACT III

[SCENE I.—*A plain in Syria.*]

Enter VENTIDIUS *as it were in triumph, with* SILIUS, *and other Romans, Officers, and Soldiers; the dead body of* PACORUS *borne before him.*

Ven. Now, darting Parthia, art thou struck, and now
　　Pleas'd fortune does of Marcus Crassus' death
　　Make me revenger. Bear the king's son's body
　　Before our army. Thy Pacorus, Orodes,
　　Pays this for Marcus Crassus.

Sil.　　　　　　　　　　　Noble Ventidius,　　5
　　Whilst yet with Parthian blood thy sword is warm,
　　The fugitive Parthians follow. Spur through Media,
　　Mesopotamia, and the shelters whither
　　The routed fly. So thy grand captain Antony
　　Shall set thee on triumphant chariots, and　　10
　　Put garlands on thy head.

ACT III

Scene 1

S.D. *Enter . . .*] *F, but omitting* 'with Silius . . . Soldiers.'　　5. *Sil.*] *Theobald; Romaine F.*　　8. whither] *F2; whether F.*

[*Scene* 1: See North, *post*, p. 253.]

1. *darting Parthia*] alluding to the well-known tactics of Parthian horsemen, who, having flung their darts, avoided close quarters by swift retreat, shooting flights of arrows backwards as they fled.

2. *Crassus' death*] Crassus (who formed the first triumvirate with Pompey and Cæsar) was defeated 53 B.C. in the plains of Mesopotamia, by Surenas, the general of Orodes, King of Parthia and father of Pacorus; and was treacherously killed during a con-

ference proposed by the victor. Orodes poured melted gold into the dead man's mouth, bidding him take his fill of what he had so coveted in life. This act possibly suggested II. v. 34–5 *ante.*

9. *grand captain*] as often. So e.g. John Heywood, *The Spider and the Flie*, 1556 (Spenser Soc., 1894, pp. 218, 223, etc.): 'The *graund Captaine* standing amid mong this rought, / Was the flie, that', etc.; *Roister Doister*, IV. viii. 26: 'I my selfe will mounsire *graunde captaine* undertake.'

94

Ven.   O Silius, Silius,
I have done enough. A lower place, note well,
May make too great an act. For learn this, Silius;
Better to leave undone, than by our deed
Acquire too high a fame, when him we serve's away.   15
Cæsar and Antony have ever won
More in their officer than person: Sossius,
One of my place in Syria, his lieutenant,
For quick accumulation of renown,
Which he achiev'd by the minute, lost his favour.   20
Who does i' the wars more than his captain can,
Becomes his captain's captain: and ambition,
The soldier's virtue, rather makes choice of loss,
Than gain which darkens him.
I could do more to do Antonius good,   25
But 'twould offend him. And in his offence
Should my performance perish.
Sil.   Thou hast, Ventidius, that
Without the which a soldier and his sword
Grants scarce distinction. Thou wilt write to Antony?
Ven. I'll humbly signify what in his name,   30
That magical word of war, we have effected;
How with his banners, and his well-paid ranks,
The ne'er-yet-beaten horse of Parthia
We have jaded out o' the field.

12–13. *A lower . . . act*] Subordinate
position may make an achievement
too great for safety.

20. *by the minute*] continually.

lost his favour] There is possibly no
authority for this statement. It is not in
North (see *post*, p. 254) or Plutarch, as
was kindly pointed out to me by Professor A. C. Bradley.

22. *captain's captain*] So is Desdemona called (*Oth.*, II. i. 74).

22–3. *ambition . . . virtue*] Cf. *Oth.*,
III. iii. 350: 'the big wars / That make
ambition virtue!'

24. *darkens him*] him, i.e. the soldier,
as ambition and the rest shows; otherwise it is equally true that he who becomes his captain's captain darkens

him. With *darkens*, cf. *Cor.*, IV. vii. 5:
'And you are *darken'd* in this action,
sir, / Even by your own.'

29. *Grants scarce*] equivalent to
'scarcely admit of.' Warburton first
explained lines 28–9 to mean, that,
without discretion, there would be
very little difference between a soldier
and his sword. Steevens quotes *Cor.*,
I. iv. 52–4: 'O noble fellow! / Who
sensibly out-dares his senseless sword, /
And, when it bows, stands up.'

31. *word of war*] Cf. II. ii. 44 *ante*.

34. *jaded*] 'driven like worn-out
nags' (Kittredge). Cf. Beaumont and
Fletcher, *Philaster*, I. i. 179: 'Oh! this
same whorson Conscience, how it
jades us!'

Sil.   Where is he now?

Ven. He purposeth to Athens, whither, with what haste   35
     The weight we must convey with 's will permit,
     We shall appear before him. On there, pass along!
                                    [*Exeunt.*

[SCENE II.—*Rome. An ante-chamber in Cæsar's house.*]

Enter AGRIPPA *at one door,* ENOBARBUS *at another.*

Agr. What, are the brothers parted?

Eno. They have despatch'd with Pompey, he is gone,
     The other three are sealing. Octavia weeps
     To part from Rome; Cæsar is sad, and Lepidus,
     Since Pompey's feast, as Menas says, is troubled   5
     With the green-sickness.

Agr.   'Tis a noble Lepidus.

Eno. A very fine one: O, how he loves Cæsar!

Agr. Nay, but how dearly he adores Mark Antony!

Eno. Cæsar! Why he's the Jupiter of men.

Agr. What's Antony? The god of Jupiter.   10

Eno. Spake you of Cæsar? How, the nonpareil?

Agr. O Antony, O thou Arabian bird!

Eno. Would you praise Cæsar, say 'Cæsar,' go no
     further.

Agr. Indeed he plied them both with excellent praises.

Eno. But he loves Cæsar best, yet he loves Antony: 15

11. Spake] *F;* Speak *F3.*

6. *green-sickness*] the form of anæmia supposed peculiar to lovesick damsels. 'Lepidus, it is insinuated, is languishing for love of Cæsar and Antony' (L. in *The Eversley Shakespeare*). And they are parodying his ecstasies.

7. *A very fine one*] This comment was possibly evoked by the sound of the word *Lepidus*, which, to me, at least, is rather suggestive of some kind of sea creature of the inerter type. But perhaps this is seeing too much: († and

why not evoked by the Latin *meaning* of *lepidus* = elegant? [R]) Lepidus is presently a 'shard-borne beetle' (line 20 *post*).

12. *Arabian bird*] a frequent phrase for the fabulous phœnix, of which but one was supposed to exist at a time. Cf. *Cym.*, I. vi. 17.

13. *'Cæsar,' go no further*] So 'Cæsar' implies the perfection of generous clemency in III. xiii. 55 *post*: 'Further than he is Cæsar.'

Hoo! hearts, tongues, figures, scribes, bards, poets,
    cannot
Think, speak, cast, write, sing, number, hoo,
His love to Antony. But as for Cæsar,
Kneel down, kneel down, and wonder.

Agr.   Both he loves.
Eno. They are his shards, and he their beetle, so: 20
                                 [*Trumpet within*]
This is to horse. Adieu, noble Agrippa.
Agr. Good fortune, worthy soldier, and farewell.

     Enter CÆSAR, ANTONY, LEPIDUS, *and* OCTAVIA.

Ant. No further, sir.
Cæs. You take from me a great part of myself;
    Use me well in 't. Sister, prove such a wife   25
    As my thoughts make thee, and as my farthest band
    Shall pass on thy approof. Most noble Antony,

16, 17. Hoo] *F1–3;* Ho *F4.*   16. figures] *Hanmer;* Figure *F.*   20. beetle, so:] *F;* beetle; [*Trumpet within*] so, *Capell, and, with minor modifications, most edd. No trumpet in F.*

16–17. *Hoo! hearts . . . Think . . .*]
I retain *Hoo!* of F as characteristic of
the speaker and also appropriate to the
semi-hysterical adulation of Lepidus
which he mimics. A common practice
of sonneteers is aimed at in the ensuing correspondence of a succession of
nouns with another of verbs, in separate lines. Cf. B. Griffin, *Fidessa,* 1596,
Sonnet xlvii: 'I see, I hear, I feele, I
know, I rue, / My fate, my fame, my
praise, my losse, my fall;' etc.

   figures] metaphors and similes.

   17. *cast*] compute. Cf. II. vi. 54 *ante.*
number] versify, put into 'numbers.'

   20. *They . . . beetle*] Steevens: 'They
are the *wings* that raise this *heavy lumpish insect* from the ground. So, in *Macbeth* [III. ii. 42]: "the *shard-borne beetle.*"'
See also *Cym.,* III. iii. 20, 'The *sharded
beetle.*' The shards are properly the
horny cases or sheaths of the insect's
wings.

   beetle, so.] † I can see no good reason
for deserting the pointing of F, though

from Capell various editors have inclined to insert the S.D. (which is not
in F) between *beetle* and *so,* making the
latter a part of Enobarbus' comment
on the trumpet-call. [R]

   21–2.] It looks as though there must
have been some second thoughts here.
Two more unmistakable exit lines it
would be hard to find, but the passage
of asides later in the scene is effective.

   26–7. *as my farthest band . . . approof*] such as I would stake anything
that you will prove to be. *Band* is frequent for *bond,* as in *Two Wise Men,*
etc., 1619, I. i (see Chapman, ed. 1875,
Poems, etc., p. 388, col. 1, line 46: 'a
friend of mine must use a thousand
pound and intreats my *band*'; etc. For
approof indicating the proved possession of a quality, compare *All's W.,* II.
v. 3: 'Of very valiant *approof.*' † And
for *pass on* cf. *Meas.,* II. i. 22–3: 'what
knows the laws / That thieves do *pass
on* thieves?' about which there has

Let not the piece of virtue which is set
Betwixt us, as the cement of our love
To keep it builded, be the ram to batter   30
The fortress of it; for better might we
Have lov'd without this mean, if on both parts
This be not cherish'd.

Ant.   Make me not offended
In your distrust.

Cæs.   I have said.

Ant.   You shall not find,
Though you be therein curious, the least cause   35
For what you seem to fear: so, the gods keep you,
And make the hearts of Romans serve your ends!
We will here part.

Cæs. Farewell, my dearest sister, fare thee well,
The elements be kind to thee, and make   40
Thy spirits all of comfort! fare thee well.

---

31. for better] *F;* for far better *Capell.*

been needless difficulty, since it does not mean that thieves pass laws, but that the law takes no cognizance of the fact that thieves (in the jury) may be *passing verdicts on* thieves (in the dock). [R]

28. *piece of virtue*] So in *Tp.*, I. ii. 56: 'The mother was a *piece of virtue*'; Sir T. Browne, *Hydriotaphia*, Epistle Ded.: 'A complete *piece of Virtue* must be made from the Centos of all Ages, as all the beauties of *Greece* could make but one handsome *Venus.*' *Piece* often = masterpiece, as here (most probably) and in v. ii. 99 *post*, but is also used merely for 'creature' and the like words. So in *The Taming of a Shrew* (*Six Old Plays*, Nichols, 1779, p. 212): '*Ferando.* 'Tis wel done, *Kate. Emelia.* I sure, and like a loving *peece*,' etc.

29. *cement*] accented on first syllable, like the verb in II. i. 48 *ante*. So commonly.

31. *for*] †Capell's emendation is graphically easy, and tempting. [R]

32. *mean*] *mean* and *means* were used indifferently. Cf. Adlington's *Apuleius*,

1566, chap. xxii (Tudor Trans., p. 124): 'shewing a *mean* to Psyches to save her life,' etc. †But I suspect that *mean* here has the sense of 'intermediary.' [R]

33–4. *Make . . . In your distrust*] This does not seem to = 'In your distrust of me, don't offend me,' but rather 'Make me not offended *with*, or *at* your mistrust,' the use of *in* being comparable to one or other of those remarked by Abbott (*Shakespearian Grammar*, §162). Cf. *Troil.*, II. iii. 150: '*In* second voice we'll not be satisfied.'

35. *curious*] particular, minute in inquiry. The word is used of careful or over-exactness of any kind. See *Rom.*, I. iv. 31, 'What *curious* eye doth quote deformities.'

40–1. *The elements . . . comfort*] Most likely a parting wish for favourable weather; Mason quotes *Oth.*, II. i. 45. Johnson, however, thought that the elements composing the human body are invoked to act harmoniously and induce cheerfulness. See on v. ii. 288 *post*.

Oct. My noble brother!

Ant. The April's in her eyes, it is love's spring,
    And these the showers to bring it on. Be cheerful.

Oct. Sir, look well to my husband's house; and—

Cæs.   What,   45
    Octavia?

Oct.   I'll tell you in your ear.

Ant. Her tongue will not obey her heart, nor can
    Her heart inform her tongue—the swan's down feather,
    That stands upon the swell at the full of tide,
    And neither way inclines.   50

Eno. [*Aside to Agr.*] Will Cæsar weep?

Agr. [*Aside to Eno.*]   He has a cloud in's face.

Eno. [*Aside to Agr.*] He were the worse for that were he a horse,
    So is he being a man.

Agr. [*Aside to Eno.*]   Why, Enobarbus?
    When Antony found Julius Cæsar dead,
    He cried almost to roaring; and he wept   55
    When at Philippi he found Brutus slain.

---

49. at the full] *F;* at full *F2, and many edd.*   51–9. *Aside . . .*] *Capell.*

43–4. *The April's . . . on*] Cf. Bodenham's *Belvedere,* 1600 (Spenser Soc., 1875, p. 28): '*MAY is not loues month, MAY is full of flowers, | But dropping APRIL: Loue is full of showers.*'

47–8. *nor can . . . her tongue*] Cleopatra, at parting, is similarly at a stand in I. iii. 89: 'something it is I would,—'

48–50. *the swan's . . . inclines*] It is not clear whether Octavia's heart is the swan's down feather, swayed neither way on the full tide of emotion at parting with her brother to accompany her husband, or whether it is merely the *inaction* of heart and tongue, which is compared to that of the feather. (†Surely *the full of tide* = slack water, just before the ebb starts. [R]

52. *were he a horse*] According to Madden (*Diary of Master William Silence*) 'a cloud' was simply the absence of a white star. His authorities are Gervase Markham (*Cavalarice*) for the star as 'an excellent good marke'

and the viciousness of 'the horse that hath no white at all'; and Sadler, *De Procreandis,* etc., *equis,* 1587: *Equus nebula (ut vulgo dicitur) in facie, cujus vultus tristis est et melancholicus, jure vituperatur.* Such a horse he says later (p. 339 in 1907 ed.) is Arcite's unlucky steed in *The Two Noble Kinsmen,* v. iv. 63, 'a blacke one, owing / Not a hayre worth of white,' etc. The Duke of Newcastle, who wrote both on horsemanship and the management of horses, uses the phrase something like Shakespeare in *The Triumphant Widow or The Medley of Humours. A comedy,* 1677 (see extracts in Lamb's *Specimens,* Bohn's ed., p. 511), of a footpad going to execution: '*2nd Woman.* Look, what a down look he has! *1st Woman.* Ay, and what a cloud in his forehead, goody Twattle, mark that. *2nd Woman.* Ay, and such frowning wrinkles, I warrant you; not so much as a smile from him.'

Eno. [*Aside to Agr.*] That year, indeed, he was troubled with
    a rheum;
    What willingly he did confound, he wail'd,
    Believe 't, till I wept too.

Cæs.   No, sweet Octavia,
    You shall hear from me still; the time shall not   60
    Out-go my thinking on you.

Ant.   Come, sir, come;
    I'll wrestle with you in my strength of love:
    Look here I have you, thus I let you go,
    And give you to the gods.

Cæs.   Adieu; be happy!

Lep. Let all the number of the stars give light   65
    To thy fair way!

Cæs.   Farewell, farewell!   [*Kisses Octavia.*
Ant.   Farewell!
               [*Trumpets sound. Exeunt.*

---

59. wept] *Theobald;* weepe *F.*

57. *a rheum*] a running at the eyes.
Cf. D'Avenant, *The Just Italian,* IV.
(*Works,* i. 258 in *Dramatists of Restoration*): 'This is a sickly *rheum,* and not /
Compunction in my eyes'; and *Oth.,*
III. iv. 52, 'salt and sullen *rheum.*'

58. *What willingly . . . wail'd*] Cf.
v. i. 28–30 *post.*

59. *wept*] Steevens and Capell retain
weep of F. The latter unaccountably
thinks it out of character for Enobarbus to weep, and says on *Believe't till I
weep too,* 'Which he thought would be
never.' The former defends it as implying something like this: Believe it
till you see me weeping on the like
occasion, and then I'll thank you for
the same undeserved credit for compassion.

61. *Out-go . . . you*] outstrip, etc., i.e.
my loving thought of you shall keep
pace with the passage of time.

62. *I'll wrestle . . . love*] After what

precedes, this gives the impression of
meaning that Antony would contend
with Cæsar—with whom Octavia was
finding it so hard to part—by putting
forth the strength of his love to separate
them; till we read the next line (63)
which seems to confine Antony's expression of love to Cæsar, whom he
embraces. *Wrestle* thus refers at once to
their embrace and rivalry in mutual
goodwill.

63–6. † The speech distribution does
not seem wholly satisfactory. Lepidus'
'thy' must surely be addressed to
Octavia, as Cæsar's 'Adieu; be happy'
presumably also is. But I feel that 'thus
I let you go, and give you to the gods'
is much more appropriate from Cæsar
to Octavia than from Antony to
Cæsar. However, any attempts at readjustment, even if one could find any
warranty for them, only create new
difficulties. [R]

[SCENE III.—*Alexandria. Cleopatra's palace.*]

Enter CLEOPATRA, CHARMIAN, IRAS, *and* ALEXAS.

Cleo. Where is the fellow?
Alex.   Half afeard to come.
Cleo. Go to, go to. Come hither, sir.

Enter the Messenger as before.

Alex.   Good majesty,
Herod of Jewry dare not look upon you,
But when you are well pleas'd.
Cleo.   That Herod's head
I'll have: but how, when Antony is gone,   5
Through whom I might command it? Come thou near.
Mess. Most gracious majesty!
Cleo.   Didst thou behold
Octavia?
Mess.   Ay, dread queen.
Cleo.   Where?
Mess.   Madam, in Rome;
I look'd her in the face, and saw her led
Between her brother and Mark Antony.   10
Cleo. Is she as tall as me?
Mess.   She is not, madam.
Cleo. Didst hear her speak? is she shrill-tongu'd or low?
Mess. Madam, I heard her speak; she is low-voic'd.
Cleo. That's not so good: he cannot like her long.

Scene III

3. *Herod of Jewry*] See on I. ii. 28 *ante*.

14. *That's . . . good*] That is less favourable news. Those who suppose the words to mean 'That is no great commendation,' on the strength of what immediately follows, and of 'dull of tongue' (line 16), perhaps do not sufficiently consider Cleopatra's hopeful mood after her recent despair. 'He cannot like her long' is probably merely a rebound from a momentary doubt, and = Nevertheless, he cannot, etc. As to 'dull of tongue'—in her new mood of interpreting everything to her own advantage, she so presently construes *low-voic'd*, just as she degrades any lower stature than her own to *dwarfish*, though she would doubtless have preferred the messenger to say 'shrill-tongued.' Cf. I. i. 32 *ante*. On the contrary supposition, Malone (as in II. v. 82–3) again applauds a suggestion of Queen Elizabeth in Cleopatra, because, forsooth, the Continuator of Stowe's *Chronicle* says: 'She was *tall of stature*, . . . her *voyce loud and shrill.*' († I think Case got entangled in his own argument, and that the second explanation is the right one. [R])

Char. Like her? O Isis! 'tis impossible   15
Cleo. I think so, Charmian: dull of tongue, and dwarfish!
    What majesty is in her gait? Remember,
    If e'er thou look'st on majesty.
Mess.   She creeps:
    Her motion and her station are as one:
    She shows a body, rather than a life,   20
    A statue, than a breather.
Cleo.   Is this certain?
Mess. Or I have no observance.
Char.   Three in Egypt
    Cannot make better note.
Cleo.   He's very knowing,
    I do perceive 't, there's nothing in her yet.
    The fellow has good judgment.
Char.   Excellent.   25
Cleo. Guess at her years, I prithee.
Mess.   Madam,
    She was a widow—
Cleo.   Widow? Charmian, hark.
Mess. And I do think she's thirty.
Cleo. Bear'st thou her face in mind? is 't long or round?
Mess. Round, even to faultiness.   30
Cleo. For the most part, too, they are foolish that are so.
    Her hair what colour?
Mess.   Brown, madam: and her forehead
    As low as she would wish it.

18. look'st] *F;* lookd'st *Pope.*

19. *station*] manner of standing, as in
Ham., III. iv. 58.
28. *she's thirty*] † Cleopatra passes on
without comment. She was herself
38 (see North, *post*, p. 246). [R]
30–1. *Round . . . so*] Steevens derives
Cleopatra's comment from the old
writers on physiognomy, quoting in-
exactly Hill's *Pleasant History*, etc.
(1613), p. 218. The information is
given repeatedly of both head and
face: 'The face very *rounde*, argueth
such an one to be foolish,' etc. (p.
86*b*); 'The head spericall or thoroughly *round*, doth denote a quicke mouing,

vnstableness, forgetfulnesse, small discretion, and little wit in that person'
(p. 26*b*); 'The head short and very
round, to be forgetfull and foolish. The
head long in fashion to the Hammer,
to be prudent and wary' (p. 218,
wrongly paged 118); 'The face very
little and *round*, to be foolish' (p. 220,
wrongly 120). In Mabbe's *Celestina*,
1613, i (Tudor Trans., p. 32), Calisto,
enumerating Melibea's beauties, says:
'The forme of her face rather long then
round.'
32. *hair what colour*] See II.v. 114 *ante.*
33. *As low . . . it*] 'The phrase em-

Cleo.   There's gold for thee,
 Thou must not take my former sharpness ill,
 I will employ thee back again; I find thee   35
 Most fit for business. Go, make thee ready,
 Our letters are prepar'd.   *[Exit Messenger.*
Char.   A proper man.
Cleo. Indeed he is so: I repent me much
 That so I harried him. Why, methinks by him,
 This creature's no such thing.
Char.   Nothing, madam.   40
Cleo. The man hath seen some majesty, and should know.
Char. Hath he seen majesty? Isis else defend!
 And serving you so long.
Cleo. I have one thing more to ask him yet, good Charmian:
 But 'tis no matter, thou shalt bring him to me   45
 Where I will write; all may be well enough.
Char. I warrant you, madam.   *[Exeunt.*

[SCENE IV.—*Athens. A room in Antony's house.*]

Enter ANTONY *and* OCTAVIA.

Ant. Nay, nay, Octavia, not only that,—
 That were excusable, that and thousands more
 Of semblable import,—but he hath wag'd
 New wars 'gainst Pompey; made his will, and read it

---

37. *Exit . . .*] *Hanmer; not in* F.

ployed by the Messenger is still a cant
one. I once overheard a chambermaid
say of her rival,—"that her legs were as
thick *as she could wish them*"' (Steevens).
A low forehead discredits beauty in
1 Antonio and Mellida, IV. i. 179: 'Her
beautie is not half so ravishing / As you
discourse of; she hath a freckled face, /
A *lowe* forehead, and a lumpish eye.'
Similarly in *The City Wit*, IV. i (Pearson's *Brome*, i. 339): 'Rufflit here, he
writes that you [i.e. Josina] have a
grosse body, a dull eye, a *lowe* forehead,
a black tooth, a fat hand, and a most
lean purse.'

39. *harried*] harassed, maltreated;
from the original sense ravaged, laid
waste. Minshew, *The Guide to the
Tongues*, 1617 (cited by Malone), has
'to *Harrie, turmoile or vex.*'
 by him] from his account.

Scene IV

3. *semblable*] similar; as in *2H4*, V. i.
72. It sometimes appears as a noun; so
in Day's *English Secretarie* (1599), p. 35:
'whereof no hystorie hath the *semblable*, no region the match,' etc.

4–5. *made his will . . . ear*] In Plutarch
it is *Antony's* will which Cæsar reads:

To public ear: 5
Spoke scantly of me: when perforce he could not
But pay me terms of honour, cold and sickly
He vented them; most narrow measure lent me:
When the best hint was given him, he not took't,
Or did it from his teeth.

Oct.   O my good lord,   10
Believe not all, or if you must believe,
Stomach not all. A more unhappy lady,
If this division chance, ne'er stood between,
Praying for both parts:
The good gods will mock me presently,   15
When I shall pray, 'O, bless my lord, and husband!'
Undo that prayer, by crying out as loud,
'O, bless my brother!' Husband win, win brother,
Prays, and destroys the prayer, no midway
'Twixt these extremes at all.

Ant.   Gentle Octavia,   20
Let your best love draw to that point which seeks
Best to preserve it: if I lose mine honour,
I lose myself: better I were not yours
Than yours so branchless. But, as you requested,
Yourself shall go between's: the mean time, lady,   25

6-7. me: when . . . honour, cold] *Rowe's pointing (approx.);* me, When . . . Honour: cold *F.*   8. them; most] *Rowe;* then most *F.*   8-9. measure lent me: When . . . him,] *Rowe's pointing (approx.);* measure: lent me, When . . . him: *F.*   9. not took't] *Theobald (Thirlby conj.);* not look't *F;* had look't *F2;* o'er-look'd *Rowe.*   16. pray] *F;* praying *Rowe.*   24. yours] *F2;* your *F.*

see North, *post,* p. 261. †It is unlike Shakespeare to desert North on so specific a point, and I think there is certainly corruption. The vagaries of F's punctuation, as well as other awkwardnesses, suggest an unusually difficult passage in MS. [R]

9. *not took 't*] The emendation is too probable to be rejected, although *not look't* might signify 'took no notice'.

10. *from his teeth*] Cf. 'Frae the teeth forward [Not from the heart]' (Henderson's *Scottish Proverbs,* ed. 1876, p. 110). Pye quotes *The Wild Gallant,* iv.

i (see Scott's *Dryden,* 1808, ii. 78): 'I am confident she's angry but *from the teeth* outwards.'

12. *Stomach*] resent. So in Danett's *Comines,* bk ii, chap. viii: 'whereof scoffes arise, which they that are scoffed *stomacke.*' Cf. also II. ii. 9 *ante.*

12-20.] Octavia's 'situation and sentiments' are compared with those of Blanche in *John,* III. i. 327 *et seq.,* and Volumnia in *Cor.,* v. iii. 97 *et seq.* Cf. also North, *post,* pp. 254-5.

15. *presently*] on the instant, immediately, as in II. ii. 159 *ante.*

    I'll raise the preparation of a war
    Shall stain your brother: make your soonest haste;
    So your desires are yours.
Oct.   Thanks to my lord.
    The Jove of power make me most weak, most weak,
    Your reconciler! Wars 'twixt you twain would be   30
    As if the world should cleave, and that slain men
    Should solder up the rift.
Ant. When it appears to you where this begins,
    Turn your displeasure that way, for our faults
    Can never be so equal, that your love   35
    Can equally move with them. Provide your going,
    Choose your own company, and command what cost
    Your heart has mind to.   [*Exeunt.*

30. Your] *F2;* You *F.*   32. solder] *Pope;* soader *F.*   38. has] *F2;*
he's *F.*

27. *stain your brother*] i.e. belittle him by comparison, eclipse any preparations in his power. Cf. *Tottel's Miscellany*, 1557 (Arber's repr., p. 163): 'one whose face will *staine* you all'; *Robert Laneham's Letter*, ed. Furnivall, 1871, pp. 60–1: 'And, too say truth: what, with myne eyz, az I can amorously gloit it, . . . my deep diapason, my wanton warblz, my running, my tuning, and my twynkling, I can gracify the matters az well az the prowdest of them; and waz yet neuer *stayned*, I thank God'; Churchyard, *The Worthiness of Wales*, 1587 (repr. 1776, p. 98): 'What newe things now, . . . can *staine* those deedes, our fathers old have done.' Boswell's conjecture *stay* has found adopters; but even were the metaphor in the text less common, its source is obvious.

28. *So your desires are yours*] †I suppose simply 'So you have what you want.' But it could equally well mean 'Granted that this is what *you* want, and not something that your brother has instigated you to want.' [R]

32. *solder . . . rift*] 'I heard that the Earl of Northumberland liues apart againe from his lady now shee hath brought him an heire, which he sayd was the *soder* of their reconcilement'; etc. (*Manningham's Diary*, 1602, Camden Society ed., p. 79).

34–6. *for our faults . . . them*] i.e. for our faults cannot possibly be so equally balanced that your love for the one or the other of us will not be lessened. ('Spoken resentfully, these words are his own condemnation, and he knows it'—D.W.)

[SCENE V.—*The same. Another room.*]

Enter ENOBARBUS *and* EROS, *meeting.*

Eno. How now, friend Eros?

Eros. There's strange news come, sir.

Eno. What, man?

Eros. Cæsar and Lepidus have made wars upon Pompey.

Eno. This is old, what is the success?   5

Eros. Cæsar, having made use of him in the wars 'gainst
    Pompey, presently denied him rivality, would not
    let him partake in the glory of the action, and not
    resting here, accuses him of letters he had formerly
    wrote to Pompey; upon his own appeal, seizes   10
    him; so the poor third is up, till death enlarge his
    confine.

Eno. Then, world, thou hast a pair of chaps, no more,
    And throw between them all the food thou hast,
    They'll grind the one the other. Where's Antony?   15

Eros. He's walking in the garden—thus, and spurns
    The rush that lies before him; cries, 'Fool Lepidus!'

Scene v

S.D. *meeting*] *Capell; not in* F.   13. world] *Hanmer;* would F.   hast] *Hanmer;*
hadst F.   chaps,] *Theobald; no comma* F.   15. the one the other] *Capell*
(*Johnson conj.*)*; the other* F.

5. *success*] issue. See on II. iv. 9 *ante.*

7. *rivality*] equality, the rank and
rights of a partner. For *rivals* = associates, cf. *Ham.*, I. i. 13: 'The *rivals* of
my watch.'

10. *his own appeal*] his own (Cæsar's)
accusation or impeachment. Cf. *R2*,
I. i. 4: 'the boisterous late *appeal.*'

11. *up*] shut up; as appears from
'till death enlarge his confine.' Cf.
Brome, *The Antipodes*, IV. xii *ad fin.*:
'*Ioy.* Sure your Lordship / Meanes not
to make your house our prison. *Let.*
By / My Lordship but I will for this one
night. / See, sir, the keyes are in my
hand. Y'are *up*, / As I am true Letoy';
and Beaumont and Fletcher, *The
Island Princess*, v. i (Camb., VIII. 158)
which is almost a gloss: 'You hear

Armusia's *up*, honest Arm: / Clapt up
in prison, . . .' Lepidus was compelled
to live at Circeii under strict observation, but not deprived of his private
wealth or office of Pontifex Maximus.

13–15. *Then, world . . . other*] *chaps* =
jaws. 'Cæsar and Antony will make
war on each other, though they have
the world to prey upon between them'
(Johnson). A metaphor related to that
of the 'pair of chaps,' though different,
occurs at the close (III. 487) of Jonson's
Sejanus, and is derived from Suetonius,
Tiberius, cap. 21 : '. . . The Roman race
most wretched, that should live /
Between so slow jaws, and so long a
bruising.'

16–17. *spurns The rush*] Cf. *Ham.*, IV.
v. 6: '*Spurns* enviously at straws.'

And threats the throat of that his officer
That murder'd Pompey.
Eno.   Our great navy's rigg'd.
Eros. For Italy and Cæsar. More, Domitius,   20
My lord desires you presently: my news
I might have told hereafter.
Eno.   'Twill be naught,
But let it be. Bring me to Antony.
Eros. Come, sir.   [*Exeunt.*

[SCENE VI.—*Rome. Cæsar's house.*]

Enter AGRIPPA, MÆCENAS, *and* CÆSAR.

Cæs. Contemning Rome he has done all this, and more
In Alexandria: here's the manner of't:
I' the market-place, on a tribunal silver'd,
Cleopatra and himself in chairs of gold
Were publicly enthron'd: at the feet sat   5
Cæsarion, whom they call my father's son,

18–19. *officer . . . Pompey*] Pompey, defeated in Sicily, escaped to the East, and there, failing in designs on Antony's provinces, met his fate, in all probability by Antony's orders, however he might throw the obloquy of the deed on his lieutenants. See North, *Cæsar Augustus*, in *The Lives of Epaminondas*, etc. 1610, pp. 1166–7: 'Whilst *Antonius* made warre with the Parthians, or rather infortunately they made warre with him to his great confusion: his Lieutenant *Titius* found the meanes to lay hands vpon *Sextus Pompeius* that was fled into the Ile of Samos, and then fortie yeares old: whom he put to death by *Antonius* commandement: for which fact he was so hated of the people of Rome, that though he had giuen them the pastime of certaine playes at his owne cost and charges, they draue him out of the Theater.'

21. *presently*] at once. See II. ii. 159; III. iv. 15 *ante*.

22–3. *'Twill be naught, But . . . be*] Presumably: 'Twill be something of no consequence he wants me for: but no matter: unless Enobarbus foresees a disastrous issue of the expedition. Thiselton, I take it, implies this in giving references here 'for Enobarbus' prescience'; and by including III. viii. 11 (i.e. III. x. 1 *post* in the present text) among them, perhaps intends us to notice the very expression there, 'Naught, naught,' etc.

Scene VI

[See North, *post*, p. 271.]
S.D.] † I have no suggestion to make about the odd order of entrance, except the highly conjectural one that there may at some stage have been a brief interchange between Agrippa and Maecenas, covering the entrance and also giving Cæsar a point of departure for his statement, which at present begins somewhat in mid-air. [R]

6. *Cæsarion*] See on II. ii. 228 *ante*.

And all the unlawful issue that their lust
Since then hath made between them. Unto her
He gave the stablishment of Egypt, made her
Of Lower Syria, Cyprus, Lydia,   10
Absolute queen.

Mæc.   This in the public eye?

Cæs. I' the common show-place, where they exercise.
His sons he there proclaim'd the kings of kings;
Great Media, Parthia, and Armenia,
He gave to Alexander; to Ptolemy he assign'd   15
Syria, Cilicia, and Phœnicia: she
In the habiliments of the goddess Isis
That day appear'd, and oft before gave audience,
As 'tis reported, so.

Mæc.   Let Rome be thus inform'd.

Agr. Who, queasy with his insolence already,   20
Will their good thoughts call from him.

Cæs. The people knows it; and have now receiv'd
His accusations.

Agr.   Who does he accuse?

Cæs. Cæsar, and that having in Sicily
Sextus Pompeius spoil'd, we had not rated him   25
His part o' the isle. Then does he say, he lent me
Some shipping unrestor'd. Lastly, he frets
That Lepidus of the triumvirate

---

13. he there] *Johnson;* hither *F.*   kings of kings] *Rowe;* King of Kings *F.*
19. reported, so] *F2;* reported so *F.*   23. Who] *F;* Whom *F2.*   28. trium-
virate] *F2;* Triumpherate *F.*

---

10. *Lydia*] So North; but Plutarch, *Libya,* which Upton pointed out and Johnson adopted. Bocchus is king of Libya in line 69 *post* and in North and Plutarch.

13. *he there*] F's *hither* is, as Dover Wilson points out, very probably a compositor's handling of an MS *hether* (cf. the frequent printing of *whether* for *whither*) so crowded that the space had disappeared; if so, Johnson's emendation is nearer to the original than at first glance looks likely.

17. *Isis*] See on I. ii. 61 *ante.*

19-21. *As 'tis . . . from him*] †I have

retained F's lineation, since Hanmer's regularization (making the lines *As 'tis . . . thus. Inform'd . . . insolence, Already . . . from him*), though adopted by almost all editors but Knight, creates so unnaturally jerky a rhythm that irregularity seems preferable. [R]

22. *knows*] See on I. iv. 21 *ante. Have now,* etc., appears to show that *people* is not a singular collective here.

25. *rated*] apportioned by estimate, a rare extension of the usual meaning 'computed,' 'valued.' See on III. xi. 69 *post.*

Should be depos'd, and, being, that we detain
All his revenue.

Agr.　　　　　　　　Sir, this should be answer'd.　　　　30

Cæs. 'Tis done already, and the messenger gone.
I have told him, Lepidus was grown too cruel,
That he his high authority abus'd,
And did deserve his change: for what I have conquer'd,
I grant him part: but then in his Armenia,　　　35
And other of his conquer'd kingdoms, I
Demand the like.

Mæc.　　　　　　He'll never yield to that.

Cæs. Nor must not then be yielded to in this.

Enter OCTAVIA *with her Train.*

Oct. Hail, Cæsar, and my lords! Hail, most dear Cæsar!

Cæs. That ever I should call thee castaway!　　　40

Oct. You have not call'd me so, nor have you cause.

Cæs. Why have you stol'n upon us thus? You come not
Like Cæsar's sister: the wife of Antony
Should have an army for an usher, and
The neighs of horse to tell of her approach,　　　45
Long ere she did appear. The trees by the way
Should have borne men, and expectation fainted,
Longing for what it had not. Nay, the dust
Should have ascended to the roof of heaven,
Rais'd by your populous troops: but you are come　　　50
A market-maid to Rome, and have prevented

29. and, being, that] and being, that *Rowe;* And being that, *F.*　　39. lords!]
L. *F.*　　42. have you] *F;* hast thou *F2.*　　us] *F;* me *F2.*

29. *and, being, that*] Boswell (1821 Var.) reads *and, being that.* This, in sense, corresponds with the reading of F, but makes clumsy both rhythm and construction.

32. *too cruel*] Shakespeare is following North (see p. 259, *post*) but 'cruelty is the last vice we should associate with his mild Lepidus' (D.W.).

39. *lords*] †I owe to Dr Brooks the suggestion that F's *L.* stands for the plural, and not, as most editors take it, for the singular. Octavia thus greets both Maecenas and Agrippa—as she naturally would—instead of only one of them. [R]

50. *populous*] similarly used in Hall's *Chronicle* (1548), Richard III, yere ii, fol. xvi [*b*]: 'where the duke not far of lay encamped wyth a *populous* army and a host of great strength and vigor,' etc.; and again, *ibid.*, yere iii, fol. xxix [*a*].

51. *prevented*] come too soon to allow: or possibly just in the modern sense.

The ostentation of our love; which, left unshown,
Is often left unlov'd: we should have met you
By sea, and land, supplying every stage
With an augmented greeting.

Oct.   Good my lord,   55
To come thus was I not constrain'd, but did it
On my free will. My lord, Mark Antony,
Hearing that you prepar'd for war, acquainted
My grieved ear withal; whereon I begg'd
His pardon for return.

Cæs.   Which soon he granted,   60
Being an abstract 'tween his lust and him.

Oct. Do not say so, my lord.

61. abstract] *F; obstruct Theobald (Warburton) and most edd.*

52. *ostentation*] public manifestation,
full display. Theobald read *ostent,* and
S. Walker conjectured *ostention,* for
metrical reasons.

52–3. *which, left . . . unlov'd*] As it
stands the text might conceivably
mean: which, if not outwardly mani-
fested, is often left without return, un-
reciprocated; but it much more probably signifies: a feeling which, if not
openly exercised, often ceases to be
felt at all. The ungenerous sentiment
in a brother must be put down to
Cæsar's momentary displeasure, unless we take *our* (line 52) to include
Octavia, which much modifies its
force. †But Cæsar is displeased, not
with Octavia, but with Antony, who
has slighted her, and I have no doubt
that the required sense is 'love which is
unshown is often thought to be unfelt,'
unlov'd being a sort of passive construction of a cognate accusative. Along
these lines the Collier MS *held unlov'd,*
or, even better, Singer's *felt* (a transposition error), adopted by Hudson,
are tempting. But I think the sense is
possible even with F's reading, taking
left = written off as. [R]

61. *abstract*] F's *abstract* has found
plenty of defenders, beginning with
Henley and Steevens. Knight thinks it
refers to Octavia as 'something separ-

ating him [Antony] from the grati-
fication of his desires.' Schmidt, who
calls *obstruct* 'an idle conjecture of
modern editors,' explains *abstract* as
'the shortest way for him and his
desires, the readiest opportunity to
encompass his wishes.' Presumably,
this is suggested by the sense of *abstract*
as a brief or epitome. See on I. iv. 9
ante. †It is true that *obstruct* (as Case
admitted, while accepting it) is found
nowhere else, and that it makes the
syntax awkward, since it must refer to
Octavia (an absolute construction,
'you being an obstruct') whereas
abstract refers directly to Octavia's
return. But (i) Shakespeare often uses
verbs as nouns, e.g. *Gent.,* IV. iii. 8,
'your ladyship's *impose,*' *2H6,* III. i.
160, 'false *accuse,*' and (ii) both sense
and elliptical syntax feel to me pecu-
liarly Shakespearean, and I have retained F's reading only on the principle
that one should not accept an emendation on mere 'preferability.' [R based
on Case's material.] But it is also possible that *abstract* is being used not in
Schmidt's sense, but simply = ab-
stracting, or removal, so that the sense,
admittedly compressed, could be,
'Your return being the removal of
something (which stood in the way
between his lust and him).' [R]

Cæs.   I have eyes upon him,
And his affairs come to me on the wind.
Where is he now?

Oct.   My lord, in Athens.

Cæs. No, my most wronged sister, Cleopatra   65
Hath nodded him to her. He hath given his empire
Up to a whore, who now are levying
The kings o' the earth for war. He hath assembled
Bocchus, the king of Libya, Archelaus
Of Cappadocia, Philadelphos, king   70
Of Paphlagonia; the Thracian king Adallas;
King Manchus of Arabia, King of Pont,
Herod of Jewry; Mithridates, king
Of Comagene, Polemon and Amyntas,
The kings of Mede and Lycaonia,   75
With a more larger list of sceptres.

Oct.   Ay me most wretched,
That have my heart parted betwixt two friends,
That does afflict each other!

Cæs.   Welcome hither:
Your letters did withhold our breaking forth
Till we perceiv'd both how you were wrong led,   80
And we in negligent danger. Cheer your heart;

78. does] *F;* do *F2.*   80. wrong led] *F;* wrong'd *Capell and several edds., reading* perceived *for metre.*

69–75. Upton points out some confusion of kings and kingdoms here. Cf. North, *post,* p. 262.

72. *Manchus*] So in North; F reads *Mauchus,* and Plutarch *Malchus.*

78. *does*] See on i. iv. 21 *ante.*

80. *wrong led*] † I doubt if we are justified in emending, and Capell's emendation assumes a compositor's error not so easy to account for as at first sight it looks, since, apart from the error in *perceived* it involves the supposed insertion by the compositor of a space and two letters—*two* letters, both *l* and *e,* since Shakespeare would not write *wronged* just to produce a feminine ending, but *wrongd*—and insertions of this kind are less natural than omissions. On the other hand it is impossible to be happy with F's reading. Not only does it produce a very awkward rhythm, but it makes it almost impossible to put the stress on *you* which is demanded by the contrast with *we* in the next line.

I wonder whether we ought to consider this alongside the *wrangle* in *Tp.,* v. i. 174, where the word must, I think, however slight the support of dictionaries, mean 'play false'. To mis-read *wrangled* as *wrong led* would have been much more natural than so to mis-read *wrongd,* though we should still be left with the need to alter *perceiv'd.* [R]

81. *negligent danger*] danger through negligence. For the transferred epithet, compare *Wint.,* i. ii. 397: 'In ignorant concealment.'

Be you not troubled with the time, which drives
O'er your content these strong necessities,
But let determin'd things to destiny
Hold unbewail'd their way. Welcome to Rome,   85
Nothing more dear to me. You are abus'd
Beyond the mark of thought: and the high gods,
To do you justice, makes his ministers
Of us, and those that love you. Best of comfort,
And ever welcome to us.
Agr.   Welcome, lady.   90
Mæc. Welcome, dear madam.
Each heart in Rome does love and pity you,
Only the adulterous Antony, most large
In his abominations, turns you off,
And gives his potent regiment to a trull,   95
That noises it against us.

88. makes] *F;* make *F2.*   his] *F;* them *Capell and most edd.;* their *Theobald.*

84–5. *let determin'd . . . their way*] † Let
predestined events go unbewailed to
their appointed end. The sentence
would not be worth comment if it were
not that some editors want to take *to
destiny* with *determin'd,* as 'things deter-
mined-to-destiny,' i.e. 'predestined'—
which seems to me awkward in syntax
and redundant in sense. [R]

87. *Beyond the mark*] beyond the
reach; probably a metaphor from
archery, as Deighton points out.

88. *makes his*] So F. *Makes* (plural) is
probably correct (see on I. iv. 21 *ante*),
and its identity with the singular form
may be responsible for *his* of the folios;
but if the reading had been *its* instead
of *his,* there would have been no doubt
that Collier (1843), who retained *his,*
did right in referring it to justice instead of to *the high gods.* In 1858, he
meekly accepted Singer's rebuke and
objection that justice is not personified
here, and that if it were, *his* would still
be inapplicable (presumably, as not
feminine), apparently not reflecting
that if *his*=its, as often, both objections
are invalid: cf. *Ham.,* IV. v. 124–5:
'treason . . . Acts little of *his* will.'

Why did F2 alter *makes* and not *his*?

93. *large*] *large* in *Ado,* referring to
language, II. iii. 217, '*large* jests,' and
IV. i. 52, 'word too *large*' = free, licen-
tious, a sense often attributed here.
More probably it is here = wide,
unbounded. The *OED* has: 1574,
Hellowes, *Guevara's Fam. Ep.* (1577),
63, 'It is not a just thing to be *large* in
sinning, and short in praying.' See also
Mac., III. iv. 11 : 'Be *large* in mirth.'

95. *regiment*] rule, authority. Very
frequent. So Jonson, *New Inn,* II. vi.
251 : '*Host.* A royal sovereign! / *Lord
L.* And a rare stateswoman! I admire
her bearing / In her new regiment.'

trull] harlot: the commonest but not
invariable sense of the word. Cf. *The
Four Elements* (Hazlitt's *Dodsley,* i. 44) :
'For to satisfy your wanton lust, / I
shall appoint you a *trull* of trust,' with
Phaer and Twyne's *Virgil* (this reference is Steevens's), [bk xi, sig. R7 in
1607 ed.] : 'Pure virgins, with Tarpeia
weilding glittring axe in fight / Italian
trulls,' etc.

96. *noises it*] makes a noise, is cla-
morous. Mabbe, *Celestina,* 1631, I
(Tudor Trans., p. 39) has: 'Not one

Oct.   Is it so, sir?

Cæs. Most certain. Sister, welcome: pray you,
    Be ever known to patience. My dear'st sister!   [*Exeunt.*

[SCENE VII.—*Near Actium. Antony's camp.*]

Enter CLEOPATRA *and* ENOBARBUS.

Cleo. I will be even with thee, doubt it not.
Eno. But why, why, why?
Cleo. Thou hast forspoke my being in these wars,
    And say'st it is not fit.
Eno.   Well, is it, is it?
Cleo. If not denounc'd against us, why should not we   5
    Be there in person?

Scene VII

5. If . . . denounc'd] *Boswell* (*Malone conj.*)*;* If not, denounc'd *F; Is't not
denounc'd Rowe; If not, denounc't Malone; Is't not? Denounce Steevens, 1793
(Tyrwhitt conj.*).

stone that strikes against another, but presently *noyseth* out, Old whore'; Milton (*Paradise Regained*, iv. 488) describes certain terrors as '*noising* loud / And threatning nigh.'

98. *known to patience*] Cf. this circumlocution for 'patient' with the scriptural 'acquainted with grief.'

Scene VII

3. *forspoke*] spoken against. See North, *post*, p. 260. The verb commonly = curse, bewitch, as in *Look About You*, 1600, sc. 26 (Hazlitt's *Dodsley*, vii. 465): 'I think I was *forespoken* at the teat, / This damn'd rogue serv'd me thus!' but also occurs in senses forbid, speak against, speak evil of. *OED* quotes: 1579, J. Stubbes, *Gaping Gulf*, E viij (*b*), 'If he should speede (which God *forespeake*)'; 1611, W. Sclater, *Key* [*to the Key of Scripture*] (1629), 84: 'The fashion of most men, in such judgements, is to cry out of ill tongues that have *forespoken* them.'

5–6. *If not denounc'd . . . person*] If the war were not proclaimed against me,

why should I not be there in person? i.e. even if the sufficient reason that the war is proclaimed against me—as you well know—did not exist for my presence, what objection could you find to it? I suggest this as at least a possible interpretation of Malone's text, because (1) the simpler 'If the war is not proclaimed against me, why,' etc., would contain a hypothesis clean contrary to the fact, the war having been proclaimed against Cleopatra and, indeed, Cleopatra alone, excluding Antony, as sufficiently appears in North (see *post*, p. 261), and (2) because Malone's own interpretation, 'If there be no particular denunciation against me, why should we not be there in person?' obscures the relation of *denounc'd* to *these wars*, tacitly making *denounc'd* impersonal; whereas the uses of *denounce* and *denounce against* make that relation almost inevitable. See, for example, Herbert of Cherbury, *Poems* (ed. Collins, 1881, p. 77): '*Denounce* an open war'; Florio's *Montaigne*, i. v (Temple Classics, i. 31):

Eno. [*Aside*]   Well, I could reply:
If we should serve with horse and mares together,
The horse were merely lost; the mares would bear
A soldier and his horse.
Cleo.   What is 't you say?
Eno. Your presence needs must puzzle Antony,   10
Take from his heart, take from his brain, from's time,
What should not then be spar'd. He is already
Traduc'd for levity, and 'tis said in Rome
That Photinus, an eunuch, and your maids

6. *Aside*] *Johnson.*   14. Photinus, an] *Delius; no comma in* F.

'the custome beareth, that they never undertake a warre, before the same be *denounced,*' etc. The same objections apply to Deighton's further step, in: 'If there is no special injunction against my taking part in these wars, why should I not be present in person?' Rowe's reading, '*Is't not denounc'd against us?*' (in Hanmer, '. . . 'gainst us?*') gives an excellent sense, and is adopted in one or the other form by some editors. The other conjectures *denounc't* and *denounce* need not disturb the folio comma after *If not*, and depend on the use of *denounce* as in Turbervile's translation of Ovid's Epistle from Phyllis to Demophoon (Steevens's reference), '*Denounce to me what I have doone,*' etc.; but they, too, have to infer disconnection between *denounc'd* and *wars.* I record Mr A. E. Thiselton's explanation of the exact folio text, retaining the comma, though unable to accept it. He says '"if not" is equivalent to "*otherwise,*" and the meaning is "it must be fit, for since the wars are *declared* against us personally, how can it be improper for us to take the field in person?" Cf. lines 16–18.' † The commentators are, I think, almost all too much preoccupied with the (admittedly common) association of 'denounce' and 'war'. If for the moment we forget that, is not Cleopatra's meaning perfectly clear (as it evidently was to Deighton)? 'If there is no express prohibition

against my being in the field, can you give me any valid reason why I should not be there?' Enobarbus gives two reasons, one in an aside, and then one direct to her, a purely military reason, with not so much as an allusion to the question whether the war had been declared against Cleopatra or not. [R]

7–9. *If we should . . . his horse*] † another example of commentators' silence. I have to admit that I do not see the precise point of Enobarbus' (presumable) ribaldry. There is perhaps a play on 'serve' in its breeders' as well as in its military sense, but this is not very helpful. The critical word here is 'bear,' which has apparently never had the specific meaning ('be mounted by') which is here needed and which 'take' (see *OED*) has had since 1577 (though that meaning is no doubt *suggested* by Cleopatra at I. v. 21). (See *OED*, but see also *H5*, III. vii. 50, and *Rom.*, I. iv. 94.) And Shakespeare's bawdry, though sometimes complicated, is almost always precise. When one is puzzled it is, I think, better to admit it than pass over without comment a passage which may be puzzling to other readers besides oneself. [R]

8. *merely*] utterly. So, often. Cf. *Ham.*, I. ii. 137: 'things rank . . . / Possess it *merely.*'

14. *Photinus, an eunuch*] If Shakespeare strictly followed the corre-

Manage this war.

Cleo.   Sink Rome, and their tongues rot   15
That speak against us! A charge we bear i' the war,
And as the president of my kingdom will
Appear there for a man. Speak not against it,
I will not stay behind.

Enter ANTONY *and* CANIDIUS.

Eno.   Nay, I have done,
Here comes the emperor.

Ant.   Is it not strange, Canidius,   20
That from Tarentum, and Brundusium
He could so quickly cut the Ionian sea,
And take in Toryne? You have heard on't, sweet?

Cleo. Celerity is never more admir'd
Than by the negligent.

Ant.   A good rebuke,   25
Which might have well becom'd the best of men,
To taunt at slackness. Canidius, we
Will fight with him by sea.

Cleo.   By sea, what else?

Can. Why will my lord do so?

Ant.   For that he dares us to't.

Eno. So hath my lord dar'd him to single fight.   30

Can. Ay, and to wage this battle at Pharsalia,
Where Cæsar fought with Pompey. But these offers,
Which serve not for his vantage, he shakes off,
And so should you.

Eno.   Your ships are not well mann'd,

---

23. Toryne] *F2;* Troine *F.*

sponding passage in North, as given *post,* p. 261, to which Delius—who is responsible for the comma after Photinus—drew attention, the words 'an eunuch' do not describe Photinus (the eunuch who was the cause of Pompey the Great's murder), but stand for Mardian. Plutarch gives 'Pothinus', as does North in his life of Cæsar.

16. *A charge . . . war*] See North, *post,* p. 260.

23. *take in Toryne*] occupy, etc. Cf. i.

i. 23 *ante.* See North, *post,* p. 263, and for Tarentum and Brundusium, *ibid.*

26. *becom'd*] So in *Cym.,* v. v. 407; *A Report,* etc., 1591 (*The Revenge,* ed. Arber, p. 28) : 'And no man could haue lesse *becommed* the place of an Orator for such a purpose, then this *Morice of Desmond.*'

27. *To taunt at*] 'to cast as a taunt at' (Deighton). The gerundial infinitive.

30–2. *So hath . . . Pompey*] See North, *post,* p. 263.

Your mariners are muleters, reapers, people   35
Ingross'd by swift impress. In Cæsar's fleet
Are those that often have 'gainst Pompey fought,
Their ships are yare, yours heavy; no disgrace
Shall fall you for refusing him at sea,
Being prepar'd for land.

Ant.   By sea, by sea.   40

Eno. Most worthy sir, you therein throw away
The absolute soldiership you have by land,
Distract your army, which doth most consist
Of war-mark'd footmen, leave unexecuted
Your own renowned knowledge, quite forgo   45
The way which promises assurance, and
Give up yourself merely to chance and hazard,
From firm security.

Ant.   I'll fight at sea.

Cleo. I have sixty sails, Cæsar none better.

Ant. Our overplus of shipping will we burn,   50
And, with the rest full-mann'd, from the head of
    Actium
Beat the approaching Cæsar. But if we fail,
We then can do 't at land.

---

35. muleters] Muliters *F2;* Militers *F.*   51. Actium] *F2;* Action *F.*

35. *muleters*] the contemporary form. Cf. Peele, *Battle of Alcazar,* IV. i. 8: 'Three thousand pioners, and a thousand coachmen, / Besides a number almost numberless / Of drudges, negroes, slaves, and *muleters,*' etc. See also, and for the passage generally, North, *post,* p. 263.

36. *impress*] press-gang work, as in *Troil.,* II. i. 107.

38. *yare*] nimble, easily manœuvred. Cf. II. ii. 211 *ante,* III. xiii. 131, v. ii. 282 *post,* and Gorges' *Lucan* (1614), lib. 3, p. 109: 'But the *Massilian* gallies are / Of saile and stirrage much more *yare,* / Nimble and light to leaue or take, / And on their staies quick speed can make,' etc. ('on their staies . . .'= 'come round quickly,' when tacking).

39. *fall*] befall, as in *John,* I. i. 78, 'Fair *fall,*' etc.

43. *Distract*] *Distract* had the senses 'confuse,' as now, and 'disjoin,' 'divide.' See the example on line 76 *post,* and also the participle in *A Lover's Complaint,* 231. Schmidt assigns the latter here, and although 'confuse' sorts suspiciously well with the ensuing appeal to the nature of the army, which consisted—as the soldier says, line 65 *post*—of men who 'Have used to conquer standing on the earth, / And fighting foot to foot,' the passage in North, *post,* p. 264, confirms his view. The speech is there given to Canidius.

44. *leave unexecuted*] give no scope for the use of.

47. *merely*] utterly, as in line 8 *ante.*

52–3. *if we fail, We then can do't at land*] † a dangerous doctrine in war. We may remember the ill-fated at-

Enter a Messenger.

                                    Thy business?
Mess. The news is true, my lord, he is descried,
      Cæsar has taken Toryne.   55
Ant. Can he be there in person? 'Tis impossible;
      Strange, that his power should be. Canidius,
      Our nineteen legions thou shalt hold by land,
      And our twelve thousand horse. We'll to our ship,
      Away, my Thetis!

Enter a Soldier.

                              How now, worthy soldier?   60
Sold. O noble emperor, do not fight by sea,
      Trust not to rotten planks: do you misdoubt
      This sword, and these my wounds? Let the Egyptians
      And the Phœnicians go a-ducking: we
      Have us'd to conquer standing on the earth,   65
      And fighting foot to foot.
Ant.   Well, well, away!
                  [*Exeunt Antony, Cleopatra, and Enobarbus.*
Sold. By Hercules I think I am i' the right.
Can. Soldier, thou art: but his whole action grows
      Not in the power on 't: so our leader's led,
      And we are women's men.
Sold.   You keep by land   70
      The legions and the horse whole, do you not?

---

69. leader's led] *Theobald;* Leaders leade *F.*

tempt to force the Gallipoli straits by
sea, and what followed. [R]

57. *power*] forces, as below, line 76,
and commonly.

58–9. *nineteen legions . . . horse*] See
North, *post*, p. 267.

60. *Thetis!*] 'Antony may address
Cleopatra by the name of this sea-
nymph, because she had just promised
him assistance in his naval expedition;
or perhaps in allusion to her voyage
down the Cydnus, when she appeared
like *Thetis* surrounded by the Nereids'
(Steevens, confusing with *Tethys*).

61–6.] See North, *post*, p. 264.

64. *a-ducking*] as a result of 'rotten
planks' perhaps, though Deighton explains: 'take to the water like ducks.'
Cf. Beaumont and Fletcher, *The Scornful Lady*, II. ii. 112: ''Tis your turn next
to sink, you shall *duck* twice before I
help you.'

68–9. *his . . . power on 't*] His course
in the war is shaped without regard
to where his real strength lies, or,
more closely, his action does not
spring from the sources of its possible
strength.

Can. Marcus Octavius, Marcus Justeius,
          Publicola and Cælius, are for sea:
          But we keep whole by land. This speed of Cæsar's
          Carries beyond belief.
Sold.   While he was yet in Rome,   75
          His power went out in such distractions as
          Beguil'd all spies.
Can.   Who's his lieutenant, hear you?
Sold. They say, one Taurus.
Can.   Well I know the man.

Enter a Messenger.

Mess. The emperor calls Canidius.
Can. With news the time's in labour, and throws forth,   80
          Each minute, some.   [*Exeunt.*

72. *Can.*] *Pope; Ven. F.*   78. Taurus] *Theobald; Towrus F throughout.*   Well
I] *Rowe (ed. 3);* Well, I *F.*   80. in] *Rowe;* with *F.*   throws] throwes *F;*
throes *Theobald.*

72–4. *Marcus Octavius,* etc.] See
North, *post,* p. 265; *whole by land,*
p. 267.
    75. *Carries*] from the language of
archery, as Steevens suggests. Cf.
with the whole passage, Daniel, *A
Funerall Poeme Vpon the Earle of Devon-
shire,* lines 217–20 (*Works,* Grosart, i.
180): 'Here is no roome to tell with
what strange speed / And secrecy he
vsed to preuent / The enemies designes,
nor with what heed / He marcht before report,' etc.
    78. *Taurus*] in North, *post,* p. 265.
    † F's spelling suggests our 'modern'
pronunciation. (Henslowe, by the
way, contrariwise spells Faustus as
'Fostus'.) [R]
    80. *in*] † Rowe's emendation is, I
think, so probable as to merit insertion

in the text. The compositor would
easily pick up and repeat the *with* from
five words before, and *with labour* is an
almost impossible phrase. [R]
    throws] † Theobald's emendation (or
rather re-spelling, since *throwe* is common Elizabethan spelling for *throe*) has
been almost universally accepted, but
is less convincing on examination than
at first sight. Steevens quotes in support *Tp.,* II. i. 238 (one of the very rare
occurrences of *throe* as a *verb*): 'a birth
indeed / Which *throes* thee much to
yield' where again F reads *throwes.* But
the image here is of a difficult birth,
and the object of the verb is the person
in labour. Here the object is the thing
born, and the image is that of a *series* of
births, with no question of difficulty, as
of an animal producing a litter. [R]

[SCENES VIII–X.—*A plain near Actium.*]

[SCENE VIII]

Enter CÆSAR *and* TAURUS, *with his army, marching.*

Cæs. Taurus!

Taur. My lord?

Cæs. Strike not by land, keep whole, provoke not battle
Till we have done at sea. Do not exceed
The prescript of this scroll: our fortune lies   5
Upon this jump.   [*Exeunt.*

[SCENE IX]

Enter ANTONY *and* ENOBARBUS.

Ant. Set our squadrons on yond side o' the hill,
In eye of Cæsar's battle, from which place
We may the number of the ships behold,
And so proceed accordingly.   [*Exeunt.*

[SCENE X]

CANIDIUS *marcheth with his land army one way over the stage,
and* TAURUS, *the lieutenant of* CÆSAR, *the other way. After
their going in, is heard the noise of a sea-fight.
Alarum. Enter* ENOBARBUS.

Eno. Naught, naught, all naught, I can behold no longer:

Scene VIII
S.D. *Enter . . .*] *Cambridge edd.; F has no* and Taurus.

Scene VIII

6. *jump*] hazard. The noun occurs here only in Shakespeare, but the verb in *Mac.*, I. vii. 7, and elsewhere. *OED* has s.v.: 1601, Holland, *Pliny*, ii. 219, 'It [hellebore] putteth the Patient to a *jumpe* or great hazzard.'

Scene IX

1–4.] Cf. IV. x. 4–9 *post*.
1. *squadrons*] bodies of troops, not necessarily cavalry; cf. *Oth.*, I. i. 22–4: 'That never set a squadron in the field, / Nor the division of a battle

knows, / More than a spinster.'
2. *battle*] embattled army, as very often. More particularly it applies to the main body. So in Harington's *Nugæ Antiquæ* (1769), i. 51: 'The order was this, Captain Lister led the forlorn hope; Sir Alexander Ratcliffe and his regiment had the vauntguard; my Lord of Dublin led the *battle*: Sir Arthur Savage the rear; the horse,' etc.

Scene X

[See North, *post*, p. 265.]
S.D.] F, though it has '*Enter Scarrus*'

The Antoniad, the Egyptian admiral,
With all their sixty fly, and turn the rudder:
To see't, mine eyes are blasted.

Enter SCARUS.

Scar.   Gods and goddesses,
All the whole synod of them!
Eno.   What's thy passion?   5
Scar. The greater cantle of the world is lost
With very ignorance, we have kiss'd away
Kingdoms, and provinces.
Eno.   How appears the fight?
Scar. On our side, like the token'd pestilence,
Where death is sure. Yon ribaudred nag of Egypt,—   10

---

10. ribaudred] *F1–3;* ribauldred *F4;* ribauld *Rowe, and others.*

---

at line 4, also brings him in along with
Enobarbus at the opening of the scene.
This is probably an example of the not
uncommon 'anticipatory' S.D. (cf. v.
ii. 318 and 327).

1. *Naught*] i.e. come to naught,
ruined. D.W. well compares *Cor.,* III.
i. 230.

2. *The Antoniad . . . admiral*] See
North, pp. 261–2. *Admiral* occurs commonly for the most considerable ship
of a fleet or as the equivalent of our
'flagship'. See *A Report,* etc. 1591 (*The
Revenge,* Arber's repr., p. 18): 'The
names of her Maiesties shippes were
these as followeth: the *Defiaunce,* which
was Admirall, the *Reuenge* Vice-
admirall,' etc.; also *1H4,* III. iii. 28.

5. *synod*] nearly always, as here, of
an assembly of the gods. So in *Cor.,* v.
ii. 73: 'The glorious gods sit in hourly
synod about thy particular prosperity,'
etc.

6. *cantle*] originally = corner, and
so portion, piece, etc. Here (see *OED*)
'a segment of a circle or sphere.' See
also *1H4,* III. i. 101, and *The Magni-
ficent Entertainment,* etc. (Bullen's *Middleton,* vii. 223): 'The FOUR ELEMENTS,
in proper shapes, artificially and aptly
expressing their qualities, . . . went
round in a proportionable and even

circle, touching that *cantle* of the Globe
(which was open) to the full view of his
Majesty:' etc.

7. *With*] by, as often. Cf. North,
post, p. 251, line 8.

9. *token'd pestilence*] Certain red spots
have always been reckoned extremely
ominous symptoms in plague, and, as
Steevens tells us, were considered and
called 'God's tokens' of speedy death,
in Shakespeare's time. He quotes
LLL., v. ii. 424, and *Two Wise Men,*
etc., 1619, IV. ii. See Chapman, *Minor
Poems,* etc., ed. 1875, p. 405, col. 1,
line 19: 'A will and a tolling bell are as
present death as God's *tokens.*' Sylvester (*Du Bartas, The Tropheis,* near
the end) calls them '*Tokens* of Terror',
and Dekker, *The Bel-man of London,*
1608 (Temple Classics ed., p. 241) has:
'where the dore of a poore Artificer (if
his child had died but with one *Token*
of death about him) was close ram'd
up,' etc. Yet Dr Forman lived to record
in his *Diary,* under 1592: 'and the 6 of
Julie I toke my bed and had the plague
in both my groines, and some moneth
after I had the red *tokens* on my feet as
brod as halfepence, and yt was 22
wickes before I was well again, the
which did hinder me moch.'

10. *ribaudred nag*] foul, wanton jade:

Whom leprosy o'ertake!—i' the midst o' the fight,
When vantage like a pair of twins appear'd
Both as the same, or rather ours the elder,—
The breeze upon her, like a cow in June,
Hoists sails, and flies.   15

14. The breeze . . . her] *In parentheses in F.*   June] *F2* (Iune); Inne *F.*

Malone, Collier (ed. 1), Knight, adopt Steevens's conjecture *ribald-rid*, but 'A *ribaudrous* and filthie tongue'—first quoted by Steevens from Baret's *Alvearie*, 1580, and urged by Singer with addition from Horman's *Vulgaria*: 'Refrayne fro such foule and *rebaudry* wordes'—makes *ribaudred* a probable form. Gould's conjecture *ribanded* would else attract, as a natural expression of disgust at the 'flying flags' which seem to have impressed Enobarbus (III. xiii. 11 *post*), and because race-horses were decked with ribands, as also, for sale purposes, unserviceable jades. Cf. *The Country Captain*, 1649, 1 (*Captain Underwit*, Bullen's *Old Plays*, ii. 333): 'What thing's this that looks so like a race Nagg trick'd with *ribbands*?' That the flags deck the ship, not Cleopatra, is of little consequence. Collier (ed. 2) and Singer adopt Tyrwhitt's conjecture, *hag* for *nag*, in view of *magic*, line 19; but *nag* for a runaway, and as applied to women (see *2H4*, II. iv. 207), is too probable. Cf. also *Swetnam the Woman Hater*, etc., 1620, I. ii: 'Those that have good wives ride to Hell Vpon ambling Hackneyes, and all the rest Vpon trotting Iades to the devill.' † This last quotation gives some support to Steevens's *ribald-rid* (i.e.—though most of the editors who adopt it are too delicate to explain what the odd word means—'a trollop whom every casual debauchee can "mount"'—but the objections to it are, I think, two: it is too complicated, though effective, a derogatory image for Scarus' state of mind, and it is feeble in sound, so that no actor, I believe, would hesitate a moment between it and *ribaudred*. Scarus means, I fancy, little more than

the modern colloquial 'bloody'. [R]

11. *leprosy*] Steevens seems to think the word used in a sense appropriate to the stigma in *ribaudred*. See Donne, *Elegy IV*, line 60: 'By thee the silly amorous sucks his death / By drawing in a *leprous* harlot's breath' and Fairfax, *Eclogue the Fourth* (*The Muses Library*, 1741, p. 373): 'But such the Issue was of that Embrace, / That deadly Poyson thro' her Body spread, / Rotted her Limbs, and *leprous* grew her Face.' As Johnson observes, however, leprosy was 'an epidemical distemper of the Ægyptians.' See Sylvester's *Du Bartas*, *The Furies*, lines 513–16: 'So *Portugall* hath *Phthisiks* most of all, / Eber Kings-euils; Arné the Suddain-Fall; / Sauoy the Mumps; West-India, Pox; and Nyle / The Leprosie'; etc.

13. *the elder*] Steevens compares *Cæs.*, II. ii. 46: 'We are two lions littered in one day, / And I *the elder* and more terrible.'

14–15. *The breeze . . . flies*] † *breeze* = gadfly, though there may be a pun on the ordinary sense. The picture seems clear enough—a gadfly-stung cow in the heat of summer suddenly charging across a meadow—but it has provoked a spate of comment and question (rather of the 'When is a cow not a cow? When it's a nag' variety): is it the nag that is stung, or the cow? who hoists sails, the nag, the cow, or Cleopatra? Staunton proposed a heroic, if unwise, cutting of one of the knots by reading *tail* for *sails*. But the trouble all arises from failure to realize Shakespeare's frequent high-handedness with metaphor, and the speaker's state of mind. Scarus is furiously angry, and when he gets to the cow he has forgotten all about his first derogatory

Eno. That I beheld:
    Mine eyes did sicken at the sight, and could not
    Endure a further view.
Scar.   She once being loof'd,
    The noble ruin of her magic, Antony,
    Claps on his sea-wing, and (like a doting mallard)   20
    Leaving the fight in heighth, flies after her:
    I never saw an action of such shame;
    Experience, manhood, honour, ne'er before
    Did violate so itself.
Eno.   Alack, alack!

Enter CANIDIUS.

Can. Our fortune on the sea is out of breath,   25
    And sinks most lamentably. Had our general
    Been what he knew himself, it had gone well:
    O, he has given example of our flight,
    Most grossly by his own!
Eno. Ay, are you thereabouts? Why, then, good-night   30
    Indeed.

---

21. heighth] *F;* height *Theobald and edd.*   28. he] *F2* (hee)*; his F.*

nag—anyway leprosy and a pair of twins have already intervened. And I suppose that if Enobarbus had been pedantic enough to challenge his syntax he would have said that Cleopatra, momentarily compared to a cow, was the subject of *hoists.* For the image, cf. Jonson, *The New Inn,* v. iii. 3: 'Runs like a heifer, bitten with the brieze.' [R]

    18. *loof'd*] † usually taken, and often printed, as *luffed.* To luff is to bring a ship's head up into the wind, and therefore whether this manœuvre is preparatory to disengaging, or, as it well might be, to engaging more closely, depends entirely on where the wind is. And I find it hard to believe that the man who could write the storm scene of *Tp.* would ever use a specific technicality so loosely. North uses the phrase 'to loof off' as though it meant simply 'to disengage', i.e. as though he were connecting it with 'aloof' in the general sense (whether or not 'aloof' is originally derived from the technical sense). [R]

    20. *mallard*] wild drake. Rolfe compares *1H4,* II. ii. 111: 'there's no more valour in that Poins than in a wild-duck,' and *ibid.,* IV. ii. 21; but the allusion here is rather to the drake's aptness to follow the coy female than to his timidity.

    27. *Been . . . himself*] It is not very clear whether this is literally, Been what he knew himself to be—another way of saying, acted in character, displayed the courage and skill he consciously possessed—or whether *formerly* is implied in *knew,* as Delius seems to think, and the sense consequently, *either* Been the man he once knew in his own person, *or* Been the man he was once conscious of being. North has, 'as if he had not oftentimes proved both the one and the other fortune,' etc. (*post,* p. 267).

Can.   Toward Peloponnesus are they fled.
Scar. 'Tis easy to 't, and there I will attend
          What further comes.
Can.   To Cæsar will I render
          My legions and my horse, six kings already
          Show me the way of yielding.
Eno.   I'll yet follow   35
          The wounded chance of Antony, though my reason
          Sits in the wind against me.   [*Exeunt.*

          [SCENE XI.—*Alexandria. Cleopatra's palace.*]

          Enter ANTONY *with Attendants.*

Ant. Hark, the land bids me tread no more upon 't,
          It is asham'd to bear me. Friends, come hither:
          I am so lated in the world that I
          Have lost my way for ever. I have a ship,
          Laden with gold, take that, divide it; fly,   5
          And make your peace with Cæsar.
All.   Fly? not we.
Ant. I have fled myself, and have instructed cowards
          To run, and show their shoulders. Friends, be gone,

---

37. *Exeunt*] *not in* F.

32–3. *'Tis easy . . . comes*] † a very odd
remark from Scarus. It looks as though
it must mean 'It's easy enough to get
there, and I'll make my way there and
watch events.' But that is certainly not
what Scarus does, and the last thing
one would expect him to do. See IV.
vii, viii, x, and xii *post*. I wonder
whether all that really belongs to
Scarus is a scornful aside, "'Tis easy
to't,' and the rest belongs to Canidius,
to whose present frame of mind it is
perfectly appropriate. [R]

36. *wounded chance*] 'broken fortunes'
(Malone, comparing v. ii. 173 *post*).
Chance = fortune is common. Cf.
Countess of Pembroke, *Antonie*, 1595,
Act v: 'Follow we our *chance*'; Church-
yard, *A Tragicall Discourse of the Vn-*

happy Man's Life, stanza 53 (*Chippes*,
1575): 'This *chaunce* is she some say
that leads men out / And brings them
home, when least they looke therefore,' etc.

37. *Sits . . . wind*] Shakespeare often
uses *sits* of the wind itself, to denote its
quarter, as in *Mer.V.*, I. i. 18: 'Plucking
the grass, to know where *sits* the wind.'
We make free with the wind like Enobarbus in the colloquialism, 'There's
something in the *wind*.'

Scene XI

[1–24: See North, *post*, p. 266.]

3. *lated*] belated, benighted. So in
Mac., III. iii. 6: 'Now spurs the *lated*
traveller apace.'

8. *show their shoulders*] Cf. Beaumont

I have myself resolv'd upon a course,
Which has no need of you. Be gone,   10
My treasure's in the harbour. Take it: O,
I follow'd that I blush to look upon:
My very hairs do mutiny; for the white
Reprove the brown for rashness, and they them
For fear, and doting. Friends, be gone, you shall   15
Have letters from me to some friends, that will
Sweep your way for you. Pray you, look not sad,
Nor make replies of loathness; take the hint
Which my despair proclaims. Let that be left
Which leaves itself: to the sea-side straightway;   20
I will possess you of that ship and treasure.
Leave me, I pray, a little: pray you now,
Nay, do so: for indeed I have lost command,
Therefore I pray you: I'll see you by and by.   [*Sits down.*

Enter CLEOPATRA *led by* CHARMIAN *and* EROS; IRAS
following.

Eros. Nay, gentle madam, to him, comfort him.   25
Iras. Do, most dear queen.
Char. Do, why, what else?

19–20. that . . . leaves itself] *Capell;* them . . . leaues it selfe *F.*

and Fletcher, *A King and no King*, III. ii.
29: 'I was never at battle but once, and
there I was running, but *Mardonius*
cudgel'd me: yet I got loose at last, but
was so afraid that I saw no more than
my *shoulders* do,' etc.

13–15. *My very hairs . . . doting*] † Cf.
IV. viii. 19–20 *post*, where he is in a very
different mood. [R]

19. *that*] Antony himself.

20. *leaves itself*] is no longer itself.

23. *for . . . command*] Johnson supposed Antony to refer to his own rising
emotion, which does, in fact, become
uncontrollable, and is perhaps already
indicated by his short-breathed speech;
and this accords with his request for
merely temporary solitude. Steevens's
interpretation, however, is probable
and generally accepted: 'I *entreat* you

to leave me, because I have lost all
power to *command* your absence.' Cf.
Beaumont and Fletcher, *A King and no
King*, I. i. 313: 'I pray you leave me,
Sirs. I'm proud of this, / That you will
be intreated from my sight.'

24–5.] † There has been a general
tendency of editors not only to complete F's S.D. by the necessary addition of Iras, but also to change it, by
having Cleopatra led in by Charmian
and Iras, with Eros following. This, I
think, misses the point. Not only is he
the first to speak, so that his entry
behind the other three is awkward, but
he has, one imagines, been instru-
mental in persuading Cleopatra to
come to comfort his master, and it is
therefore appropriate that he should
conduct her. [R]

Cleo. Let me sit down. O Juno!

Ant. No, no, no, no, no.

Eros. See you here, sir?　　　　　　　　　　　　30

Ant. O fie, fie, fie!

Char. Madam!

Iras. Madam, O good empress!

Eros. Sir, sir!

Ant. Yes, my lord, yes; he at Philippi kept　　　　35
　　　His sword e'en like a dancer, while I struck
　　　The lean and wrinkled Cassius, and 'twas I
　　　That the mad Brutus ended: he alone
　　　Dealt on lieutenantry, and no practice had
　　　In the brave squares of war: yet now—No matter.　　40

Cleo. Ah, stand by.

Eros. The queen, my lord, the queen.

Iras. Go to him, madam, speak to him.

---

29. *No . . . no*] perhaps in rejection of Eros' attempt, as Delius says; but possibly only an audible fragment of Antony's bitter reflections.

35. *Yes, my lord, yes*] To an imaginary collocutor, according to Delius; but Hudson refers it to Cæsar, whom, certainly, Antony might now in bitter irony call 'my lord.'

35–6. *he at Philippi . . . dancer*] Steevens explains that Cæsar is charged with wearing his sword for ornament only, undrawn, like a dancer, and compares *Tit.*, II. i. 38: 'Why boy, although our mother unadvis'd / Gave you a *dancing-rapier* by your side.' Malone added *All's W.*, II. i. 32: '. . . and no sword worn / But one to *dance* with.' See also the extracts from 'A Paire of Spy-knaves' in the preface to *The Four Knaves* by S. Rowlands (Percy Society, no. xxxiv, p. xi): 'Bid him trim up my walking rapier neat, / My *dancing* rapier's pummell is too great;' etc. On Cæsar at Philippi, see North, *post*, p. 244.

37. *The lean . . . Cassius*] Cf. *Cæs.*, I. ii. 193, etc.

37–8. *I . . . mad Brutus ended*] not to be taken literally. See North, *post*, p.

244. Brutus' high, unselfish aims, and ascription of the like to others, perhaps account for the epithet *mad*.

39. *Dealt on lieutenantry*] 'fought by proxy' (Steevens). Cf. III. i. 16–17 and North, *post*, p. 253. *Dealt on* seems to be = to acted *or* proceeded in dependence on, unless it corresponds with our disparaging use of *to deal in, traffic in*. Steevens and Malone quote passages containing *deal upon*, but this in all these = deal with *or* 'set to work upon' (*OED*), as in *R3*, IV. ii. 75.

39–40. *no practice . . . squares of war*] Cf. the Countess of Pembroke's *Antonie* (1595), Act III: 'A man . . . in Mars' school who never lesson learned'; and again: 'A man who never saw enlaced pikes / With bristled joints against his stomach bent. / Who fears the field and hides him cowardly / Dead at the very noise the soldiers make.' For *squares* = squadrons, cf. *H5*, IV. ii. 28: 'our *squares* of battle'; Markham's *Sir Richard Grinuile*, 1595 (p. 65 in Arber's repr.): 'In foure great battailes marcht the *Spanish* hoast, / The first of *Siuill*, led in two great *squares*,' etc.

He is unqualitied with very shame.
Cleo. Well then, sustain me: O!   45
Eros. Most noble sir, arise, the queen approaches,
    Her head's declin'd, and death will seize her, but
    Your comfort makes the rescue.
Ant. I have offended reputation,
    A most unnoble swerving.
Eros.   Sir, the queen.   50
Ant. O, whither hast thou led me, Egypt? See,
    How I convey my shame out of thine eyes,
    By looking back what I have left behind
    Stroy'd in dishonour.
Cleo.   O my lord, my lord,
    Forgive my fearful sails! I little thought   55
    You would have follow'd.
Ant.   Egypt, thou knew'st too well,
    My heart was to thy rudder tied by the strings,
    And thou shouldst tow me after. O'er my spirit
    Thy full supremacy thou knew'st, and that

---

44. He is] *F2*; Hee's *F.*   47. seize] *F2*; cease *F.*   54. Stroy'd] *F*; Strow'd
or Strew'd *Capell conj.*   58. tow] *Rowe* (towe); stowe *F.*   59. Thy] *Theobald*
(*ed. 2*); The *F.*

---

44. *unqualitied*] unmanned, not himself. *Qualited* occurs twice in *The Passionate Morrice*, 1593 (New Shakespeare
Soc., 1876, pp. 82, 85): 'They that
were wealthy were meanely *qualited*,
and they that had many good properties were moniles'; 'an exquisite
proper *qualited* Squire.'

47. *seize*] *cease* for *seize*, as in F, is
common. Cf. Marston, *The Dutch
Courtesan* (1605), III. i (III. ii. 30 in
Gifford): 'mischiefe and a thousand
divells *cease* him!'

but] unless. So Peele, *The Battle of
Alcazar*, III. iv. 28: 'The hellish prince
... Ding down my soul to hell ... *But*
I perform religiously,' etc.

52-4. *How I convey ... dishonour*] See
how I take my disgrace out of your
sight by giving myself up to solitary
brooding over the wreck of my fortunes and my honour. For *stroy'd*, cf.
Sir T. Wyatt, *Of the meane and sure*

estate, etc. line 14: 'And when her store
was *stroyed* with the floode'; *A Collection
of ... Ballads and Broadsides* (1559-97),
1867, p. 122: 'Let not the wicked
thus preuayle, / To vexe thy church
and sayntes; / But *stroy* them from
the head to tayle,' etc. Both the
infinitives *stroyen* and *destroyen* exist-
ed in Middle English. Some print
the contraction *'stroy'd* here. It is
used by Henry More, *Philosophicall
Poems* (1647), p. 111, line 5: 'For
she may deem herself *'stroyed* quite,'
etc.

57. *the strings*] i.e. the heart strings.
Cf. the passage in the Countess of
Pembroke's *Antonie* (1595), Act II,
quoted by Steevens, and containing
the lines: 'Forgetful of his charge (as if
his soul / Unto his ladies soul had been
enchained),' etc. Shakespeare makes
the image more concrete with rudder
and strings.

Thy beck might from the bidding of the gods   60
    Command me.
Cleo.   O, my pardon!
Ant.   Now I must
To the young man send humble treaties, dodge
And palter in the shifts of lowness, who
With half the bulk o' the world play'd as I pleas'd,
Making and marring fortunes. You did know   65
How much you were my conqueror, and that
My sword, made weak by my affection, would
Obey it on all cause.
Cleo.   Pardon, pardon!
Ant. Fall not a tear, I say, one of them rates
    All that is won and lost: give me a kiss,   70
    Even this repays me. We sent our schoolmaster,
    Is a' come back? Love, I am full of lead:
    Some wine within there, and our viands! Fortune knows,
    We scorn her most, when most she offers blows.   [*Exeunt.*

62. *treaties*] propositions. So in *John*, II. i. 480: 'Why answer not the double majesties / This friendly *treaty* of our threaten'd town?'

62–3. *dodge . . . lowness*] shuffle and hedge in those devices to which the man who has lost his power is reduced.

65. *Making and marring*] Nothing is commoner than the collocation of *make* and *mar*, and 'To make *or* mar' is a proverbial phrase. Yet, in conjunction with 'play'd' (line 64), there seems to be an allusion here to a game of some kind. Rushton, *Shakespeare Illustrated by the Lex Scripta* (1870), p. 57, cites: '. . . places for bowling, tennis, dicing, white and black, *making and marring*, and other unlawful games prohibited by the laws and statutes of this realm, . . . 2 and 3 Philip and Mary, cap. ix.'

69. *Fall*] transitively used, as in *Tp.*, II. i. 304, and often. Cf. R. Chester, *Love's Martyr*, 1601 (New Shake-

peare Soc. 1878, p. 125): '*Fall* thou a teare, and thou shalt plainly see, / Mine eyes shall answer teare for teare of thine.'

rates] 'estimates, expresses the value of, is worth' (Schmidt, who observes that the passage is peculiar). The ordinary meaning (to assess, value) is seen in *Cym.*, I. iv. 88: '*Post.* I praised her as I *rated* her: so do I my stone. *Iach.* What do you esteem it at?' See also on III. vi. 25 *ante*.

71. *schoolmaster*] Euphronius, the tutor of his children by Cleopatra. See North, *post*, p. 268.

73. *Some wine . . . knows*] † The line is unmetrical, which would be less suspicious if it were not the first line of a concluding couplet. F, which has made an unmetrical jumble of the preceding two lines, gets the couplet 'right' by putting *some wine* at the end of the 'line' before, and starting the couplet with *Within there.* [R]

[SCENE XII.—*Egypt. Cæsar's camp.*]

Enter Cæsar, Agrippa, Dolabella, *and* Thidias,
with others.

Cæs. Let him appear that's come from Antony.
    Know you him?
Dol.   Cæsar, 'tis his schoolmaster,
    An argument that he is pluck'd, when hither
    He sends so poor a pinion of his wing,
    Which had superfluous kings for messengers,   5
    Not many moons gone by.

Enter Ambassador from Antony.

Cæs.   Approach, and speak.
Amb. Such as I am, I come from Antony:
    I was of late as petty to his ends,
    As is the morn-dew on the myrtle-leaf
    To his grand sea.

Scene XII

1. from] *F;* for *F2.*

[See North, *post*, pp. 268–9.]

S.D. *Agrippa.*] Many editors omit him, on the grounds that he does not speak. But Shakespeare not infrequently includes a non-speaker, either (perhaps) because he at first intended him to speak and then forgot or changed his mind, or (as more probable here) because it was natural for the character to be there.

5. *kings for messengers*] Cf. III. xiii. 91 and IV. ii. 13 *post.*

10. *To his grand sea*] Tyrwhitt conjectures *this* for *his*, supposing the sea visible from Cæsar's camp, but, as Steevens says, *his* = its, and the sea is the morn-dew's, as being its source, or, I imagine, as being its goal after exhalation by the sun. This latter would give—besides the usual interpretation, 'in comparison with "the sea from which the dew-drop is exhaled"' (Steevens)—an alternative, substituting *to which . . . passes* for *from which . . . is exhaled.* I have not seen it

suggested that the simile may be elliptic, and = as petty to his purposes as the morn-dew to those of the great sea it comes from (i.e. as an insignificant part of it), *or* passes to (i.e. as an insignificant contributor to it). † I think that Steevens and Case were wrong about *his* meaning 'its' here (though it often does), and that the words mean 'to the great sea which is Antony.' [R] For *grand* = great, cf. III. i. 9 *ante*, and Sylvester's *Du Bartas*, third day, first week, line 184: 'Whither the Sea, which we *Atlantick* call, / Be but a peece of the *Grand Sea* of all'; etc. In the preceding day, line 501 *et seq.*, we have the contemporary idea about dew: 'Two sorts of vapours by his heat exhales / From floating Deeps, and from the flowry Dales: / . . . / And if this vapour fair and softly sty [ascend], / Not to the cold Stage of the middle Sky, / But 'boue the Clouds, it turneth (in a trice) / In *April*, Deaw; in *Ianuary*, Ice.'

Cæs.   Be't so, declare thine office.   10
Amb. Lord of his fortunes he salutes thee, and
      Requires to live in Egypt, which not granted,
      He lessens his requests, and to thee sues
      To let him breathe between the heavens and earth,
      A private man in Athens: this for him.   15
      Next, Cleopatra does confess thy greatness,
      Submits her to thy might, and of thee craves
      The circle of the Ptolemies for her heirs,
      Now hazarded to thy grace.
Cæs.   For Antony,
      I have no ears to his request. The queen   20
      Of audience nor desire shall fail, so she
      From Egypt drive her all-disgraced friend,
      Or take his life there. This if she perform,
      She shall not sue unheard. So to them both.
Amb. Fortune pursue thee!
Cæs.   Bring him through the bands. 25
                              [*Exit ambassador.*
      [*To Thidias*] To try thy eloquence, now 'tis time,
          despatch;
      From Antony win Cleopatra, promise,
      And in our name, what she requires; add more,
      From thine invention, offers: women are not
      In their best fortunes strong; but want will perjure 30
      The ne'er-touch'd vestal: try thy cunning, Thidias;

13. lessens] *F2;* Lessons *F.*   26. *To Thidias*] *Rowe; not in F.*

12. *Requires*] requests (not 'demands').

13. *lessens*] Thiselton defends *Lessons*
of F on the supposition that the initial
capital indicates an emphasis scarcely
appropriate in the case of *lessens*; and
observes: 'The fact that the ambassador is on this occasion a schoolmaster
should have been sufficient to have
warded off the sacrilegious hand of the
emendator.'

18. *circle*] crown, as in *John,* v. i. 2.

19. *Now . . . grace*] the retention of
which now depends on your favour.

28–9. *add . . . offers*] S. Walker conjectures *and more . . . offer.* But, after all,

in rapidly worded directions, *offers*
comes in naturally enough where it
stands in the text. It merely reinforces,
by an emphatic word, what has been
already expressed. †The most attractive emendation is Hanmer's, *As thine
invention offers.* [R]

31. *Thidias*] †The name so appears
consistently in F. Rowe and Pope
were content to leave it. Theobald, on
the grounds that North has Thyreus,
supplanted Thidias by Thyreus, and
almost all editors since, except Dover
Wilson, have followed him. But North
can have no authority (not even that
of Plutarch, who has Thyrsus) against

Make thine own edict for thy pains, which we
Will answer as a law.
Thid.   Cæsar, I go.
Cæs. Observe how Antony becomes his flaw,
And what thou think'st his very action speaks   35
In every power that moves.
Thid.   Cæsar, I shall.   [*Exeunt.*

[SCENE XIII.—*Alexandria. Cleopatra's palace.*]

Enter CLEOPATRA, ENOBARBUS, CHARMIAN, *and* IRAS.

Cleo. What shall we do, Enobarbus?
Eno.   Think, and die.

F. Why or how *Thidias* was arrived at
is another question. Dover Wilson suggests that Shakespeare made the alteration, because 'the Thyreus he found
in North was so difficult for the actor
to speak.' I should have thought that,
if anything, it was the other way
round; and rhythmically *Thyreus* is
surely preferable. [R]

32–3. *Make . . . law*] Put your own
valuation on your services: I will conform to what you decree as to a law.
The usual sense of *answer* in connection
with law is, 'meet the charge,' 'justify
the fact,' as in Brome, *The Court Beggar*,
IV. ii (Pearson's *Brome*, i. 244): '*Doct.*
You cannot answer it. / *Gou.* Better by
Law then you can the intent / Of rape
upon the Lady.' 'Edicts at Rome were
rules promulgated by magistrates
upon entry into office; and when the
practice became common of magistrates adopting the edicts of their predecessors, these edicts practically had
the force of ordinary laws' (Deighton).

34. *becomes his flaw*] bears himself as
a broken (*or* disgraced, as in line 22
above) man. Cf. the verb in *H8*, I. i.
95: 'For France hath *flaw'd* the
league'; and see Day's *English Secretarie*, 1599, pt i, p. 76: 'Whilst there is
yet but one craze or slender *flaw* in the

touchstone of thy reputation, peece it
up, and new flourish again by a greater
excellencie, the square of thy workmanship.'

35–6. *And . . . power that moves*] and
what may be augured of his state of
mind from a close observation of his
behaviour. *Power that moves*, faculty of
body or mind that is put in action.
Steevens compares *Troil.*, IV. v. 55–7:
'There's language in her eye, her
cheek, her lip, / Nay her foot speaks;
her wanton spirits look out / At every
joint and *motion* of her body.' See also
Sylvester's *Du Bartas*, 1621 ed. (*Baby-
lon*, p. 262): 'mine eys . . . / By peece-
meal close; all *moving powrs* be still; /
From my dull fingers drops my faint-
ing quill'; etc.

Scene XIII

1. *Think, and die*] Hanmer read
Drink, and Tyrwhitt at first proposed
Wink, on the strength of the bidding
wink and die in Fletcher's *Sea Voyage*, I.
i. (Camb. IX. 3). There are other
instances, e.g. *2H4*, I. iii. 33: 'winking,
leap'd into destruction'; D'Avenant,
To Endymion Porter, etc. (*Works*, 1673,
p. 235): 'there I / (Scarce griev'd for by
my self) would winke and *die*'; Sir R.
Howard, *Poems*, 1696, p. 16: 'But like

Cleo. Is Antony, or we, in fault for this?
Eno.   Antony only, that would make his will
         Lord of his reason. What though you fled,
         From that great face of war, whose several ranges   5
         Frighted each other? why should he follow?
         The itch of his affection should not then
         Have nick'd his captainship, at such a point,

a Covvard wink't and fought'; but the question is rather whether to infer from *Think, and die* that death is to be the result of thinking and no other agency (as apparently was later the case with Enobarbus, IV. vi. 35–6 *post*, which see), or to be self-inflicted after a melancholy view of a hopeless situation. The former sense, i.e. 'Become a prey to melancholy and die of it,' is favoured by IV. vi. 35–6 (see note), but even the passage from *Cæs.* (II. i. 186), quoted by Steevens, does not certainly decide the question in its favour: 'If he love Cæsar, all that he can do / Is to himself, take thought and *die* for Cæsar.'

5. *face of war*] So in Beaumont and Fletcher, *The Queen of Corinth*, IV. iii. (Camb. VI. 56): 'Fear nothing that this *face of arms* presents.'

ranges] the lines of the opposing fleets. For this noun, not elsewhere in Shakespeare, cf. Hall's *Chronicle*, 1548, Henry VIII, v. yere, f. xxxiii: 'The frenchmen came on in iii *ranges*, xxxvi mens thickness'; *Historie of the Arrivall of Edward IV*, etc. (Camden Society, 1838, p. 20): 'assayled them, in the mydst and strongest of theyr battaile, . . . and, than, turned to the *range*, first on that one hand, and than on that othar hand, in lengthe, and so bet and bare them downe, so that,' etc. Fairfax's Tasso, *Godfrey of Bulloigne* (1600), vi. 107: 'And breaking through the ranks and *ranges* long.'

8. *nick'd*] There are sundry possible sources of this expression, and (1) I seem to be alone in suggesting that of gaming, whence—from a *nick* being a winning throw in the game of hazard

—*to nick* came to mean to cheat, or merely *to get the better of*. So, in many passages, e.g.—with a play on words— in *Barnavelt*, v. ii (Bullen's *Old Plays*, ii. 303), where the headsman is said to have '*Nickt* many a worthie gamester'; *Two Wise Men*, etc. (1619), vi. iv (said by an inn-chamberlain of a guest who will order nothing): 'but we'll *nick* him well enough in his horse-meat and scurvy sheets'; and Borrow, *The Romany Rye* (1857), II. xiv, p. 213: 'his reverence chated me, and I chated his reverence; the ould thaif knew every trick that I knew, and one or two more; but in daling out the cards I *nicked* his reverence; scarcely a trump did I ever give him, Shorsha, and won his money purty freely.' The *Eng. Dial. Dict.* has many examples of the senses 'cheat' and 'steal.' (2) From the simple sense of *nick'd*, i.e. notched, is obtained maimed. So Staunton (emasculated), Deighton (marred, disfigured), Herford (properly cut in notches, here 'curtailed'). (3) Steevens, comparing *Err.*, v. i. 175: 'His man with scissors *nicks* him like a fool,' gives 'set the mark of folly on,' which has satisfied most editors.

† I have almost no doubt that Case's own interpretation is the right one. *OED* (which had not reached the word when Case wrote his note) gives 'cut short', with reference to this passage, as does Onions. But it cites no earlier instance, and none later till 1787—i.e. it derives its meaning from the very passage which is in dispute. On the other hand, for Case's interpretation, besides quoting *Barnavelt*, it goes back to 1553. [R]

When half to half the world oppos'd, he being
The mered question. 'Twas a shame no less   10
Than was his loss, to course your flying flags,
And leave his navy gazing.

Cleo.   Prithee, peace.

Enter the Ambassador, with ANTONY.

Ant. Is that his answer?
Amb. Ay, my lord.
Ant. The queen shall then have courtesy, so she   15
Will yield us up.
Amb.   He says so.
Ant.   Let her know 't.
To the boy Cæsar send this grizzled head,
And he will fill thy wishes to the brim,
With principalities.
Cleo.   That head, my lord?
Ant. To him again, tell him he wears the rose   20
Of youth upon him; from which, the world should note
Something particular: his coin, ships, legions,
May be a coward's, whose ministers would prevail
Under the service of a child, as soon
As i' the command of Cæsar: I dare him therefore   25
To lay his gay comparisons apart

10. mered] meered *F; see note.*   26. comparisons] *F;* caparisons *Pope.*

10. *mered question*] whole or sole ground of quarrel, if Mason is correct in supposing a coinage from *mere.* Cf. Middleton, *The Widow,* v. i. 142: 'Signor Francisco, whose *mere* object now / Is woman at these years,' etc. and for *question, Ham.,* I. i. 111. Johnson cites *mere* a boundary, and some make *mered question* = 'the matter to which the dispute is limited,' comparing Spenser, *Ruins of Rome,* xxii: 'When that brave honour of the Latin name, / Which *mear'd* her rule with Africa and Byze,' etc. The boundaries (strips of grass or banks) in the common fields of Shakespeare's day were called *meers,* whence a verb to mark off land, which may appear in extended usage here. Johnson also conjectured *mooted*;

moved (often *meued* or *meevid* thirty years or so before this play) is nearer in form and just as probable: 'But which part should begin sute: that peace to moue,' etc. (John Heywood, *The Spider and the Flie,* 1556, Spenser Society ed., p. 370).

20–1. *rose Of youth*] Cf. *All's W.,* I. iii. 137: 'this thorn / Doth to our rose of youth rightly belong'; and *Ham.,* III. i. 155.

26. *gay comparisons*] the showy supports in which he excels me. Most editors similarly understand *comparisons* (with Johnson) as = comparative superiority in fortune, and Malone quotes *Mac.,* I. ii. 55: 'Till that Bellona's bridegroom, lapp'd in proof, / Confronted him with *self-comparisons,*'

And answer me declin'd, sword against sword,
Ourselves alone. I'll write it: follow me.

[*Exeunt Antony and Ambassador.*

Eno. [*Aside*] Yes, like enough! High-battled Cæsar will
Unstate his happiness, and be stag'd to the show   30
Against a sworder! I see men's judgments are
A parcel of their fortunes, and things outward
Do draw the inward quality after them,
To suffer all alike, that he should dream,
Knowing all measures, the full Cæsar will   35
Answer his emptiness; Cæsar, thou hast subdued
His judgment too.

Enter a Servant.

Ser.   A messenger from Cæsar.

28. S.D. *Exeunt* . . .] *Capell; not in* F.   29. *Aside*] *Capell.*

etc. but a few adopt Pope's reading *caparisons.* There is a play on the two words in *Sir Gyles Goosecappe,* IV. ii (*Old Plays,* Bullen, iii. 64): '*Foul.* A my life a most rich *comparison.* *Goos.* Never stirre if it be not a richer *Comparison* then my Lorde my Cosin wore at Tilt,' etc. Perhaps it may support the text to note that *comparisons* are inferred between youth and age, fortune with its gifts and naked misfortune; and that while the gay, glittering ones, the gifts, can be set aside, the advantage in years and flush of success must remain.

27. *declin'd*] i.e. in fortune, and probably also 'into the vale of years' (*Oth.,* III. iii. 266 *q.v.*). In the Countess of Pembroke's *Antonie,* iii, A. says he proffered combat: 'Though he in prime and I by feeble age / Mightily weakened both in force and skill.' The 20th stanza of A. Copley's *A Fig for Fortune* (1596) begins: 'There is no hell like to *declined* glorie.'

29. *High-battled*] master of noble armies. See on III. ix. 2 *ante,* and compare *Tit.,* IV. iv. 35: 'High-witted Tamora.'

30. *Unstate his happiness*] i.e. strip it of state and dignity. See *Lr,* I. ii. 110: 'I would *unstate* myself to be in a due

resolution' = 'give up my position as a duke, forfeit my rank and fortune' (Craig). The context in both passages supports this view of *unstate,* which otherwise might merely equal unsettle, disestablish, as *stated* occurs in the sense, constituted, firmly fixed. So in Felltham's *Resolves* (ed. 1631), xxiv: 'a soul that is rightly *stated*'; xxvi: 'Nature is motive in the quest of ill; / *Stated* in mischief,' etc.

30–1. *stag'd . . . sworder*] Henley notes the allusion to the public combats of gladiators. And, as Kittredge points out, prize fights with swords were common shows in London. With *stag'd,* cf. *Meas.,* I. i. 67: 'I love the people / But do not like to *stage* me to their eyes'; for *sworder,* *2H6,* IV. i. 135: 'A Roman *sworder* and banditto slave.'

32. *A parcel of*] 'of a piece with' (Steevens), literally, a part of.

32–4. *and things outward . . . alike*] Cf. *Sonn.* cxi: 'And almost thence my nature is subdued / To what it works in, like the dyer's hand.'

34. *that*] †seeing that: the general truth (*things outward . . .*) is exemplified by the particular instance. [R]

35. *Knowing all measures*] being so good a judge of men's 'capacities'.

Cleo. What, no more ceremony? See, my women,
Against the blown rose may they stop their nose,
That kneel'd unto the buds. Admit him, sir.   40
                                        [*Exit Servant.*
Eno. [*Aside*] Mine honesty, and I, begin to square.
The loyalty well held to fools does make
Our faith mere folly: yet he that can endure
To follow with allegiance a fall'n lord,
Does conquer him that did his master conquer,   45
And earns a place i' the story.

                    Enter THIDIAS.

Cleo.   Cæsar's will.
Thid. Hear it apart.
Cleo.   None but friends: say boldly.
Thid. So haply are they friends to Antony.
Eno. He needs as many, sir, as Cæsar has,
Or needs not us. If Cæsar please, our master   50
Will leap to be his friend: for us, you know,
Whose he is, we are, and that is, Cæsar's.
Thid.   So.
Thus then, thou most renown'd, Cæsar entreats,
Not to consider in what case thou stand'st
Further than he is Cæsar.
Cleo.   Go on: right royal.   55
Thid. He knows that you embrac'd not Antony
As you did love, but as you fear'd him.

40. S.D. *Exit . . .*] *Capell; not in* F.   41. *Aside*] *Capell.*   51. us, you] us you *F;*
as you *F2.*   55. Cæsar] *F2; Cæsars.* F.   56. embrac'd] *Hudson (Capell conj.);*
embrace *F.*

41. *square*] quarrel. See on II. i. 45
ante; and cf. our phrase 'he squared up
to his opponent.'
50. *Or needs not us*] Heath: 'or else he
needs not even us, whose small number
and want of power render us incapable, without other assistance, of being
of any service to him'; Deighton: 'or
has no *need* for any friends, i.e. his case
is beyond hope.' Is Enobarbus' speech,
however, dictated by his meditated
defection, and do these words signify:

or does not *need* us, for we are among
them (viz. Cæsar's friends)? What
follows contradicts this if 'Whose he is'
= whose friend he is, but not necessarily if it = whose creature (i.e. at
whose discretion) he is, in which
sense both commentators understood
it.
55. *Further . . . Cæsar*] beyond the fact
that it is Cæsar, and no harsh conqueror, with whom you have to do.
57. *as you fear'd him*] † Cleopatra, in

Cleo.   O!

Thid. The scars upon your honour, therefore, he
        Does pity, as constrained blemishes,
        Not as deserv'd.

Cleo.   He is a god, and knows   60
        What is most right. Mine honour was not yielded,
        But conquer'd merely.

Eno. [*Aside*]   To be sure of that,
        I will ask Antony. Sir, sir, thou art so leaky
        That we must leave thee to thy sinking for
        Thy dearest quit thee.   [*Exit*.

Thid.   Shall I say to Cæsar   65
        What you require of him? for he partly begs
        To be desir'd to give. It much would please him,
        That of his fortunes you should make a staff
        To lean upon. But it would warm his spirits
        To hear from me you had left Antony,   70
        And put yourself under his shroud,
        The universal landlord.

Cleo.   What's your name?

Thid. My name is Thidias.

Cleo.   Most kind messenger,
        Say to great Cæsar this in deputation:

---

62. *Aside*] *Hanmer*.   74. this in deputation:] this in disputation, *F; * this; in
deputation *Theobald* (*Warburton*), *and edd*.

North, during the scene in which she
deludes Cæsar, says the same of herself (see p. 275). This may help to
clarify the way in which Cleopatra's
O! should be delivered. [R]

    61. *right*] true.
    62. *merely*] utterly.
    66. *require*] request (no hint of
demand).
    71. *shroud*] shelter. See Kyd, *Works*
(ed. Boas), *The Hovsholders Philosophie*,
p. 248, line 9: 'vnder the shade of a
Tree, or *shroude* of a Church'; *ibid*.
p. 240: '"The wrath of *Fortune* and of
mightie me[n] I shun, howbeit I am
eftsoones *shrowded* vnder the estate of
Sauoy." "Vnder a magnanimous, just,
and gratious Prince you soiourne
then" (quoth he).'

    74. *in deputation:*] in deputed auth-
ority, as my representative. I have
been guided by the folio punctuation,
seeing no necessity for the accepted
arrangement due to Warburton,
which places the colon after *this*, and
makes the sense: 'I kiss his conquering
hand by proxy.' Other passages hardly
favour it. Cf. *1H4*, IV. iii. 86: 'Of all the
favourites that the absent king / In
deputation left behind him here,' etc.;
ibid. IV. i. 32: 'And that his friends by
deputation could not / So soon be
drawn.' See also *Troil*., I. iii. 152.
Steevens (pointing as Warburton)
believed that F's *disputation* might be
retained, suggesting the sense: 'I own
he has the better in the controversy.'
The probabilities seem to me, how-

I kiss his conquering hand: tell him, I am prompt   75
To lay my crown at's feet, and there to kneel:
Tell him, from his all-obeying breath I hear
The doom of Egypt.

Thid.   'Tis your noblest course.
Wisdom and fortune combating together,
If that the former dare but what it can,   80
No chance may shake it. Give me grace to lay
My duty on your hand.

Cleo.   Your Cæsar's father oft,
When he hath mus'd of taking kingdoms in,
Bestow'd his lips on that unworthy place,
As it rain'd kisses.

Enter ANTONY *and* ENOBARBUS.

Ant.   Favours? By Jove that thunders!   85
What art thou, fellow?

Thid.   One that but performs
The bidding of the fullest man, and worthiest
To have command obey'd.

Eno. [*Aside*]   You will be whipp'd.

Ant. Approach there! Ah, you kite! Now, gods and devils,
Authority melts from me: of late, when I cried 'Ho!'   90

88, 94. *Aside*] *Capell.*   90. me: of late, when] *Johnson* (me. Of); me of late.
When F.

ever, in favour of *dis* being a result of
the attractive proximity of *this* and
kiss.

77. *all-obeying*] 'which all obey.'
With *obeying* = obeyed, cf. *Lucr.*, 993,
'unrecalling crime', i.e. crime past
recall.

78. *doom of*] judgment on.
Egypt] myself.

80. *former . . . shake it*] If a man is
wise enough to limit his daring to the
possible, he is secure.

83. *taking . . . in*] Cf. i. i. 23; iii. vii. 23
ante.

87. *fullest*] Here, I think, not only,
most completely endowed with man's
best qualities, but also with the gifts of
fortune. See line 35 *ante. Full* is particularly applied in *Oth.*, ii. i. 36: 'Like

a *full* [i.e. complete] soldier.' With the
rest of the speech, compare Decretas
on Antony, v. i. 6–7 *post.*

89. *Ah, you kite*] probably addressed
to Cleopatra. Mr Craig quotes this
line on *Lr*, i. iv. 286, 'Detested kite,'
and says of *kite*: 'a term of strong
opprobrium, when by Shakespeare
applied to women. . . Turberville in
his *Book of Faulconrie*, 1575, describes
kites as "base, bastardly, refuse,
hawks."' On the other hand, Thidias
might be so addressed. Cf. *Ralph
Roister Doister*, v. v. 9: 'Roister Doister
that doughtie *kite*'; and Sylvester's *Du
Bartas*, ed. 1621, p. 217 (*The Furies*):
'whose *Siren*-notes / Inchant chaste
Susans, and like hungry *Kite* / Flie at all
game, they *Louers* are behight.'

Like boys unto a muss, kings would start forth,
And cry 'Your will?' Have you no ears?
I am Antony yet.

Enter Servants.

                    Take hence this Jack, and whip him.
Eno. [*Aside*] 'Tis better playing with a lion's whelp,
Than with an old one dying.
Ant.   Moon and stars,   95
Whip him. Were't twenty of the greatest tributaries
That do acknowledge Cæsar, should I find them
So saucy with the hand of she here,—what's her name,
Since she was Cleopatra? Whip him, fellows,
Till like a boy you see him cringe his face,   100
And whine aloud for mercy. Take him hence.
Thid. Mark Antony!
Ant.   Tug him away: being whipp'd

93. S.D. *Enter Servants*] *Dyce; Enter a servant. F, after* him.   94. *Aside*]
Capell.

91. *a muss*] a scramble. So Jonson, *Bart. Fair*, IV. ii. 33: 'Cokes. Gods so! *a muss, a muss, a muss, a muss!* [Falls a-scrambling for the pears].' Cotgrave, defining another word, has 'The boyish scrambling for nuts, etc., cast on the ground; a Musse'; and Onions points out that *muss* = scramble survives in Leicestershire and Warwickshire. Grey pointed out the inclusion by Rabelais (I. xxii) of *muss* among the games of Gargantua, and a mention again, in III. xl, where are these details: 'I found them all [i.e. the high treasurers of France] recreating and diverting themselves at the play called *musse, . . .* provided that *hic not.* that the game of the musse is honest, healthful, ancient, and lawful, *a Muscho inventore, . . . & muscarii*, such as play and sport it at the musse, are excusable in and by law . . . And at the very same time was master Tielman Picquet one of the players of that game of musse. There is nothing that I do better remember; for he laughed heartily when his fellow-members of the aforesaid judicial chamber spoiled their caps in swindging of his shoulders'; etc. (*Works*, Chatto & Windus, n.d., p. 354). With the succeeding reference to kings, cf. III. xii. 5 *ante* and IV. ii. 13 *post*.

93. *Jack*] fellow, impudent rascal. The frequency of the name led to its use for clown, peasant, etc. (as now for sailor), and so in more or less contemptuous senses. Cf. our *Jacks-in-office*, and with it the corresponding phrase in 'And I may set up for an *Author*, I hope, among the *Crowd* . . . where *Licensers, Correctors*, and *Criticks*, are made but *Jacks* in an Office' (*The Parliament of Criticks*, 1702, p. 2).

whip him] See North, *post*, p. 269.

100. *cringe his face*] OED quotes for this transitive use of *cringe*, in addition to the present passage, Bishop Hall, *Satires*, 1598, IV. ii [ed. Singer, 1824, p. 85]: 'And shake his head, and *cringe* his neck and side'; Taylor, the Water Poet, *Red Herring, circa* 1630: 'They, *cringing* in their necks, like rats, smothered in the hold, poorly replied.'

Bring him again: this Jack of Cæsar's shall
Bear us an errand to him.   [*Exeunt servants with Thidias.*
You were half blasted ere I knew you: ha?   105
Have I my pillow left unpress'd in Rome,
Forborne the getting of a lawful race,
And by a gem of women, to be abus'd
By one that looks on feeders?

Cleo.   Good my lord,—

Ant. You have been a boggler ever,   110
But when we in our viciousness grow hard—
O misery on't!—the wise gods seel our eyes,
In our own filth drop our clear judgments, make us
Adore our errors, laugh at's while we strut
To our confusion.

---

103. this] *Pope;* the *F.*   112–13. eyes, In our own filth drop] eyes: In our own filth drop *Warburton;* eyes in our owne filth, drop *F.*

---

107. *Forborne . . . race*] not the fact. See North, *post*, p. 254.

108. *gem*] Headley (*Select Beauties*, etc. ed. 1810, i. 161) quotes this passage to illustrate, 'My chosen pheare, my *gem*, and all my joy,' from G. Gascoigne's *Poems*, p. 141, 1587, 4to. He considers *gem* 'An expression of endearment of great beauty.'

109. *feeders*] servants. Similarly they are called *cormorants*; 'I . . . forgot to bring one of my *cormorants* to attend me' (Jonson, *E.M.O.*, v. i. 8); *beef-eaters*: 'Begone yee greedy *beefe-eaters*' (*Histriomastix*, III. i. 99); '*eaters of broken meats*' (*Lr*, II. ii. 15); *eaters*: 'tall *eaters* in blue coats' (D'Avenant, *The Wits*, III. i; *Works*, 1872, ii. 167); *mouths*: 'Where are all my eaters? my *mouths* now? [*Enter Servants*' (Jonson, *The Silent Woman*, III. v. 33). To the last two, quoted by Steevens, Gifford adds from Fletcher, *The Nice Valour*, III. i (Camb. X, p. 164): 'Now servants he has kept, lusty tall *feeders*'; and in *AYL.*, II. iv. 100: 'I will your very faithful *feeder* be,' the word is mostly taken as = servant. It is noteworthy that in none of these passages are eating propensities *apropos*, so that the terms are general; and though it is otherwise in

Tim., II. ii. 168: 'When all our offices have been oppress'd / With riotous *feeders*,' the sense of the word is determined here too, as Steevens pointed out, by its conjunction with *offices* or servants' quarters. The weight of evidence is wholly against Delius' and Schmidt's explanation, *parasites*. Cf. also lines 123–4, 157 *post*.

110. *boggler*] waverer, shifty one. See *All's W.*, v. iii. 234: 'You *boggle* shrewdly,' etc.

112. *seel*] The term in falconry for sewing up a hawk's eyelids temporarily to prepare it for the use of the hood. Often used figuratively as here. Cf. Jonson, *Catiline*, I. 297: 'Are your eyes yet *unseel'd*? dare they look day / In the dull face?' The practice had other uses. Among amusements provided by Zelmane (Sidney's *Arcadia*, bk i, ed. 1725, p. 99) this figures: 'Now she brought them to see a *seeled* dove, who, the blinder she was, the higher she strove.'

113. *In . . . judgements*] Probability and Steevens's illustration from *H5*, III. v. 59: 'He'll *drop* his heart into the *sink* of fear,' negative the pointing of F, to which Knight adheres.

Cleo.   O, is't come to this?   115
Ant. I found you as a morsel, cold upon
          Dead Cæsar's trencher: nay, you were a fragment
          Of Gnaeus Pompey's, besides what hotter hours,
          Unregister'd in vulgar fame, you have
          Luxuriously pick'd out. For I am sure,   120
          Though you can guess what temperance should be,
          You know not what it is.
Cleo.   Wherefore is this?
Ant. To let a fellow that will take rewards,
          And say, 'God quit you!', be familiar with
          My playfellow, your hand; this kingly seal,   125
          And plighter of high hearts! O that I were
          Upon the hill of Basan, to outroar
          The horned herd, for I have savage cause,
          And to proclaim it civilly, were like
          A halter'd neck, which does the hangman thank   130
          For being yare about him.

Enter a Servant with THIDIAS.

                         Is he whipp'd?
Ser. Soundly, my lord.
Ant.   Cried he? and begg'd 'a pardon?
Ser. He did ask favour.

132. 'a] a *F;* he *Capell and most edd.*

116–17. *morsel . . . trencher*] Cf. the
metaphor for Cleopatra, 'his Egyptian
dish,' II. vi. 123 *ante*, and Cleopatra's
own description of herself as 'a morsel
for a monarch,' I. v. 31 *ante*.

117. *fragment*] left scrap or morsel.
Cf. the plural in *Cym.*, v. iii. 44.

118. *Gnaeus Pompey's*] Cf. IV. xii.
13 *post*, and see North, *post*, p.
246.

120. *Luxuriously*] lustfully. So the
adjective = lustful, as in *Tit.*, v. i. 88:
'O most insatiate and *luxurious*
woman!' and the noun, 'lust', as in
Ham., I. v. 83, in Shakespeare and his
contemporaries.

124. *quit*] reward. Cf. Browne,
Britannia's Pastorals, II. iv. 964: 'You

whose flocks . . . / By my protection
quit your industry.'

125. *seal*] So in *MND.*, III. ii. 143–
4: 'thy hand . . . this *seal* of bliss!'

127–8. *Basan . . . herd*] Steevens
quotes the Prayer-book versions of
Psalms lxviii. 15 and xxii. 12: 'As the
hill of *Basan*, so is God's hill: even an
high hill, as the hill of *Basan*'; 'Many
oxen are come about me: fat bulls of
Basan close me in on every side.' With
the inevitable allusion to *horned*, cf. I.
ii. 4 *ante*. Antony means that he is the
champion cuckold of the world.

131. *yare*] adroit, quick. Cf. II. ii.
211, III. vii. 38 *ante*; v. ii. 282 *post*.

132. '*a*] For *a* = he in F, cf. II. vii. 90,
133 *ante*.

Ant. If that thy father live, let him repent
    Thou wast not made his daughter, and be thou sorry 135
    To follow Cæsar in his triumph, since
    Thou hast been whipp'd for following him: henceforth
    The white hand of a lady fever thee,
    Shake thou to look on 't. Get thee back to Cæsar,
    Tell him thy entertainment: look thou say   140
    He makes me angry with him. For he seems
    Proud and disdainful, harping on what I am
    Not what he knew I was. He makes me angry,
    And at this time most easy 'tis to do 't:
    When my good stars, that were my former guides,   145
    Have empty left their orbs, and shot their fires
    Into the abysm of hell. If he mislike
    My speech, and what is done, tell him he has
    Hipparchus, my enfranched bondman, whom
    He may at pleasure whip, or hang, or torture,   150
    As he shall like to quit me. Urge it thou:
    Hence with thy stripes, begone!   *Exit Thidias.*
Cleo. Have you done yet?
Ant.   Alack, our terrene moon
    Is now eclips'd, and it portends alone
    The fall of Antony!
Cleo.   I must stay his time.   155
Ant. To flatter Cæsar, would you mingle eyes

---

137. whipp'd for] *Theobald;* whipp'd, for *Rowe;* whipt. For *F.*

141–7. *He . . . angry*, etc.] See North, *post*, p. 269.

142–3. *what I am . . . was*] Cf. *Arden of Feversham*, i. 322, for the reverse idea: 'Measure me *what I am*, not what I *was*.'

144. *do't:*] †so F; most edd. print a comma. F is right, I think, marking the pause before he amplifies *this time*. [R]

146. *orbs*] spheres. See on II. vii. 14–16 *ante*, IV. xv. 10 *post*, and *MND.*, II. i. 153.

149. *Hipparchus*] See North, *post*, pp. 266, 269. Antony is not abandoning an innocent man thus, but a revolter.

enfranched] Only here in Shakespeare. *OED* also cites Marbeck, *Book of Notes* (1581), p. 193: 'By him we be *enfraunched* from the captivitie and thraldome of the Divell.'

151. *quit me*] pay me out, requite me. Cf. line 124 *ante*.

153–4. *moon . . . eclips'd . . . portends*] He has already, in his anger, referred to Cleopatra as no longer herself (line 99 *ante*); now similarly, but in softer mood, he figures her as a moon darkened, lustreless, and hence, according to the common superstition, portending evil. See *Lr*, I. ii. 115. Capell supposes him to think of Cleopatra as Isis. See on I. ii. 61 and cf. III. vi. 17 *ante*.

155. *stay his time*] be patient till he comes to himself.

With one that ties his points?
Cleo.   Not know me yet?
Ant. Cold-hearted toward me?
Cleo.   Ah, dear, if I be so,
From my cold heart let heaven engender hail,
And poison it in the source, and the first stone   160
Drop in my neck: as it determines, so
Dissolve my life; the next Cæsarion smite
Till by degrees the memory of my womb,
Together with my brave Egyptians all,
By the discandying of this pelleted storm,   165
Lie graveless, till the flies and gnats of Nile
Have buried them for prey!
Ant.   I am satisfied.
Cæsar sits down in Alexandria, where
I will oppose his fate. Our force by land
Hath nobly held, our sever'd navy too   170
Have knit again, and fleet, threatening most sea-like.

158. me?] *F;* me! *Theobald.*   162. Cæsarion smite] *Rowe* (Cæsario) *;* Cæsarian
smile *F.*   165. discandying] *Theobald* (*Thirlby conj.*) *;* discandering *F.*
168. sits] *Johnson;* sets *F.*

157. *one that . . . points*] a contemptuous phrase for a menial, like *feeder,* line
109 *ante. Points* were the tagged laces
with which the parts of a man's or
woman's dress were fastened together. See *1H4,* II. iv. 242; *Kemps nine
daies vvonder,* 1600 (Camden Society,
1840, p. 17): 'it was the mischaunce of
a homely maide, that, belike, was but
newly crept into the fashion of long
wasted peticotes tyde with *points,*' etc.
   his] Cæsar's.
158. *Cold-hearted toward me?*] † I am
inclined to think that Theobald and
other editors who follow his reading
were right, and that Antony, not yet
relenting, is bitterly answering Cleopatra's question: 'Yes, only too well I
know your cold heart.' [R]
161. *determines*] comes to an end, dis-
solves. See *Cor.,* III. iii. 42: 'Must all
determine here?'
162. *Cæsarion*] Cf. III. vi. 6 *ante.*
165. *discandying*] melting. This and
discandy, IV. xii. 22 *post,* seem to be the

only known instances, but the opposite idea is common. Cf. Sylvester's
Du Bartas, The Lawe, 1621 ed., p. 362:
'As thick, or thicker then the Welkin
pours / His *candi'd* drops vpon the ears
of Corn,' etc. The conceit seems to be
that the poison in the hail (line 160) is
liberated by the melting. The wish
which follows resembles that in v. ii.
57–60 *post.*
   pelleted] occurs also in *Compl.,* 18:
'the brine / That season'd woe had
pelleted in tears.'
   166–7. *flies . . . prey*] Deighton well
compares *Mac.,* III. iv. 72–3: 'our
monuments shall be the maws of kites.'
   169. *his fate*] Cf. *H5,* II. iv. 64: 'and
let us fear / The native mightiness and
fate of him.'
   171. *fleet*] float. Very common; so
T. Hudson, *Du Bartas's Judith,* 1584
(p. 793 in Sylvester, 1621 ed.): 'When
Seas are calme, and thousand vessels
fleet / Vpon the sleeping seas with passage sweet'; etc. *Selimus,* 1594, ed.

Where hast thou been, my heart? Dost thou hear, lady?
If from the field I shall return once more
To kiss these lips, I will appear in blood,
I, and my sword, will earn our chronicle: 175
There's hope in't yet.
Cleo. That's my brave lord!
Ant. I will be treble-sinew'd, hearted, breath'd,
And fight maliciously: for when mine hours
Were nice and lucky, men did ransom lives   180
Of me for jests: but now, I'll set my teeth,
And send to darkness all that stop me. Come,
Let's have one other gaudy night: call to me

175. our] *F*; my *F2*.

Grosart, 467: 'a quiet road for *fleeting ships*.'

172. *heart*] With Delius, I understand this as courage, spirit, and not as addressed to Cleopatra.

174. *in blood*] Besides the obvious sense, Deighton detects 'an allusion to the phrase as used of a stag when in full vigour,' and compares *1H6*, IV. ii. 48, and *Cor.*, IV. v. 225: 'But when they shall see, sir, his crest up again, and the man *in blood*, they will,' etc. See also *Sejanus*, II. 385: 'The way to put / A prince *in blood*, is to present the shapes / Of dangers greater than they are,' etc.

175. *our chronicle*] a record of our deeds. Cf. line 46 *ante*, and Beaumont and Fletcher, *Philaster*, v. iii. 130: 'Well, my dear Countrymen, What-you-lacks, if you continue, and fall not back upon the first broken shin, I'll have you *chronicled* and *chronicled*, and cut and *chronicled*, and all-to-be-prais'd and sung in Sonnets,' etc.

178. *breath'd*] Some print *breathed* and explain 'exercised', a frequent sense; but here a treble strength of breath goes with the like of heart and sinews.

180. *nice*] The favoured sense of *nice* here is Warburton's 'delicate', or the like (cf. Minshew, 1617, 'Nice, *or daintie . . . or effeminate*'), and Schmidt well supports with *2H4*, I. i. 145:

'Hence, thereafter, thou *nice* crutch! / A scaly gauntlet now with joints of steel / Must glove this hand'; etc. A slight objection to this and most senses suggested is that as Antony is speaking of his former *fighting* temper, his hours, however lucky, could only have been dainty, etc., in a very relative sense. Johnson preferred the modern 'just fit for my purpose, agreeable to my wish'; and it is perhaps worth remarking that 'nice and lucky' as a colloquialism nowadays would mean extremely, or satisfactorily, lucky. Other suggestions are, 'trifling' (Steevens), as in *Rom.*, v. ii. 18, etc.—and 'jests' would certainly suit hours that were trivial compared with the present crisis—'amorous, or wanton', Douce, who quotes Stowe, of one Mary Breame in 1583, who 'had been *accused* by her husband to bee a *nice woman of her body*.' As *nice* comes from *nescius*, ignorant, this is a probable degradation of the word. †I fancy that *nice* has here the sense of 'finicky', 'choosy', and that Antony means 'When I was lucky, I could afford to pick and choose at my caprice.' [R]

183. *gaudy*] festive. Feast days are still called 'gaudy days' at Oxford. Reed quotes Blount's *Glossographia* [see for the following, ed. 4, 1674]: 'In the Inns of Court there are four of these in

All my sad captains, fill our bowls once more;
Let's mock the midnight bell.

Cleo.   It is my birth-day,   185
I had thought t' have held it poor. But since my lord
Is Antony again, I will be Cleopatra.

Ant. We will yet do well.

Cleo. Call all his noble captains to my lord.

Ant. Do so, we'll speak to them, and to-night I'll force   190
The wine peep through their scars. Come on, my queen,
There's sap in 't yet. The next time I do fight
I'll make death love me; for I will contend
Even with his pestilent scythe.   [*Exeunt all but Enobarbus.*

Eno. Now he'll outstare the lightning; to be furious   195
Is to be frighted out of fear, and in that mood
The dove will peck the estridge; and I see still,

---

194. *Exeunt . . . Enobarbus*] *Camb. edd.; Exeunt. F.*

---

the year, that is, one in every Term, viz. *Ascension-day* in *Easter* Term, *Midsummer-day* in *Trinity* Term, *All-Saints-day* in *Michaelmas* Term, and *Candlemas-day* in *Hillary* Term; these four are no days in Court, and on these days double Commons are allowed, and Musick on *All-Saints* and *Candlemas-day*, as the first and last of *Christmas*. The Etymology of the word may be taken from Judge *Gawdy*, who (as some affirm) was the first institutor of those days, or rather from *gaudium*, because (to say truth) they are days of *joy*, as bringing good cheer to the hungry Students. In Colledges, they are most commonly called *Gaudy*, in Inns of Court, *Grand days*, and at Court, *Coller days*.' See Bullen's *Middleton*, viii. 43–4, *The Black Book*, where 'Pierce Pennyless, exceeding poor scholar, that hath made clean shoes in both universities' is spoken of as not 'once munching commons but only upon *gaudy*-days'; and, for the general use, Edward Phillips's *Life of John Milton*, 1694 (Appendix to Godwin's *Lives of Edward and John Philips*, 1815, p. 365): 'with these gentlemen, he would so far make bold with his body,

as now and then to keep a *gawdy*-day.'

185. *birth-day*] See North, *post*, p. 270.

193–4. *contend . . . scythe*] equal the slaughter of even his scythe of pestilence (i.e. the plague).

197. *estridge*] goshawk. See on the word here and in *1H4*, IV. i. 98, Douce (*Illustrations of Shakespecre*, 1807, i. 436), who appeals to *3H6*, I. iv. 41: 'So doves do peck the falcon's piercing talons,' and quotes the Romance of Guy of Warwick, of which the *Early English Text Soc.* editions, 1883, have (pt i, p. 12, lines 175–6) from Auchinleck MS: 'Michel he couþe of hauk and hounde, / Of estriche faucons of gret mounde.' Nares (*Glossary*, 1822) under *Astringer*, cites Blount's *Tenures*, ed. 1784, p. 166: 'A goshawk is in our records termed by the several names of *osturcum, hostricum, estricium, asturcum,* and *austurcum*' (in which list *estricium* is the significant form, while *hostricum* suggests a possible reason for the 'ostrich' confusion), and Halliwell (*Dict. Archaic and Provincial Words*) explains the word in the text as Douce. Editors have entirely ignored all this, and are kept in countenance by *OED*,

A diminution in our captain's brain
Restores his heart; when valour preys on reason,
It eats the sword it fights with: I will seek   200
Some way to leave him.   [*Exit.*

199. preys on] *Rowe;* prayes in *F.*   201. *Exit*] *Rowe; Exeunt. F.*

in which the sense 'goshawk' is un-noticed, and our text illustrates that of *ostrich,* for which *estridge* commonly appears. In Professor Littledale's re-issue of Dyce's *Glossary to Shakespeare,* the correction is made in the Appendix, but ascribed to Madden (*Diary of Master William Silence,* pp. 144–5, etc.).

† I do not understand why editors are for the most part so reluctant to admit that *estridge* can mean goshawk, as well as ostrich.

Dover Wilson does his best to support the meaning 'ostrich' here by saying that it is appropriate to Egypt. That, to begin with, is not so, unless the limits of the ostrich's geographical distribution were in Shakespeare's day further north than they are now. But in any case would Shakespeare have given a moment's thought to the geographical appropriateness of the ostrich—or for that matter of the gos-hawk? He was concerned with an image, and an image which he uses elsewhere. In *Mac.* (IV. ii. 9–11) the wren, in defence of her young, will fight against the owl, and (II. iv. 12–13) a mousing owl hawks at and kills a falcon. And the passage quoted above from *3H6* is seen to be even more closely relevant to the present passage when quoted complete, since it deals with the *mood* in which the dove will turn upon the bird of prey: 'So cowards fight when they can fly no further: / So doves do peck the falcon's piercing talons.' Suppose for a moment that *estridge* had been a ἅπαξ λεγόμενον, occurring in this passage only. Would any commentator with the other Shakespearean passages before him have doubted that it meant some kind of bird of prey, or, with the 'estriche' and 'estricium' passages before him, that it probably meant specifically a goshawk? [R]

ACT IV

[SCENE I.—*Before Alexandria. Cæsar's camp.*]

Enter CÆSAR, AGRIPPA, *and* MÆCENAS, *with his Army;*
CÆSAR *reading a letter.*

Cæs. He calls me boy, and chides as he had power
    To beat me out of Egypt. My messenger
    He hath whipp'd with rods, dares me to personal
        combat,
    Cæsar to Antony: let the old ruffian know,
    I have many other ways to die; meantime   5
    Laugh at his challenge.
Mæc.   Cæsar must think,
    When one so great begins to rage, he's hunted
    Even to falling. Give him no breath, but now
    Make boot of his distraction: never anger
    Made good guard for itself.
Cæs.   Let our best heads   10
    Know, that to-morrow the last of many battles
    We mean to fight. Within our files there are,

ACT IV
Scene I

3. combat.] *F;* combat, *most edd.*

3–4.] † I think F's punctuation very probably right. *Cæsar to Antony* is then the opening of his reply (as though he was dictating a letter). But for *to* (awkward in modern idiom) meaning 'versus', cf. *1H6*, I. ii. 47, 'Blue coats to tawny coats.' [R]

6. *Cæsar must think*] † Apart from the halting rhythm, this is an oddly third-personal way for Maecenas to address Cæsar (which he is clearly doing, and not delivering a comment aside).

Should we perhaps read *Cæsar, we must think*? [R]

9. *Make boot of*] take advantage of. See on II. v. 71 *ante*.

12. *files*] 'It must be added that the file was, in those days, the unit (to use a modern phrase) in which the strength of an army was expressed. Men took their places in the *files*, not in the *ranks* of an army' (*Shakespeare's England*, Oxford, 1916, I. iv, p. 114).

Of those that serv'd Mark Antony but late,
Enough to fetch him in. See it done,
And feast the army; we have store to do 't,   15
And they have earn'd the waste. Poor Antony! [*Exeunt.*

[SCENE II.—*Alexandria. Cleopatra's palace.*]

Enter ANTONY, CLEOPATRA, ENOBARBUS, CHARMIAN,
IRAS, ALEXAS, *with others.*

Ant. He will not fight with me, Domitius?
Eno.   No.
Ant. Why should he not?
Eno. He thinks, being twenty times of better fortune,
He is twenty men to one.
Ant.   To-morrow, soldier,
By sea and land I'll fight: or I will live,   5
Or bathe my dying honour in the blood
Shall make it live again. Woo't thou fight well?
Eno. I'll strike, and cry 'Take all.'

Scene II

1. Domitius?] Domitius. *Rowe and others; Domitian? F.*

14. *fetch him in*] capture him, as in *Cym.*, IV. ii. 140: 'and swear / He 'ld *fetch us in.*'

16. *waste*] needless expenditure.

Scene II

[See North, *post*, p. 271.]

5. *or*] either.

6. *Or bathe . . . blood*] perhaps an allusion to baths of blood as a remedy. Mr C. Crawford refers me to Jonson's *Discoveries*, line 1058: '*Morbi.* The Body hath certaine diseases, that are with lesse evil, tolerated, then remov'd. As if to cure a Leprosie a man should *bathe* himselfe with the warme *blood* of a murthered Child, so,' etc., on which Professor Schelling refers, *inter alia*, to '*Gesta Romanorum*, ed. Osterley, No. 230, in which a girl afflicted with leprosy, only to be cured by her *bathing*

in royal *blood*, accepts the sacrifice of her royal lover, who allows so much blood to be taken from him that it causes his death.' In a citation of Carlyle's (*French Rev.*, I. i. 2) from Lacretelle, *Histoire de France*, etc., occurs: 'an absurd and horrid rumour rises among the people; it is said that the doctors have ordered a Great Person to take *baths* of young human *blood* for the restoration of his own, all spoiled by debaucheries.'

7. *Woo 't*] a common form = *wilt.* Cf. IV. xv. 59 *post*; *Ham.*, v. i. 298; S. Rowlands, *The Knave of Clubbs* (Percy Society, 1843, No. xxxiv, pp. 9–12 *passim*): 'Why doe and *t' woot*,' etc.

8. '*Take all*'] Johnson: 'Let the survivor *take all.* No composition; victory or death.' No doubt the expression comes, as Collier says, from the

Ant.   Well said, come on,
    Call forth my household servants, let's to-night

Enter three or four Servitors.

    Be bounteous at our meal. Give me thy hand,   10
    Thou hast been rightly honest;—so hast thou,—
    Thou,—and thou,—and thou: you have serv'd me well,
    And kings have been your fellows.
Cleo. [*Aside to Eno.*]   What means this?
Eno. [*Aside to Cleo.*] 'Tis one of those odd tricks which
        sorrow shoots
    Out of the mind.
Ant.   And thou art honest too.   15
    I wish I could be made so many men,
    And all of you clapp'd up together in
    An Antony; that I might do you service,
    So good as you have done.
All.   The gods forbid!
Ant. Well, my good fellows, wait on me to-night: 20
    Scant not my cups, and make as much of me
    As when mine empire was your fellow too,
    And suffer'd my command.
Cleo.   [*Aside to Eno.*] What does he mean?
Eno [*Aside to Cleo.*] To make his followers weep.
Ant.   Tend me to-night;
    May be it is the period of your duty,   25
    Haply you shall not see me more, or if,
    A mangled shadow. Perchance to-morrow

13, 14. *Aside* . . .] *Capell.*   23, 24. *Aside* . . .] *Capell.*

language of gaming. See *A Warning for Faire Women*, ii. 683 (Simpson, *School of Shakspere*, ii. 295): '*Yong San.* Come, Harrie, shall we play a game? *Har.* At what? *Yong San.* Why, at crosse and pile. *Har.* You have no Counters. *Yong San.* Yes, but I have as many as you. *Har.* Ile drop with you; and he that has most, *take all*.' A proverbial expression, 'the longer liver *take all*,' occurs in *Rom.*, I. v. 19, and elsewhere.

9–10. S.D.] † The majority of editors from Dyce onwards have put this S.D. after 'meal,' a good example of the difference in placing S.D.s required by the different depths of the Elizabethan and modern stages. F's placing avoids the awkward pause which, on the deep Elizabethan stage, would have intervened between the entry and Antony's 'Give me thy hand.' [R]

13. *kings . . . fellows*] Cf. III. xii. 5 and xiii. 91 *ante*.

25. *period*] end (full stop), as in IV. xiv. 107 *post*.

You'll serve another master. I look on you,
As one that takes his leave. Mine honest friends,
I turn you not away, but like a master   30
Married to your good service, stay till death:
Tend me to-night two hours, I ask no more,
And the gods yield you for't!

Eno.   What mean you, sir,
To give them this discomfort? Look, they weep,
And I, an ass, am onion-ey'd; for shame,   35
Transform us not to women.

Ant.   Ho, ho, ho!
Now the witch take me, if I meant it thus!
Grace grow where those drops fall, my hearty friends;
You take me in too dolorous a sense,
For I spake to you for your comfort, did desire you   40
To burn this night with torches: know, my hearts,
I hope well of to-morrow, and will lead you
Where rather I'll expect victorious life,
Than death, and honour. Let's to supper, come,
And drown consideration.   [*Exeunt.* 45

38. fall, my . . . friends;] fall (my . . . Friends) *F;* fall! My . . . friends,
Theobald.

30–1. *but like a master . . . stay till death*] † I suppose this must mean 'You have served me well and I will remain your master till I die,' but I think that the *like* is slightly awkward, and that the natural sense (though it cannot be extracted from the text) would be 'I ask you to stay with me till I die' (which, the whole context implies, will be soon). It is perhaps worth considering a 'transposed pointing' so that the passage will read: 'I turn you not away, but like a master / Married to your good service: stay till death, / Tend me. . .' Then, taking *but* = except, the lines will mean 'I am not turning you away except as any master would warn loyal servants of his approaching death: stay with me till death comes.' [R]

33. *yield*] pay, requite, the original sense. Cf. *AYL.*, III. iii. 81: 'God*'ild* you for your last company,' etc.

35. *And I . . . onion-ey'd*] Cf. I. ii. 167.

36. *Ho, ho, ho*] After his brief indulgence in sentiment and pathos, Antony laughs it off. Holt White seriously produces many instances of a single *ho* = stop, to show that *stop* or *desist* is the sense here.

37. *the witch take me*] may I be bewitched! For *take* = bewitch, exert a malignant influence on, cf. *Ham.,* I. i. 163: 'No fairy *takes*, nor witch hath power to charm'; *Wiv.*, IV. iv. 33, of Herne the hunter: 'And then he blasts the tree and *takes* the cattle,' etc.; *Gammer Gurton's Needle* (1575), I. ii. 26: 'As though they had ben *taken* with fairies, or els with some il sprite.'

38. *Grace grow . . . fall*] Steevens quotes *R2* [III. iv. 104–5]: 'Here did she fall a tear; here in this place / I'll set a bank of rue, sour herb of *grace*.'

44. *death, and honour*] refers to IV. ii. 6 *ante*.

[SCENE III.—*The same. Before the palace.*]

Enter a Company of Soldiers.

First Sold. Brother, good night: to-morrow is the day.

Sec. Sold. It will determine one way: fare you well.

Heard you of nothing strange about the streets?

First Sold. Nothing: what news?

Sec. Sold. Belike 'tis but a rumour, good night to you. 5

First Sold. Well, sir, good night.

They meet other Soldiers.

Third Sold. Soldiers, have careful watch.

First Sold. And you: good night, good night.

[*They place themselves in every corner of the stage.*

Sec. Sold. Here we: and if to-morrow

Our navy thrive, I have an absolute hope

Our landmen will stand up.

First Sold. 'Tis a brave army, 10

And full of purpose.

[*Music of the hautboys is under the stage.*

†I have retained throughout the scene the stage-directions and speech-headings of F, except immediately after the entry of the 'other soldiers' where one of the two speeches (given by F to '2' and '1' respectively) must, I think, be given to one of the new-comers. I can see no valid reason elsewhere for joining in the game of musical chairs played by the eight-eenth century editors with the rest of the speeches. Capell up to a point saw, I think, what is supposed to be hap-pening. His stage-directions are *Enter two Soldiers, to their guard:* then *Enter two other Soldiers.* Shakespeare, I think, meant there to be four or five soldiers in each group, even though only two in each are vocal, and his '*they meet*' indicates that the second group come in by the other door. But Capell then ob-scures the situation by giving, instead of '*They place themselves . . .*,' '*The two first go to their posts,*' rather as though they went off-stage to their posts—

which, from his own subsequent stage-directions, they clearly do not. He saw, however, that all the soldiers are on guard. Dover Wilson complicates matters further by saying that the dialogue makes it plain that the first two are going off guard and the second pair coming on (though he retains F's stage-directions) and therefore has to accept Capell's redistribution of speeches in lines 9–12. But Shake-speare's intentions are, I suggest, per-fectly clear. A number of sentries meet, as they go on their way to their posts, and exchange greetings. They then distribute themselves to their posts, which are, by the space-destroy-ing conventions of the Elizabethan stage, improbably close together (cf. the tents of Richard and Richmond in *R3*, v. iii). Thus they are in a position not only to hear the music, which in fact they could have done, but to inter-change comments on it, which in fact they could not. [R]

5. *Belike*] probably, as in I. ii. 35 *ante.*

Sec. Sold.   Peace, what noise?
First Sold.   List, list!
Sec. Sold. Hark!
First Sold.   Music i' the air.
Third Sold.   Under the earth.
Fourth Sold. It signs well, does it not?
Third Sold.   No.
First Sold.   Peace, I say:
    What should this mean?
Sec. Sold. 'Tis the god Hercules, whom Antony lov'd,   15
    Now leaves him.
First Sold.   Walk, let's see if other watchmen
    Do hear what we do.
Sec. Sold.   How now, masters? [*Speak together.*
All.   How now?
    How now? do you hear this?
First Sold.   Ay, is 't not strange?
Third Sold. Do you hear, masters? do you hear?
First Sold. Follow the noise so far as we have quarter.   20
    Let's see how it will give off.
All.   Content. 'Tis strange.
                                  [*Exeunt.*

17. S.D. *and* All] *Speak together.* Omnes. F; All [*Speaking together*] *most edd.*

11. *noise*] possibly = music here, as understood in *Mac.*, IV. i. 106: 'and what *noise* is this? [*Hautboys.*'; but the word in North (see *post*, p. 271) applies generally, including the cries and sounds of a multitude, as well as music, and the marginal note is, 'Strange *noises* heard, and nothing seene.'

13. *signs well*] signifies good luck.

15. *Hercules . . . lov'd*] See on I. iii. 84 *ante*. Upton and Capell note that Shakespeare varies from Plutarch here (see extracts, *post*, p. 271) in substituting Hercules, Antony's supposed ancestor, for Bacchus, the object of his 'singular devotion,' etc. In recounting the signs and wonders antecedent to Actium, Plutarch says (North, *Tudor*

Trans., vi. 63): 'And at the citie of Athens also, . . . the statue of Bacchus with a terrible winde was throwen downe in the Theater. It was sayd that Antonius came of the race of Hercules, as you have heard before, and in the manner of his life he followed Bacchus: and therefore he was called the new Bacchus.' Cf. also North extracts, *post*, p. 247.

17. Speak together] another 'imperatival' S.D. Cf. II. v. 73.

20. *as . . . quarter*] as the post assigned to us (i.e. our watch) extends. Cf. *John*, v. v. 20: 'Well: keep good *quarter* and good care to-night.'

21. *give off*] cease (in modern northern dialect 'give over').

[SCENE IV.—*The same. A room in the palace.*]

Enter ANTONY *and* CLEOPATRA, CHARMIAN, *and others attending.*

Ant. Eros! mine armour, Eros!
Cleo.　　　　　　　　　　Sleep a little.
Ant. No, my chuck. Eros! come, mine armour, Eros!

Enter EROS *with armour.*

Come, good fellow, put thine iron on:
If fortune be not ours to-day, it is
Because we brave her. Come.
Cleo.　　　　　　　　Nay, I'll help too.　　　　5
What's this for?
Ant.　　　　　　　Ah, let be, let be! thou art

Scene IV

S.D. *Enter . . .*] *Malone; Enter Anthony and Cleopatra, with others. F.*　2. S.D.
with armour] *added by Capell.*　3. thine] *F;* mine *Hanmer and many other edd.*
5–8. Nay . . . must be] *As Malone (Capell's suggestion); in F all assigned to Cleo.
reading* Nay, I'll help too, *Anthony. See note.*

S.D.] F's omission of Charmian may be just an oversight, but it may suggest that Charmian's few words and Cleopatra's two words of rejoinder (line 35) were an after-thought.

2. *chuck*] This term of fondness (= chick) was used of either sex. So Mistress Potluck in Cartwright's *Ordinary*, 1651, I. ii: 'Thou must keep nothing from thy Rib, good *Chuck.*' And cf. *Mac.*, III. ii. 45.

3. *thine iron*] †I see no justification for changing F, but some at least of the editors who retain it adduce a weak reason, namely that a third *mine* would be repetitive. Why not? But Antony is, I think, being slightly humorous: 'Come on, Eros, put your whole ironmonger's shop on me.' [R]

5–8. †I think Capell's suggestion must be, in the main, right. F reads:
Cleo. Nay, Ile helpe too, *Antony.*
What's this for? Ah let be, let be,
　　thou art
The Armourer of my heart: False,
　　false: This, this,

Sooth-law Ile helpe: thus it must bee.
It is quite clear that this does not all belong to Cleopatra, and fairly clear that from 'Ah let be' down to at any rate 'False, false,' and probably to 'This, this' belongs to Antony, while the italic *Anthony* was a speech heading, and not a proper name, in the text, but found its way into the wrong place. Dover Wilson suggests that Antony's speech was added in the margin, which is possible enough, but does not, I think, go far enough, since if we then take what remains for Cleopatra it is awkward, running:
Cleo. Nay, Ile helpe too, what's this
　　for?
　　Sooth-law Ile helpe: thus it
　　must be.
I suggest that 'Sooth-law Ile helpe' was also part of the addition, with the appropriate speech-heading for Cleopatra, and that her speech originally stood simply:
Cleo. Nay, Ile helpe too, what's this
　　for? Thus it must bee. [R]

The armourer of my heart: false, false; this, this.
Cleo. Sooth, la, I'll help: thus it must be.
Ant.   Well, well,
We shall thrive now. Seest thou, my good fellow?
Go, put on thy defences.
Eros.   Briefly, sir.   10
Cleo. Is not this buckled well?
Ant.   Rarely, rarely:
He that unbuckles this, till we do please
To daff't for our repose, shall hear a storm.
Thou fumblest, Eros, and my queen's a squire
More tight at this than thou: despatch. O love,   15
That thou couldst see my wars to-day, and knew'st
The royal occupation, thou shouldst see
A workman in't.

Enter an armed Soldier.

                      Good morrow to thee, welcome:
Thou look'st like him that knows a warlike charge:
To business that we love, we rise betime,   20
And go to't with delight.
Sold.   A thousand, sir,
Early though 't be, have on their riveted trim,
And at the port expect you.   [*Shout. Trumpets flourish.*

13. daff't] *Dyce;* daft *F;* doft *F2.*

6–7. *thou . . . heart*] 'your work is to
steel my *heart* with courage, not,' etc.
(Deighton).

7. *false, false*] 'That is all wrong'
(Deighton).

10. *Briefly*] in a moment.

13. *daff't*] doff it, put it off. For the
form, cf. *Ado,* II. iii. 187; v. i. 78.

15. *tight*] deft, adroit. So the adverb
in Massinger, *The Picture,* v. iii. 58:
'You shall see I am experienced at the
game, / And can play it *tightly*'; and
Spence's *Lucian* (1684), i. 70: 'Vulcan.
[To Jupiter] Take heed we don't commit some Absurdity, for I shall not
manage you so *tightly* as a Midwife
wou'd.' *Tight* sometimes improperly
represents the adverb *tite* = quickly.

18. *A workman*] a real craftsman.

22. *riveted trim*] *trim* = any kind of
dress or finery (cf. *Sonn.* xcviii) († but
surely there is here something of the
sense in which a ship or her sails are
'trimmed', i.e. properly adjusted.
[R]). See *Jack Drum's Entertainment,*
1616, v (Simpson's *School of Shakspere,*
ii. 200) and *H5,* IV, prol. 13: 'The ar-
mourers, accomplishing the knights, /
With busy hammers closing rivets up,'
on which Douce: 'This does not
solely refer to the business of *riveting* the
plate armour before it was put on, but
in part to when it was on. Thus,' etc.
See *Illustrations of Shakespeare,* 1807, or
H5 (Arden Shakespeare), *ad. loc.*

23. *port*] gate. So in *2H4,* IV. v. 23:

Enter Captains, and Soldiers.

Capt. The morn is fair: good morrow, general.
All. Good morrow, general.
Ant.   'Tis well blown, lads.   25
This morning, like the spirit of a youth
That means to be of note, begins betimes.
So, so; come, give me that: this way; well said.
Fare thee well, dame, whate'er becomes of me:
This is a soldier's kiss: rebukeable,   [*Kisses her.* 30
And worthy shameful check it were, to stand
On more mechanic compliment; I'll leave thee
Now like a man of steel. You that will fight,
Follow me close, I'll bring you to't. Adieu.
          [*Exeunt Antony, Eros, Captains, and Soldiers.*
Char. Please you retire to your chamber?
Cleo.   Lead me: 35
He goes forth gallantly: that he and Cæsar might
Determine this great war in single fight!
Then Antony—; but now—Well, on.   [*Exeunt.*

24. *Capt.*] *Rowe; Alex. F.*   28. well said] *F2;* well-sed *F.*   30. *Kisses her*]
Johnson; not in F.   34. S.D. *Exeunt . . .*] *Capell (substantially); Exeunt. F.*

'the *ports* of slumber,' and Chapman's
Hesiod, *Georgics,* i, p. 216, col. 1, note:
'He calls this seven-*ported* Thebes, to
distinguish it from that of Egypt, that
had a hundred *ports,*' etc. See also on
1. iii. 46 *ante.*

24. *Capt.*] Rowe's necessary substitution for F *Alex.* See IV. vi. 12
post.

25. '*Tis well blown*] Delius and Rolfe
refer this to the trumpets (which blow
a 'Good Morrow': see *Oth.,* III. i. 2,
Arden Shakespeare), Hudson and
Deighton to the morning; 'the metaphor being employed of night blossoming into day' (Hudson). The former
explanation is simple and unforced,
the latter forced: yet, as it has some
excuse in lines 26–7, it at least demands
record.

28. *So, so . . . said*] Antony is still
putting on his armour, and the 'that'
is a piece of it. 'Well said' signalizes the
completion of the arming.

well said] well done; as often in
Shakespeare, approving action, not
speech: 'Well said, Hal! to it, Hal!'
(*1H4,* v. iv. 75, where Hal is not saying
anything but fighting for his life),
'Well said, i'faith, Wart.' (*2H4,* III. ii.
298, Wart not having opened his
mouth), 'Now masters, draw. (*They
shoot*). O! well said, Lucius!' (*Tit.,* IV.
iii. 63). The phrase is, in fact, just the
equivalent of 'Attaboy!'

32. *mechanic*] From the contemptuous application to artisans, as in v. ii.
208 *post,* 'mechanic slaves', the word
came to mean 'vulgar', 'common';
and this sense, or 'journeyman-like', is
assigned here. It does not seem altogether satisfactory; I should prefer to
take 'to stand on more mechanic
compliment' as = to stand on ceremony, were evidence forthcoming for
the early use of *mechanic* for unspon-
taneous, and so ceremonious or con-
ventional.

[SCENE V.—*Alexandria. Antony's camp.*]

Trumpets sound. Enter ANTONY *and* EROS; *a soldier meeting them.*

Sold. The gods make this a happy day to Antony!

Ant. Would thou, and those thy scars had once prevail'd
To make me fight at land!

Sold.   Hadst thou done so,
The kings that have revolted, and the soldier
That has this morning left thee, would have still   5
Follow'd thy heels.

Ant.   Who's gone this morning?

Sold.   Who?
One ever near thee; call for Enobarbus,
He shall not hear thee, or from Cæsar's camp
Say 'I am none of thine.'

Ant.   What sayest thou?

Sold.   Sir,
He is with Cæsar.

Eros.   Sir, his chests and treasure   10
He has not with him.

Ant.   Is he gone?

Sold.   Most certain.

Ant. Go, Eros, send his treasure after, do it,
Detain no jot, I charge thee: write to him—
I will subscribe—gentle adieus, and greetings;

S.D. *a Soldier meeting them*] *Theobald; not in* F.   1. *Sold.*] *Theobald (Thirlby conj.); Eros.* F.   3, 6. *Sold.*] *Eros.* F.

S.D. and speech-headings] † There is some confusion here, and confusion for which it is not easy to account. One might suppose that Shakespeare had intended to operate with only Antony and Eros, but found that later he wanted another speaker, and hurriedly inserted a soldier. But this will not account for the opening lines since 'those thy scars' makes it certain that this is the soldier of III. vii. 61, with his 'these my wounds', and the second

speech which F attributes to Eros must therefore from the outset have been the soldier's. [R]

1. *happy*] lucky.

2–3. *Would . . . land*] See III. vii. 61–6.

7. *Enobarbus*] In Plutarch (see North, *post*, p. 264) Enobarbus deserts prior to Actium. It is the brave man-at-arms whom Antony calls Scarus in scenes vii and viii *post* who presently decamps with his reward; see North, p. 270.

Say, that I wish he never find more cause   15
To change a master. O, my fortunes have
Corrupted honest men. Despatch.—Enobarbus.

[*Exeunt.*

[SCENE VI.—*Alexandria. Cæsar's camp.*]

Flourish. Enter AGRIPPA, CÆSAR, *with* ENOBARBUS,
and DOLABELLA.

Cæs. Go forth, Agrippa, and begin the fight:
Our will is Antony be took alive;
Make it so known.
Agr. Cæsar, I shall.   [*Exit.*
Cæs. The time of universal peace is near: 5
Prove this a prosperous day, the three-nook'd world

17. Despatch.—Enobarbus] *See note.*

Scene VI

4. *Exit.*] *not in F.*

16–17. *O, my fortunes . . . men*] See note on III. xiii. 32–4 *ante.*

17. *Despatch.—Enobarbus*] F has *Dispatch Enobarbus*; F2 *Dispatch Eros,* whence Pope, *Dispatch my Eros*; Steevens, 1793 (Ritson conj.) *Eros, despatch.* Steevens (1773) reads *Dispatch. Enobarbus!* Capell *Dispatch.—O Enobarbus!* Thiselton says the reading of F means 'Get fully quit of Enobarbus by sending his belongings after him,' a sense which would need much softening to put it in harmony with what precedes. For Antony's conduct, cf. North, *post,* p. 264. According to Plutarch, Cæsar similarly treated Labienus on his desertion to Pompey (*Life of Julius Cæsar*).

Scene VI

S.D.] † The placing of Agrippa first may be due to mere carelessness, but does it perhaps indicate that Agrippa is to enter by a different door (on his return from seeing that the troops are ready for action, or the like)? [R]

6. *three-nook'd*] three-cornered; alluding, perhaps, to the world's having been divided between the Triumvirs. See also *Cæs.,* IV. i. 14. A trine aspect of the world was familiar to contemporary poets apart from such associations. See Pearson's *Heywood,* iii. 242 (*The Brazen Age*): 'Il'e make her Empresse ore the *triple* world'; *Locrine,* III. iv. 36: 'Stout Hercules . . . / That tam'd the monsters of the *three-fold* world'; *ibid.* v. iv. 5: 'The great foundation of the *triple* world, / Trembleth,' etc. In such cases the phrase was probably caught from the *triplex mundus* of Ovid, *Metam.,* xii. 40, involving sky, land, and sea. Du Bartas (Sylvester, 1621 ed.) speaks of the earth as divided 'in *three* vnequall Portions' by the sea and its arms (p. 49) and again (p. 268), of 'this spacious Orb' as parted by the Creator 'Into *three* Parts,' east, south, and west, 'Twixt *Sem,* and *Cham,* and *Japeth.*'

Shall bear the olive freely.

Enter a Messenger.

Mess.   Antony
Is come into the field.
Cæs.   Go charge Agrippa,
Plant those that have revolted in the vant,
That Antony may seem to spend his fury   10
Upon himself.   [*Exeunt all but Enobarbus.*
Eno. Alexas did revolt; and went to Jewry on
Affairs of Antony, there did dissuade
Great Herod to incline himself to Cæsar,
And leave his master Antony. For this pains,   15
Cæsar hath hang'd him; Canidius and the rest
That fell away, have entertainment, but
No honourable trust: I have done ill,
Of which I do accuse myself so sorely,
That I will joy no more.

Enter a Soldier of CÆSAR'S.

Sold.   Enobarbus, Antony   20

---

9. vant] *F; van F2 and edd.*   11. *Exeunt . . .] Exeunt. F.*   13. dissuade] *F*
(disswade); persuade *Rowe.*   20. more] *F2; mote F.*

---

7. *bear*] bring forth. Cf *2H4*, iv. iv.
87: 'But Peace puts forth her olive
everywhere.' Mason—in favour of
bear = carry—ignores metaphor in
objecting that Augustus' success 'could
not make the olive-tree grow without
culture in all climates'; but Schmidt
also explains *wear*. So D'Avenant sings
in *The first dayes entertainment at Rutland
House*: 'Did ever war so cease / That all
might olive *wear?*'

9. *vant*] the old form of the word,
short for *vantwarde*, whence *vanguard*
and so *van*.

12. *and*] † ? '*a* (= he). Alexas clearly
did not revolt *before* he went to Jewry.
[R]

13. *dissuade*] Johnson thought *dissuade* of F probably right. North (*post*,
p. 269) has *persuaded*, but it is not impossible that the thought of dissuation

from Antony's service determined the
word here. When King John's emissary pander, in Drayton's *Legend of
Matilda*, becomes threateningly per-
suasive, the heroine does not describe
herself, during her hesitation, as by
fear *persuaded*, but 'By fear disswaded,
menaced by murder' (stanza 74), not
thinking of persuasion to unchasteness
—the natural sequence—but dis-
suasion from chastity. *Dissuade* can be
followed by the infinitive: *OED* quotes
Camden's *Remains*, ed. 1637, p. 246:
'Some *disswaded* him to hunt that day.'

17. *entertainment*] employment. Cf.
All's W., iv. i. 16: 'He must think us
some band of strangers i' the adversary's *entertainment*'; *A Report*, etc., 1591
(*The Revenge*, ed. Arber, p. 27): 'A
notable testimonie of their rich *entertainment* and great wages.'

Hath after thee sent all thy treasure, with
His bounty overplus. The messenger
Came on my guard, and at thy tent is now
Unloading of his mules.

Eno.   I give it you.

Sold. Mock not, Enobarbus,   25
I tell you true: best you saf'd the bringer
Out of the host; I must attend mine office,
Or would have done't myself. Your emperor
Continues still a Jove.   [*Exit.*

Eno. I am alone the villain of the earth,   30
And feel I am so most. O Antony,
Thou mine of bounty, how wouldst thou have paid
My better service, when my turpitude
Thou dost so crown with gold! This blows my heart:
If swift thought break it not, a swifter mean   35
Shall outstrike thought, but thought will do't, I feel.
I fight against thee? No, I will go seek
Some ditch, wherein to die: the foul'st best fits
My latter part of life.   [*Exit.*

---

36. do't, I feel.] *Rowe;* doo't. I feele *F.*

23. *on my*] while I was on.

26. *true: best*] † ? *'twere* has dropped out before *best*, by confusion with *true.* [R]

saf'd] conducted safely. Cf. Chapman's *Homer, Odyssey,* iv (ed. Shepherd, p. 332b): 'Neptune . . . / *Saft* him unwrack'd to the Gyræan isle.' *Safe* = make safe, occurs in I. iii. 55 *ante.*

31. *And feel . . . most*] and am he who most realizes it.

32. *mine of bounty*] Cf. *1H4,* III. i. 167: 'as bountiful As *mines* of India.'

34. *blows*] swells, 'makes it full to bursting' (Schmidt). Cf. *blown* = swollen, v. ii. 347 *post* (if that is what it means there), and Jonson, *Catiline,* IV. 18: 'It is our base petitionary breath

That *blows* 'em to this greatness.'

† But may it not mean simply 'beats upon'? [R]

35. *mean*] See on III. ii. 32 *ante.*

35, 36. *thought*] melancholy. See on III. xiii. 1 *ante,* and cf. 'in great trowble, *thought,* and hevines' (p. 13) with 'right great trowble, sorow, and hevines' (p. 17) in *Historie of the Arrivall of Edward IV,* etc. (Camden Society, 1838). Cf. *Ham.,* IV. v. 187 and Brome, *A mad Couple well Match'd* (Pearson's *Brome,* i. 16): 'And can you be so mild? then farwell *thought,*' the exclamation of a husband whose wife has inquired into the cause of his melancholy and forgiven its offensive nature when confessed.

[SCENE VII.—*Field of battle between the camps.*]

Alarum. Drums and trumpets. Enter AGRIPPA and others.

Agr. Retire, we have engag'd ourselves too far:
Cæsar himself has work, and our oppression
Exceeds what we expected.   [*Exeunt.*

Alarums. Enter ANTONY, and SCARUS wounded.

Scar. O my brave emperor, this is fought indeed!
Had we done so at first, we had droven them home   5
With clouts about their heads.
Ant.   Thou bleed'st apace.
Scar. I had a wound here that was like a T,
But now 'tis made an H.   [*Retreat afar off.*
Ant.   They do retire.
Scar. We'll beat 'em into bench-holes, I have yet
Room for six scotches more.   10

Enter EROS.

Scene VII

S.D. *Enter . . . others.*] *Steevens, 1778; Enter Agrippa. F.*   2. *and our oppression*]
F; our opposition *Hanmer.*   8. *Retreat afar off*] *Capell; Far off. (after* heads,
line 6) *F.*

2. *our oppression*] †our difficulties—
but Hanmer's *opposition* is tempting.
[R]
4. *Scarus*] As Capell notes, the name
is not from Plutarch, the hero of this
sally being merely 'one of his [An-
tony's] men of armes.' The character,
as he further says, was a necessity, in
order to fill up the place about Antony
left vacant by Enobarbus.
6. *clouts*] cloths, bandages. The suggested 'cuffs', or 'blows' is not blood-
thirsty enough for Scarus or for the
wounds of the scene, received and
meditated (line 12).
8. *an H*] Scarus' jocular allusion to
the enlargement of his wound is supposed to include a play on *H* and *ache*,
once often pronounced alike. Cf. *Ado,*
III. iv. 55. There would be more con-

fidence about it if we could find any
particular reason for selecting T just
before. (†But a T with an extra stroke
(wound) at the bottom *is* an H on its
side, if we are thinking of printed
capitals. And see Dover Wilson's note
ad loc. giving Maunde Thompson's
comment on the minuscule letters in
'secretary' hand. [R]
9. *bench-holes*] holes of privies. Cf.
North-ward Hoe, 1607, v (Pearson's
Dekker, iii. 78): 'The Trab [i.e. *drab*]
will driue you (if she put you before
her) into a *pench hole*'; Fletcher,
Woman Pleased, IV. iii (Camb. VII.
291): 'That I were a Cat now, / Or
anything could run into a *Bench-hole.*'
Malone quotes Cecil's *Secret Correspondence* (ed. Lord Hailes, 1766): 'I will
leave it like an abort in a *bench-hole.*'

Eros. They are beaten, sir, and our advantage serves
　　　For a fair victory.
Scar.　　　　　　　　　Let us score their backs,
　　　And snatch 'em up, as we take hares, behind,
　　　'Tis sport to maul a runner.
Ant.　　　　　　　　　　　　I will reward thee
　　　Once for thy spritely comfort, and ten-fold　　　　15
　　　For thy good valour. Come thee on.
Scar.　　　　　　　　　　　I'll halt after.
　　　　　　　　　　　　　　　　　[Exeunt.

[SCENE VIII.—*Under the walls of Alexandria.*]

Alarum. Enter ANTONY *again, in a march;* SCARUS, *with others.*

Ant. We have beat him to his camp: run one before,
　　　And let the queen know of our gests: to-morrow
　　　Before the sun shall see's, we'll spill the blood
　　　That has to-day escap'd. I thank you all,
　　　For doughty-handed are you, and have fought　　　5
　　　Not as you serv'd the cause, but as't had been
　　　Each man's like mine: you have shown all Hectors.
　　　Enter the city, clip your wives, your friends,
　　　Tell them your feats, whilst they with joyful tears
　　　Wash the congealment from your wounds, and kiss　　10
　　　The honour'd gashes whole.

Enter CLEOPATRA.

　　　　　　[*To Scarus*] Give me thy hand;
　　　To this great fairy I'll commend thy acts,

---

13. hares, behind] *Theobald;* Hares behinde *F.*

Scene VIII

2. gests] *Theobald (Warburton);* guests *F.*　　11. *To Scarus*] *Rowe; not in F.*

15. *spritely*] cheerful, high-spirited. It has a 'solider' connotation than our modern rather effervescent one. Cf. IV. xiv. 52 *post, our sprightly port.*

Scene VIII

[See North, *post*, p. 270.]
2. *gests*] deeds. So Heywood, *The Exemplary Lives . . . of Nine, the most*

worthy Women of the World, 1640, sig. **3: 'Of History there be foure species, either taken from place, as Geography; from time, as Chronologie; from Generation, as Genealogie; or from *gests* really done,' etc.
8. *clip*] hug; as frequently. So in *Cor.*, I. vi. 29: 'O let me *clip* ye,' etc.
12. *fairy*] enchantress. Used of

Make her thanks bless thee. O thou day o' the world,
Chain mine arm'd neck, leap thou, attire and all,
Through proof of harness to my heart, and there 15
Ride on the pants triumphing!

Cleo. Lord of lords,
O infinite virtue, com'st thou smiling from
The world's great snare uncaught?

Ant. My nightingale,
We have beat them to their beds. What, girl, though grey
Do something mingle with our younger brown, yet ha' we 20
A brain that nourishes our nerves, and can
Get goal for goal of youth. Behold this man,
Commend unto his lips thy favouring hand:
Kiss it, my warrior: he hath fought to-day
As if a god in hate of mankind had 25
Destroy'd in such a shape.

Cleo. I'll give thee, friend,
An armour all of gold; it was a king's.

Ant. He has deserv'd it, were it carbuncled

---

18. My] *F2;* Mine *F.* 23. favouring] *Theobald;* savouring *F.*

Venus by Sylvester, *Du Bartas, The Magnificence,* ed. 1621, p. 461: 'But O, fair *Faëry,* who art thou?'; by Braithwaite, of a courtesan, *Strappado for the Diuell,* 1615, *The Conyburrow:* 'Now my (prodigious *faery*) that canst take / Vpon occasion a contrary shape'. In Shirley's *The Brothers,* II. i (*Works,* 1833, i. 217), Carlos says of a girl: 'Ha! turn away / That *fairy,* she's a witch, the count talks with her.' Delius says Cleopatra is so called as dispenser of the good fortune which Scarus had deserved by his valour, such being the light in which the fairies were regarded in Shakespeare's time.

15. *proof of harness*] proof-armour, in which sense *proof* alone usually appears. Cf. *Rom.,* I. i. 216: 'And in strong *proof* of chastity well arm'd.'

16. *Ride . . . triumphing*] Fletcher imitates this in *The False One,* IV. ii. 126: '*Cleo.* . . . I love with as much

ambition as a Conqueror, / And where I love, will triumph. / *Cæsar.* So you shall; / My heart shall be the chariot that shall bear ye,' etc. For the accentuation, *triumphing,* cf. *R3,* III. iv. 88.

17. *virtue*] valour (the Latin *virtus*), as in *Lr,* v. iii. 104: 'Trust to thy single *virtue,*' etc.

18. *world's great snare*] 'i.e. the war' (Steevens). (†less limited, I think, and nearer to 'all the snares the world can set.' [R])

19-20. *though grey . . . brown*] †in his present mood he can laugh about his greying hair: cf. III. xi. 13-15 *ante.* [R]

22. *Get goal . . . youth*] 'At all plays of barriers, the boundary is called a *goal*; to *win a goal* is to be a superior in a contest of activity' (Johnson).

25. *mankind*] 'Accented mostly on the last syllable in *Timon of Athens,* on the first in the other plays' (Schmidt).

28-9. *carbuncled . . . car*] Cf. *Cym.,*

Like holy Phœbus' car. Give me thy hand,
Through Alexandria make a jolly march,   30
Bear our hack'd targets like the men that owe them.
Had our great palace the capacity
To camp this host, we all would sup together,
And drink carouses to the next day's fate,
Which promises royal peril. Trumpeters,   35
With brazen din blast you the city's ear,
Make mingle with our rattling tabourines,
That heaven and earth may strike their sounds
      together,
Applauding our approach.   [*Exeunt.*

v. v. 190, 'a *carbuncle* of Phœbus' wheel.' In the description in Ovid, *Metam.* ii, which probably suggests the simile, the yoke of Phœbus' chariot is set with chrysolite and gems, his palace with carbuncles. See also Fairfax's *Tasso*, 1600, xvii. 34: 'Her chariot like *Auroraes* glorious waine, / With *Carbuncles* and Iacinthes glistred round.'

30. *jolly*] Professor Warwick Bond credits the word here with an approach to the 'sense of proud bearing,' in a note on *Shr.*, III. ii. 215 (Arden ed.), where he gives examples of *jolly* = arrogant, overbearing. This is possible; but the ordinary sense, as in 'Be jolly, lords,' II. vii. 59 *ante*, is, I think, more likely here.

31. *owe*] own, as very often. The whole line admits of two senses; Johnson's straightforward: 'Bear . . . with spirit and exultation, such as becomes the brave warriors that own them,' and Warburton's interpretation of 'hack'd targets,' etc., as = 'hack'd as much as the men to whom they belong.' Abbott (*Shakespearian Grammar*, §419a) includes the line as a probable case of such transposition of adjectival phrases.

34. *drink carouses*] drain bumpers. A German adverb *garaus* = right out is the ultimate source of *carouse*, etc., and underwent little or no modification at first as English adverb, verb,

noun. See, e.g. Fynes Moryson, *An Itinerary*, 1617, pt iii, p. 90: 'did at the very beginning of supper, drinke great *garausses*,' etc. B. Rich, *The Irish Hubbub* (see p. xix, Introduction to *The Honestie of this Age*, Percy Society, 1844) begins a description of '*Healths*' thus: 'In former ages they had no conceits whereby to draw on drunkennesse; their best was, I drinke to you, and I pledge yee, till at length some shallow-witted drunkard found out the *Carowse*, which shortly afterwards was turned into a hearty draught.' Each of the company drank a full cup quite out, or a carouse, in turn, after much ceremony and then, turning the cup bottom upward, 'in ostentation of his dexteritie,' filliped it 'to make it cry *Twango*.' 'Hearty draught' was a new name mockingly employed by the convivial, since *Quaffing* and *Carowsing* were reprobated. See Gascoigne, *A Delicate Diet for daintie mouthde Droonkardes*, 1576.

37. *tabourines*] Cf. *Troil.*, IV. v. 277. The commentators very naturally explain, 'small drums', but the tabourine appears to have been 'the full-sized military drum, corresponding to the modern side-drum,' while the tabor was a little drum, chiefly devoted to peaceful amusements. See Naylor, *Shakespeare and Music*, 1896, pp. 161–2, and Cowling, *Music on the Shakespearian Stage* (1913), c. iii, p. 42.

[SCENE IX.—*Cæsar's camp.*]

Enter a Sentry and his company; ENOBARBUS *follows.*

Sent. If we be not reliev'd within this hour,
　　　We must return to the court of guard: the night
　　　Is shiny, and they say we shall embattle
　　　By the second hour i' the morn.
First Watch.　　　　　　　　　This last day was
　　　A shrewd one to's.
Eno.　　　　　　　O bear me witness, night—　　　　5
Sec. Watch. What man is this?
First Watch.　　　　　　Stand close, and list him.
Eno. Be witness to me, O thou blessed moon,
　　　When men revolted shall upon record
　　　Bear hateful memory: poor Enobarbus did

Scene IX

† I have retained the stage-directions and speech-headings of F throughout the scene, with the exception of F's spelling '*Centerie*', and the additions of '*dies*' and '*with the body*,' though indeed the latter is so clearly implied in the text that it is hardly needed. The usual stage-directions, deriving from Capell and Malone, are an amusing example of what was apt to happen when the eighteenth-century editors really got to work. Capell started off with *Sentinels upon their posts*, distributed the speeches as he thought best among three '*soldiers*' (giving the first speech, oddly enough, to the third), but adhered to F by giving *Enter Enobarbus* at the beginning of the scene, instead of, like later editors, bringing him in just before his opening words in line 5.

Now, in the first place, *Sentinels upon their posts* is an impossible stage-direction for the Elizabethan curtain-less stage, which precluded ringing up on actors already in position, and on which everyone must 'enter.' In the second place, Shakespeare did not bring on just any three soldiers, but rather an N.C.O. and the two men

who with him were to form the sentry-group, and it is moderately clear from his speeches that the 'Sentry' is the leader. Lastly, Enobarbus' entry in line 5 is awkward, partly because he too patently enters merely to deliver his farewell speeches, and partly because an abrupt entry after the watchmen are more or less in position ought to be the occasion for a challenge. Shakespeare brought him wandering in almost on the heels of the group, so that when he begins to speak they might have fancied that he had been there before them. [R]

2. *court of guard*] guard-room, or other place of muster, as in *1H6*, II. i. 4; Heywood, ΓΥΝΑΙΚΕΙΟΝ, 1624, p. 408: 'his officers leave the *court of guard* and come to know the matter'; and cf. *Oth.*, II. iii. 218. According to *OED*, a perversion of *Corps de garde*, which came to mean guard-room, as well as the guard itself. In the original sense, it occurs several times in Greene's *Orlando Furioso* (*Works*, Dyce, ed. 1883, pp. 94–6), e.g. 'The *court-of-guard* is put unto the sword.' The forms *court de (du) guard* also occur.

5. *shrewd*] ill, curst; the old sense. So in *All's W.*, III. v. 68: 'a *shrewd* turn.'

Before thy face repent.

Sent.   Enobarbus?

Sec. Watch.   Peace!   10
  Hark further.

Eno. O sovereign mistress of true melancholy,
  The poisonous damp of night dispone upon me,
  That life, a very rebel to my will,
  May hang no longer on me. Throw my heart   15
  Against the flint and hardness of my fault,
  Which being dried with grief, will break to powder,
  And finish all foul thoughts. O Antony,
  Nobler than my revolt is infamous,
  Forgive me in thine own particular,   20
  But let the world rank me in register
  A master-leaver, and a fugitive:
  O Antony! O Antony!

First Watch.   Let's speak to him.

Sent. Let's hear him, for the things he speaks
  May concern Cæsar.

Sec. Watch.   Let's do so; but he sleeps.   25

Sent. Swoons rather, for so bad a prayer as his
  Was never yet for sleep.

First Watch.   Go we to him.

Sec. Watch. Awake, sir, awake, speak to us.

First Watch.   Hear you, sir?

Sent. The hand of death hath raught him.

                    [*Drums afar off.*] Hark, the drums
  Demurely wake the sleepers. Let us bear him   30

23.] *Rowe inserted S.D. 'Dies'; not in F.*

12. *O . . . melancholy*] the moon; so apostrophized for her 'wanne' face, and supposed influence in mental disease.

13. *dispone*] drop, as from a sponge. Browne, *Britannia's Pastorals*, I. ii. 239, has: 'The hand of Heaven his *spongy* clouds doth strain,' etc.

20. *in . . . particular*] as far as you yourself are concerned. Cf. I. iii. 54 *ante.*

22. *master-leaver*] it was a serious offence for an apprentice, or servant, to abscond.

fugitive] deserter, as in Latin.

27. *for*] a prelude to.

29. *raught*] = *reached*, but here most likely used in the further sense of *snatched away.* So *2H6*, II. iii. 43, and Middleton, *Mayor of Queenborough*, IV. ii. 154: 'I was surpris'd / By villains, and so *raught.*'

30. *Demurely*] solemnly (Warburton), soberly, gravely (Schmidt), in a subdued manner (*OED*). Perhaps the soldier inconsistently treats the mellowed sound, that reaches him at a

To th' court of guard: he is of note: our hour
Is fully out.
Sec. Watch. Come on then, he may recover yet.

[*Exeunt with the body.*

[SCENES X–XII.—*Between the two camps.*]

[SCENE X]

Enter ANTONY *and* SCARUS, *with their Army.*

Ant. Their preparation is to-day by sea,
We please them not by land.
Scar.   For both, my lord.
Ant. I would they'ld fight i' the fire, or i' the air,
We'ld fight there too. But this it is; our foot
Upon the hills adjoining to the city   5
Shall stay with us (order for sea is given,
They have put forth the haven),

33. S.D. *with the body*] *added by Capell.*

Scene x
6–7. us (order . . . haven)] *vs.* Order . . . Hauen: *F.*

distance, as if it were similarly heard by those in camp. Hanmer reads *din early wakes*; Collier MS and ed. 2, *Do early wake*; Dyce conjectures *Do merrily wake.*
31. *court of guard*] See on line 2 above.

Scene x
† Just as a reminder of the vexatiousness of modern scene-divisions with their 'Between the two camps'—'Another part of the same'—'Another part of the same,' I have omitted any further indications of place after the numbers of scenes xi and xii. [R]
6–7. (*order . . . haven*),] Most editors consider line 7 incomplete, and some out of many rash conjectures have even appeared in the text, as: *Further on*, Rowe; *Let's seek a spot*, Malone; *—forward, now*, Dyce, etc. If *Where* (line 8) has the force of *Whither*, as

most of them assume, the sense might be: They have . . . haven, *to a place where* we may best observe their array and watch their efforts; but *best* would be improbably applied save to Antony's choice of a vantage-point for observation, and bearing in mind that the situation is very like that in III. ix *ante*, *Where* in line 8, here, seems to refer to *hills* (line 5) almost as inevitably as *from which place* to *yond side o' the hill* in that passage. Like Staunton, who, nevertheless, believed line 7 incomplete, I tentatively adopt the parenthesis of Knight, Collier, and Singer, as affording a plain sense in a practically undisturbed text.
† R. G. White, though he used the reference to justify an insertion, refers, I think decisively, *against* the need for insertion, to the relevant passage in North (*post*, p. 271): 'he went to set those few footemen he had in order

Where their appointment we may best discover,
And look on their endeavour.   [*Exeunt.*

[SCENE XI]

Enter CÆSAR, *and his Army.*

Cæs. But being charg'd, we will be still by land,
Which, as I take it, we shall, for his best force
Is forth to man his galleys. To the vales,
And hold our best advantage.   [*Exeunt.*

[SCENE XII]

Alarum afar off, as at a sea-fight.

Enter ANTONY *and* SCARUS.

Ant. Yet they are not join'd: where yond pine does stand,

Scene XII

S.D. *Alarum* . . .] *F; placed later in scene by most edd. See note.*

---

upon the hills adjoyning unto the citie; and there he stoode to behold his gallies which departed from the haven.' [R]

Scene XI

1–2. *But . . . shall*] except being charged, etc., i.e. Unless we are assailed, we will remain quiescent by land, which I expect we shall be left to do. Cf. *but* as a preposition in such phrases as 'We were all *but* killed *or* being killed.'

4. *hold . . . advantage*] occupy the best position we can.

Scene XII

S.D. Alarum . . .] †Most editors have felt it necessary to transpose this S.D. either (as Dover Wilson) to just after Antony's exit at line 3, or (as Steevens and most others, but, I think, less happily) to just before his re-entry in line 9, on the grounds that it is an awkward opening to the scene, particularly in view of Antony's first words. Dover Wilson suggests that it

may have been written 'somewhat indefinitely' in the margin. This is no doubt possible, but since it is also quite possible that its position represents Shakespeare's intention, it is worth examining the point, not least because it well illustrates the troubles that are sometimes created by the post-Elizabethan division into scenes. F prints as follows:

> . . . our best advantage.   *exeunt.*
> *Alarum afarre off, as at a Sea-fight.*
> *Enter Anthony, and Scarrus.*
> *Ant.* Yet they are . . .

That is to say, the S.D. does not belong to either 'scene,' but occupies the empty-stage interval between *exeunt* and *Enter*. And we may, if we like, assume that the producer faded out the alarum just before Antony's entrance, so that his opening words are not absurd, but the audience knows that he is wrong, which has a certain effectiveness. [R]

1. *pine*] The conspicuous tree probably supplies Antony with the meta-

I shall discover all: I'll bring thee word
Straight, how 'tis like to go.   [*Exit.*

Scar.   Swallows have built
In Cleopatra's sails their nests. The augurers
Say, they know not, they cannot tell, look grimly,   5
And dare not speak their knowledge. Antony
Is valiant, and dejected, and by starts
His fretted fortunes give him hope and fear
Of what he has, and has not.

Re-enter ANTONY.

Ant.   All is lost:
This foul Egyptian hath betrayed me: 10
My fleet hath yielded to the foe, and yonder
They cast their caps up, and carouse together
Like friends long lost. Triple-turn'd whore, 'tis thou
Hast sold me to this novice, and my heart

4. augurers] *Capell;* Auguries *F.*

phor for himself in line 23 below, as
Thiselton notes. His further deduc-
tions I cannot follow.

3. *Swallows*, etc.] This omen is transferred from before Actium. See North,
post, p. 262; and for the rest of the
scene, p. 271.

4. *augurers*] †I have adopted the
usual emendation of F's *auguries*.
There are no doubt plenty of places in
Shakespeare where an abstract is used
for a concrete, but seldom, I think,
where the abstract is immediately followed by a run of verbs which seem to
demand a concretely personal subject.
But I rather suspect that the true reading is *augures*, a Latin plural, like 'pyramides' in v. ii. 61. [R]

8. *fretted*] chequered. To *fret* is to
interlace, and the noun *fret*—originally, a grille or grating—signifies
heraldic or architectural ornament
partaking of the nature of trelliswork.
Hence the figurative use in the text to
express mingled or varied fortune, a
sense which the context seems to indicate in preference to that of *harassed*,

impaired, from the verb *fret* = gnaw,
corrode. In *Cæs.*, II. i. 104: 'and yon
grey lines / That *fret* the clouds are
messengers of day' we encounter the
word in the like, though not figurative,
sense of chequer, variegate.

8–9. *hope and fear Of . . . not*] i.e.
probably, hope of keeping and fear of
losing the power he still has, and hope
of recovering and fear of not recovering what he has no longer. It seems
better not to apply hope and fear
separately, that is to *has not* and *has*
respectively, supposing an irregular
correspondency as in IV. xv. 25–6 *post*.

13. *Triple-turn'd*] Cf. III. xiii. 116–18
ante. Staunton's acuteness reconciled
this epithet with the fact that Cleopatra had more than three lovers, if
Octavius was to be reckoned as one.
He says: 'From Julius Cæsar to Cneius
Pompey, from Pompey to Antony,
and, as he suspects now, from him to
Octavius Cæsar.' Previous commentators had disputed as to whether
Pompey or Octavius was to be left out
of the application.

Makes only wars on thee. Bid them all fly: 15
For when I am reveng'd upon my charm,
I have done all. Bid them all fly, be gone.   [*Exit Scarus.*
O sun, thy uprise shall I see no more,
Fortune and Antony part here, even here
Do we shake hands. All come to this? The hearts   20
That spaniel'd me at heels, to whom I gave
Their wishes, do discandy, melt their sweets
On blossoming Cæsar: and this pine is bark'd,
That overtopp'd them all. Betray'd I am.
O this false soul of Egypt! this grave charm,   25
Whose eye beck'd forth my wars, and call'd them
    home;
Whose bosom was my crownet, my chief end,

17. *Exit Scarus*] *Capell; not in F.*   20. hands.] *Capell; hands? F.*   21. spaniel'd]
Hanmer; pannelled F.

16. *charm*] abstract for concrete,
charmer or enchantress. Cf. *charmer* =
enchantress in *Oth.*, III. iv. 58, and
charm, line 25, *spell*, line 30 *post*.

21. *spaniel'd*] In support of this
emendation of Hanmer's Tolet urges
the frequent spelling *spannel* for *spaniel*
[see, e.g., *spannell* in Lyly's *Campaspe*, v.
i] and quotes *MND.*, II. i. 203 *et seq.*:
'I am your *spaniel*,' etc. Halliwell supplies an example closely resembling
the text, from Copley's *Fig for Fortune*,
1596, p. 64: 'I *spanield* after Cate-
chrysius' foot.' Cf. also *The Buggbears*,
II. i. 19–20 (*Early Plays from the Italian*,
1911, R. Warwick Bond, p. 99): '. . .
they shold not run & lackie like
spaniells at my stirrop, but shold ride
everye iornye,' etc.; and Pepys' Diary,
26 May 1660: 'My Lord dined with
the Vice-Admiral to-day (who is as
officious, poor man! as any spaniel can
be.)' Upton defended F *pannelled* on
the ground that a panel of wainscot,
being inset, comes behind the main
surface; and Theobald, more reasonably, adopted Warburton's conjecture
pantler'd me for 'ran after me like footmen or pantlers,' comparing the contemptuous application of the noun in

Cym., II. iii. 129. But, as has been
observed, *pantler* does not mean servant
or footman, and therefore one likely to
follow at heel, but the servant who has
the care of bread.

22. *discandy*] See on III. xiii. 165 *ante*.
23. *bark'd*] stripped, and so destroyed.
25. *grave charm*] Steevens: 'deadly or
destructive piece of witchcraft.' Pope
changed the epithet to *gay*, but *grave* in
the above or some allied sense is far
more beautiful and appropriate than
this or other suggestions, as *great*
(Collier MS), *grand* (Singer, ed. 2),
brave (Deighton conj.). In support of it
Steevens adduces two passages from
Chapman's Homer, viz. *Iliad*, xix, and
Odyssey, xxii [see Herne Shepherd's
ed., 1875, pp. 237*b*, 510*b*], containing
'thy *grave* ruin' and 'Their *grave* steel'
respectively. It is also possible, especially in view of the next line, that the
word = potent or commanding.
Chapman (*Odyssey*, xxii, *ibid.*, p. 509*b*]
makes Minerva say to Ulysses:
'Priam's broad way'd town / By thy
grave parts was sack'd and over-
thrown.'

27. *crownet*] i.e. coronet: the object

Like a right gipsy, that at fast and loose
Beguil'd me, to the very heart of loss.
What, Eros, Eros!

Enter CLEOPATRA.

            Ah, thou spell! Avaunt!   30
Cleo. Why is my lord enrag'd against his love?
Ant. Vanish, or I shall give thee thy deserving,
   And blemish Cæsar's triumph. Let him take thee,
   And hoist thee up to the shouting plebeians,

and reward of my toils. Cf. the use of *crown*, in various senses of fulfilment and superlativeness, in IV. xv. 63 *post*; Chapman's Homer (Steevens's reference), *Iliad*, ii [ed. Herne Shepherd, 1875, p. 33*a*]: 'and all things have their *crown*'; *ibid.*, p. 29*b*: 'We fly, not putting on the *crown* of our so long held war.' The form *crownet* recurs in v. ii. 91 *post*; in Peele, *Arraignment of Paris*, I. i. 76: 'Her robes, her lawns, her *crownet*, and her mace'; and often.

28–9. *Like a right . . . of loss*] †An interesting example of differences of punctuation. The accepted modern punctuation is: 'Like a right gipsy, hath, at fast and loose, / Beguil'd me to the very heart of loss.' I think that F, throwing heavier emphasis on to the last six words, is more effective. [R]

   28. *right*] true, typical.

   gipsy] Hawkins notes 'a kind of pun . . . arising from the corruption of the word *Ægyptian* into *gipsy*.' The gipsies were falsely supposed from Egypt: hence this name *via* Middle English *Egyptien*, and *Gipsen*, instanced by Skeat, *Etymol. Dict.*, from Spenser, *Mother Hubberd's Tale*, line 86. See *Oth.*, III. iv. 57, and Jonson, *The Gipsies Metamorphos'd*, First Song (line 124): 'Thus the Ægyptians throng in clusters'; and other passages as line 60: 'Gaze upon them, as on the offspring of Ptolemy, begotten upon several Cleopatras,' and: 'And Queene *Cleopatra*, / The *gipsyes* grand-matra' (the Patrico's

speech, line 173). Egyptian may still be heard for gipsy among the lower classes.

   fast and loose] a cheating game thus described by Sir I. Hawkins (1821 Variorum): 'A leathern belt is made up into a number of intricate folds, and placed edgewise upon a table. One of the folds is made to represent the middle of the girdle, so that whoever should thrust a skewer into it would think he held it fast to the table; whereas, when he has so done, the person with whom he plays may take hold of both ends, and draw it away.' There is a play on the game and hanging in Whetstone's *1 Promos and Cassandra*, II. v: 'Heare are new ropes: how are my knots? I faith syr, slippery. / At *fast or loose* with my Giptian, I mean to have a cast'; and again in Harvey's *The Trimming of Thomas Nashe Gentleman*, etc., 1597, near the end. The name was applied to any trick of apparent knots, and its figurative use is as familiar today as ever. Cf. also *LLL.*, I. ii. 162, III. i. 109; and Suckling, 'Upon my Lord Brohall's Wedding': 'How weak is lover's law! / The bonds made there (like gipsies' knots) with ease / Are *fast and loose*, as they that hold them please.'

   29. *heart of loss*] So Jonson, *Sejanus*, I. 250: 'I do not know / The *heart* of his designs.'

   34. *plebeians*] The accent is similarly on the first syllable in *Cor.*, I. ix. 7; v. iv. 40.

Follow his chariot, like the greatest spot   35
Of all thy sex. Most monster-like be shown
For poor'st diminutives, for dolts, and let
Patient Octavia plough thy visage up
With her prepared nails.   [*Exit Cleopatra.*
                              'Tis well th' art gone,
If it be well to live. But better 'twere   40
Thou fell'st into my fury, for one death
Might have prevented many. Eros, ho!
The shirt of Nessus is upon me, teach me,
Alcides, thou mine ancestor, thy rage.
Let me lodge Lichas on the horns o' the moon,   45

35. *spot*] Cf. Bunyan, *The Pilgrim's Progress*: 'They say you are a spot among Christians, and that Religion fareth the worse.'

36. *monster-like*] like a 'curiosity' (fat woman, child with six toes, etc.) at a travelling show. Cf. *Tp.*, II. ii. 29–36; *Mac.*, v. vii. 54: 'We'll have thee, as our rarer monsters are, / Painted upon a pole, and underwrit, "Here may you see the tyrant."'

37. *For . . . diminutives, for dolts*] to poor undersized weaklings, to fools. Though some who accept Thirlby's ingenious *doits* for *dolts* also explain *diminutives* thus, with most editors the change involves interpreting *diminutives* as small pieces of money, for which no instance is adduced; whereas as applied to persons, we have 'Such a *diminutive?*' (Chapman, *Byron's Conspiracy*, v. i. 88), *diminutives of nature* (*Troil.*, v. i. 38). The change also rather interrupts the sequence of ideas, which seems wholly concerned with (1) the triumph; (2) the vengeance of Octavia, as is the case also in later reminiscences of the passage; one in general terms, IV. xv. 23–9 *post*, and two in particular, v. ii. 52–7, and 207 *et seq. post*, all of which persuade that the showing is in the procession and in that only, maugre a reference in the last to puppet-shows, of which—as Gifford says—shows of monsters were the constant concomitants. Certain

passages alone cause hesitation, viz. *Tp.*, II. ii. 29–35, concluding: 'when they will not give a doit to relieve a lame beggar, they will lay out ten to see a dead Indian'; and this new one (Chapman, *Bussy D'Ambois*, III. i. 26): 'the sly charms / Of the witch Policy makes him [i.e. sin] like a monster / Kept only to show men for servile money:' etc. This passage immediately follows that which corresponds with IV. xiv. 2–7 *post* (see note there), and increases the probabilities in favour of *doits*; but such do not justify tampering with a text clear and reasonable in sense as it stands.

39. *prepared*] 'Suffered to grow for this purpose,' as Warburton says, or may be, sharpened.

43. *shirt of Nessus*] Hercules shot the centaur Nessus with a poisoned arrow. Nessus gave Deianira, Hercules' wife, a shirt soaked with his poisoned blood for use at need as a love charm. Sent to Hercules later, it caused his torture and self-destruction. See on 45 *infra*.

44. *mine ancestor*] See on I. iii. 84 *ante*.

45. *Let . . . Lichas . . . moon*] Lichas, who innocently brought the shirt to Hercules, was flung skyward by his infuriated master, and fell into the sea, after being turned into pebble-stone by the force of his despatch. See Golding, Ovid's *Metam.*, bk ix, and for a dramatization of the story, Heywood's *Brazen Age*. In *The Actor's Vindication*,

And with those hands that grasp'd the heaviest club,
Subdue my worthiest self. The witch shall die,
To the young Roman boy she hath sold me, and I fall
Under this plot: she dies for 't. Eros, ho!   [*Exit.*

[SCENE XIII.—*Alexandria. Cleopatra's palace.*]

Enter CLEOPATRA, CHARMIAN, IRAS, MARDIAN.

Cleo. Help me, my women! O, he's more mad
Than Telamon for his shield, the boar of Thessaly
Was never so emboss'd.

Scene XIII

1. he's] *F* (hee's); he is *F2.*

n.d., p. 30, Heywood relates the story
of Julius Cæsar's realistic personation
of Hercules, even to the actual slaying
of the representative of Lichas. Cf. for
the hyperbole in the text for extreme
height, *Cor.*, I. i. 219, and Fletcher,
The Sea Voyage, I. i. 5: 'I saw a Dolphin
hang i' the *horns o' th' moon,* / Shot from
a wave.' etc. Warburton thought it
derived in this case from Seneca's
Hercules Oetæus. John Studley translates: 'With Lycas thus his labours end
throwne vp to heauen they say, / That
with his dropping bloud the cloudes he
stayned all the way' (*Seneca, His Tenne
Tragedies,* etc., 1581, p. 201).

47. *worthiest*] Rolfe explains '*worthiest* of being *subdued* or destroyed'; but
Antony in lines 45–7 expresses the fury
he seeks to show, in terms of the actions
of his ancestor, the last of which was to
destroy himself. His own 'worth' (i.e.
his heroic nature) is, therefore, that of
Hercules: but, apart from that, there
is no reason why he should not assert it
in a passage expressive of rage and
resentment, and not of humiliation.

48. *young Roman boy*] † The line is
hypermetric, and though it is possible
to regularize it by a slurring rapidity of
delivery, that seems not consonant
with the rest of the speech. We should
perhaps omit *young*, conjecturing that

Shakespeare first wrote *young boy*, then
saw that it was redundant, and that
Roman boy would give a double point
(betrayal to one who was both an
enemy and a mere boy), wrote in
Roman but did not make clear his
deletion of *young.* [R]

Scene XIII

2. *Telamon*] Ajax Telamon, who
went mad and slew himself when
Ulysses, and not he, was awarded the
armour and famous shield of Achilles
as bravest of the Greeks. Heywood
treats the story in *The Iron Age*, pt i,
Act v.

boar of Thessaly] The boar—whose
'eies did glister bloud and fire' (Golding, Ovid's *Metam.*, bk viii)—sent by
Diana in revenge for omitted sacrifices
to ravage the territories of the king
of Caledon, and slain by his son
Meleager, the brother of Deianira.
The story is one of the themes of
Heywood's *Brazen Age.*

3. *emboss'd*] a term of the chase,
sometimes used merely for 'driven to
extremity', sometimes to signify that
the quarry showed signs of exhaustion
by foaming at the mouth. Cf. *1 King
Edward IV* (Pearson's *Heywood*, i. 40):
'*Dutch.* Cam'st thou not downe the
wood? *Hobs.* Yes mistriss; that I did.

Char.   To the monument,
There lock yourself, and send him word you are dead.
The soul and body rive not more in parting   5
Than greatness going off.
Cleo.   To the monument!
Mardian, go tell him I have slain myself:
Say, that the last I spoke was 'Antony,'
And word it, prithee, piteously. Hence, Mardian,
And bring me how he takes my death to the
monument.   [*Exeunt.*   10

[SCENE XIV.—*The same. Another room.*]

Enter ANTONY *and* EROS.

Ant. Eros, thou yet behold'st me?
Eros.   Ay, noble lord.
Ant. Sometime we see a cloud that's dragonish,

---

10. death to the monument.] *F* (to' th') *; death; To the monument! Pope.*

Dutch. And sawest thou not the deere *imbost?*' with Lyly, *Midas*, IV. iii. 26: '*Pet.* There was a boy leasht on the single because when he was *imbost*, he tooke soyle. *Licio.* What's that? *Pet.* Why, a boy was beaten on the taile with a leathern thong, bicause when he fomde at the mouth with running, he went into the water'; and P. Fletcher, Psalm xlii (*Poems*, ed. Grosart, iii. 248): 'Look as an hart with sweat and bloud embrued / Chas'd and *embost*, thirsts in the soil to be.' In our text are meant the similar tokens of rage. The term is often applied to animals other than the quarry, and to men, in the sense of 'spent,' 'visibly heated by exertion.' So in *Shr.*, Ind. i. 17, 'the poor cur is emboss'd' and *Albumazar*, v. ii. 12 (Hazlitt's *Dodsley*, xi. 406): 'I am *emboss'd* / With trotting all the streets to find Pandolfo'; and *Swetnam the Woman Hater* (1620), I. ii: 'Hast thou been running for a wager, Sirrah? / Thou art horribly *imbost.*' While both senses at the head of this note are

thought to derive from a verb whose primary sense is 'to take shelter in a wood,' the second of the two is probably influenced by another verb *emboss*, to form protuberances, or bosses, to which blobs of foam have some resemblance. See *OED, s.v.*

3–4. *To the monument*, etc.] See North, *post*, p. 271.

5–6. *The soul . . . off*] Malone compares *H8* [II. iii. 12–16]. The idea in line 5 also occurs in *Arden of Feversham*, III. i. 19–20, and Chapman, *Bussy D'Ambois*, II. ii (Parrott I. 564*b*): 'I must utter that / That will in parting breake more strings in me, / Than death when life parts;' etc.

10. † I have, with some hesitation, retained F's punctuation. It makes good sense, but Pope's emendation does undoubtedly provide a more emphatic exit. [R]

Scene XIV

2–7. *Sometime we see*, etc.] Several passages have been suggested as the

A vapour sometime, like a bear, or lion,
A tower'd citadel, a pendent rock,
A forked mountain, or blue promontory   5
With trees upon 't, that nod unto the world,
And mock our eyes with air. Thou hast seen these signs,
They are black vesper's pageants.

Eros.   Ay, my lord.

Ant. That which is now a horse, even with a thought
The rack dislimns, and makes it indistinct   10

4. tower'd] *Rowe;* toward *F.*   10. dislimns] *Theobald;* dislimes *F.*

source of this fancy, but its beautiful
and striking use to illustrate man's unstable hold of his very entity seems
to occur here only. The passages are
Aristophanes, *Nubes,* 346 [in Theobald's version, *The Clouds,* 1715, p. 20:
'In looking upon the Sky, have you
never seen a Cloud resemble a Centaur, a Leopard, a Wolf or a Bull?']
(Sir W. Rawlinson); Holland's Pliny,
Natural History, II. iii, where the shapes
are of chariot, bear, bull (Steevens);
Chapman's *Monsieur D'Olive,* II. ii. 91:
'our great men / Like to a mass of
clouds that now seem like / An elephant, and straightways like an ox, /
And then a mouse,' etc. (Steevens);
where, indeed, as in the text, the
dwindling of the great is expressed;
Chapman's *Bussy D'Ambois,* III. i. 23–5,
where the shapes are dragons, lions,
elephants (Malone); *A Treatise of
Spectres,* etc., 4to, 1605: 'The *cloudes*
sometimes will seem to be monsters,
lions, bulls, and wolves; painted and
figured albeit . . . nothing but a
moyst humour mounted in the ayre,' etc.
(Malone). I have met with passages
anterior to these last in Sylvester's *Du
Bartas* (1598), *The Imposture* (in 1621
ed., p. 189): 'For, as the Air, with
scattred clouds bespred, / Is heer and
there black, yellow, white and red, /
Resembling Armies, Monsters, Moun-
tains, Dragons, / Rocks, fiery Castles,
Forrests, Ships, and Wagons, / And
such to vs through glass transparent
clear / From form to form varying it
doth appear:' etc.; and Fairfax's

Tasso, 1600, bk xvi, st. 69: 'As oft the
clouds frame shapes of castles great /
Amid the aire, that little time do last, /
But are dissolu'd by winde or Titans
heat'; etc. Examples later than *Ant.*
occur in Ford, etc., *The Witch of Ed-
monton,* v. i. 15; *The City Nightcap,* IV. i
(Bullen's *Davenport,* p. 150).

8. *pageants*] The following from
Whetstone's *2 Promos* and *Cassandra,*
1578, I. v (Nichols, *Six Old Plays,* 1779,
p. 65), explains the allusion: '*Phallax.*
With what strange showes doo they
their *Pageaunt* grace? / *Bedell.* They have
Hercules of monsters conquerying, /
Huge great *Giants* in a forest fighting /
With *Lyons, Beares, Wolves, Apes, Foxes,*
and *Grayes,* / *Baiards, Brockes,* &c.'
According to Singer, Boswell somewhere (not in 1821 Variorum) cites
'the following apposite passage from a
sermon by Bishop Hall': 'I feare some
of you are like the *pageants* of your
great solemnities, wherein there is a
show of a solid body, whether of a lion,
or elephant, or unicorne; but if they be
curiously look'd into, there is nothing
but cloth, and sticks, and ayre.'
Pageants were originally the movable
stages on which Miracle Plays were
represented, then the plays themselves, and so moving shows or
spectacles in general.

9. *even with a thought*] as fast as
thought. So in *Cæs.,* v. iii. 19: 'I will be
here again, *even with a thought.*'

10. *The rack dislimns*] the drifting
clouds efface. Cf. Jonson, *Masque of
Hymen:* 'Here the upper part of the

As water is in water.

Eros. 　　　　　　It does, my lord.

Ant. My good knave Eros, now thy captain is
Even such a body: here I am Antony,
Yet cannot hold this visible shape, my knave.
I made these wars for Egypt, and the queen,　　　　15
Whose heart I thought I had, for she had mine:
Which whilst it was mine, had annex'd unto't
A million moe, now lost: she, Eros, has
Pack'd cards with Cæsar, and false-play'd my glory
Unto an enemy's triumph.　　　　　　20

---

18. moe] *F;* more *Rowe and many edd.*　　19. Cæsar] *Rowe;* Caesars *F.*

scene, which was all of clouds and made artificially to swell, and ride like the *rack*, began to open:' etc. *Dislimns* reverses *limns* (i.e. *paints*), and is not found elsewhere till imitated in the nineteenth century. See *OED.*

12. *knave*] boy, servant, as often; the former is the original meaning.

15. *Egypt*] Cleopatra. So in I. iii. 41, 78 *ante*, etc.

18. *moe*] more *in number*, while *more* referred to degree. Originally an adverbial comparative.

19. *Pack'd . . . Cæsar*] ensured good hands for herself and Cæsar by false dealing, i.e. treacherously conspired with Cæsar. Cf. Cartwright, *The Ordinary*, 1651, II. iii, p. 28: 'For Cards you may . . . without the cut or shuffle, / Or the *packt* trick, have what you will yourself'; Southey, *Commonplace Book*, 4th series, 1850, p. 275: 'The Lady Cheatabell, playing at hunt the Knave out of town, *packed* the cards, and gave herself the Knave of Hearts, being Jack'; and for a figurative use, as in the text, *The Parliament of Criticks*, 12mo, 1702, p. 16: 'The *Cards* are *pack'd* by Authority, and Dominion turns up what *Trump* it pleases.' We still speak of *packing* a jury. Thiselton observes that 'knave' and 'queen' (lines 14, 15) possibly suggested the metaphor from cards.

19–20. *false-play'd . . . triumph*] Warburton was probably right in seeing in

triumph—as well as the obvious sense— an allusion to the trump card, or *triumph* as it was originally called. Cf. French *triomphe*. Halliwell cites Cotgrave, who has 'Triomphe: f. The card-game called Ruffe, or Trump; also the Ruffe, or Trump at it' [1660 ed.]; and Warburton's reference to Latimer's *Sermons on the Card* yields: 'The game that we will play at shall be called the *triumph*,' etc. (Parker Society ed., p. 8): 'Let therefore every christian man and woman play at these cards, that they may have and obtain the *triumph*; you must mark also that the *triumph* must apply to fetch home unto him all the other cards, whatsoever suit they be of' (pp. 8–9). Later on he employs 'trump' (pp. 12, 13), but so that we may identify it with the triumph, that fetches 'home the other cards'; 'Now turn up your trump, your heart (hearts is trump, as I said before), and cast your trump, your heart, on this card'; etc. The objection of Malone and others that playing false to an *adversary*'s trump would be meaningless here, does not hold. Cæsar, in Antony's view, is only *in show* Cleopatra's adversary. Ostensibly Antony's partner, Cleopatra not only unfairly helps Cæsar to secure good cards, but *false-plays* those in her own power (involving Antony's glory) to encounter them. The form *triump* occurs in *The Interlude*

Nay, weep not, gentle Eros, there is left us
Ourselves to end ourselves.

Enter MARDIAN.

                              O, thy vile lady!
She has robb'd me of my sword.
Mar.   No, Antony.
My mistress lov'd thee, and her fortunes mingled
With thine entirely.
Ant.   Hence, saucy eunuch, peace!   25
She hath betray'd me, and shall die the death.
Mar. Death of one person can be paid but once,
        And that she has discharg'd. What thou wouldst do
        Is done unto thy hand: the last she spake
        Was 'Antony! most noble Antony!'   30
        Then in the midst a tearing groan did break
        The name of Antony; it was divided
        Between her heart, and lips: she render'd life
        Thy name so buried in her.
Ant.   Dead, then?
Mar.   Dead.
Ant. Unarm, Eros, the long day's task is done,   35

35. Unarm] Vnarme *F;* Unarm me *Rowe and many edd.*

of Youth (Hazlitt's *Dodsley*, II. 34):
'Also at the cards I can teach you to
play, At the *triump* and one-and-thirty,
Post, pinion, and also aums-ace,' etc.
Whiter quotes Jonson, *The Fortunate
Isles*, line 362: 'Except the four knaves
entertained for the guards, / Of the
kings and the queens that *triumph* in
the cards.'

26. *die the death*] See on *Cym.*, IV. ii.
96, and *MND.*, I. i. 65, in Arden
Shakespeare.

31–4. *Then in the midst*, etc.] The like
of this is cleverly ridiculed by Sheridan
in *The Critic*, near the end: '*Whisk*. . . .
And Whiskerandos quits this bustling
scene / For all eter——— *Beef*. ———nity
—he would have added, but stern
death / Cut short his being, and the
noun at once!' and cf. *1H4*, v. iv.
86.

35. *Unarm*] See North, *post*, p. 272.
Unarm, Eros] † It is one of the curi-
osities of editing that so many editors
(Dover Wilson indeed, though erro-
neously, says 'all editors') have followed Rowe in reading *Unarm me,
Eros*, and even more remarkable that
the arguments pro and con have been
almost entirely metrical. The emendation is, of course, graphically easy, and
the intrusive *me*, though I think it produces a rhythm less suiting to the
context, is metrically quite defensible
(it is more awkward if we are pro-
nouncing the name as Ērŏs rather than
Ĕrōs). But it changes the force of Antony's words. They are more general
(like the echo, *the bright day is done*, in
v. ii. 192) than a command to unarm
him. He is saying 'All is over; our
"occupation's gone".' [R]

And we must sleep. [*To Mar.*] That thou depart'st
  hence safe
Does pay thy labour richly; go.   [*Exit Mardian.*
                                Off, pluck off,
The seven-fold shield of Ajax cannot keep
The battery from my heart. O, cleave, my sides!
Heart, once be stronger than thy continent,   40
Crack thy frail case! Apace, Eros, apace!
No more a soldier: bruised pieces, go,
You have been nobly borne. From me awhile.
                                    [*Exit Eros.*
I will o'ertake thee, Cleopatra, and
Weep for my pardon. So it must be, for now   45
All length is torture: since the torch is out,

36. *To Mar.*] *Globe; not in F.*

38. *seven-fold shield of Ajax*] the shield
of brass, backed with seven folds of
ox-hide, which defied the lance of
Hector (Homer, *Iliad*, vii. 222, 245,
etc.): 'Six folds th' untamed dart
strook through, and in the *seventh*
tough hide / The point was check'd'
(see Chapman's *Homer*, 1598, ed. R. H.
Shepherd, 1875, pp. 95–6). See also
Ovid, *Metam.*, xiii. 2: 'The owner of
the *seauenfold shield*, to these did Ajax
rise' (Golding, ed. 1593).

39. *The battery . . . heart*] The sense
generally received here is Boswell's:
'the battery proceeding from my
heart, which is strong enough to break
through the seven-fold shield of Ajax,'
which depends on the ensuing 'O
cleave,' etc. However probable, it is,
nevertheless, as I think, unconvincing.
The sense of oppression from the
heart's agitation would explain 'Off,
pluck off' if it stood alone, but it is
natural to suppose it repeats the
thought in 'Unarm, Eros,' etc., line 35,
the source of which is entirely different. If that be so, it is as safe to interpret
'No external arms—even the strongest
—can defend me from the assault of
such a calamity as this,' regarding line
35 and disregarding line 39 ('O cleave,'

etc.), as to regard the latter and disregard the former with Boswell. Cf.
Kyd, *The Spanish Tragedie*, i. iii. 57:
'My *hart* growne hard gainst mischiefes
battery.' A shield, moreover, is not so
placed as to curb inward batteries. We
should rather expect a reference to
armour, as in i. i. 6–8 *ante*, and Marston, *i Antonio and Mellida*, v. i. 311,
where Andrugio, entering 'in armour',
says: 'And twere not hoopt with steele,
my brest wold break.'

40–1. *Heart . . . case*] For this appeal,
cf. *Lr*, ii. iv. 200: 'O sides, you are too
tough.' †Antony is not asking his
heart to break (as in *Lr*, v. iii. 314) but
to have for once the strength to break
out into freedom from the confining
body. [R]

40. *thy continent*] what contains thee.
So *Lr*, iii. ii. 57: 'close pent-up guilts /
Rive your concealing *continents*,' etc.
Sandys, *A Paraphrase*, etc., 1638, *Job*,
chap. xxxii, p. 41: 'My Bowels boyle
like wine that hath no vent; / Ready to
breake the swelling *Continent*.'

46. *length*] i.e. of time *or* life, duration. So in *R2*, v. i. 94: 'there is such
length in grief,' etc.

torch] i.e. the light of his life's travel,
Cleopatra.

Lie down and stray no farther. Now all labour
Mars what it does: yea, very force entangles
Itself with strength: seal then, and all is done.
Eros!—I come, my queen:—Eros!—Stay for me,   50
Where souls do couch on flowers, we'll hand in hand,
And with our sprightly port make the ghosts gaze:
Dido, and her Æneas, shall want troops,
And all the haunt be ours. Come, Eros, Eros!

Re-enter EROS.

Eros. What would my lord?
Ant.   Since Cleopatra died,   55
I have liv'd in such dishonour that the gods
Detest my baseness. I, that with my sword
Quarter'd the world, and o'er green Neptune's back
With ships made cities, condemn myself, to lack
The courage of a woman, less noble mind   60

48–9. *very force . . . strength*] even the power of strength serves only to embarrass it. Dover Wilson well compares *Sonn.* xxiii, lines 3–4, 7–8.

49. *seal then*, etc.] For the metaphor from sealing and thus *completing* agreements, cf. *H5*, iv. vi. 26; *Ham.*, iii. ii. 41; Daniel, *Cleopatra*, iv, line 1024 (*Works*, ed. Grosart, vol. iii): 'My blood must *seale* th' assurance of his state.'

51. *Where souls . . . flowers*, etc.] So in a delightful passage depicting 'deaths Ioyes' in *Nero*, 1624, iv [Scene vii] (Bullen's *Old Plays*, i. 81): 'Mingled with that faire company shall we / On bankes of *Violets* and of *Hiacinths*, / Of loves devising, sit and gently sport'; etc. With *couch*, cf. *Ado*, iii. i. 45: 'as fortunate a bed, / As ever Beatrice shall *couch* upon.'

52. *sprightly*] high-spirited, full of vitality—stronger and more dignified than our 'spritely.' Cf. iv. vii. 15 *ante*.

53. *Dido, and her Æneas*] Successive commentators tell us that Shakespeare forgot that Virgil (*Æneid*, vi. 467–74) consorts Dido with her husband, Sichæus, in Hades, and makes her

repel Æneas during his visit to the shades. But Shakespeare was not likely, any more than others, to uncouple a famous pair of lovers for a pedantic scruple. Theobald long ago quoted the jailor's daughter in *The Two Noble Kinsmen*, iv. iii. 16: 'For in the next world will *Dido* see *Palamon*, and then will she be out of love with *Æneas*.' The ingenious author of *Nero*, in the passage quoted in the last note, even reconciles Lucrece and Tarquin in Elysium; and Thomas May, *Antony and Cleopatra*, v. 1639, sig. D12, makes Antony say: 'I'll follow thee, / And beg thy pardon in the other world. / All crimes are there for evermore forgot. / There *Ariadne* pardons *Theseus* falsehood, / *Dido* forgives the perjur'd Prince of Troy, / And *Troilus* repentant *Cressida*.'

54. *all the haunt be ours*] not 'we shall possess all the region,' but 'we shall be the people run after.'

Re-enter Eros] For the rest of the scene, cf. North, *post*, p. 272.

60. *less noble mind*] probably in apposition with *I*, line 57, in which case there is scarcely need to suppose any

Than she which by her death our Cæsar tells
'I am conqueror of myself.' Thou art sworn, Eros,
That when the exigent should come, which now
Is come indeed: when I should see behind me
The inevitable prosecution of   65
Disgrace and horror, that, on my command,
Thou then wouldst kill me. Do't, the time is come:
Thou strik'st not me, 'tis Cæsar thou defeat'st.
Put colour in thy cheek.

Eros.   The gods withhold me,
Shall I do that which all the Parthian darts,   70
Though enemy, lost aim, and could not?

Ant.   Eros,
Wouldst thou be window'd in great Rome, and see
Thy master thus with pleach'd arms, bending down
His corrigible neck, his face subdued
To penetrative shame; whilst the wheel'd seat   75

---

ellipse, as is usual if it be made to depend on *condemn myself* or *to lack*. Rowe,
Pope, Dyce, for *mind* read *minded*, but
the corresponding passage in North
supports the noun. See *post*, p. 272.
Malone, comparing, e.g. *Wint.*, III. ii.
55–8, supposes an inaccurate use of
less after *to lack*, making Antony say
'that he is *destitute of a less noble mind*
than Cleopatra,' when he meant to
'acknowledge he *has* a less noble mind
than she.'

63. *exigent*] exigency, emergency. Cf.
Cæs., v. i. 19; Sidney's *Arcadia*, bk ii
(ed. 1725, i. 169): 'Now was *Zelmane*
brought to an *exigent*,' etc.

65. *inevitable prosecution*] pursuit admitting no escape. For *inevitable*, cf. S.
Marmion, *Cupid and Psyche*, 1637 (repr.
1820, p. 72): 'What darkness can pro-
tect me? what disguise / Hide me from
her *inevitable* eyes?'

68. *defeat'st*] frustratest. Cf. v. i. 65
post. Some—I think unnecessarily—
explain by *destroyest*, comparing such
passages as *Oth.*, IV. ii. 160: 'And his
unkindness may *defeat* my life.'

71. *enemy*] here an adjective as in
Cor., IV. iv. 24: 'This *enemy* town';

Lr, v. iii. 222: 'Follow'd his *enemy*
king.'

73. *pleach'd*] folded or intertwined.
Cf. *Ado*, I. ii. 12: 'a thick-*pleached* alley';
III. i. 7: 'the *pleached* bower,' etc. Delius
suggests that Antony thus indicates
the together-bound arms of a captive.
With the whole passage Steevens
compares Kyd, *Cornelia*, III. ii. 12–15:
'Now shalt thou march (thy hands fast
bound behind thee), / Thy head hung
downe, thy cheeks with teares be-
sprent, / Before the victor; Whyle thy
rebell sonne, / With crowned front,
tryumphing followes thee.' In this passage, unlike that in the text, the proper
order of captives ('Before the victor')
in a Roman triumph is observed.

74. *corrigible*] 'submissive to correction'. *OED* cites 1583, Babington,
Commandm., iii (1637), 28: 'If hee be
corrigible, not euen in the Lords cause
should I curse my brother.' It is used
in an active sense = 'corrective' in
Oth., I. iii. 330.

75. *penetrative*] penetrating. Not elsewhere in Shakespeare. The *Century
Dict.* cites Sir T. Elyot, *Castle of Health*,
ii: 'The rayne water . . . if it be re-

  Of fortunate Cæsar, drawn before him, branded
  His baseness that ensued?
Eros.   I would not see't.
Ant. Come then: for with a wound I must be cur'd,
  Draw that thy honest sword, which thou hast worn
  Most useful for thy country.
Eros.   O, sir, pardon me! 80
Ant. When I did make thee free, swor'st thou not then
  To do this when I bade thee? Do it at once,
  Or thy precedent services are all
  But accidents unpurpos'd. Draw, and come.
Eros. Turn from me then that noble countenance, 85
  Wherein the worship of the whole world lies.
Ant. Lo thee!   [*Turning from him.*
Eros. My sword is drawn.
Ant.   Then let it do at once
  The thing why thou hast drawn it.
Eros.   My dear master,
  My captain, and my emperor: let me say 90
  Before I strike this bloody stroke, farewell.
Ant. 'Tis said, man, and farewell.
Eros. Farewell, great chief. Shall I strike now?
Ant.   Now, Eros.
Eros. Why, there then: thus I do escape the sorrow
  Of Antony's death.   [*Kills himself.*
Ant.   Thrice-nobler than myself, 95
  Thou teachest me, O valiant Eros, what
  I should, and thou couldst not; my queen and Eros

---

87. *Turning . . .*] *Rowe; not in F.* 95. *Kills . . .*] *Opposite Eros, line 93, in F.*

ceyued pure and cleane, it is most
subtyl and *penetrative* of any other
waters'; Sir H. Wotton, *Reliquiæ Wot-
tonianæ* [1672], p. 7: '. . . the Aire . . .
That it be not too *gross*, nor too
penetrative.'

 76-7. *branded . . . ensued*] rendered
conspicuous, as by a brand, the abject
condition of him who followed. With
ensued, cf. Queen Elizabeth, *Translation
out of Seneca, Nugæ Antiquæ* (1769), i.
137: 'The cleare daies followes the

darck clowdes; the rowghest seas *insues*
the greattest calmes.'

 81. *swor'st thou not,* etc.] Cf. the
inferior scene between Cassius and
Pindarus in *Cæs.,* v. iii. 36-50.

 86. *worship . . . world*] that majesty
which the whole world reveres as a
god's. Johnson's 'dignity, authority',
scarcely give the force of *worship*
here.

 87. *Lo thee*] So in *H8,* I. i. 202: '*Lo,*
you, my lord,' etc.

Have by their brave instruction got upon me
A nobleness in record. But I will be
A bridegroom in my death, and run into't　　　100
As to a lover's bed. Come, then; and, Eros,
Thy master dies thy scholar; to do thus
　　　　　　　　　　　　　[*Falling on his sword.*
I learnt of thee. How, not dead? not dead?
The guard, ho! O, despatch me!

　　　　Enter a Guard; DECRETAS *following them.*

First Guard.　　　　　　　　　　What's the noise?
Ant. I have done my work ill, friends: O make an end　　105
Of what I have begun.
Sec. Guard.　　　　　　　　　The star is fall'n.
First Guard. And time is at his period.
All.　　　　　　　　　　　　Alas, and woe!
Ant. Let him that loves me, strike me dead.
First Guard.　　　　　　　　　　　Not I.
Sec. Guard. Nor I.

---

102. S.D. *Falling . . .*] *Rowe; not in F.
Enter . . .*] *Enter a Guard. F. See note.*

104. ho!] *Theobald;* how? *F.*　　S.D.

98–9. *Have . . . record*] have, as my
tutors in courage, *or*, by teaching me a
lesson in bravery, won for themselves
[from me] a noble place in story. Perhaps 'got upon me' would justify the
comparative, 'a nobler place'. Rolfe's
'forestalled me in gaining' is a very
attractive explanation, for which he
compares 'win upon me' in II. iv. 9
ante. But the case does not strike me
as parallel, and I should rather compare Milton, *Samson Agonistes*, 470:
'all these boasted trophies won on
me.'

104. *ho*] The F spelling (*how* for *ho*)
is frequent. Cf. I. ii. 110 *ante*, and
'Peace, *how*, peace! I charg you, keep
the peace!' (*Sir Thomas More*, p. 25,
Shakes. Society, 1844), on which
Dyce comments: 'One of a hundred
passages in old plays, which shew how
improperly the two latest editors
[Knight and Collier] of Shakespeare

have followed the folios in printing,
"The guard!—*how?*" *Ant.*, act IV.
sc. 12.'

S.D. Enter . . .] †F has only *Enter a
Guard.* We clearly have to get Decretas
on at some point, and the usual
method has been to give 'Enter
Decretas (or Dercetas or Dercetus)
and Guard' but that rather suggests
that he is in command of the guard,
which he pretty clearly is not. We can
bring him in after the guard's exit at
line 110, but that makes his first speech
abrupt—he needs a short while in
which to take in the situation. I suggest therefore that he comes in behind
the guard (like Enobarbus in IV. viii),
and watches and listens. [R]

Decretas] for the variations in this
character's name, see note on V. i. 3
post.

107. *period*] end, full stop, as in IV. ii.
25 *ante.*

Third Guard. Nor any one. [*Exeunt Guard.* 110
Dec. Thy death and fortunes bid thy followers fly.
    This sword but shown to Cæsar with this tidings,
    Shall enter me with him.

Enter DIOMEDES.

Dio. Where's Antony?
Dec.   There, Diomed, there.
Dio.   Lives he?
    Wilt thou not answer, man? [*Exit Decretas.* 115
Ant. Art thou there, Diomed? Draw thy sword, and give me
    Sufficing strokes for death.
Dio.   Most absolute lord,
    My mistress Cleopatra sent me to thee.
Ant. When did she send thee?
Dio.   Now, my lord,
Ant.   Where is she?
Dio. Lock'd in her monument; she had a prophesying fear
    Of what hath come to pass: for when she saw— 121
    Which never shall be found—you did suspect
    She had dispos'd with Cæsar, and that your rage
    Would not be purg'd, she sent you word she was dead;
    But fearing since how it might work, hath sent 125
    Me to proclaim the truth, and I am come,
    I dread, too late.
Ant. Too late, good Diomed: call my guard, I prithee.
Dio. What ho; the emperor's guard, the guard, what ho!
    Come, your lord calls. 130

Enter four or five of the Guard of ANTONY.

Ant. Bear me, good friends, where Cleopatra bides,
    'Tis the last service what I shall command you.
First Guard. Woe, woe are we, sir, you may not live to wear

---

110. *Exeunt Guard*] *Pope; Exeunt. F.*   111. *Dec.*] *Dercetus. F.*   114. *Dec.*]
Decre. F.   115. *Exit Decretas*] *no exit in F.*

114.] Dover Wilson adds a good
stage-direction for Decretas, *hiding the
sword in his cloak.*

123. *dispos'd*] made arrangements *or*
dispositions, came to terms. This is

the only example of this sense in *OED.*

124. *purg'd*] expelled [by assertions
of innocence]. See on I. iii. 53 *ante.*
The figure is perhaps continued in
work, next line.

All your true followers out.

All.   Most heavy day!

Ant. Nay, good my fellows, do not please sharp fate   135
To grace it with your sorrows: bid that welcome
Which comes to punish us, and we punish it
Seeming to bear it lightly. Take me up;
I have led you oft, carry me now, good friends,
And have my thanks for all. [*Exeunt, bearing Antony.* 140

[SCENE XV.—*The same. A monument.*]

Enter CLEOPATRA *and her maids aloft, with* CHARMIAN
and IRAS.

Cleo. O Charmian, I will never go from hence.

Char. Be comforted, dear madam.

Cleo.   No, I will not:
All strange and terrible events are welcome,
But comforts we despise; our size of sorrow,
Proportion'd to our cause, must be as great   5
As that which makes it.

Enter, below, DIOMEDES.

                              How now? is he dead?

Dio. His death's upon him, but not dead.
Look out o' the other side your monument,

Scene xv

6. S.D. *Enter . . .*] *Collier; Enter Diomed. F.*

---

136. *To grace*] a gerund = by grac-
ing. So in *R2*, II. ii. 95: 'But I shall
grieve you to report the rest.' See
Abbott (*Shakespearian Grammar*, §356).
  bid] the not uncommon imperative-
conditional—'if we bid . . . we punish it.'

Scene xv

[See North, *post*, pp. 272–3, and for
the staging see Appendix IV.]
  S.D. aloft] i.e. to the balcony at the
rear, which was a special feature of the
old stage. A well-known sketch of

the interior of the Swan Theatre in
1596 (?) by a Dutch traveller, repro-
duced in Mr Ordish's *Early London
Theatres* and *Shakespeare's London*, represents it as a sort of stage box divided
by five pillars, occupying the length of
the tiring house—at some height above
its doors—at the back of the stage.

  7.] Steevens thought that respect for
the questioner, as well as metre, neces-
sitated the insertion of *madam* after
him; Keightley reads 'but *he is* not
dead.'

His guard have brought him thither.

Enter, below, ANTONY, *borne by the Guard.*

Cleo.   O sun,
Burn the great sphere thou mov'st in, darkling stand   10
The varying shore o' the world. O Antony,
Antony, Antony! Help, Charmian, help, Iras, help:
Help, friends below, let's draw him hither.

9. S.D. *Enter . . .*] *Collier; Enter Anthony, and the Guard. F.*

10–11. *Burn the great sphere . . . world*]
See on II. vii. 14–16 *ante*. In the system
there described, 'the sun was a planet,
and was whirled round the earth by
the motion of a solid sphere in which it
was fixed.—If the sun therefore was to
set fire to the sphere, so as to consume
it, the consequence must be, that itself,
for want of support, must drop
through, and wander in endless space;
and in this case the earth would be
involved in endless night' (Heath).
For *darkling*, i.e. in darkness, cf. *Lr*, I.
iv. 240. Warburton explains *The varying shore o' the world* as the shore 'of the
earth, where light and darkness made
an incessant *variation*.' Hudson applauds and adopts a conjecture of
Staunton's (*Athenæum*, 1873) of *star*
(*starre*) for *shore*, making 'the varying
star' = the changing moon. He observes that Shakespeare uses *star*, with
some epithet, such as *moist* or *watery*,
for the moon; but that is not the same
thing as calling it 'the varying star o'
the world.' If 'darkling stand,' etc. is a
consequence, Cleopatra would make
it apply to the orb that held herself and
Antony rather than to the moon.
12–13. *Help . . . hither*] † Dover Wilson regards this line and a half as 'indubitable interpolation'; in the region
of conjecture, 'indubitable' is an un-
duly positive word, against which a
reader rightly reacts unfavourably,
but he makes a strong case (see pp.
128–30 of his edition). If the words
stand here, then lines 30–1 are awkwardly repetitive, whereas they are

effective if they propose, *for the first
time*, the drawing of Antony up as the
alternative to Cleopatra coming down.
Further, Antony's *Peace!* at the end of
line 13 follows more naturally on Cleopatra's repeated *Antony!* if nothing
else intervenes. Dover Wilson accounts
for the 'interpolation' by assuming
that the passage originally ran as we
have it, but without this line and a half,
and that then a proposed cut was indicated from line 13, *Peace!* to line 31,
good friends: but the cutter, finding that
he had now no text left to correspond
to the drawing up of Antony, wrote in
the substance of lines 30–1 at lines 12–
13 in a version of his own. (It is just
worth remark that Cleopatra's triple
Antony! in lines 11–12 is all in one line
in F, so that *Help, Charmian* starts a new
line.) The weakness of the argument
(unless I misunderstand the details of
it) is that it posits an unskilful, and
even silly, cutter, who gave himself
more trouble than there was any need
for. Why did he not simply stop his cut
at the end of line 29 (*Antony*), and
relieve himself of the job of rewriting
Shakespeare for the insertion at line
12? But there is another possibility,
which is, I think, more likely, namely,
that Shakespeare, having brought
Antony in, and written Cleopatra's
impassioned greeting (line 9, *O sun*
down to the third *Antony* in line 12),
first intended to have Antony immediately hoisted up, and wrote the
appropriate lines for Cleopatra; that
he then saw the advantages of a brief

Ant.   Peace!
    Not Cæsar's valour hath o'erthrown Antony,
    But Antony's hath triumph'd on itself.   15
Cleo. So it should be, that none but Antony
    Should conquer Antony, but woe 'tis so!
Ant. I am dying, Egypt, dying; only
    I here importune death awhile, until
    Of many thousand kisses, the poor last   20
    I lay upon thy lips.
Cleo.   I dare not, dear,
    Dear my lord, pardon: I dare not,
    Lest I be taken: not the imperious show
    Of the full-fortun'd Cæsar ever shall
    Be brooch'd with me, if knife, drugs, serpents, have   25

---

22. dare not] *F;* dare not descend *Malone;* dare not open *D. Wilson.*

---

interchange before the hoisting up, and wrote lines 13 (*Peace!*)–31 (*good friends*); and that either he forgot to delete the now worse than unwanted *Help, Charmian . . . hither,* or his indications of deletion were neglected. (Something of the same kind almost certainly happened in *LLL.,* IV. iii, where a speech of twenty-two lines (296–317) is immediately followed by an elaborated version of the same speech (318–54), where it is reasonable to assume that the deletion of the first version was either forgotten or neglected.) We shall still need the cutter to account for the repetition of Antony's *I am dying, Egypt, dying* (if we are determined to be rid of its second occurrence—see note on line 41 below), but at least he need no longer be a fool. [R]

16–17. *that none . . . Antony*] Cf. Ovid, *Metam.,* xiii. 390: 'That none may Ajax overcome save Ajax' (Golding's Ovid), and *Cæs.,* v. v. 56.

19. *importune death awhile*] *importune* seems to be used with much latitude here. Johnson explains: 'I *solicit* death to delay *or* I trouble death by keeping him in waiting.'

22. *dare not*] †The line halts and

though completion is not essential the sense is improved if Cleopatra makes plain what it is she 'dare not,' and Malone's *descend* is as easy an addition as any. But I am not sure that the improvement in sense, and metre, is not bought with a loss in effectiveness. There is a compression, or ellipse, in Cleopatra's words as they stand: it is not that she dare not take his last kiss—though that is what she says—but that even for that she dare not come down. [R]

25. *brooch'd*] adorned; a brooch being always an ornament, as Ritson observes. Cf. *Ham.,* IV. vii. 93: 'he is the *brooch* indeed / And gem of all the nation.' Steevens cites Jonson, *The Staple of News,* III. ii. 265: 'The very *brooch* o' the bench, gem o' the city'; *The Magnetic Lady,* I. vii. 33: 'The *brooch* to any true state-cap in Europe.' In the last passage, the brooch is the last of several ornaments, to which 'the jewel / Of all the court, close Master Bias' is compared, and the prevailing mode of wearing a brooch in the front of the cap or hat is alluded to, as also in *The Poetaster,* I. ii. 161: 'honour's a good *brooch* to wear in a man's hat, at all times.'

Edge, sting, or operation. I am safe:
Your wife Octavia, with her modest eyes,
And still conclusion, shall acquire no honour
Demuring upon me: but come, come, Antony,—
Help me, my women,—we must draw thee up: 30
Assist, good friends.

Ant.   O quick, or I am gone.

Cleo. Here's sport indeed! How heavy weighs my lord!
Our strength is all gone into heaviness,
That makes the weight. Had I great Juno's power,
The strong-wing'd Mercury should fetch thee up,   35
And set thee by Jove's side. Yet come a little,
Wishers were ever fools, O, come, come, come.

[*They heave Antony aloft to Cleopatra.*

And welcome, welcome! Die when thou hast liv'd,
Quicken with kissing: had my lips that power,

---

33. heaviness,] *F*; heaviness; *Cambridge edd.*   38. when] *F*; where *Pope.*

26. *sting, or operation*] Hanmer reads *operation, or sting* to correspond in order with *drugs, serpents*; but for disregard of such nicety, cf. *Ham.*, III. i. 160.

28. *still conclusion*] composed and silent censure, quiet formation of opinion. The idea seems to be one of disapproval following on inspection, instinctively felt by its object, maugre silence and 'modest eyes' or demure looks. Cf. v. ii. 54 *post.*

29. *Demuring upon me*] looking demurely upon me, with an air of innocence. *Demuring* is not found elsewhere. It is just possible that it may be from *demur* (see *OED demur*), and thus used to indicate the leisurely consideration of Octavia, the deliberation, as of one doubtful, with which she would appear to draw her conclusions. Cf. Sir John Harington, *Epigrams* (ed. 1633, bk i. 37): 'Once, by mishap, two Poets fell a squaring, / The Sonnet and our Epigram comparing; / And *Faustus* having long *demur'd* upon it, / Yet at the last gave sentence for the Sonnet,' etc.

32. *Here's sport indeed*] The grim humour of this exclamation was lost on

Johnson, who took it for a rebuke of trifling efforts! and others have positively suggested emendations. Possibly, as Malone suggests, there is a thought of their former fishing diversions. Cf. II. v. 13–15 *ante*: 'and, as I draw them up, / I'll think them every one an Antony, / And say, "Ah, ha! you're caught."'

33. *heaviness*] Malone 'equivocally for sorrow and weight.' See the passages cited on IV. vi. 36 *ante*. Cf. for the thought, Daniel, *Cleopatra*, 1607 (*Works*, ed. Grosart, III. 8): 'Whose surcharg'd heart more then her body wayes.'

37. *Wishers . . . fools*] This sounds like a proverb. In Ray's collection occurs, 'Wishers and woulders are never good householders.'

38. *when*] †Few commentators (Rowe and Dover Wilson among them) have adhered to F's *when*, but I think they are right. The sense is then 'live once more before you die,' and a point, otherwise awkwardly lacking, is given to *Quicken with kissing*. [R]

39. *Quicken*] gain life or vitality. Cf. *Oth.*, III. iii. 277.

Thus would I wear them out.

All.   A heavy sight!   40

Ant. I am dying, Egypt, dying.

Give me some wine, and let me speak a little.

Cleo. No, let me speak, and let me rail so high,

That the false huswife Fortune break her wheel,

Provok'd by my offence.

Ant.   One word, sweet queen: 45

Of Cæsar seek your honour, with your safety. O!

Cleo. They do not go together.

Ant.   Gentle, hear me,

None about Cæsar trust but Proculeius.

Cleo. My resolution, and my hands, I'll trust,

None about Cæsar.   50

Ant. The miserable change now at my end

Lament nor sorrow at: but please your thoughts

In feeding them with those my former fortunes

Wherein I liv'd: the greatest prince o' the world,

---

54. liv'd: the] liued. The *F; liv'd the *Theobald.

40. *A heavy*] †perhaps *Ah, heavy*
(Rowe emends to *Oh*). [R]

41. *I am dying, Egypt, dying*] †This
also Dover Wilson regards as an interpolation (see note to lines 12–13 of this
scene), arguing that the cutter, feeling
that he had left Antony's dying condition insufficiently stressed, lifted a
significant phrase from the cut (line
18) and inserted it. If one accepts the
general hypothesis of the cut, this
seems convincing. The exact repetition of the famous phrase weakens it,
and further, the lines which follow its
first occurrence are so immeasurably
more effective than those which follow
its second. [R]

44. *huswife*] Here, as often, *huswife*
has a bad sense: jilt, wanton, etc. Cf.
H5, v. i. 85: 'Doth Fortune play the
huswife with me now?' *Huswiverie* is
similarly used, e.g. mistrust in husbands is said to 'plante newe trickes of
huswiuerie in their wiues consciences'
(*Tell-Trothes New-yeares Gift*, 1593,
New Shakespeare Soc., 1876, p. 22).

In this speech, lines 43–5, Cleopatra
seems to strike a false note. The tone
of line 44, which Johnson calls 'this
despicable line,' is in keeping with
AYL., i. ii. 34; here it savours of un-
couth early dramas.

†But perhaps Shakespeare knew
better than his editors how men and
women talk under stress: cf.Malcolm's
surprising 'O by whom?' in *Mac.*, ii.
iii. 107. [R]

54–7. *liv'd . . . countryman:*] F's full-
stops are disconcerting to the modern
reader, since they are syntactically
very awkward, and he is used to syntactical punctuation. They may, of
course, be mere blunders, and many
editors have emended them. But they
may, I think more probably, come
from the original, and if so, the colons
of the present text (lightening F's colon
after *noblest*, to maintain the distinction in length of pause) perhaps come
as near as modern notation will permit to representing Shakespeare's intention without undue distraction to

The noblest; and do now not basely die,   55
Not cowardly put off my helmet to
My countryman: a Roman, by a Roman
Valiantly vanquish'd. Now my spirit is going,
I can no more.
Cleo.   Noblest of men, woo't die?
Hast thou no care of me, shall I abide   60
In this dull world, which in thy absence is
No better than a sty? O, see, my women:
The crown o' the earth doth melt.   [*Antony dies.*]
                    My lord?
O, wither'd is the garland of the war,
The soldier's pole is fall'n: young boys and girls   65
Are level now with men: the odds is gone,
And there is nothing left remarkable

---

63. *Antony dies*] Capell, *after* women, *line 62; Rowe after* more, *line 59; not in F.*

the reader. Antony is, literally, at the last gasp, and his utterance is broken, with heavy pauses.

56–8. *Not cowardly put*, etc.] See North, *post*, p. 273. Rowe placed a comma after *cowardly* with F4, thus connecting it with *die*, and changed *not* to *nor*. This is defensible; but surely those who, with Pope, read *Nor cowardly put off* . . . weaken the connection of the negative with *cowardly*: to which alone it applies and not to *put off*, etc.

59. *woo't*] See on IV. ii. 7 *ante*.

63. *crown*] Cf. next note, and see on IV. xii. 27 *ante*.

S.D.] †I have inserted the usual S.D. for Antony's death, though at a place slightly later than the usual. But I am not clear that we should not do better to follow F and dispense with it altogether. Antony's death occurs, presumably, somewhere between Cleopatra's 'woo't die?' and her 'O, wither'd . . .', and the precise instant of it matters very little. [R]

64. *garland of the war*] Cf. *Cor.*, I. i. 189: 'And call . . . Him vile that was your *garland*'; Quarles, *Argalus and Parthenia*, bk i (ed. 1701, p. 35): 'he

that is the crown / Of prized virtue, honour and renown, / The flower of Arts, the *Cyprian* living story, / *Arcadia's Garland*, and great *Greece's* glory'.

†But surely, as Deighton and Furness saw, there is a suggestion of the maypole. [R]

65. *pole*] perhaps standard, which the aptitude of the metaphor supports. Boswell gets the credit of the suggestion, really Beckett's (*Concordance*, 1787, p. 445). Schmidt and the Temple and Eversley editors explain by 'lodestar', and, certainly, the second guard in IV. xiv. 106 *ante* says 'The star is fall'n,' while the use of *pole* in simile or metaphor is common. Cf. Richard James (1592–1638), *Poems*, ed. Grosart, 1880, p. 124: 'This [i.e. Faith and True Religion] was the *Pole*, the Pillar, and the light,' etc.

66. *the odds is gone*] There is no distinction left between great and small, cf. *Troil.*, iii. 23–8, 83–126; and *No-body and Some-body*, lines 107–8 (Simpson's *School of Shakspere*, i. 281): 'if your highnesse note his leg and mine, there is *ods*; and for a foot, I dare compare.'

67. *remarkable*] Staunton receives

    Beneath the visiting moon.   [*Faints.*

Char.   O quietness; lady!

Iras. She's dead too, our sovereign.

Char.   Lady!

Iras.   Madam!

Char. O madam, madam, madam!

Iras.   Royal Egypt: 70
    Empress!   [*Cleopatra stirs.*

Char. Peace, peace, Iras!

Cleo. No more but e'en a woman, and commanded
    By such poor passion as the maid that milks,
    And does the meanest chares. It were for me   75
    To throw my sceptre at the injurious gods,
    To tell them that this world did equal theirs,
    Till they had stol'n our jewel. All's but naught:

---

68. *Faints.*] *She Faints. Rowe; not in F.*
not in F.   73. e'en] *Johnson; in F.*

71. *Cleopatra stirs*] D. *Wilson (she stirs);*

credit for observing that this word had, when this play was written, a more impressive sense, far worthier of the occasion, than the present one of merely 'observable or noteworthy,' but he had the remark from Gifford. See the latter's *Massinger*, 1805, i. 157, note on *The Unnatural Combat*, II. i. Malone compares with lines 66–8, *Mac.*, II. iii. 99–103: 'from this instant / There's nothing serious in mortality'; etc.

69–73.] † There are various small points in these lines. Rowe's S.D. is clearly justified, since otherwise there is no point of reference for Iras' first speech, and so is Wilson's, as the occasion for Charmian's *Peace, peace, Iras!* (if that should be hers). I think that Charmian's *O quietness* is addressed to Iras, and her *Lady!* to Cleopatra, like her own and Iras' subsequent exclamations, and I have punctuated accordingly. I think that Cleopatra's *No more but e'en a woman* is a correction of Iras' *Empress!*, and if so Charmian's *Peace, peace, Iras!* must be given as a rapid aside. But it is very tempting to attribute the words to Cleopatra her-

self, comparing her *Peace, peace!* at v. ii. 307 *post*, where also the words check an excited address. [R]

73. *No more but e'en a woman*] As Malone observes, this responds to the words of Iras, without noticing those of Charmian. But is the sense, as he takes it—placing with most editors (Johnson's conjecture) a comma after *more*—No more (i.e. no longer) an empress, but just a woman; or merely No more than just a woman, as Hudson evidently interprets? One can only be guided here by an instinctive preference, and specious as the first explanation is, my impulse is to read with Hudson, as in the text above. The words seem to me not so much an answer to Iras, as the outcome of a train of thought suggested by Iras.

e'en] † In support of Johnson's emendation, cf. F's frequent *bin* for *been*. [R]

75. *chares*] tasks. A *char* or *chare* is a turn, and hence, a turn of work. Cf. *char-woman*. The word is used by Shakespeare only in this play but was very common in his time. See Peele, *Edward I*, VI. 119: 'Why, so, this *chare* is chared'; (again in v. ii. 230 *post*).

Patience is sottish, and impatience does
Become a dog that's mad: then is it sin,   80
To rush into the secret house of death,
Ere death dare come to us? How do you, women?
What, what, good cheer! Why, how now, Charmian?
My noble girls! Ah, women, women. Look,
Our lamp is spent, it's out. Good sirs, take heart,   85
We'll bury him: and then, what's brave, what's noble,
Let's do it after the high Roman fashion,
And make death proud to take us. Come, away,
This case of that huge spirit now is cold.
Ah, women, women! come, we have no friend   90
But resolution, and the briefest end.
                    [*Exeunt; those above bearing off Antony's body.*

83. what, good cheer!] what good cheere? *F.*   87. do it] *Pope;* doo't *F.*
91. S.D. *Exeunt . . .*] *Capell (substantially); Exeunt, bearing of Anthonies body. F.*

79. *sottish*] foolish, mere stupidity. Not elsewhere in Shakespeare, but common; so in The Epistle Dedicatorie, *Mirrour for Magistrates*, 1587: 'not coūted wise, righteous, and constant, but *sottish*, rude and desperate.'
79–80. *does Become*] is characteristic of.
85. *Our lamp*] one of the many echoes of which the play is full; cf. the preceding scene, line 46, *the torch is out.*
Good sirs] to the women. Cf. *Sirrah*

Iras, v. ii. 228 *post*, and Whetstone, *1 Promos and Cassandra*, IV. vii. 6: '*Grimball* . . . kysse me for acquaintaunce. / *Dalia.* If I lyke your manhoode, I may do so perchaunce. / [*She faynes to looke in his basket. Grimball.* Bate me an ase, quoth *Boulton*: Tush your minde I know: / Ah *Syr*, you would, belike, let my cocke sparrowes goe.' Dyce quotes examples from Beaumont and Fletcher, *A King and no King*, II. i. 250; *Philaster*, IV. iii. 54.

ACT V

[SCENE I.—*Alexandria. Cæsar's camp.*]

Enter CÆSAR, AGRIPPA, DOLABELLA, MÆCENAS, GALLUS,
PROCULEIUS, *and others, his council of war.*

Cæs. Go to him, Dolabella, bid him yield.
    Being so frustrate, tell him, he mocks
    The pauses that he makes.
Dol.   Cæsar, I shall.   [*Exit.*

Enter DECRETAS, *with the sword of* ANTONY.

ACT V
Scene I

S.D. *Enter* . . .] *Globe; Enter Cæsar, Agrippa, Dolabella, Menas, with his Counsell of Warre. F.*   3. *Exit.*] *not in* F.

[*Scene* I: See North, *post,* pp. 273-4.]
S.D. Enter . . . *Mæcenas* . . .] Theobald (Thirlby conj.) first substituted *Mæcenas* for *Menas* of F, pointing out not only that the speeches of the character are marked *Mec.* in the margin, but also that though when Menas died he was a partisan of Cæsar, his death occurred five years before Antony's own.

2. *frustrate*] baffled. So *Tp.,* III. iii. 10: 'Our *frustrate* search on land.' Perhaps pronounced as a trisyllable. Compare *mistress,* II. v. 27 *ante.*

2–3. *he mocks . . . makes*] his delays are mere mockery. Steevens suggested this very probable sense, which seems capable of being deduced from the text. I can imagine a phrase 'to mock pauses' as equivalent to 'to make mocking pauses,' i.e. pauses mocking either the maker or another, according

to the sense required by the context; and perhaps 'to mock' here is a condensation for something like 'to make ineffectually', or 'to make ridiculously'. Malone evaded the difficulty by reading '*mocks* us by'.

† Cæsar's meaning is, I think, plain (and Malone therefore is on the wrong tack): 'tell him his pauses—i.e. his shifts, evasions, attempts to postpone the moment of surrender—are idle,' which is substantially Case's interpretation, but not very easy to elicit from the text as it stands. [R]

3. S.D. *Decretas.*] † I do not know that it matters much what we call this unimportant character, but I think that Dover Wilson's note about him merits a moment's consideration. He says: 'I follow Shakespeare and read "Decretus," which is the form he gives to Plutarch–North's "Dercetaeus" at

189

Cæs. Wherefore is that? and what art thou that dar'st
    Appear thus to us?
Dec.   I am call'd Decretas,   5
    Mark Antony I serv'd, who best was worthy
    Best to be serv'd: whilst he stood up, and spoke,
    He was my master, and I wore my life
    To spend upon his haters. If thou please
    To take me to thee, as I was to him   10
    I'll be to Cæsar, if thou pleasest not,
    I yield thee up my life.
Cæs.   What is't thou say'st?
Dec. I say, O Cæsar, Antony is dead.
Cæs. The breaking of so great a thing should make
    A greater crack. The round world   15
    Should have shook lions into civil streets,
    And citizens to their dens. The death of Antony
    Is not a single doom, in the name lay
    A moiety of the world.
Dec.   He is dead, Cæsar,
    Not by a public minister of justice,   20
    Nor by a hired knife, but that self hand
    Which writ his honour in the acts it did,

4.4.111, and not like Pope and later editors "Dercetas," which lies half way between North and the spelling "Decretas" that crops up in F at 5.1.3 (S.D.) and 5.1.5, and is in fact the sort of conflation that pre-Pollardian editors loved.' I think this is somewhat misleading. The facts are these: the name occurs in full three times, once in a speech-heading (IV. xiv. 111) as Dercetus, once in a stage-direction (v. i. 3) as Decretas, and once in the text (v. i. 5) also as Decretas; an abbreviated form occurs four times, at IV. xiv. 114 (Decre.) and v. i. 5, 13, 19 (Dec.). Admittedly a confusion between the two forms of the name would be easy enough, but I think that we are more likely to be 'following Shakespeare' if we accept the 6–1 majority of F in favour of Decretas. [R]

5. *thus*] i.e. as Delius observes, with a naked, bloody sword.

6–7. *who best . . . serv'd*] Cf. Thidias on Cæsar, III. xiii. 87–8 *ante*.

15.] An omission has been generally suspected here, and made the subject of many conjectures. Steevens suggested: 'A greater crack than this: the ruin'd world.' As the sense is plain, may not the short line have been intentional? a pause here would be natural and impressive. For the thought, cf. *Cæs.*, I. iii. 3–4, 20–2.

19. *moiety*] half, the strict sense of the word, as in *All's W.*, III. ii. 69. Often merely = share, portion, as in *Lr*, I. i. 7.

21. *self*] same, as in *Err.*, v. i. 10: 'that *self* chain about his neck'; *Lr*, IV. iii. 36, etc. Cf. also *The Three Lords*, etc. (Hazlitt's *Dodsley*, vi. 376): 'Not all our ships sail for one *self* haven.'

Hath, with the courage which the heart did lend it,
Splitted the heart. This is his sword,
I robb'd his wound of it: behold it stain'd   25
With his most noble blood.

Cæs.   Look you sad, friends?
The gods rebuke me, but it is a tidings
To wash the eyes of kings.

Agr.   And strange it is,
That nature must compel us to lament
Our most persisted deeds.

Mæc.   His taints and honours   30
Wag'd equal with him.

Agr.   A rarer spirit never
Did steer humanity: but you gods will give us
Some faults to make us men. Cæsar is touch'd.

Mæc. When such a spacious mirror's set before him,
He needs must see himself.

Cæs.   O Antony,   35
I have follow'd thee to this, but we do launch
Diseases in our bodies. I must perforce
Have shown to thee such a declining day,
Or look on thine: we could not stall together,

26. Look . . . sad, friends?] *Hanmer;* sad friends; *Theobald;* Looke you sad friends, *F;* Look you, sad friends, *F3.*   27. is a tidings] *F2* (Tydings); is Tydings *F.*   28, 31. *Agr.*] *Theobald; Dol. F*   31. Wag'd] *F;* way *F2;* weigh'd *Rowe, and many others.*   36. launch] *F;* lance *Theobald and edd.*

24. *Splitted*] Cf. *2H6,* III. ii. 411; *Err.,* I. i. 103; v. i. 309: 'O time's extremity, / Hast thou so crack'd and *splitted* my poor tongue,' etc.

27. *a tidings*] †F's rhythm is so awkward that we may without much compunction, I think, accept F2, particularly since a too gramatically-minded compositor might easily, thinking *a Tydings* a solecism, have dropped the *a* in the interest of supposed correctness. [R]

28–30. *And strange . . . deeds*] Cf. III. ii. 58 *ante.*

31. *Wag'd equal*] Steevens: 'were an equal match, i.e. were opposed to each other in just proportions, like the

counterparts of a wager.' This explanation is confirmed by *Per.,* IV. ii. 34: 'The commodity *wages not* with the danger.'

36. *launch*] *launch* or *lanch* is the old and common form of 'lance'. Cf. Nashe, *Christ's Tears* (McK. II. 156, line 19): 'and even as *Archabius* the Trumpeter had more giuen him to cease then to sound (the noise that he made was so harsh) so wil they giue them more . . . to corrupt them then to make them sound, to feede their sores than to *launch* them'; and see note on *Lr,* II. i. 52 (Arden Shakespeare).

39. *stall*] dwell. See Whetstone, *2*

In the whole world. But yet let me lament   40
With tears as sovereign as the blood of hearts,
That thou my brother, my competitor,
In top of all design; my mate in empire,
Friend and companion in the front of war,
The arm of mine own body, and the heart   45
Where mine his thoughts did kindle;—that our stars,
Unreconciliable, should divide
Our equalness to this. Hear me, good friends,—
But I will tell you at some meeter season,
The business of this man looks out of him,   50
We'll hear him what he says.

Enter an Egyptian.

                              Whence are you?
Egyp. A poor Egyptian yet; the queen my mistress
Confin'd in all she has, her monument,
Of thy intents desires instruction,
That she preparedly may frame herself   55
To the way she's forc'd to.

52. Egyptian yet; the] *Rowe (ed. 3);* Egyptian yet, the *F; Hunter, followed by
D. Wilson, reads* Egyptian, yet the   56. to] *F2;* too *F.*

Promos and Cassandra, III. ii (Nichols,
Six Old Plays, 1779, p. 83): 'Well, ere
I leave, my poorest subjects shall /
Both lyve and lyke, and by the richest
stawl.'

41. *sovereign . . . blood*] See on IV. ii. 6
ante, the thought being, perhaps, of a
sovereign remedy.

42. *competitor*] Perhaps here =
friendly rival, [thou] who viedst with
me, rather than merely—as in I. iv. 3
and II. vii. 70 *ante*—associate.

43. *In top . . . design*] 'In top of'
means 'in height of', and expresses the
superlative degree of whatever is in
question, as in *A Lover's Complaint*, 55:
'This said, *in top of* rage the lines she
rents,' etc. Hence, possibly, it may be
allowable to paraphrase here: 'in the
daring (*or* supreme) conception and
conduct of all enterprise.'

46. *Where . . . kindle*] No one seems
to find a difficulty here. *His*, of course
= its, but does 'Where my heart did

kindle its thoughts' = Where I found
inspiration, or merely indicate the
close commune of friends?

47–8. *divide . . . this*] sunder us, who
were thus equal associates in everything, so widely and so fatally.

50. *The business . . . him*] Cf. *Cym.*,
v. v. 23: 'There's business in these
faces'; and *Mac.*, I. ii. 47: 'What a
haste looks through his eyes!'

52. *A poor Egyptian yet*] Taken in connection with what follows, this reply
seems equivalent to: 'From what is yet
Egypt, till your intents pronounce its
fate.' Johnson's explanation is: 'Yet a
servant of the Queen of Egypt, though
soon to become a subject of Rome.'
A new suggestion is made by Deighton,
viz.: 'one who, though conquered, still
boasts himself an Egyptian.' Schmidt
prefers the F reading, explaining 'A
poor Egyptian yet, the queen,' as 'My
queen, who is now no more than a
poor Egyptian.'

Cæs.   Bid her have good heart;
She soon shall know of us, by some of ours,
How honourable, and how kindly we
Determine for her. For Cæsar cannot live
To be ungentle.

Egyp.   So the gods preserve thee!   [*Exit.*   60
Cæs. Come hither, Proculeius. Go and say
We purpose her no shame: give her what comforts
The quality of her passion shall require,
Lest, in her greatness, by some mortal stroke
She do defeat us. For her life in Rome   65
Would be eternal in our triumph: go,
And with your speediest bring us what she says,
And how you find of her.

Pro.   Cæsar, I shall.   [*Exit.*
Cæs. Gallus, go you along. [*Exit Gallus.*] Where's Dolabella,
To second Proculeius?

All.   Dolabella!   70
Cæs. Let him alone: for I remember now
How he's employ'd: he shall in time be ready.
Go with me to my tent, where you shall see
How hardly I was drawn into this war,

---

59. live] *Rowe (ed. 3) and Southern MS;* leaue *F;* learn *Dyce (Tyrwhitt conj.).*
60. ungentle] *F;* gentle *Capell, reading* Leave *transferred to this line.*   69. *Exit
Gallus*] *Theobald; not in F.*

59–60. *live To be ungentle*] †The
Southern–Rowe emendation has been
almost universally accepted. It is fairly
easy graphically (especially if we
accept Dover Wilson's suggestion of
a MS *leue*, a spelling which would
account for F's *love* for *leave* in I. ii. 177)
and even easier auditorily; and it
makes quite adequate sense. None the
less *leave* has to me a more Shakespearean 'feel', with the sense 'stop
being gentle' or even more nearly
'stop being himself so as to become
ungentle'. But the first involves an
almost impossible (in spite of Capell)
emendation, and the second an almost
impossible ellipse. [R]

65–6. *her life . . . triumph*] Not 'her
abode in Rome would perpetuate my

triumph,' but 'her presence *alive*, at
my triumph in Rome, would make it
everlastingly memorable.' The sense of
life is not here 'continuous existence,'
but merely contains the idea of life, as
opposed to that of death involved in
'some mortal stroke.' We may, perhaps, regard *eternal* here as having become merely intensive, and explain:
'her presence . . . would contribute in
the highest degree to my triumph.'
Expressions like 'an eternal swindle'
may be heard nowadays. See also an
eternal villain in *Oth.,* IV. ii. 130 (Arden
Shakespeare). Cf. North, *post,* p.
274.

67. *with your speediest*] as quickly as
you can. Cf. 'with your earliest,' *Oth.,* II.
iii. 7.

How calm and gentle I proceeded still   75
In all my writings. Go with me, and see
What I can show in this.   [*Exeunt.*

[SCENE II.—*Alexandria. A room in the monument.*]

Enter CLEOPATRA, CHARMIAN, *and* IRAS.

Cleo. My desolation does begin to make
A better life: 'tis paltry to be Cæsar:
Not being Fortune, he's but Fortune's knave,
A minister of her will: and it is great
To do that thing that ends all other deeds,   5
Which shackles accidents, and bolts up change;
Which sleeps, and never palates more the dung,
The beggar's nurse, and Cæsar's.

Scene II

7. dung] *F; dug Theobald* (dugg) *and many other edd.*

Scene II

[For the staging of this scene see Appendix IV.]

S.D. Enter *Cleopatra . . .*] † F brings in Mardian also. Much as I dislike tinkering with F's S.D.s, I think that he must be omitted. (*a*) He says nothing throughout the scene; not a strong argument, in view of Agrippa in III. xi. (*b*) North (see p. 277) stresses the absence of everyone but the two waiting-women; a trifle stronger, but not at all decisive. (*c*) There is no place that I can see where we can restore a supposedly omitted 'Exit Mardian,' so that if he is to be there we must imagine him as a silent spectator throughout. But there are two points at which, if he is there, one would expect some notice to be taken of him, first at the moment of Cleopatra's farewell (line 291), second after Cæsar's entry (line 332), where he would naturally be questioned. I fancy that Shakespeare intended to include him in the dialogue, but then found that the scene was better without him, and forgot to delete his entry. [R]

2. *A better life*] i.e. a life in which Fortune's gifts are rightly estimated and despised, and the contemplation of one crowning and emancipating deed restores a sense of confidence, and superiority over Fortune's minion.

3. *knave*] servant, as in IV. xiv. 12.

7–8. *Which . . . Cæsar's*] Fortune's favour has just been scorned: it remains to decry life, which Cæsar and the beggar must retain by the same means. 'Which sleeps,' etc. (line 7) is a bold equivalent for: Which is a sleep, emancipated from need of the base food on which depends as much the life of Cæsar as a beggar's. Johnson says: 'The difficulty of the passage, if any difficulty there be, arises only from this, that the act of suicide, and the state which is the effect of suicide, are confounded. Voluntary death, says she, is an act *which bolts up change*; it produces a state . . . which has no longer need of the gross and terrene sustenance, in the use of which Cæsar and the beggar are on a level. The speech is abrupt, but perturbation in

Enter PROCULEIUS.

Pro. Cæsar sends greeting to the Queen of Egypt,
      And bids thee study on what fair demands   10
      Thou mean'st to have him grant thee.
Cleo.   What's thy name?
Pro. My name is Proculeius.
Cleo.   Antony
      Did tell me of you, bade me trust you, but
      I do not greatly care to be deceiv'd
      That have no use for trusting. If your master   15
      Would have a queen his beggar, you must tell him,
      That majesty, to keep decorum, must
      No less beg than a kingdom: if he please
      To give me conquer'd Egypt for my son,
      He gives me so much of mine own, as I   20
      Will kneel to him with thanks.
Pro.   Be of good cheer:
      Y'are fall'n into a princely hand, fear nothing,
      Make your full reference freely to my lord,
      Who is so full of grace, that it flows over
      On all that need. Let me report to him   25
      Your sweet dependency, and you shall find
      A conqueror that will pray in aid for kindness,

8. S.D. *Enter Proculeius*] F; *Enter, to the gates of the monument, Proculeius, Gallus, and Soldiers. Capell.*

such a state is surely natural.' For *palates* = tastes, cf. *Troil.*, IV. i. 59: 'Not *palating* the taste of her dishonour.' A little earlier (IV. xv. 62) Cleopatra has described the world as now 'No better than a sty', and in I. i. 35–7 *ante*, Antony contrasts the nobleness of life in love with kingship over clay: 'our dungy earth alike,' he says, 'feeds beast as man': and as the play is full of reminiscences, we have probably one such here. And it is probably the attraction of an inoffensive for an unpleasant idea, repulsive to modern refinement, rather than the association with the word *nurse*, which has caused so many editors to read *dug* for *dung* with Warburton.

8. Enter . . . *Proculeius* . . .] With what follows, to line 46, cf. North, *post*, p. 274. And see Appendix IV.

14. *care to be deceiv'd*] i.e. care whether I am deceived or not (Delius).

20. *as*] = that, after *so*. Cf. *R3*, III. iv. 37 (Q): 'And finds the testy gentleman so hot, / *As* he will lose his head ere give consent,' etc., and see Abbott, *Shakespearian Grammar*, §109.

23. *Make your . . . reference*] refer your case.

27. *pray in aid*] a legal term, as Hanmer pointed out. Here, with the context, equivalent to beg your assistance in order that he may omit no kindness. 'This word (Ayde) is also particularly used in matter of Plead-

Where he for grace is kneel'd to.

Cleo.   Pray you, tell him
I am his fortune's vassal, and I send him
The greatness he has got. I hourly learn   30
A doctrine of obedience, and would gladly
Look him i' the face.

Pro.   This I'll report, dear lady.
Have comfort, for I know your plight is pitied
Of him that caus'd it.

Enter GALLUS *and soldiers behind.*

Gal. You see how easily she may be surpris'd: 35
[*To Proculeius and the Guard*] Guard her till Cæsar come.
                                                    [*Exit.*

Iras. Royal queen!
Char. O Cleopatra, thou art taken, queen.
Cleo. Quick, quick, good hands.   [*Drawing a dagger.*

34. S.D.] *not in F. See App. IV.*   35. *Gal.*] *Malone; Pro. F; Char. F2. See note.*
36. *To Proculeius . . .*] *Malone; not in F.*   S.D. *Exit*] *Exit Gallus. Malone; not
in F.*   39. *Drawing . . .*] *Theobald; not in F.*

ing, for a Petition made in Court for the calling in of help from another that hath an interest in the cause in question, and is likely both to give strength to the Party that prayeth in ayd of him, and also to avoid a prejudice growing toward his own right, except it be prevented.' So Cowel's *Interpreter*, enlarged by Manley, ed. 2, 1684, under *Ayde*. The meaning of the term seems to admit of the above 'beg *your* assistance' instead of merely 'seek assistance,' and in lines 185–6 *post*, Cæsar says: 'For we intend so to dispose you as / *Yourself shall give us counsel.*' The simpler sense occurs in Bacon's essay 'Of Friendship': 'But yet without *praying in aid* of alchemists,' etc.

29–30. *I send . . . got*] Johnson: 'I allow him to be my conqueror; I own his superiority with complete submission.'

35–6. Gal. *You . . . come*] Theobald

was the first to see, by reference to Plutarch, that line 35 belongs to Gallus. Line 36, however, 'Guard her,' etc., he left to Proculeius, inserting a corresponding stage-direction after line 34: 'Here Gallus, and Guard, ascend the Monument by a ladder, and enter at a back-window.' See *post*, p. 274, for the passage in North which justifies Malone in assigning line 36 also to Gallus, by showing that Proculeius, with two of his men, was now within the monument in presence of Cleopatra, while Gallus remained without.

† See Appendix IV. I have left the original note standing, as an example of the dangers of equating North and Shakespeare. There is nothing in Shakespeare to show that Proculeius ever had two or any other number of men with him, or that he is now anywhere else than he has been throughout. [R]

Pro.   Hold, worthy lady, hold:
                                 [*Seizes and disarms her.*
Do not yourself such wrong, who are in this   40
Reliev'd, but not betray'd.
Cleo.   What, of death, too,
That rids our dogs of languish?
Pro.   Cleopatra,
Do not abuse my master's bounty, by
The undoing of yourself: let the world see
His nobleness well acted, which your death   45
Will never let come forth.
Cleo.   Where art thou, death?
Come hither, come; come, come, and take a queen
Worth many babes and beggars!
Pro.   O, temperance, lady!
Cleo. Sir, I will eat no meat, I'll not drink, sir,—
If idle talk will once be necessary,—   50
I'll not sleep neither. This mortal house I'll ruin,

39. S.D. *Seizes . . .*] *Malone; not in* F.   42. languish] *F;* anguish *Johnson conj.*
49–50. sir,— . . . necessary,—] *See note;* sir, . . . necessary *F.*

42. *languish*] the miserable drooping condition caused by disease or injury. See *Rom.,* I. ii. 50. A late example is cited in *OED*: 'A long record of perishable *languish*' (H. Coleridge, *Poems,* 1851, i. 118).
50. *If . . . necessary,* —] I prefer to regard this line as parenthetical, with Singer and Kinnear. Most editors point, *sir; If . . . necessary, I'll neither:* F has no stop save comma after *sir* and full stop after *neither*. Hitherto (and she reverts to this course in her interview with Cæsar) Cleopatra has silently nursed her purpose and deceived her conquerors. Now, shaken out of her self-possession she reveals it in threats, idle talk, as she calls them by contrast with her settled and previously dissembled purpose. 'Words,' says Daniel's Cleopatra, 'are for them that can complaine and liue' (*Works,* Grosart, iii. 73, *Cleopatra,* IV, line 1154). The line will then mean: 'If for once

I must weakly deal in words': and it seems more naturally to follow the first threats than to be confined to that of not sleeping. Steevens suggested: 'If it be necessary, for once, to talk of performing impossibilities, why, I'll not sleep neither.' Malone and Ritson believed a line to be lost after *necessary*, such as—according to the former—'I'll not so much as syllable a word.' Hanmer has *accessary*, and so, too, the Collier MS and Staunton, the last-named explaining: 'and if idle talk will for the nonce be assistant, I'll not sleep.' Capell reads *speak* for *sleep*. The omission of the line (50), as one cancelled by Shakespeare but retained by the printer, has also been suggested. With Cleopatra's threats, cf.: 'I neuer will nor eate, nor drinke, nor taste / Of any Cates that may preserue my life / I neuer will nor smile, nor sleepe, nor rest.' *A Woman Kilde with Kindnesse,* 1607 (Pearson's *Heywood,* ii. 151).

Do Cæsar what he can. Know, sir, that I
Will not wait pinion'd at your master's court,
Nor once be chastis'd with the sober eye
Of dull Octavia. Shall they hoist me up,   55
And show me to the shouting varletry
Of censuring Rome? Rather a ditch in Egypt
Be gentle grave unto me, rather on Nilus' mud
Lay me stark-nak'd, and let the water-flies
Blow me into abhorring; rather make   60
My country's high pyramides my gibbet,
And hang me up in chains.
Pro.   You do extend
These thoughts of horror further than you shall
Find cause in Cæsar.

Enter DOLABELLA.

Dol.   Proculeius,
What thou hast done thy master Cæsar knows,   65
And he hath sent for thee: for the queen,
I'll take her to my guard.
Pro.   So, Dolabella,
It shall content me best: be gentle to her;
[*To Cleo.*] To Cæsar I will speak what you shall please,
If you'll employ me to him.
Cleo.   Say, I would die.   70
                                    [*Exit Proculeius.*

---

56. varletry] Varlotry *F2;* Varlotarie *F.*   66. for the queen] *F;* as for . . . *F2.*
69. *To Cleo.*] *Hanmer.*

52–7.] Cf. IV. xii. 33–9 *ante,* and
v. ii. 207 *et seq. post.*

53. *pinion'd*] with wings clipped (not
'manacled').

58–60.] Cf. the wish in III. xiii.
166–7 *ante.*

61. *high pyramides*] Though *pyramids*
occurs in *Mac.,* IV. i. 57, the classical
and quadrisyllabic plural was the pre-
valent form. Cf. e.g. *Locrine,* III. iv. 32:
'the high *pyramides,* / Which with their
top surmount the firmament'; and
Heywood, *The Actor's Vindication,* n.d.,
London, by G. E. for W. C., p. 7:

'Hercules . . . on his high *Pyramides*
writing *Nil ultra*,' etc.

64. Enter *Dolabella*] In North (see
post, p. 275) it is Epaphroditus who is
sent at this stage. For *Dolabella,* see
ibid., p. 276, the source of lines 196,
206 *post.*

70. Exit Proculeius] This in F is
after *to him,* an interesting illustration
of the time which an exit (like an entrance) took on the Elizabethan stage.
He begins his exit as he concludes his
speech, and Cleopatra speaks to him
as he moves to the door.

Dol. Most noble empress, you have heard of me?
Cleo. I cannot tell.
Dol.   Assuredly you know me.
Cleo. No matter, sir, what I have heard or known:
      You laugh when boys or women tell their dreams,
      Is't not your trick?
Dol.   I understand not, madam.   75
Cleo. I dreamt there was an Emperor Antony.
      O such another sleep, that I might see
      But such another man!
Dol.   If it might please ye,—
Cleo. His face was as the heavens, and therein stuck
      A sun and moon, which kept their course, and lighted
      The little O, the earth.
Dol.   Most sovereign creature,—   81
Cleo. His legs bestrid the ocean, his rear'd arm
      Crested the world: his voice was propertied
      As all the tuned spheres, and that to friends:

71. me?] *Capell;* me. *F.*   81. O, the] *Steevens;* o' th' *F;* O o'th' *Theobald.*

71. *empress*] 'It owns her Antony's widow and ignores Octavia' (Barker).

81. *O, the earth*] This reading squares with Shakespeare's use of O for anything circular, as in *H5*, Prol. 13: 'Within this wooden *O*,' for the first Globe theatre, a round building. See also *MND.*, III. ii. 188; *LLL.*, v. ii. 45. Hanmer has 'orb *o' th' earth*,' as in *Cor.*, v. v. 127.

82. *His legs ... ocean*] Cf. *Cæs.*, I. ii. 134: 'Why man, he doth bestride the narrow world / Like a Colossus,' etc. and Webster, *Appius and Virginia*, III. i. 84: 'The high Colossus that bestrides us all.'

83. *Crested the world*] Percy: 'Alluding to some of the old crests in heraldry where a raised arm on a wreath was mounted on the helmet.'

83–4. *was propertied ... spheres*] was as musical in quality as, etc. 'Pythagoras (saith Censorinus) asserted, that this whole World is made according to musical proportion, and that the seven Planets, betwixt Heaven and the

Earth, which govern the Nativities of Mortals, have a harmonious motion, and Intervals correspondent to musical Diastemes, and render various sounds, according to their several heights, so consonant, that they make most sweet melody; but to us inaudible, by reason of the greatness of the noise, which the narrow passage of our Ears is not capable to receive' (Stanley, *History of Philosophy*, ed. 3, 1701, p. 393, pt ix, sect. iv, chap. iii). See also on II. vii. 14–16 *ante*. This sphere-music is the subject of a poetical scene (the last of Act III) in *Lingua* (Hazlitt's *Dodsley*, ix. 406–10) and recurs constantly in Elizabethan poetry. For *propertied*, cf. *The English Traveller*, I. i. (Pearson's *Heywood*, iv. 9): 'This approues you, / To be most nobly *propertied*, that,' etc.

84. *and that to friends*] Theobald read *when that* with no advantage. Anon. conj. *addrest;* Staunton, *and sweet;* Elze, *and soft.* Cf. Middleton's *The Roaring Girl*, IV. ii. 109: 'when *friends* meet, /

But when he meant to quail, and shake the orb,   85
He was as rattling thunder. For his bounty,
There was no winter in 't: an autumn 'twas
That grew the more by reaping: his delights

87. autumn 'twas] *Thirlby conj.; Theobald, independently; Anthony* it was F.

The music of the spheres sounds not more sweet / Than does their conference.'

85. *quail*] often, as here, transitive; cow, overpower. Cf. *The Three Ladies of London*, 1584 (Hazlitt's *Dodsley*, vi. 266): 'She cannot *quail* me, if she came in likeness of the great devil.'

87. *an autumn 'twas*] † This brilliant emendation is graphically easy (no more than the rectification of two minim errors) if (but only if) we assume, with Dover Wilson, an MS spelling *Automne*, misread by the compositor as *Antonie*.

There is no doubt that *autumn* gives admirable sense, and that the turn of imagination is thoroughly Shakespearean, whereas *Antony* gives no sense at all. For the word, Jonson's use of it in *Volpone*, v. vi. 18, is illustrative: 'You should ha' some would swell now, like a wine-fat, / With such an *Autumn*—Did he gi' you all, Sir?' while for the thought, and particularly the coupling of *bounty* with the idea of autumn, Malone's quotation from *Sonn*. liii brings one near to conviction: 'Speak of the spring, and foison of the year; / The one doth shadow of your beauty show, / The other as your bounty doth appear.'

The real trouble about the emendation is implied in 'but only if' above. The evidence of F is strong that, unless we are to suppose that he altered the spelling of the name every time he came to it, what the compositor had in front of him in his copy was regularly *Anthony* (very occasionally *Anthonie*). And easy though the *Automne-Antonie* confusion would be, to misread *Automne* as a word containing (probably) *y*, and (almost certainly) distinctive long-tailed *h*, would be much

less natural. Further, if, whatever the normal spelling, the copy (whether Shakespeare's autograph or transcript) indicated proper names for italicization, the absence of such indication for the hypothetical *Automne* ought to have made the compositor suspicious. However, as Dr Brooks points out, F's reading at III. xiii. 162, where the compositor apparently took *Cæsarion* as an adjective, suggests that the copy was at least not consistent in such indication. And, for what it is worth, there is no such indication in the 'three pages' of *Sir Thomas More*.

But graphical considerations have much stronger positive than negative force. To show that a blunder was graphically easy is cogent support for an emendation; but to show that it was not easy is slender evidence against an emendation which on other grounds is convincing. Experience of the vagaries of compositors, modern as well as Elizabethan, makes one progressively surer that no blunder is 'impossible'—a word, I think, too readily used in dismissing an emendation on graphical grounds. And I have little doubt that *Automne* is what Shakespeare wrote. [R]

88–90. *his delights . . . in*] This seems to mean that not even the sea of pleasure in which he lived could conceal the strength and greatness of the man, which his very pastimes displayed. Delius explains that Antony was not submerged in his pleasures, but knew how to keep himself always above them. By reading *their back* for *his back* Hanmer made the delights into consistent dolphins but spoiled the sense. With the image, Steevens compares a poem ['Being Absent from his Mistresse,' etc.] from Lodge's *William*

Were dolphin-like, they show'd his back above
The element they lived in: in his livery   90
Walk'd crowns and crownets: realms and islands were
As plates dropp'd from his pocket.

Dol.   Cleopatra!

Cleo. Think you there was, or might be such a man
As this I dreamt of?

Dol.   Gentle madam, no.

Cleo. You lie up to the hearing of the gods.   95
But if there be, or ever were one such,
It's past the size of dreaming: nature wants stuff
To vie strange forms with fancy, yet to imagine

96. or] *F3; nor F, F2.*

Longbeard, 1593 (see *Glaucus and Scylla,* etc., Chiswick Press, 1819, p. 115): 'Oh, faire of fairest, dolphin-like, / Within the riuers of my plaint, / With labouring finnes the waue I strike,' etc. In the explanation of the frontispiece to a work on the 'Law of Drinking,' quoted in Braithwaite's *Barnabee's Journal* (ed. Hazlitt, 1876, pp. 44–5 *note*), occurs: 'Next adjoyning stands the signe of the Dolphin with a bush and upon the signe this impreze, TEMULENTIS LÆTOR IN UNDIS.'

91. *crownets*] coronets, as in IV. xii. 27 *ante, q.v.* Crowns and crownets are put for their wearers, as often drum for drummer and the like.

92. *plates*] silver coins or pieces, a sense derived from the Spanish form (*plata*) of *plate.* Cf. *Christmas Carols,* from a collection 'probably printed between 1546 and 1552' (*Bibliographical Miscellanies,* Oxford, 1813, p. 51: 'For .xxx. *plates* of money / His mayster had he solde,' etc. Steevens quotes Marlowe's *Jew of Malta,* line 865: 'What, can he steale that you demand so much? / Belike he has some new tricke for a purse / And if he has, he is worth 300 *plats.*' And again, immediately after: 'Ratest thou this Moore but at 200 *plats*?' The Spanish original reappears in *Tom Cringle's Log,* 1834, chap. xiii: 'and last of all we got

two live land-crabs from the servants, by dint of persuasion and a little *plata,* and clapped one into each stocking foot.'

96. *or*] Mr Thiselton thinks *nor* of F, F2 'has been unwarrantably changed to *or,* owing to its being overlooked that this line is in direct contrast with the preceding, and that *nor* implies an ellipsis of *neither* or *not.*' 'Cleopatra would ask,' he says, ' "But assuming for the moment you are right, how came I to dream of such a one?" ' This is ingenious, but Shakespeare's ellipses of *neither* are always unmistakable and cause no ambiguity.

97. *It's past . . . dreaming*] No dream can come up to the reality. The thought is not unlike *Oth.,* II. i. 63–5 (F as usually emended): 'One that excels the quirks of blazoning pens, / And in the essential vesture of creation / Does tire the ingener.' Cf. 'size of words,' *Tim.,* v. i. 71.

98. *To vie . . . fancy*] to compete with fancy in the creation of strange forms. 'To vie' in gaming was to stake or counter-stake, originally (see Skeat, *Etymol. Dict.*) 'to draw on or invite a game' by staking a sum, *vie* and *invite* being different forms of one original. Cf. *Shr.,* II. i. 303, and *Swetnam the Woman Hater,* 1620, IV. iii, where the tying of Misogynus to a post and

An Antony were nature's piece, 'gainst fancy,
Condemning shadows quite.

Dol.   Hear me, good madam:
Your loss is as yourself, great; and you bear it   101
As answering to the weight: would I might never
O'ertake pursued success, but I do feel,
By the rebound of yours, a grief that smites
My very heart at root.

Cleo.   I thank you, sir: 105
Know you what Cæsar means to do with me?

Dol. I am loath to tell you what, I would you knew.

Cleo. Nay, pray you, sir,—

Dol.   Though he be honourable,—

Cleo. He'll lead me then in triumph.

Dol. Madam, he will, I know 't.   110

[*Flourish and shout within,* "Make way there: Cæsar!"

Enter PROCULEIUS, CÆSAR, GALLUS, MÆCENAS, *and
others of his Train.*

104. smites] *Capell;* suites *F;* shoots *Pope.*   109. triumph.] *F;* triumph? *Pope.*
110. S.D.s] *See note.*

pricking him with pins is jocularly treated as a game of Post and Pair: '*Scold.* First, stake. *Mis.* Oh, oh, oh, oh, . . . *Aur.* Againe, for me too, I will *vye* it'; also Braithwaite, *Strappado for the Diuell,* 1615 (repr. 1878), p. 146: 'from his eyes / Her teares by finde their renew'd supplies, / Both *vie* as for a wager, which to winne,' etc.

99–100. *were nature's piece . . . quite*] would be a masterpiece of conception which would entirely discredit the unsubstantial creations of fancy. For *piece,* see on III. ii. 28 *ante,* and cf. Mabbe, *Celestina,* 1631, IV (Tudor Trans., p. 97): 'Not a woman that sees him, but praiseth Nature's workmanship, whose hand did draw so perfect a *piece*'; etc.

102–3. *would I might . . . but I do*] may I never achieve my aim if I do not. . .

104. *smites*] Pope's reading (shoots), which Malone and Boswell adopt, relying on the once similar pronuncia-

tion of *suits* and *shoots,* is further supported by Mr Thiselton's reference to *Cor.,* v. i. 45: 'grief-shot / With his unkindness.' But it does not agree with 'at root,' as *smites* does, †and also produces an impossible assonance. [R] Cf. *smites me,* line 170 *post.*

110–11. Enter *Proculeius,* etc.] With what follows, down to line 189, cf. North, *post,* pp. 275–6.

S.D.s] † F reads here as follows:

Dol. Madam, he will, I know't.
                          Flourish.

*Enter Proculeius, Cæsar, Gallus,
Mecenas, and others of his Traine.*

All. Make way there *Cæsar.*

This is all puzzling. In the first place, one feels that the 'Make way' must surely precede Cæsar's entry. And in the second place what is Proculeius doing apparently leading the procession? The usual modern method of dealing with it has been to have a 'shout within' along with the flourish,

Cæs. Which is the Queen of Egypt?

Dol. It is the emperor, madam.   [*Cleopatra kneels.*

Cæs. Arise, you shall not kneel:
   I pray you, rise, rise, Egypt.

Cleo.   Sir, the gods
   Will have it thus, my master and my lord   115
   I must obey.

Cæs.   Take to you no hard thoughts;
   The record of what injuries you did us,
   Though written in our flesh, we shall remember
   As things but done by chance.

Cleo.   Sole sir o' the world,
   I cannot project mine own cause so well   120
   To make it clear, but do confess I have
   Been laden with like frailties, which before
   Have often sham'd our sex.

Cæs.   Cleopatra, know,
   We will extenuate rather than enforce:
   If you apply yourself to our intents,   125

and to demote Proculeius to a humbler place. This will serve, and perhaps gives the modern reader (and producer) as near as we can get to what was intended. But it is not wholly satisfying, and one or two observations fall to be made. First, on the Elizabethan stage the 'Make way' would need to precede Cæsar's appearance at the entrance door by very little, if at all. He still has to make his way some distance down stage, and a certain amount of noise and bustle would not be amiss. Second, the guard have presumably, from the time of Cleopatra's capture, been lining the back of the stage, guarding the exits, and it is they who have to make way. Is it possible that Proculeius does in fact enter first, perhaps with a few soldiers, as a kind of advance party, and that the 'Make way' comes from the guard, clearing the doors under his instructions, and not from 'voices off'? [R]

120. *project*] frame or set forth. The projector of Shakespeare's day was the promoter of ours, one who framed or planned a scheme and set it forth to the best advantage. The extension of the sense from *plan* to *set forth* seems, therefore, natural, but I have not met with another example of the latter. The former is common. Cf. Nabbes, *Covent Garden*, IV. iii (*Works*, Bullen, i. 67): 'A countrey Gentleman to sell his land, is as it were to change his copie: leave his knowne trade to *project* a better profit'; and Quarles, *Argalus and Parthenia*, bk i (ed. 1701, p. 14): '*Projects* and casts about which way to find / The progress of young Parthenia's heart.'

121. *clear*] clear of blame.

124. *enforce*] press home, emphasize [frailties]. Cf. II. ii. 99 *ante*; and *Cæs.*, III. ii. 42: 'his glory not extenuated, wherein he was worthy, nor his offences *enforced*, for which he suffered death.'

125. *If . . . intents*] if you conform yourself to my intentions, fall in with my designs.

Which towards you are most gentle, you shall find
A benefit in this change, but if you seek
To lay on me a cruelty, by taking
Antony's course, you shall bereave yourself
Of my good purposes, and put your children   130
To that destruction which I'll guard them from,
If thereon you rely. I'll take my leave.
Cleo. And may through all the world: 'tis yours, and we
   Your scutcheons, and your signs of conquest shall
   Hang in what place you please. Here, my good lord. 135
Cæs. You shall advise me in all for Cleopatra.
Cleo. [*handing a paper.*] This is the brief: of money, plate,
   and jewels,
   I am possess'd of, 'tis exactly valued,
   Not petty things admitted. Where's Seleucus?

Enter SELEUCUS.

Sel. Here, madam.   140
Cleo. This is my treasurer, let him speak, my lord,

---

133. *And may . . . world*] As Delius
remarks, Cleopatra takes *leave* in a
wider sense than Octavius. She tells
him that liberty to do his will is now
his without restriction of place; or,
perhaps, says, as Deighton puts it: 'the
whole world is yours and therefore you
are free to go through it from end to
end.'

134. *scutcheons*] shields, or represen-
tations of them, showing the armorial
bearings. Cf. *1H4*, v. i. 142: 'Honour
is a mere *scutcheon*'; *LLL.*, v. ii. 565.

137. S.D.] † Craig added the useful
'*Giving a scroll*' at this point, Dover
Wilson '*she proffers a paper*' two lines
earlier. I think Craig is right. 'Here,
my good lord' is said as Cleopatra gets
ready to hand the paper, and Cæsar's
line, which has nothing to do with the
paper but is an anticipation of lines
185–6, really interrupts continuous
speech and action on her part. [R]

brief] concise list, schedule. See
MND., v. i. 42: 'There is a *brief* how
many sports are ripe,' etc. Also in

sense of *abstract* or *summary*, as in
Edward III, ii. i. 82: 'Whose body as an
abstract or a *brief*, / Contains each
general virtue in the world'; Jonson,
A Tale of a Tub, v. ii. 52: 'Give me the
brief of your subject.'

139. *admitted*] because Cleopatra
immediately calls Seleucus to witness
that she has reserved nothing. Theobald reads, 'Not petty things *omitted*';
'for this declaration,' he says, 'lays
open her falsehood; and makes her
angry when her treasurer detects her
in a direct lie.' But her anger, as Johnson observes, is because 'she is accused
of having reserved more than petty
things.' Warburton, Hanmer, and
Capell read as Theobald.

Enter *Seleucus*] † Capell, followed by
most editors since, brought on Seleucus
in Cæsar's train at line 110. But what
is he doing there? And if he had
already gone over to Cæsar why does
Cleopatra here explain who he is? For
the episode which follows, see pp.
275–6. [R]

Upon his peril, that I have reserv'd
To myself nothing. Speak the truth, Seleucus.

Sel. Madam,
    I had rather seel my lips, than to my peril   145
    Speak that which is not.

Cleo.   What have I kept back?

Sel. Enough to purchase what you have made known.

Cæs. Nay, blush not, Cleopatra, I approve
    Your wisdom in the deed.

Cleo.   See, Cæsar! O behold,
    How pomp is follow'd! mine will now be yours,   150
    And should we shift estates, yours would be mine.
    The ingratitude of this Seleucus does
    Even make me wild. O slave, of no more trust
    Than love that's hir'd? What, goest thou back?
        thou shalt
    Go back, I warrant thee: but I'll catch thine eyes   155
    Though they had wings. Slave, soulless villain, dog!

---

145. seel] *F* (seele), *Johnson, and some others;* seal *F3* (seale) *and most edd.*   156.
soulless villain] *Pope* (soul-less); Soule-lesse, Villain *F.*

145. *seel*] †*seel* in its technical sense is to close a hawk's eyelid by a stitch. I see no reason for deserting F, and some for retaining it. (i) Out of the seventy-one occurrences in Shakespeare of *seal* (verb or noun), in the ordinary sense or a metaphorical sense derived from it, there is not a single instance of the spelling with *ee* (apart from one misprint *steale* and one *seal* it appears always as *seale* or *Seale*), and the same is true of the twenty-six occurrences of the past participle. It seems a gratuitous assumption that this is the one instance of error out of 100. (ii) The emendation (for it is an emendation, and not, as the above count shows, merely a matter of accepting one of two spellings commonly confused) is usually supported by the statement that *seel* is used only of the eyes. This statement—unless it means that the word in its technical sense is only so used, which is so obvious as to be hardly worth stating

—is just not true. Of the four occurrences of *seele* or *seeling* in F, three have to do with the eyes, but in the fourth, *Oth.*, 1. iii. 270, the speculative and officed instrument which (if we accept F rather than Q as giving us Shakespeare's word) is to be *seeled* is much more than the eyes. And in any case if we are going to confine Shakespeare's metaphorical use of a word to the limits of its everyday use we are going to find ourselves in deep waters. (iii) In the matter of appropriateness to the context, *seal* makes Seleucus say, in effect, 'I would rather keep my mouth shut than tell lies,' a sufficiently vapid remark, whereas *seel* allows him to say 'I would rather submit to a painful operation than tell lies.' [R]

150. *mine*] i.e. my followers.

154–6. *What, goest thou back? thou shalt,* etc.] said as Seleucus recoils before Cleopatra's threatening advance.

156. *soulless villain*] † F's *Soule-lesse,*

O rarely base!
Cæs.   Good queen, let us entreat you.
Cleo. O Cæsar, what a wounding shame is this,
That thou vouchsafing here to visit me,
Doing the honour of thy lordliness   160
To one so meek, that mine own servant should
Parcel the sum of my disgraces, by
Addition of his envy. Say, good Cæsar,
That I some lady trifles have reserv'd,
Immoment toys, things of such dignity   165
As we greet modern friends withal, and say

Villain, can no doubt be defended, but it seems to weaken the crescendo of invective from a creature despicable but still human, through something barely human, to something not human at all. [R]

161. *meek*] Malone: 'tame, subdued by adversity . . . Cleopatra, in any other sense, was not eminent for meekness.'

162-3. *Parcel . . . envy*] *OED* observes that the verb here has not been satisfactorily explained, and cites the versions of Johnson ('To make up into a mass') and Schmidt ('To enumerate by items, specify'). Johnson does not explain how he takes *addition*, on which much depends and, in any case, if *parcel* means what he says, *sum* is rather unnecessary. Schmidt, like Delius, takes *addition* as 'the summing up of numbers,' which suits his sense of *parcel* and yields, practically, 'reckons up my disgraces by his malicious adding up *or* counting.' But Seleucus had not done this: what he did was to increase the number of disgraces by one more, a sense at least met by Malone—whom most editors follow—with 'add one more parcel or *item* to the sum of my disgraces, namely, his own malice.' The difficulty is the doubtful possibility of Malone's interpretation of 'parcel by addition.' After the morris dance in Nashe's *Summer's Last Will* (III, p. 240, line 209) *Ver* says: 'May it please my lord, this is the grand capitall summe: but there are certayne parcels behind, as you shall see,' to which *Summer* rejoins: 'Nay, nay, no more: for this is all too much.' 'tis participle *parcell'd* occurs in *R3*, II. ii. 81, but in sense, distributed, severally assigned: 'Their woes are parcell'd, mine are general.'

† Since *piece* can mean 'piece out', extend by adding pieces, as in I. v. 45 *ante*, may not *parcel* mean 'extend by adding "parcels,"' i.e. extra items? [R]

165. *Immoment*] Of no moment or consequence. No other example of the word is known.

166. *modern*] ordinary, common. Cf. *Oth.*, I. iii. 109; *Mac.*, IV. iii. 170: 'where violent sorrow seems / A modern ecstasy.' See also Jonson, *The Poetaster*, v. iii. 280: 'Alas! that were no modern consequence,' etc., and *AYL.*, II. vii. 156, '*modern* instances.' The present-day sense was also in use. It is probably the sense in Marston's *Scourge of Villanie*, ix. 45: 'O what a tricksie, lerned, nicking strain / Is this applauded, senseless, *modern* vain'; and certainly in *Jack Drum's Entertainment*, 1601, iv. 37 (*School of Shakspere*, 1878, II. 183): 'Brother, how like you of our *modern* wits? How like you the new Poet *Mellidus*?' In the same play, IV. 100 (*ibid.* 185): 'Indeed I yeeld, 'tis *moderne* policie, / To kisse euen durt that plaisters vp our wants,' the sense is as likely, or more so, to be 'common'.

Some nobler token I have kept apart
For Livia and Octavia, to induce
Their mediation, must I be unfolded
With one that I have bred? The gods! it smites me   170
Beneath the fall I have. [*To Seleucus*] Prithee go hence,
Or I shall show the cinders of my spirits
Through the ashes of my chance: wert thou a man,
Thou wouldst have mercy on me.

Cæs.   Forbear, Seleucus.

                                    [*Exit Seleucus.*

Cleo. Be it known, that we, the greatest, are misthought   175
For things that others do; and when we fall,
We answer others' merits in our name,

171. *To Seleucus*] *Johnson; not in F.*   174. S.D. *Exit . . .*] *Capell; not in F.*   177.
merits in our name,] *Johnson;* merits, in our name *F.*

168. *Livia*] Cæsar's wife.

169–70. *unfolded With*] exposed by. *Unfold* has a similar sense in *Oth.*, IV. ii. 141, v. i. 21. For *with* = by, see *Wint.*, v. i. 113, v. ii. 68, *Lr*, II. iv. 308, etc.

172–3. *cinders . . . chance*] The metaphor from fire concealed under ashes is very frequent. See II. ii. 13 *ante*; Sidney's *Arcadia*, ii (1725 ed. i, p. 202): 'so truly the cold ashes laid upon my fire, did not take the nature of fire from it. Full often hath my breast swollen with keeping my sighs imprisoned,' etc.; R. Tailor's *The Hog hath lost his Pearle*, I. i (Hazlitt's *Dodsley*, xi. 431): 'I am that spark, sir, though now raked up in ashes; / Yet when it pleaseth fortune's chaps to blow / Some gentler gale upon me, I may then / From forth of embers rise and shine again.' Jonson uses it very nobly in *Sejanus*, I. 97–101. Cleopatra says that the fires of her nature are within an ace of showing that they are not utterly overwhelmed by the ashes to which her power and prosperity (see on *chance*, III. x. 36 *ante*) have been reduced; in plain English, that her misfortunes have not subdued her past a dangerous resentment. Dr Hudson, however, adopts *spirit* (S. Walker conj.

and Collier MS) for *spirits* (used III. xiii. 69 *ante*)—an unnecessary change —and Dr Ingleby's 'correction' (*Shakespeare Hermeneutics*, 1875, p. 158) of *glance* for *chance*, on the ground that 'neither *my cħance*, nor *mischance* [Hanmer], nor *my change* [S. Walker conj.], appears to answer the occasion or the speaker's mood: we seem,' he says, 'to need some word referring directly to Cleopatra's own person or personal appearance.' Why?

174. *Forbear*] equivalent to 'withdraw.' Cf. *Forbear me*, I. ii. 118 *ante*.

175. *misthought*] misjudged. Cf. *3H6*, II. v. 107: 'How will the country . . . / *Misthink* the king and not be satisfied!'

177. *We answer . . . name*] We answer (are accountable) in our own names for the demerits (or misdeeds) of others. Cf. *Stukeley*, line 1126 (Simpson's *School of Shakspere*, i. 204): 'No sir I will not, and will *answer it*.' The observation is general, or Cleopatra has forgotten that she has practically acknowledged the particular delinquency. Delius separates 'in our name' from 'answer', and makes 'others' merits in our name' = what others have misdone in our name; but the connection with 'answer' is too probable to be lightly dismissed, admitting

Are therefore to be pitied.

Cæs.   Cleopatra,
Not what you have reserv'd, nor what acknowledg'd,
Put we i' the roll of conquest: still be 't yours,   180
Bestow it at your pleasure, and believe
Cæsar's no merchant, to make prize with you
Of things that merchants sold. Therefore be cheer'd,
Make not your thoughts your prisons: no, dear queen,
For we intend so to dispose you, as   185
Yourself shall give us counsel: feed, and sleep:
Our care and pity is so much upon you,
That we remain your friend, and so adieu.

Cleo. My master, and my lord!
Cæs.   Not so: adieu.

                    [*Flourish. Exeunt Cæsar and his Train.*

Cleo. He words me, girls, he words me, that I should not   190
Be noble to myself. But hark thee Charmian.

                                    [*Whispers Charmian.*

Iras. Finish, good lady, the bright day is done,
And we are for the dark.

Cleo.   Hie thee again,

---

191. S.D. *Whispers . . .*] *Theobald; not in* F.

---

this expansion to be possible. *Merits*
and *demerits* were used interchange-
ably. Cf. Braithwaite, *Strappado for
the Diuell*, 1615 (repr. 1878, p. 174):
'That those which wil not labour they
should sterue, / For rightly so their
merits do deserue,' etc., with *Cor.*, i. i.
277: 'Opinion . . . shall / Of his *demerits*
rob Cominius,' and *Oth.*, i. ii. 22.

182. *make prize with you*] This usually
escapes comment, but Deighton explains 'with you' as 'together with
you,' quoting *R3*, iii. vii. 184: 'widow
. . . / Made *prize* and purchase of his
wanton eye.' Schmidt, however, explains *prize* as *estimation*, quoting *Cym.*,
iii. vi. 76, *Lr*, ii. i. 122, leaving us to
speculate whether he takes 'make' etc.
as make estimation 'like you' (as
Deighton understands him), *or* (referring to the goods), in the same category with you, *or*, finally, make estima-

tion along with you, i.e. enter into the
question of reservations with you
('whether 'tis exactly valued, / Not
petty things admitted'), a tempting
sense if *prize* can really equal estimation in the sense of valuation.

† But prize can also mean a contest
—see *Mer.V.*, iii. ii. 142, 'Like one of
two contending in a prize,' and though
OED does not give an example of
'make prize' = 'engage in a contest' it
seems a quite possible phrase, and is
certainly the natural sense here
required, 'to haggle.' [R]

184. *Make not . . . prisons*] Johnson:
'Be not a prisoner in imagination,
when in reality you are free.' Cf.
Bacon, *Device on the Queen's Day* (1595),
'The Hermit's Speech in the Presence';
'there is no *prison* to the *prison* of the
thoughts, which are free under the
greatest tyrants.'

I have spoke already, and it is provided,
Go put it to the haste.

Char.   Madam, I will.   195

Re-enter DOLABELLA.

Dol. Where's the queen?
Char.   Behold, sir.   [*Exit.*
Cleo.   Dolabella!
Dol. Madam, as thereto sworn, by your command
    (Which my love makes religion to obey),
    I tell you this: Cæsar through Syria
    Intends his journey, and within three days   200
    You with your children will he send before:
    Make you best use of this. I have perform'd
    Your pleasure, and my promise.
Cleo.   Dolabella,
    I shall remain your debtor.
Dol.   I your servant.
    Adieu, good queen, I must attend on Cæsar.   205
Cleo. Farewell, and thanks.   [*Exit Dolabella.*
                    Now, Iras, what think'st thou?
    Thou, an Egyptian puppet shall be shown
    In Rome as well as I: mechanic slaves
    With greasy aprons, rules, and hammers shall

---

196. *Exit*] *not in F; Exit Charmian placed here by Capell; line 195 Theobald.*   206.
Exit . . .] *Capell; Exit. F, after* Cæsar.   207. shall] *F;* shalt *F2 and edd.*

195. *the haste*] Cf. *i' the haste* for 'in great haste' (*Lr*, II. i. 26).

196. Exit] †another example of Elizabethan exit, not easy to indicate, as the discrepancy between Theobald and Capell interestingly shows. Charmian begins to move off on *Madam, I will*, and meets Dolabella on her way to the door. [R]

196–206. *Dolabella! . . .*] Cf. North, *post*, p. 276.

207. *an Egyptian puppet*] an allusion to the innumerable puppet shows of the time, which drew their subjects from contemporary events, as well as popular plays, and history, sacred and profane. See Jonson, *Bartholomew Fair*,

v. i. 6: 'O the motions, that I Lanthorn Leatherhead have given light to, in my time, since my Master Pod died! Jerusalem was a stately thing; and so was Nineveh, and the City of Norwich, and Sodom and Gomorrah; with the rising of the prentices; and pulling down the bawdy-houses there, upon Shrove-Tuesday; but the *Gunpowder-plot*, there was a get-penny!' etc. With what follows, cf. IV. xii. 33 *et seq.* and v. ii. 55–7 *ante*.

209. *rules*] instruments for ruling straight lines, and measuring short lengths, used by carpenters, etc. Cf. *Cæs.*, I. i. 7: 'Where is thy leather apron and thy *rule*?' and Sylvester's *Du*

Uplift us to the view. In their thick breaths,   210
Rank of gross diet, shall we be enclouded,
And forc'd to drink their vapour.
Iras.   The gods forbid!
Cleo. Nay, 'tis most certain, Iras: saucy lictors
Will catch at us like strumpets, and scald rhymers
Ballad us out o' tune. The quick comedians   215
Extemporally will stage us, and present
Our Alexandrian revels: Antony
Shall be brought drunken forth, and I shall see
Some squeaking Cleopatra boy my greatness
I' the posture of a whore.
Iras.   O the good gods!   220
Cleo. Nay, that's certain.

---

215. Ballad] *F2;* Ballads *F.*   o'] *Theobald;* a *F.*   219. squeaking Cleopatra
boy] *F* (Boy)*;* speaking-Cleopatra-Boy *F2.*

Bartas, The Magnificence, 1621 ed., p. 447: 'Where e'r she [Wisdom] go, she never goes without / Compasse and *Rule,* Measure and weights about.'

212. *drink*] inhale. Cf. Jonson, *E.M.I.,* III. v. 137: 'The most divine tobacco that ever I drunk,' or (in case that suggests a Robinson Crusoe decoction), Purchase, *Pilgrimage,* IX. i. 820, 'after they have drunke the smoke of a certain herbe.'

213. *lictors*] As Dover Wilson points out, Shakespeare is probably equating lictors with beadles, who officially dealt with strumpets, cf. *Lr,* IV. vi. 166.

214. *scald*] scabbed, scurvy. So in *H5,* v. i. 5: 'the rascally, *scald,* beggarly, lousy, pragging knave, Pistol,' etc.

215. *Ballad us*] Cf. *Andromana,* v. ii (Hazlitt's *Dodsley,* xiv. 267): 'I shall be grown discourse for grooms and foot-boys, / Be *balladed,* and sung to filthy tunes.' Massinger deplores the plague of ballads at the end of *The Bondman,* in a longer passage containing these lines: 'Let but a chapel fall, or a street be fired, / A foolish lover hang himself for pure love, / Or any such like acci-

dent, and, before / They are cold in their graves, some damn'd ditty's made,' etc.

quick] Malone: 'lively, inventive, quick-witted,' for Johnson's 'gay, inventive.'

216. *stage us, and present*] So Jonson, *Poetaster,* III. iv. 197: 'I hear you'll bring me o' the *stage* there; you'll play me, they say; I shall be presented by a sort of copper-laced scoundrels of you: life of Pluto! an you *stage* me, stink-ard,' etc.

219. *boy*] English, unlike continental practice, confined female parts to boys or young men on public stages, till a clause in the patent granted to D'Avenant in Jan. 1662–3 provided: 'That, whereas the women's parts in plays have hitherto been acted by men in the habits of women, at which some have taken offence, we permit and give leave for the time to come, that all women's parts be acted by women.' See D'Avenant, *Works,* 1872, I. lxvii (*Prefatory Memoir*). In 1656, he had already experimented by giving the part of Ianthe in his musical piece, *The Siege of Rhodes,* to Mrs Coleman. See *ibid.,* lxiv.

Iras. I'll never see't! for I am sure my nails
    Are stronger than mine eyes.
Cleo.   Why, that's the way
    To fool their preparation, and to conquer
    Their most absurd intents.

Re-enter CHARMIAN.

                        Now, Charmian!   225
Show me, my women, like a queen: go fetch
My best attires. I am again for Cydnus,
To meet Mark Antony. Sirrah Iras, go
(Now noble Charmian, we'll dispatch indeed),
And when thou hast done this chare, I'll give thee leave
To play till doomsday: bring our crown, and all.   231
         [*Exeunt Charmian and Iras. A noise within.*
Wherefore's this noise?

Enter a Guardsman.

Guard.   Here is a rural fellow,
    That will not be denied your highness' presence,
    He brings you figs.
Cleo. Let him come in.   [*Exit Guardsman.*
           What poor an instrument   235

---

222. my] *F2;* mine *F.*   224. to conquer] *F;* conquer *F2.*   225. absurd] *F;*
assur'd *Theobald;* abhorr'd *Kinnear;* obscene *D. Wilson conj.*   228–9. go (Now
. . . indeed,)] *F; Rowe removed parentheses.*   231. S.D.] *F has no exit; Exit Iras.
Malone; Exit Iras. Charmian falls to adjusting Cleopatra's Dress. Noise within. Capell.
See App. IV.*   235. What] *F;* How *F2.*

225. *absurd*] †Why this desire for
emendation? *Absurd* is surely triumphantly proleptic, 'the intents that I
am going to make look silly'; cf. *ass,
Unpolicied* in lines 306–7. [R]

227. *I . . . Cydnus*] See II. ii. 187 *et seq.,
ante.*

228. *Sirrah*] Women were often ad-
dressed thus. Cf. *Ralph Roister Doister,*
IV. viii. 2: 'Ah *sirrha* now, Custance,'
etc. Philippa calls Violetta *sirrah* in
Middleton's *The Widow,* III. ii. 28. See
also on IV. xv. 85 *ante,* and examples in
Pearson's *Dekker,* ii. 383, illustrating
Westward Hoe, p. 292.

230. *chare*] See on IV. xv. 75 *ante,* and

cf. *Sir Thomas More* (Shakespeare Soc.,
1844, p. 37): 'This *charre* being charde,
then all our debt is payd.'

231. Exeunt] See Appendix IV.

232, etc. *Here . . . rural fellow . . .*] See
North, *post,* p. 277.

235. *What poor an instrument*] Abbott
(*Shakespearian Grammar,* §422) treating
of transposition of the article, observes
on this passage that 'we can say "how
poor an instrument," regarding "how"
as an adverb, and "how poor" as an
adverbialised expression, but not
"what poor an instrument," because
"what" has almost lost with us its
adverbial force.'

May do a noble deed! he brings me liberty:
My resolution's plac'd, and I have nothing
Of woman in me: now from head to foot
I am marble-constant: now the fleeting moon
No planet is of mine.

Re-enter Guardsman, with Clown bringing in a basket.

Guard.   This is the man.   240
Cleo. Avoid, and leave him.   [*Exit Guardsman.*
  Hast thou the pretty worm of Nilus there,
  That kills and pains not?
Clown. Truly I have him: but I would not be the party
  that should desire you to touch him, for his biting is   245
  immortal: those that do die of it, do seldom or never
  recover.
Cleo. Remember'st thou any that have died on 't?
Clown. Very many, men and women too. I heard of one
  of them no longer than yesterday, a very honest   250
  woman, but something given to lie, as a woman
  should not do, but in the way of honesty, how she
  died of the biting of it, what pain she felt: truly, she
  makes a very good report o' the worm: but he that
  will believe all that they say, shall never be saved   255
  by half that they do: but this is most falliable, the
  worm's an odd worm.

---

239. marble-constant] *hyphened by Capell.*   240. S.D. *Re-enter . . .*] *Globe;
Enter Guardsman, and Clowne. F; with a Basket. added by Rowe.*   256. falliable] *F;
fallible F2 and edd.*

239. *marble-constant*] Philoclea, in
Sidney's *Arcadia*, bk ii, inscribed her
vows of chastity on marble; but sub-
sequently blaming her love for Zelmane, composed other verses to sub-
join to the former, confessing 'how ill
agree in one, / A woman's hand with
constant marble stone.'
  fleeting moon] As at III. xiii. 153–4,
q.v., Capell thinks that Cleopatra's
imitation of the goddess Isis, the moon
goddess, is alluded to. The suggestion
here is originally Warburton's.
  242. *worm*] snake; an old and com-

mon sense. So in *Cym.*, III. iv. 37: 'out-
venoms all the *worms* of Nile'; Jonson,
Sejanus, v. 47: 'T'express a *worm*, a
snake!'
  249. *of*] from.
  256. *falliable*] Editors read *fallible*
with F2, but the odd form may be as
intentional as the positions of *all* and
half in the preceding clause, which
Warburton wished to transpose. Cf.
infalliable in Kirk, *Secret Commonwealth*,
etc., 1691, ed. Lang, 1893, p. 48; and,
in general, the grave-diggers in
Hamlet.

Cleo. Get thee hence, farewell.

Clown. I wish you all joy of the worm. [*Setting down his basket.*

Cleo. Farewell. 260

Clown. You must think this, look you, that the worm
    will do his kind.

Cleo. Ay, ay, farewell.

Clown. Look you, the worm is not to be trusted, but in
    the keeping of wise people: for indeed, there is no 265
    goodness in the worm.

Cleo. Take thou no care, it shall be heeded.

Clown. Very good: give it nothing, I pray you, for it is
    not worth the feeding.

Cleo. Will it eat me? 270

Clown. You must not think I am so simple but I know
    the devil himself will not eat a woman: I know, that
    a woman is a dish for the gods, if the devil dress her
    not. But truly, these same whoreson devils do the
    gods great harm in their women: for in every ten 275
    that they make, the devils mar five.

Cleo. Well, get thee gone, farewell.

Clown. Yes, forsooth: I wish you joy o' the worm. [*Exit.*

Re-enter CHARMIAN *and* IRAS *with a robe, crown, and
other jewels.*

Cleo. Give me my robe, put on my crown, I have
    Immortal longings in me. Now no more 280
    The juice of Egypt's grape shall moist this lip.
    Yare, yare, good Iras; quick: methinks I hear
    Antony call. I see him rouse himself
    To praise my noble act. I hear him mock
    The luck of Cæsar, which the gods give men 285

---

259. *Setting . . .*] Capell; not in F.   278. S.D. *Re-enter . . . jewels*] no S.D. in F;
Re-enter Iras with a robe, crown, etc. Malone, *followed by most other edd. See App. IV.*

262. *his kind*] what his nature dic-
tates. Cf. 'the deed of *kind*' (*Mer. V.*, I.
iii. 86); Jonson, *The New Inn*, III. ii.
250: 'She did her *kind*, according to her
latitude'; Fuller, *The Profane State*, v.
xviii, 1648, p. 477: 'Diseases do but
their *kind*, if they kill, and an evil
expected, is the lesse evil: but no such

Torment as to die of the remedie,'
etc.

278. S.D.] See Appendix IV.

279. *robe, . . . crown*] Cf. North, *post*,
pp. 277–8.

280. *Immortal longings*] longings for
immortality.

282. *Yare, yare*] deftly.

To excuse their after wrath. Husband, I come:
Now to that name, my courage prove my title!
I am fire, and air; my other elements
I give to baser life. So, have you done?
Come then, and take the last warmth of my lips.   290
Farewell, kind Charmian, Iras, long farewell.
          [*Kisses them. Iras falls and dies.*
Have I the aspic in my lips? Dost fall?
If thou and nature can so gently part,
The stroke of death is as a lover's pinch,
Which hurts, and is desir'd. Dost thou lie still?   295
If thus thou vanishest, thou tell'st the world
It is not worth leave-taking.
Char. Dissolve, thick cloud, and rain, that I may say,
          The gods themselves do weep!

---

291. S.D. *Kisses* . . .] *Malone; Kissing them. Hanmer; Kissing them. Iras falls. Capell; not in F.*

286. *their after wrath*] nemesis, disaster sent to punish arrogance resulting from excessive good luck.

288. *my other elements*] i.e. earth and water, as man was thought to be composed of the four elements, whose relative proportions determined his character in each case. Cf. *H5*, III. vii. 22 of the Dauphin's horse: 'he is pure air and fire; and the dull *elements* of earth and water never appear in him'; *Tw.N.*, II. iii. 10; *Cæs.*, v. v. 73. There is a full discussion of the matter in Sylvester's *Du Bartas*, week 1, day 2, pp. 20–2 in 1621 ed., from which is: 'For, in our Flesh, our Bodie's Earth remains: / Our vitall spirits, our Fire and Aire possess: / And last, our Water in our humours rests.'

289. *I give . . . life*] according to Deighton, 'I leave to be eaten by worms.' I doubt the idea's being so definite. 'Fire and air' are that part of Cleopatra which she supposes to escape through death to immortal life: her other elements she leaves with the *baser* conditions she is quitting, baser whether compared with the new life or with death, by which that is to

be nobly attained. In my view it is simply life in a general sense, the abstract idea of life as opposed to death, that is implied.

291. *Charmian, Iras*] So the folio; with the result in sound of slow, unbroken movement befitting farewells and, in sense, of uniting both women in the long adieu. The usual separative pointing, *Charmian; Iras*, gains nothing but a paltry contrast of the halves of the line.

292. *aspic*] the form of the word used by North (see *post*, pp. 268, 278) and others. So in *Oth.*, III. iii. 451.

Dost fall] Steevens: 'Iras must be supposed to have applied an asp to her arm while her mistress was settling her dress, or I know not why she should fall so soon.' I am rather inclined to agree with Delius that Iras is meant to die of grief at parting from her mistress. After all, the improbability is little, if any, greater than that connected with the death of Enobarbus.

† But Dover Wilson, I think rightly, says that *This* in line 299 surely implies a self-sought death. [R]

Cleo.   This proves me base:
If she first meet the curled Antony,   300
He'll make demand of her, and spend that kiss
Which is my heaven to have. Come, thou mortal
    wretch,
[*To an asp, which she applies to her breast*] With thy sharp
    teeth this knot intrinsicate
Of life at once untie: poor venomous fool,
Be angry, and despatch. O, couldst thou speak,   305
That I might hear thee call great Cæsar ass,
Unpolicied!
Char.   O eastern star!
Cleo.   Peace, peace!
Dost thou not see my baby at my breast,
That sucks the nurse asleep?
Char.   O, break! O, break!
Cleo. As sweet as balm, as soft as air, as gentle.   310

302. S.D. *To . . .*] *Capell (substantially); To the Serpent. Pope; not in F.* 306-7.
ass, Unpolicied] *F; most edd. omit comma.*

300. *curled*] Probably she thinks of
Antony as she first saw him, 'barber'd
ten times o'er' (II. ii. 224 *ante*), again
set off to the best advantage for this
meeting, as she herself will be (lines
226–8 *ante*) in 'her best attires,' 'again
for Cydnus, / To meet Mark Antony.'
Shakespeare alludes to the fashion of
his own day, as in *Oth.*, I. ii. 68: 'The
wealthy *curled* darlings of our nation.'
Cf. Lyly, *Midas*, III. ii. 40: 'A lowe
curle on your head like a Bull or dang-
ling lock like a spaniel? . . . your love-
lockes wreathed with a silken twist, or
shaggie to fall on your shoulders?'

301. *He'll make demand . . . kiss*]
Johnson: 'He will enquire of her concerning me, and kiss her for giving him
intelligence.' (†A kindly explanation;
but Shakespeare's Cleopatra knew her
Antony better than Johnson did.
[R]

302. *mortal*] deadly. Similarly used
of a creature in *2H6*, III. ii. 263 ('The
mortal worm'), and elsewhere in
Shakespeare.

wretch] merely = creature. Cf.

Oth., III. iii. 90: 'Excellent *wretch*!'

303. *intrinsicate*] intricate. The word,
as has been pointed out, is ridiculed as
a 'new-minted epithet' in Marston's
preface to his *Scourge of Villanie*, 1598,
and affectedly used by Amorphus in
Jonson's *Cynthia's Revels* (in the 1616
folio additions), v. ii. 14: 'Yet there are
certain *puntilioes*, or (as I may more
nakedly insinuate them) certaine
intrinsecate strokes, and wardes, to
which your actiuitie is not yet mount-
ed.' See *Lr*, II. ii. 80, for *intrinse* in same
sense: 'Such smiling rogues as these, /
Like rats, oft bite the holy cords
a-twain / Which are too intrinse to
unloose.'

308. *baby*] In Peele's *Edward I*, xvi.
20–6, the same idea occurs to Queen
Elinor, when she cruelly kills the
Mayoress by applying a serpent to her
breast: 'Why, so; now she is a nurse.—
Suck on, sweet babe.' See also *Christ's
Tears*, etc., 1593–4 (Grosart's *Nashe*,
prose, iv, pp. 211–12): 'At thy breasts
(as at Cleopatraes) aspisses shall be
put out to nurse.'

O Antony! Nay, I will take thee too.

[Applying another asp to her arm.

What should I stay—   *[Dies.*

Char. In this vile world? So fare thee well.
Now boast thee, death, in thy possession lies
A lass unparallel'd. Downy windows, close,   315
And golden Phœbus, never be beheld
Of eyes again so royal! Your crown's awry,
I'll mend it, and then play.

Enter the Guard, rustling in.

First Guard. Where's the queen?
Char.   Speak softly, wake her not.
First Guard. Cæsar hath sent—
Char.   Too slow a messenger.   320

[Applies an asp.

311. S.D. *Applying . . .*] *Theobald; not in* F.   313. vile] *Capell; wilde* F.   317.
awry] *Rowe, ed. 3;* away F.   318. play.] *Capell;* play— F.   319. Where's]
F; Where is *Hanmer.*   320. S.D. *Applies . . .*] *not in* F; *Charmian and Iras apply
the asp. Rowe.*

311. Applying another . . . arm]
One aspic (biting the arm only, not
the breast) is mentioned in Plutarch,
though some Latin writers speak of
two: see *post*, p. 278; and Sir T.
Browne, *Vulgar and Common Errors*, v.
xii, 'Of the Picture describing the
death of Cleopatra,' speaking of the
breast being indicated as the place in
some writers, says: 'But herein the
mistake was easy, it being the custom
in capital malefactors to apply them
unto the breast; as the author *De
Theriaca ad Pisonem*, an eye-witness
hereof in Alexandria, where Cleopatra died, determineth; "I beheld,"
saith he, "in Alexandria, how suddenly these serpents bereave a man of
life; for when any one is condemned to
this kind of death, if they intend to use
him favourably, that is, to despatch
him suddenly, they fasten an asp unto
his breast, and bidding him walk
about, he presently perisheth thereby."' Halliwell (folio ed.) quotes this
passage.

312. *What*] *Why*, as in *Lr*, II. iv. 264,
266.

313. *vile*] F *wilde* is probably a misprint of *vilde*, a very common form of
vile; but some editors retain *wild* =
desert, savage. Cf. '*vilde* lady!', IV. xiv.
22 *ante*. Here I respect Capell's
modernization.

315. *windows*] eyelids, as in *Rom.*, IV.
i. 100: 'thy eyes' *windows* fall'; *Cym.*,
II. ii. 22, and elsewhere.

317. *awry*] †A few editors have
attempted to justify F's *away*, Furness
on the very strange grounds that *away*
is 'more smooth and liquid than the
crooked, harsh' *awry* (a good example
of the dangers of looking at a word
instead of hearing it). But the emendation is graphically easy (the comparatively frequent *a : r* confusion),
and I think that Dover Wilson's apposite quotation from Daniel's *Cleopatra*,
v. ii. 268–9, 'in her sinking down shee
wryes / The Diadem' is decisive. [R]

318. *play*] a touching reference to
her mistress's words, line 231 *ante*.

O, come apace, despatch, I partly feel thee.
First Guard. Approach ho, all's not well: Cæsar's beguil'd.
Sec. Guard. There's Dolabella sent from Cæsar; call him.
First Guard. What work is here, Charmian? Is this well done?
Char. It is well done, and fitting for a princess   325
   Descended of so many royal kings.
   Ah, soldier!   [*Dies.*

Re-enter DOLABELLA.

Dol. How goes it here?
Sec. Guard.   All dead.
Dol.   Cæsar, thy thoughts
   Touch their effects in this: thyself art coming
   To see perform'd the dreaded act which thou   330
   So sought'st to hinder.
                    [*Within* 'A way there, a way for Cæsar!'

Enter CÆSAR and all his Train, marching.

Dol. O sir, you are too sure an augurer;
   That you did fear, is done.
Cæs.   Bravest at the last,
   She levell'd at our purposes, and being royal
   Took her own way: the manner of their deaths?   335
   I do not see them bleed.
Dol.   Who was last with them?
First Guard. A simple countryman, that brought her figs:

---

324. here, Charmian? Is] heere *Charmian.* Is *F; here?—Charmian, is Capell and most edd.*

---

320. *ad fin. Cæsar hath sent—*] See North, *post*, pp. 278.

324. *What work . . .*] †Capell's emendation, usually accepted, produces a better rhythm, and, for what it is worth, a closer approximation to North; but I am not clear that we are therefore justified in deserting F. [R]

327. S.D.] F brings Dolabella in with the guard at 318, as well as giving him an entry here. Cf. III. x. S.D.

329. *Touch their effects*] meet with realization. Cf. *Lr*, IV. ii. 14.

334. *levell'd at*] guessed correctly; an image from levelling a weapon to take aim, which also occurs in *Mer. V.*, I. ii. 41. It means *aimed at* in *No-body and Some-body* (Simpson's *School of Shakspere*, i. 298): 'My thoughts are *leveld* at a bloody end'; and for the concrete sense, cf. Sylvester's *Du Bartas*, ed. 1621, week 1, day 7, lines 22–3: 'A skilfull Gunner wtih his left eye winking, / *Levels* dircctly at an oak hard by.'

337. *simple*] of humble degree. Cf. *Lr*, IV. vi. 156: 'yond *simple* thief.'

This was his basket.

Cæs.   Poison'd then.

First Guard.   O Cæsar;
This Charmian lived but now, she stood and spake:
I found her trimming up the diadem   340
On her dead mistress; tremblingly she stood,
And on the sudden dropp'd.

Cæs.   O noble weakness!
If they had swallow'd poison, 'twould appear
By external swelling: but she looks like sleep,
As she would catch another Antony   345
In her strong toil of grace.

Dol.   Here on her breast,
There is a vent of blood, and something blown,
The like is on her arm.

First Guard. This is an aspic's trail, and these fig-leaves
Have slime upon them, such as the aspic leaves   350
Upon the caves of Nile.

Cæs.   Most probable
That so she died: for her physician tells me
She hath pursued conclusions infinite

---

351. caves] caues *F;* canes *Barry conj.*

---

344. *external swelling*] Cf. North, *post*, p. 278, and see on line 311 *ante.* There are many allusions to the painlessness of the death caused by asps; in Sylvester's *Du Bartas, The Lawe* (p. 350 in 1621 ed.), the absence of swelling is also noted. 'So th' Aspick pale . . . doth spet / . . . / A drowzy bane, that inly creeps, and burns / So secretly, that without sense of pain, / Scar, wound, or swelling, soon the Partie's slain.'

347. *blown*] † This is usually explained as 'swollen', which I find very hard to accept. No doubt *blown* can mean 'swollen', but it does not appear to suit the context. It will be observed that the Guard does not say '*Here* is an aspic's trail,' as though he was looking elsewhere about the room, but '*This* is,' presumably referring to whatever Dolabella has discovered on breast and arm. I think therefore that *blown* must refer to something like the track of a snail. [R]

351. *caves*] † Though I have not ventured to promote it to the text, I think Barry's emendation almost certain. No doubt there were caves by the Nile, and no doubt 'aspics' may have left slime in them. But 'upon the caves' is an odd expression for the natural 'in the caves' or 'upon the walls of the caves,' whereas the parallel between the *canes* and the fig-leaves is appropriate. The misreading of *n* as *u* is easy. [R]

353. *conclusions*] experiments, as in *Ham.*, III. iv. 195; *Cym.*, I. v. 18, etc. So Braithwaite, *His Odes*, 1621, No. 7, verse 6: '*These, conclusions* try on man, / *Surgeon and Physician,*' etc. For the physician's information, cf. North, *post*, p. 268.

Of easy ways to die. Take up her bed,
And bear her women from the monument;   355
She shall be buried by her Antony.
No grave upon the earth shall clip in it
A pair so famous: high events as these
Strike those that make them: and their story is
No less in pity than his glory which   360
Brought them to be lamented. Our army shall
In solemn show attend this funeral,
And then to Rome. Come, Dolabella, see
High order, in this great solemnity.   [*Exeunt.*

357. *clip*] clasp. See on IV. viii. 8 *ante.*

359. *Strike . . . make them*] afflict those whose actions have caused them. A reflection corresponding with v. i. 36 *et seq., ante*: 'I have follow'd thee to this, . . . but yet let me lament,' etc.

360–1. *No less . . . lamented*] apparently elliptical for: and the tale of these events is as pitiful as the renown of him who caused their lamentable nature is glorious. But in an uncritical perusal, the mind—and perhaps rightly after all—may refer *their* in *their story* to *A pair so famous*, and understand: and there is as much to pity in their story as glory for him who made them objects of pity.

APPENDIX I

'An arm-gaunt steed' (i. v. 48)

In favour of *arm-gaunt*, or at least its first syllable, are (1) the frequent application to *horse* or *steed* of epithets from arms, as war-apparelled, barbed, harnessed, all-armed, as in Drayton's *Baron's War*, vi. 85 (ed. Morley, p. 159) 'Why fell I not from that all-armed horse On which I rode before the gates of Gaunt', etc.; (2) the existence of like compounds, as the Chaucerian *arm-greet* (as great as one's arm), *arm-strong* (strong of arm: *Locrine*, i. i; iii. i; iii. iv), etc.; and the fact that *arm* was not restricted to the limbs of man (see *OED*, *s.v.*). (*a*) From *gaunt* = lean, we have suggested meanings: worn lean by much service in war (Warburton), gaunt by bearing arms (Collier), thin-shouldered (Seward, pref. to *Beaumont and Fletcher*: in 1778 ed., p. lxxi, note), thin as one's arm (Halliwell, who compares *arm-greet*, as above), having lean fore-limbs (*Temple Shakespeare*),? with gaunt limbs (*OED*). The following from Sylvester's *Du Bartas* (*The Handycrafts*, p. 227 in 1621 ed.) favours the latter meanings in giving some characteristics of 'a gallant Horse':

> With Pasterns short, vpright (but yet in mean);
> Dry sinewie shanks; strong, flesh-less knees, and lean;
> With Hart-like legs, etc.

(*b*) From derived senses of *gaunt*: looking fierce in armour (Boswell: who conjectures a sense 'fierce' for *gaunt* from its being used of animals made savage by hunger), hungry for battle (Thiselton; relying on Jonson, *Catiline*, iii. i. 199: 'and let His own [i.e. Jove's] gaunt Eagle flie at him, to tire', a reference of Staunton's). In *OED* under sense *hungry, greedy*, etc. I find: Smollett, *Reproof*, 125, 'Gorg'd with our plunder, yet still gaunt for spoil', etc. (*c*) From *gaunt* as = gaunted, i.e. gloved, armour-gloved (Nicholson), gloved in arms (Schmidt). No evidence of the sense is adduced: *Gaunters* occurs for Glovers in the list of crafts and plays, dated 1415, pr. in *York Plays*, ed. Toulmin Smith, 1881. (*d*) Schmidt suggests also: completely armed, harnessed; *or rather* lusty in arms, full of life and martial spirits, from another *gaunt* found in Old English, the German *ganz*, signifying 'whole', 'healthful', 'lusty'. The *English Dialect Dict.* (Wright) has *ganty* (of a horse) = frisky (Sussex), and I find in Braithwaite, *Barnabee's Iournall*, pt 3 (ed. Hazlitt, 1876, sig. H3), presumably in a somewhat similar sense:

> Where were dainty Ducks, and gant ones,
> Wenches that could play the wantons, etc.

In the following, however, *gaunte* seems to mean slenderness in a maid: 'hur medyll ys bothe gaunte and small' (*Anglia*, 10 Aug. 1908, p. 315, *Songs* temp. *Henry VIII*, from Rawlinson MS c. 813).

The chief emendations proposed are: *arm-girt* (Hanmer), *termagaunt* (Mason), *war-gaunt* (Jackson), *arrogaunt* (Boaden), *rampaunt* (Lettsom). As to *arm-girt*, *guirt* is a common spelling of *girt*, and the word (which Hudson adopts) retains the article *an* of the text. Singer urges this advantage on behalf of *arrogant* (adopted by himself, Delius, and Deighton), and cites 'el cavallo arrogante' from Lope de Vega's *Auraco Domado*. In the *Times Literary Supplement*, 29 April 1920, Dr John Sampson proposed to read *armigerent*, as possibly coined by Shakespeare, 'intending to call up a picture of the horse's trappings, emblazoned with the armorial bearings of his master'. (†But challenge any actor to deliver the line as thus emended! [R].)

APPENDIX II

MISLINEATION

Here are some examples of F's mislineation, taken from II. ii. (I have modernized the spelling but retained the punctuation.)

II. ii. 8–14

> I would not shave't to day.
> *Lep.* 'Tis not a time for private stomaching.
> *Eno.* Every time serves for the matter that is then born in't.
> *Lep.* But small to greater matters must give way.
> *Eno.* Not if the small come first.
> *Lep.* Your speech is passion: but pray you stir
> No embers up. Here comes the noble *Antony*.
> *Enter Antony and Ventidius*
> *Eno.* And yonder *Cæsar*.

It may be observed that Lepidus' speeches will do very well as they are. But unless Enobarbus, who has hitherto been talking unmistakable verse, suddenly lapses into prose, his first complete 'line' ('Every time . . .') will not do at all, and to cure it involves a general reshuffle, so that modern editors, probably rightly, print

        I would not shave't to-day.
Lep.   'Tis not a time
        For private stomaching.
Eno.   Every time
        Serves for the matter that is then born in't.
Lep. But small to greater matters must give way.
Eno. Not if the small come first.
Lep.   Your speech is passion:
        But, pray you, stir no embers up. Here comes
        The noble Antony.
             Enter Antony and Ventidius
Eno.   And yonder, Cæsar.

II. ii. 118–24

Agri. Thou hast a sister by the mother's side, admir'd
        Octavia? Great *Mark Antony* is now a widower.
Cæsar. Say not, say *Agrippa*; if *Cleopater* heard you, your
        proof were well deserved of rashness.
Ant.   I am not married Cæsar: let me hear *Agrippa*
        further speak.

This is a curious passage. An oasis of prose cannot have been intended in the middle of a straight run of regular verse (which the compositor set quite correctly). All one can say is that the compositor, for whatever reason, whether difficulty with his copy (but why should the copy have been more difficult here than just before or just after?) or from a temporary fit of drowsiness, struck a bad patch, since not only does he set verse as prose, but he makes certainly two blunders (a second 'say' for 'so', with transposed comma, and *Cleopater*) and perhaps two more (a question mark and 'proof' for 'reproof'). This is usually regularized thus:

Agri. Thou hast a sister by the mother's side,
        Admir'd Octavia: great Mark Antony
        Is now a widower.
Cæs.   Say not so, Agrippa;
        If Cleopatra heard you, your reproof
        Were well deserv'd of rashness.
Ant.   I am not married, Cæsar: let me hear
        Agrippa further speak.

It is worth notice that the passage, even when regularized, contains two incomplete lines. I see no other way of dividing the lines, but this suggests that in other places there may be more than one readjustment possible, as in the next example.

II. ii. 29–37

> *Ant.* I learn, you take things ill, which are not so:
> Or being, concern you not.
> *Cæs.* I must be laugh'd at, if or for nothing, or a little, I
> Should say myself offended, and with you
> Chiefly i' the world. More laugh'd at, that I should
> Once name you derogately: when to sound your name
> It not concern'd me.
> *Ant.* My being in Egypt *Cæsar*, what was't to you?
> *Cæs.* No more than my residing here at Rome. . . .

Up to a point this is plain enough; Cæsar's first five words are clearly the completion of the preceding line, and Rowe's cure has been universally accepted

> *Ant.* I learn, you take things, ill that are not so,
> Or being, concern you not.
> *Cæs.*   I must be laugh'd at,
> If, or for nothing or a little, I
> Should say myself offended, and with you
> Chiefly i' the world: more laugh'd at that I should
> Once name you derogately,

but after this things are much less plain. Almost all editors, even those who are elsewhere earnestly and even sometimes fussily determined to extort more or less metrical lines from the most unpromising material, happily accept F's 'Once name . . . your name' as a line, and follow Capell in redistributing the rest thus:

> Once name you derogately, when to sound your name
> It not concern'd me.
> *Ant.*   My being in Egypt, Cæsar,
> What was't to you?
> *Cæs.* No more than my residing here in Rome. . . .

On this one may observe that the F line can be made metrical only by an awkwardly slurring rapidity of delivery which will reduce the six syllables 'you derogately when' to the value of two feet instead of three, and, further, that whatever we do we are going to be left with an incomplete line somewhere, so that two other redistributions are possible, one of them, I think, preferable to Capell's:

> Once name you derogately, when to sound
> Your name it not concern'd me.
> *Ant.*   My being in Egypt,
> Cæsar, what was't to you?
> *Cæs.* No more than . . .

or

> Once name you derogately, when to sound

> Your name it not concern'd me.
> *Ant.* My being in Egypt, Cæsar, what was't to you?
> *Cæs.* No more than . . .

II. ii. 158–63

> At heel of that, defy him.
> *Lepi.* Time calls upon's,
> Of us must *Pompey* presently be sought,
> Or else he seeks out us.
> *Anth.* Where lies he?
> *Cæsar.* About the Mount-Misena.
> *Anth.* What is his strength by land?
> *Cæsar.* Great, and increasing:
> But by sea he is an absolute master.
> *Anth.* So is the fame.

This is a good example of the results of the practice of starting each new speech with a new line. It looks like prose, and one might also be tempted to think that Shakespeare had intended this staccato interchange to be prose, if it were not for Lepidus' one complete line, which is unmistakable verse. The operations of the early editors were surprisingly tentative. Some adhered to F, and even Theobald produced the odd 'line' 'Great and increasing, but by sea'. But from Hanmer onwards the accepted distribution has been

> At heel of that, defy him.
> *Lep.*   Time calls upon's:
> Of us must Pompey presently be sought,
> Or else he seeks out us.
> *Ant.*   Where lies he?
> *Cæs.* About the Mount Misena.
> *Ant.*   What's his strength
> By land?
> *Cæs.*   Great and increasing, but by sea
> He is an absolute master.
> *Ant.*   So is the fame.

(Hanmer made a further, and attractive, change by attributing 'By land' to Cæsar. See the notes, *ad loc.*)

II. ii. 193–5

> Purple the sails: and so perfumed that
> The winds were love-sick.
> With them the oars were silver,
> Which to the tune of flutes kept stroke, and made
> The water . . .

This is an example of a type of mislineation rare in this play, namely of unmistakable mislineation (and incidentally of mispunctuation) occurring in the middle of a continuous piece of verse otherwise correctly set. It may be that Shakespeare had here made some alterations in the copy which confused the compositor, or simply that the correct line was too long for the narrow column and the compositor arbitrarily divided it, getting his punctuation wrong in the process. I give (in F's spelling) the next longest line in the passage, which just fills the width of the column, for purposes of comparison.

With diuers coulour'd Fannes whose winde did seeme,
The Windes were Loue-sick. With them the Owers were Silver,

[It may have been expected that on this question of mislineation I should have at least referred to the views of Dr R. Flatter, set out in *Shakespeare's Producing Hand* (1948). I shall have a good deal to say about them later, so far as they bear upon *Othello*, on the textual problems of which Dr Flatter has views both decided and remarkable, and from which he adduces a considerable number of his instances. But he adduces few from *Antony and Cleopatra*, as is indeed natural, since the problems of this play are in the main not ones to which his views are helpfully applicable. And I will therefore for the moment content myself with a brief comment. Dr Flatter is a scholar and knows Shakespeare. But I do not believe that anyone, however scholarly and however well read, can appreciate the prosodic subtleties of a language other than his own, since he has not, in the nature of the case, the indispensable native ear. When therefore Dr Flatter is dealing with metrical considerations, and basing his arguments upon them, he seems to me almost uniformly wide of the mark, and wandering in a region which he does not begin to understand. When, on the other hand, he is dealing with points of dramatic effectiveness and verisimilitude (for example, and especially, his point that, when a new speaker has had no chance of hearing what the last speaker said, it would be unreasonable of him to open with a metrical completion of an unfinished line), then I think he has a great deal that is of interest, and something that is of value, to say.]

APPENDIX III

PUNCTUATION

(*a*) I. v. 59–78. F has two misprints in words (*mans* for *man* in 61 and *Parago nagaine* for *Paragon againe*); it prints some verse as prose (63–7); and in punctuation it has one intrusive colon (after *againe* in 71) and a probably intrusive comma (after *say* in 75). The rest of the punctuation, though far from modern, is certainly not impossible. But Case, Craig, and Dover Wilson make respectively fifteen, fourteen, and thirteen alterations in punctuation. They agree in deleting three commas and a colon, in inserting at least four commas (Case six), in replacing one comma by colon or full stop, and one comma and one full stop by exclamation marks. (*b*) III. xiii. 182–201. F has one misprint (*in* for *on* in 199) and a comma (after *lightning* in 195) where even on Elizabethan principles a heavier stop would probably be better. Case, Craig, and Dover Wilson make fifteen, fourteen, and seven changes in punctuation. Case and Craig, apart from the usual insertions and deletions of commas, replace a comma by a heavier stop five times, and semi-colon or colon by the next heavier stop twice; but in the other direction they lighten a full stop or colon to semi-colon or comma three times. (*c*) v. ii. 345–64. F has one misprint (*Solmemnity* for *Solemnity* in 364), one possible misprint (*caues* for, perhaps, *canes* in 351), a comma after *monument* in 355 where a heavier stop would be more natural, and a comma after *show* in 362 but no comma after *shall* at the end of the line before. Case, Craig, and Dover Wilson make thirteen, thirteen, and ten changes. They all insert two commas and delete two; Case and Craig replace four commas by heavier stops (Dover Wilson only two); but Case and Craig both replace a full stop and a colon by the next lighter stop.

There follow some further examples of the different effect produced by the two types of punctuation.

EXAMPLES OF FOLIO PUNCTUATION

(I have throughout taken the original Arden edition's punctuation as typical of the 'usual' modern text.)

I. iii. 71–3

(Arden)   *Cleo.*   Cut my lace, Charmian, come;
                          But let it be: I am quickly ill, and well,
                          So Antony loves.

(F)   *Cleo.* Cut my Lace, *Charmian* come,
                 But let it be, I am quickly ill, and well,
                 So *Anthony loues.*

v. ii. 193-5

(Arden) *Cleo.* Hie thee again:
I have spoke already, and it is provided;
Go put it to the haste.

(Craig, by the way, even adds a comma after 'Go'.)

(F) *Cleo.* Hye thee againe,
I haue spoke already, and it is prouided,
Go put it to the haste.

In both these examples the light punctuation of F is tantamount to a stage-direction, in the first *Cleo.* (*in agitation*), in the second, *Cleo.* (*with hurried urgency*). She has no time for semi-colons.

I. iv. 12

(Arden) His faults in him seem as the spots of heaven,

(F) His faults in him, seeme as the Spots of Heauen,

Where the F comma, I think, throws the required emphasis on to *him*—in a lesser man, Lepidus means, the faults would darken all the goodness. I have made this yet plainer in the present edition by inserting the second comma which the modern reader expects, before *in*.

II. ii. 151-3

(Arden) let her live
To join our kingdoms and our hearts; and never
Fly off our loves again!

(F) Let her liue
To ioyne our kingdomes, and our hearts, and neuer
Flie off our Loues againe.

The comma after *kingdomes* points the distinction between the official union and the personal concord.

II. vii. 101-2

(Arden) but I had rather fast from all four days
Than drink so much in one.

(F) but I had rather fast from all, foure dayes, then
drinke so much in one.

The F commas emphasize the duration of the fast (in modern American idiom 'Yes, and I mean "fast"').

III. iv. 11-12

(Arden) Believe not all; or, if you must believe,
Stomach not all.

(F)   Beleeue not all, or if you must beleeue,
Stomacke not all.

Almost no one in speech would make the pause suggested by the 'logical' comma after *or*. And the same difference between speech and thought is shown in the next two examples.

IV. xiv. 62–4

(Arden)   Thou art sworn, Eros,
That, when the exigent should come,—which now
Is come indeed,—

(F)   Thou art sworne *Eros*,
That when the exigent should come, which now
Is come indeed:

IV. xiv. 85

(Arden)   Turn from me, then, that noble countenance . . .

(F)   Turne from me then that Noble countenance . . .

IV. xii. 9–20

An example of the greater rapidity of delivery suggested by F's punctuation.

(Arden) *Ant.*   All is lost;
This foul Egyptian hath betrayed me:
My fleet hath yielded to the foe; and yonder
They cast their caps up and carouse together
Like friends long lost. Triple-turn'd whore! 'tis thou
Hast sold me to this novice; and my heart
Makes only wars on thee. Bid them all fly;
For when I am revenged upon my charm,
I have done all. Bid them all fly; begone.
O sun, thy uprise shall I see no more:
Fortune and Antony part here; even here
Do we shake hands. All come to this? . . .

(F)   *Ant.* All is lost:
This fowle Egyptian hath betrayed me:
My Fleete hath yeelded to the Foe, and yonder
They cast their Caps vp, and Carowse together
Like Friends long lost. Triple-turn'd Whore, 'tis thou
Hast sold me to this Nouice, and my heart
Makes onely Warres on thee. Bid them all flye:
For when I am reueng'd vpon my Charme,
I haue done all. Bid them all flye, be gone.
Oh Sunne, thy vprise shall I see no more,
Fortune, and *Anthony* part heere, euen heere
Do we shake hands? All come to this?

v. ii. 7–8

(Arden)   Which sleeps, and never palates more the dung,
            The beggar's nurse and Cæsar's.

(F)   Which sleepes, and neuer pallates more the dung,
            The beggers Nurse, and *Cæsars*.

The comma after *Nurse* surely points the ironic levelling-down
of Cæsar.

v. ii. 158–63

(Arden)   O Cæsar, what a wounding shame is this,
            That thou, vouchsafing here to visit me,
            Doing the honour of thy lordliness
            To one so meek, that mine own servant should
            Parcel the sum of my disgraces by
            Addition of his envy!

(F)   O *Cæsar*, what a wounding shame is this,
            That thou vouchsafing heere to visit me,
            Doing the Honour of thy Lordlinesse
            To one so meeke, that mine owne Seruant should
            Parcell the summe of my disgraces, by
            Addition of his Enuy.

This is an interesting example. The modern punctuation, whatever else may be said of it, is as a rule grammatical. But here the
inserted comma after *thou* in the second line wrecks the syntactical
structure by leaving *thou* a nominative hanging over a vacuum. If
a comma was to be inserted at all it should have been after *That*,
since it is plain that *thou vouchsafing . . . doing* is an 'absolute' construction ('when you vouchsafe . . .').

v. ii. 286–7

(Arden)   Husband, I come:
            Now to that name my courage prove my title!

(F)   Husband, I come:
            Now to that name, my Courage proue my Title.

The slight pause after *name* is surely as oratorically masterly as it
is logically indefensible.

APPENDIX IV

SCENES IV. xv AND V. ii

The staging of these scenes is discussed by Granville Barker, *Prefaces to Shakespeare*, second series, pp. 162–6, by Adams, *The Globe Playhouse*, pp. 263–8, and by Jenkin in the *Review of English Studies*, xxi, pp. 1–14. All three assume the use of the inner stages, the upper for iv. xv and the lower for v. ii. But Dover Wilson points out that in both scenes dead bodies have to be carried off (the operation is explicit in the F stage-direction at the end of iv. xv *Exeunt, bearing of Anthonies body*, and implicit in the text of v. ii. 355), and that this carrying off would not be necessary with the curtainable inner stage (cf. the end of *Othello*). He therefore suggests that a temporary monument was devised, 'a square painted wooden structure, with a barred gate in front' to conform with North (see page 282 *post*) 'and a flat roof' and that this structure was 'erected by servitors at the end of iv. xiv on the outer stage over the central trap (through which Cleo. etc., could enter and thence climb to the roof by a concealed stair).' Antony's body would then be 'borne off down the stair at the end of iv. xv.' and the structure would 'remain in position during the brief interval scene (v. i.), be inexpensive to make, and quick to erect.'

This highly ingenious suggestion seems to me to create more, and more difficult, problems than it solves. (*a*) What is the audience, keyed up by Antony's attempted suicide, and waiting for his arrival 'where Cleopatra bides', supposed to be doing between the end of scene xiv and the opening of xv? Watching servitors at work on a bit of stage carpentry? 'Quick' is a relative term, and even five minutes of 'quick erection' would surely be fatally dislocating. (*b*) Would any manager or producer in his senses, having a ready built-in structure with which the two scenes can be adequately staged, go to the nuisance and expense of cluttering up his main stage with a temporary erection? (*c*) I say 'cluttering up' because v. i, cheerfully dismissed by Dover Wilson as a 'brief interval scene', has in fact seventy-seven lines, only fourteen fewer than iv. xv, and a much fuller stage, since besides five speaking characters (and Gallus, who is there only to receive an order) on the stage till a few lines from the end, the F stage-direction brings on also Cæsar's *Counsell of Warre*. There are also two entries, one of which, that of Decretas with Antony's sword, is a dramatic moment. Imagine the Elizabethan stage, with the audience round three sides of it, and this temporary structure in the centre. No part of the audience can get an uninterrupted view of the whole stage, and the only part of the stage that will be visible to all the audience will be a narrow strip in the front. The problems of the producer— to dispose a minimum of ten characters in this restricted space, and to make Decretas' entry effective—are surely insoluble.

Nor does Dover Wilson's argument appear, on examination, particularly cogent. It rests on an unwarranted assumption. It is true that the removal of dead bodies was *unnecessary* when the regular inner stage was in use, since it could be curtained off; but it does not at all follow that the removal was therefore always *undesirable*. In *Othello* there would be no dramatic gain, and some loss, in such a removal; so the tragic lodging of the bed is covered, and Othello is left alone with his wife and her faithful attendant. But in *Antony and Cleopatra* there is every possible reason why 'royal Egypt' should pass from the stage, like Hamlet, with full ceremonial honours, and there is neither mechanical nor any other reason why the bearers should not start as well from the inner as from the outer stage. Dover Wilson, driven by his fixed idea, takes Cæsar's words near the end (v. ii. 354–5): 'Take up her bed, And bear her women from the monument' and comments 'This instruction proves that the deaths take place on the outer stage'. Clearly the instruction *proves* nothing of the kind, and unless the whole stage, outer as well as inner, is by now to be thought of as inside the monument, it *implies* exactly the reverse.

Anyhow, the presence or absence of the temporary structure is irrelevant to the end of the play, except in so far as its presence would be a practical nuisance for the producer in staging the final procession. Would its presence help at any other point in either scene? I think not. (*a*) There is one point in IV. xv where it might at first sight seem to help, and oddly enough Dover Wilson does not adduce this, by far the strongest bit of supporting evidence which the text offers him. At line 8 Diomedes says 'Look out o' the other side your monument.' It is quite true that a structure such as Dover Wilson posits would have more obviously an 'other side' than the permanent 'above'. But I think that this is more than counterbalanced by the fact that the entry of the guard with Antony would be obscured from some of the audience. And there is no real difficulty in staging the episode with the existing stage. Diomedes enters by one door, and talks up to Cleopatra standing at one end of 'above'. On Diomedes' direction she moves to the other end and sees Antony, who has been carried in by the other door. (*b*) The *ad hoc* structure would, so far as I can see, do less than nothing to help with some supposed difficulties in the earlier part of v. ii, and in any case these difficulties are more apparent than real. Let us, for the moment neglecting North, examine what happens, according to F. In the first sixty-four lines of the scene, down to the entry of Dolabella, there are no stage-directions except for the entry of Cleopatra, Charmian, Iras, and Mardian at the opening, and of Proculeius at line 8. Cleopatra and her attendants are perhaps on the inner stage, and she talks to Proculeius, who enters on the outer stage. At one point two successive speeches (lines 32–4, 'This I'll report . . . caus'd it' and lines 35–6, 'You see . . . Cæsar come') are both credited to Proculeius, the speech-heading *Pro.* being repeated, and it is moderately certain that the second of these should be attributed to someone else, presumably (see later) Gallus. At line 35, while listening to Proculeius, Cleopatra is taken unawares by the entry of Cæsar's men behind her; she attempts to stab herself and is prevented by Proculeius. There is no indication in the text where the 'guards' have come from, nor does it particularly matter. It is natural, though not essential, to suppose from earlier indications that Cleopatra is locked in her monument (this is explicit in North, but I am trying for the moment to do without North), and that therefore there is a barred gate across the opening of the inner stage, through which she talks to Proculeius, and which the guard after their entry unbar from inside so that Proculeius can enter. That, I think, is all fairly plain sailing, though no doubt some stage-directions from Shakespeare would have made it plainer. The early editors, beginning with Theobald, followed by Warburton and Johnson, and later elaborated by Malone, vexed in particular by the unaccounted for appearance of the guard, went to work to remedy Shakespeare's (or F's) omissions, and called North to their aid. Here is North (see p. 282):

For Proculeius came to the gates that were very thicke and strong, and surely barred, but yet there were some cranewes through the which her voyce might be heard, and so they without understoode, that Cleopatra demaunded the kingdome of Ægypt for her sonnes: and that Proculeius aunswered her, that she should be of good cheere, and not be affrayed to referre all unto Cæsar. After he had viewed the place verie well, he came and reported her aunswere unto Cæsar. Who immediately sent Gallus to speake once againe with her, and bad him purposely hold her with talke, whilest Proculeius did set up a ladder against that highe windowe, by the which Antonius was trised up, and came downe into the monument with two of his men hard by the gate, where Cleopatra stoode to heare what Gallus sayd unto her. One of her women which was shut in her monuments with her, saw Proculeius by chaunce as he came downe, and shreeked out: O, poore Cleopatra, thou art taken. Then when she sawe Proculeius behind her as she came from the gate, she thought to have stabbed her selfe in with a short dagger she ware of purpose by her side. But Proculeius came sodainly upon her, and taking her by both the hands, said unto her:

From this Hanmer brought in Gallus along with Proculeius at line 8, and at line 35 Theobald read *Here Gallus, and Guard, ascend the Monument by a Ladder, and enter at a back-window*, and Malone *Here Proculeius, and two of the guard, ascend the Monument by a Ladder placed against a window, and having descended, come behind Cleopatra. Some of the guard unbar and open the gates.* Now the first thing to be observed about these directions, whatever their intrinsic merits, and whether it is to be Gallus or Proculeius who leads the storming party, is that, if they are placed where their authors placed them, there is no time for these scaling-ladder operations. They would take an appreciable time, during which Cleopatra must be held in talk by someone—in North it is Gallus, but Shakespeare, compressing two episodes into one, has committed himself to Proculeius. Dover Wilson, seeing this, greatly improves matters as follows: at line 9, *Enter* PROCULEIUS. *As he speaks with* CLEOPATRA *through the bars,* GALLUS *and soldiers enter, unseen by those within, mount to the top with ladders, and go down into the monument,* and after line 34, *The doors are suddenly flung open, showing a richly furnished room, with* GALLUS *and soldiers standing behind* CLEOPATRA *and her women.*

Gallus. You see how easily . . .

Now, if Gallus and the guard have to come on to the outer stage at all, that is the way to do it. They have plenty of time to get into the monument, and the audience has the pleasure of suspense while it waits for their appearance behind Cleopatra. And for this entry the temporary monument would be undeniably convenient. It is true that the unobserved escalade could be conducted on the ordinary stage, so long as Cleopatra and her attendants were kept well back on the inner stage, since to an actor even four or five feet back on the inner stage there are two segments of the outer stage which are invisible. But it would, I think, be unconvincing, whereas if conducted at the rear or one side of the hypothetical structure it would be natural enough.

But is there any reason for having Gallus and the guard on the stage at all until their sudden entry at lines 34–5? If not, F's entry for Proculeius alone at line 8 is justified, and we get rid at one sweep of most of the elaborate additions to the stage-directions. All we need will be at line 34, *Gallus and three or four soldiers enter behind Cleopatra* (and we may have to add *and unbar the gate*, to allow Proculeius to enter the inner stage, but this is a point to be considered later). The sudden irruption is effective, it has the advantage of making line 35 (otherwise a trifle awkward) more natural, as a sort of 'cover' line, explaining their arrival, and the audience will simply assume that they have broken in somewhere at the back of the monument. It is worth quoting some excellent common sense from Furness. 'I have not quoted in the Textual notes all the stage-directions given by the early editors in their vain reachings after those which would satisfy all requirements; nor have I recorded all the minor variations of the modern editors. For my own part, I see no need of any stage-direction at all. It is, at least for me, quite sufficient to see that the Romans rush in and seize the queen. In these thrilling moments, how they got in, I neither know nor care. Nor does any one in the audience ever know how they entered, and would not know, unless the stage-manager came forward and read aloud Plutarch, or Malone's directions.'

We now come to the last main problem in the staging of v. ii, one which is of considerable intrinsic importance, and the consideration of which, I think, finally demolishes the temporary structure. Where, for the first thirty-five lines of the scene, are Cleopatra and her attendants supposed to be? Malone assumed that they were on the inner stage, with a barred gate across the opening. That is all very well for the dialogue with Proculeius, and it is according to North. But it is very far from well for Cleopatra's opening speech. We do not want that to come from a sort of disembodied voice of an imperfectly visible actress. Nor does it make effective the entry of the guard, who would be even less visible. Some editors, seeing this difficulty, bring in Cleopatra *aloft*. This has, for the moment, obvious advantages. It gives Cleopatra a prominent position on the stage, she talks to Proculeius with a barrier between them, though it is one of height, not of a barred gate, and the irruption of the guard—so long as they now appear for the first time—can be made as well on the upper level as on the lower. (Some editors who add *aloft* also retain at line 35 the climb of the guard, watched apparently by Cleopatra with quiet interest.) But these momentary advantages are paid for too high by difficulties later. How does Proculeius arrive where he can prevent Cleopatra's attempt at suicide—unless he joins in the absurd climb of the guard? And at what point does Cleopatra come down from aloft for the scene with Cæsar, which must, I think, occur on the main stage? In any case, this insertion of *aloft* has no authority, and textual evidence is against it, since F's stage-direction for IV. xv specifies an entry *aloft*, and as there is no *aloft* in the v. ii stage-direction it is a reasonable inference that Shakespeare did not intend there to be one, but wished the scene to be played throughout on the lower level, whether or not the inner stage was to be used. The difficulties caused by a gate across the opening of the inner stage have already been glanced at; but consider the much greater difficulties created by a temporary monument. It is, *ex hypothesi*, a square structure, standing in the middle of the stage, with a gate on the side towards the front of the stage. Not only therefore will that part of the audience which faces it see Cleopatra imperfectly (as with the gated inner stage) but about half the audience will not see her at all, but will be looking frustratedly at one or other blank side of the structure. Which, I think, is absurd. The only solution would be to have the structure open—though with bars—on three sides, so that Cleopatra and her attendants would appear like animals in the zoo, or like Bajazeth in *Tamburlaine*. Which is yet more absurd. I think that the structure must be dismantled, along with other ingenious, but not fully thought-out, hypotheses.

If then, we dismiss both an entry aloft and a temporary monument, how is the scene to be presented? There has been an almost universal insistence by editors (except those who make the first entry *aloft*) from Capell downwards that Cleopatra's entry is to a barred inner stage, which is unbarred at line 35. And stage-direction after stage-direction (none of them in F), differing in detail but concurring in general sense, have been devoted to emphasizing this picture. I have pointed out certain weaknesses which this method of staging involves, and I said earlier 'unless the whole stage, outer as well as inner, is by now to be thought of as inside the monument'. I want to hazard the heterodox suggestion that the whole stage should be so thought of, and that if it is many of the difficulties melt into thin air.

Why, then, in the first place, such concurrence of the editors? To this there are, I think, two answers. First, they paid very natural, but excessive, attention to North. It happens that the relevant North passage is not only detailed but pictorially vivid, with the gates very thick and strong, and surely barred, and with their 'cranewes'. And it was naturally felt that Shakespeare, who elsewhere follows North so closely, must have followed him here also, in spite of F. But if Shakespeare had found matter in North which was undramatic or difficult of presentation on his stage, surely he would have jettisoned him without a second thought. (As it is he compresses two episodes of North into one, and the compression has caused part of the editorial troubles.) Second, I think that, accustomed to their own stage with scenery and properties, the editors failed to reckon with the readiness of the Elizabethan audience to change their imaginative conception of what their bare stage was at any moment supposed to represent. It is quite true that in IV. xv 'aloft' is the monument which Cleopatra dare not leave, and the outer stage, on which Antony is carried in, is the outer world. But it does not follow that this must be permanently so. And it is clear that at some point (if not from the start) in v. ii the outer stage has become a room inside the monument. Apart from the scene with Cæsar, which demands a full stage, there is the episode of the 'clown' with the figs, which is, I think, decisive. The F stage-directions are here explicit. Cleopatra is interrupted in her orders to Charmian by '*A noise within*' (i.e. off-stage). '*Enter a Guardsman*', announcing the arrival of 'a rural fellow'. 'Let him come in,' says Cleopatra. '*Exit Guardsman.*' '*Enter Guardsman, and Clowne.*' '*Exit Guardsman.*' The implications are, I think, inescapable. Cleopatra, the means of self-destruction being presumably removed, is under guard in the monument. But the guard is off-stage, not on the outer stage. Therefore the outer stage is now part of a room in the monument.

Suppose we push this conception of 'locality' back to the opening of the scene. Cleopatra and her attendants enter (I think through the curtains of the inner stage, to mark that they come from another room in the monument). She delivers her first speech in full view of the audience. *Enter Proculeius.* Here is, I think, the one real difficulty, a difficulty which some readers may think insuperable. It is that Cleopatra expresses no surprise at his entry. One rather expects her to say, in effect, 'And how, by Isis, did you get in?' I suggest, however, that if one is troubled about the problem at all, which many spectators would not be, one may assume that Cleopatra, hearing that a single emissary has come from Cæsar, has given orders for him to be admitted. (It is reasonable to suppose that Cleopatra still has servants besides her immediate attendants—the Egyptian in v. i. proves that she had at least one—and that some of them were on duty at the outer gates.) This makes it natural enough that he, and not she, opens the conversation, and that she asks as it were for his credentials—what is his name?—with perhaps the hope that he may be the one man whom Antony told her to trust. At line 35 the guards break in from behind, either through the curtains or through the ordinary doors. On these lines the scene plays straightforwardly from beginning to end, and we are relieved of the temptation to add elaborate stage-directions to those of F. Down to the entry of Cæsar at line 110 we need add only the entry of Gallus and the guard at line 34, Gallus's exit at line 36, and perhaps (though the necessary action is clear from the text) Cleopatra's drawing the dagger and Proculeius' removing it from her.

There remains only the minor problem (which has nothing to do with the major one of staging) of Gallus and the muddled speech-heading at line 35. It is, I think, a prime mistake to add Gallus to F's entry of Proculeius alone at line 8. Cæsar's orders to Gallus in v. i. 69 come, according to F's stage-direction, after Proculeius' exit, so that Proculeius supposes himself to be the sole emissary. Further, it seems to me flat contrary to the expectation created by Antony's verdict on Proculeius that we should now find him party to a design to capture the queen. Nor do his speeches feel like those of a man dishonestly playing for time, but rather like those of a man honestly presenting his master's attitude. But Gallus must, I think, be introduced somewhere, not because of North, but because Cæsar gave him orders, and it is bad craftsmanship (though Shakespeare is elsewhere guilty of it, as in *Mer. V.*) to create an expectation which is not fulfilled, and also because we must have someone to take the news to Cæsar (see line 65), and as Gallus enters with Cæsar later it is natural to suppose that he has been the someone. Hence I think it right to cut out the second *Pro.* speech-heading for line 35 ('You see how easily . . .') and give the speech to Gallus, but I suggest that the erroneous speech-heading was not just a matter of careless substitution, but rather of the transference of a proper name from text to speech-heading, and that the lines should run thus:

> *Pro.*   This I'll report, dear lady
>   Have comfort, for I know your plight is pitied
>   Of him that caus'd it. *Enter Gallus and guard behind.*
> *Gal.*   *Proculeius,*
>   You see how easily she may be surpris'd
>   Guard her till *Cæsar* come.   *Exit Gallus.*

v. ii. 231, 278, *stage-directions.* Since F has no stage-directions, editors are free to insert what they consider most consonant with the text and theatrically effective. It has been universally accepted that Capell was right in leaving Charmian on the stage. I am doubtful whether this was Shakespeare's intention and I am sure that the point is profitably arguable, since the determination of it makes a considerable difference to a dramatic moment in the play.

The argument for Iras' exit alone must rest entirely on Cleopatra's words in lines 225–31, and possibly on line 282. (Between lines 232 and 278 there is nothing in the text to indicate whether Charmian is present or absent, nor anything in line 279 to indicate whether the re-entry is of one or both attendants.) Now it is true that Iras alone is specifically ordered to 'go' (line 228), and that if we take F's brackets in line 229 to indicate a *parenthesis* the 'thou' in line 230 must be addressed to Iras, and further that if 'yare' is taken to mean no more than 'quick' the first five words of line 282 may be taken as no more than a somewhat repetitive direction to Iras to bring robe and crown more quickly from the entry door to where Cleopatra is standing.

But let us examine the two passages a little more in detail. In the first place, if lines 225–6 stood alone no one would have had any hesitation.

> Show me, my women, like a queen: go fetch
> My best attires

is clearly an instruction to *both* her attendants to bring all her royal array, and editors would inevitably, and rightly, have inserted after it, *Exeunt Charmian and Iras*. It also creates the expectation that if there are to be further instructions they will be addressed to both attendants, and not to one only. And so I think they are. It will be noticed, by the way, that if 'thou' in line 230 is Iras, the half-ironic effectiveness of the echo in line 317 (Charmian's 'Your crown 's awry, I'll mend it, and then play') is sadly weakened. As to 'Yare, yare, good Iras, quick', I doubt whether it is relevant one way or the other. 'Yare', I think, has almost never the meaning merely of 'quick'; there is a notion of deftness as well as that of speed. (A ship that is yare is one that is easily manœuvrable, not so much a fast sailer, but quick on the helm; see III. vii. 38 of this play, and *Tempest*, v. i. 226. But compare especially II. ii. 211 of this play, 'yarely frame the office'.) And I take it that the remark to Iras comes after the robing has begun, telling her to show her usual skill in adjusting the robe, and to be quick about it.

To return then to the crucial seven lines. As to Cleopatra's 'Now, Charmian', we can either follow Capell and others, read a question mark for F's full stop, and take it that Cleopatra is asking whether Charmian has been successful in the mission on which she was despatched at line 195, or take the words as a statement that she knows from Charmian's return that she has been successful and that all is in order. The first is perhaps a trifle the more effective, but I doubt whether the emendation is justified. The real crux is F's brackets, which certainly mean something, and cannot just be neglected and replaced by commas, as is mostly done (though it would, of course, greatly strengthen my case if they could). I think that they represent not a grammatical *parenthesis*, but an *aside*,

addressed to Charmian alone, apropos her confidential mission to
secure the asps, and followed up, as she waves Charmian to follow
Iras, by the rest of the speech aloud, but addressed to Charmian.

Here, along these lines, is the passage with full stage-directions,
giving first the alternative with Capell's emendation:

> Cleo.   Now, Charmian?
> > *Charmian nods*
>
> > (*triumphant*) Show me . . .
>
> or
>
> Cleo. (*knowing from Charmian's return that all is ready, and exultant*)
> Show me, my women, like a queen: go fetch
> My best attires. I am again for Cydnus,
> To meet Mark Antony. Sirrah Iras, go.
> > *Iras moves towards the door*
> (*sotto voce to Charmian*) Now, noble Charmian, we'll
> > dispatch indeed,
> (*waves Charmian to follow Iras and speaks aloud to her as she
> > moves away*)
> And when thou hast done this chare, I'll give thee leave
> To play till doomsday: bring our crown and all.
> > *Exeunt Iras and Charmian. Cleopatra is left alone.
> > Noise within.*
> Wherefore's this noise?

Cleopatra is thus left alone on the stage for her interview with the
clown. This, I think, has two dramatic advantages. First, her few
lines (235–40) in which she stiffens her resolution are, I feel, more
naturally delivered in soliloquy (like Juliet's before she drinks the
drug) than to an audience even of one. (This, I admit, may be
countered by saying that Cleopatra likes an audience, and that if
I am right this is the only time in the play at which she is even
for a moment alone.) Second, her apprehension of interruption,
which makes her impatient with the clown (she makes three in-
effective attempts to get rid of him) more strongly compels the
audience to share it if she is for the moment without the support
of even one of her women. And this is perhaps true also of 'Wherefore's this noise?', since she cannot be certain that this is only the
arrival of her means of freedom.

Finally, as to the re-entry. Cleopatra's 'and all' rather suggests
that there is more to be brought than a crown and robe—perhaps
more jewels from the regalia—even though later she mentions
those only. And I feel that the entry of both her women, equipped
to array their mistress for her last imperial exit, is more dignified
and more effective than that of a solitary and perhaps somewhat
overburdened Iras.

APPENDIX V

EXTRACTS FROM NORTH'S *PLUTARCH*
(1579)

But besides all this, he had a noble presence, and shewed a countenaunce of one of a noble house: he had a goodly thicke beard, a broad forehead, crooke nosed, and there appeared such a manly looke in his countenaunce, as is commonly seene in Hercules pictures, stamped or graven in mettell. Now it had been a speeche of old time, that the familie of the Antonii were discended from one Anton, the sonne of Hercules, whereof the familie tooke name. This opinion did Antonius seeke to confirme in all his doings: not onely resembling him in the likenes of his bodye, as we have sayd before, but also in the wearing of his garments. For when he would openly shewe him selfe abroad before many people, he would alwayes weare his cassocke gyrt downe lowe upon his hippes, with a great sword hanging by his side, and upon that, some ill favored cloke. Furthermore, things that seeme intollerable in other men, as to boast commonly, to jeast with one or other, to drinke like a good fellow with every body, to sit with the souldiers when they dine, and to eate and drinke with them souldierlike: it is incredible what wonderfull love it wanne him amongest them. And furthermore, being given to love: that made him the more desired, and by that meanes he brought many to love him. For he would further every mans love, and also would not be angry that men should merily tell him of those he loved. But besides all this, that which most procured his rising and advauncement, was his liberalitie, who gave all to the souldiers, and kept nothing for him selfe: and when he was growen to great credit, then was his authoritie and power also very great, the which notwithstanding him selfe did overthrowe by a thowsand other faults he had.

Antonius shape and presence.

The house of the Antonii discended from Hercules.

Antonius liberalitie.

. . . .

Afterwards when Pompeys house was put to open sale, Antonius bought it: but when they asked him money for it, he made it very straung, and was offended with them, and writeth himself that he would not goe with Cæsar into the warres of Africk, bicause he was not well recom-

Antonius byeth Pompeys house.

penced for the service he had done him before. Yet Cæsar
did somewhat bridle his madnes and insolencie, not
suffering him to passe his faulte so lightly away, making
as though he sawe them not. And therefore he left his
Antonius
married
Fulvia,
Clodius
widow.
Fulvia ruled
Antonius, at
home, and
abroad. dissolute manner of life, and married Fulvia that was
Clodius widowe, a woman not so basely minded to spend
her time in spinning and housewivery, and was not contented to master her husband at home, but would also
rule him in his office abroad, and commaund him, that
commaunded legions and great armies: so that Cleopatra was to give Fulvia thankes for that she had taught
Antonius this obedience to women, that learned so well
to be at their commaundement. Nowe, bicause Fulvia
was somewhat sower, and crooked of condition, Antonius
devised to make her pleasaunter, and somewhat better
disposed: and therefore he would playe her many prety
youthfull partes to make her mery.

 · · · · · · · ·

Now thinges remayning in this state at Rome, Octavius
Cæsar the younger, came to Rome, who was the sonne of
Iulius Cæsars Nece, as you have heard before, and was
left his lawefull heire by will, remayning at the tyme of
the death of his great Unkle that was slayne, in the citie
of Apollonia.

 · · · · · · · ·

This young Cæsar seeing his doings, went unto Cicero
and others, which were Antonius enemies, and by them
crept into favor with the Senate: and he him selfe sought
the peoples good will every manner of way, gathering
together the olde souldiers of the late deceased Cæsar,
which were dispersed in divers cities and colonyes.
Antonius being affrayd of it, talked with Octavius in the
capitoll, and became his friend. But the very same night
Antonius had a straunge dreame, who thought that
lightning fell upon him, and burnt his right hand. Shortly after word was brought him, that Cæsar lay in waite to
kil him. Cæsar cleered himselfe unto him, and told him
there was no such matter: but he could not make
Antonius believe the contrary. Whereuppon they became further enemies than ever they were: insomuch
that both of them made friends of either side to gather
together all the old souldiers through Italy, that were

dispersed in divers townes: and made them large promises, and sought also to winne the legions of their side, which were already in armes. Cicero on the other side being at that time the chiefest man of authoritie and estimation in the citie, he stirred up al men against Antonius: so that in the end he made the Senate pronounce him an enemy to his contry, and appointed young Cæsar Sergeaunts to cary axes before him, and such other signes as were incident to the dignitie of a Consul or Prætor: and moreover sent Hircius and Pansa, then Consuls, to drive Antonius out of Italy. These two Consuls together with Cæsar, who also had an armye, went against Antonius that beseeged the citie of Modena, and there overthrew him in battell: but both the Consuls were slaine there. Antonius flying upon this overthrowe, fell into great miserie all at once: but the chiefest want of all other, and that pinched him most, was famine. Howbeit he was of such a strong nature, that by pacience he would overcome any adversitie, and the heavier fortune lay upon him, the more constant shewed he him selfe. Every man that feleth want or adversitie, knoweth by vertue and discretion what he should doe: but when in deede they are overlayed with extremitie, and be sore oppressed, few have the harts to follow that which they praise and commend, and much lesse to avoid that they reprove and mislike. But rather to the contrary, they yeld to their accustomed easie life: and through faynt hart, and lacke of corage, do chaunge their first mind and purpose. And therefore it was a wonderful example to the souldiers, to see Antonius that was brought up in all fineness and superfluitie, so easily to drinke puddle water, and to eate wild frutes and rootes: and moreover it is reported, that even as they passed the Alpes, they did eate the barcks of trees, and such beasts, as never man tasted of their flesh before.

Antonius judged an enemy by the Senate.

Hircius and Pansa Consuls.

Antonius overthrowen in battell by the citie of Modena. Antonius patient in adversitie.

Antonius hardnes in adversitie, notwithstanding his fine bringing up.

. . . .

Now the government of these Triumviri grewe odious and hatefull to the Romanes, for divers respects: but they most blamed Antonius, bicause he being elder then Cæsar, and of more power and force than Lepidus, gave him selfe again to his former riot and excesse, when he left to deale in the affaires of the common wealth. But setting aside the ill name he had for his insolencie, he was

Antonius riot in his Triumvirate.

The praise
of Pompey
the great.

yet much more hated in respect of the house he dwelt in, the which was the house of Pompey the great: a man as famous for his temperaunce, modestie, and civill life, as for his three triumphes. For it grieved them to see the gates commonly shut against the Captaines, Magistrates of the citie, and also Ambassadors of straunge nations, which were sometimes thrust from the gate with violence: and that the house within was full of tomblers, anticke dauncers, juglers, players, jeasters, and dronkards, quaffing and goseling, and that on them he spent and bestowed the most parte of his money he got by all kind of possible extorcions, briberie and policie.

. . . .

Octavius Cæsar perceiving that no money woulde serve Antonius turne, he prayed that they might devide the money betwene them, and so did they also devide the armie, for them both to goe into Macedon to make warre against Brutus and Cassius: and in the meane time they left the government of the citie of Rome unto Lepidus. When they had passed over the seas, and that they beganne to make warre, they being both camped by their enemies, to wit, Antonius against Cassius, and Cæsar against Brutus: Cæsar did no great matter, but

The valiant-
nes of Anto-
nius against
Brutus.

Antonius had alway the upper hand, and did all. For at the first battell Cæsar was overthrowen by Brutus, and lost his campe, and verie hardly saved him selfe by flying from them that followed him. Howebeit he writeth him selfe in his *Commentaries*, that he fled before the charge was geven, bicause of a dreame one of his frends had. Antonius on the other side overthrewe Cassius in battell, though some write that he was not there him selfe at the battell, but that he came after the overthrowe, whilest his

The death
of Cassius.

men had the enemies in chase. So Cassius at his earnest request was slaine by a faithfull servaunt of his owne called Pindarus, whom he had infranchised: bicause he knew not in time that Brutus had overcomen Cæsar. Shortly after they fought an other battell againe, in the

Brutus slue
him selfe.

which Brutus was overthrowen, who afterwardes also slue him selfe. Thus Antonius had the chiefest glorie of all this victorie, specially bicause Cæsar was sicke at that time.

. . . .

For he understoode not many of the thefts and robberies his officers committed by his authoritie, in his treasure and affaires: not so muche bicause he was carelesse, as for that he over-simply trusted his men in all things. For he was a plaine man, without suttletie, and therefore overlate founde out the fowle faultes they committed against him: but when he heard of them, he was muche offended, and would plainly confesse it unto them whome his officers had done injurie unto, by countenaunce of his authoritie. He had a noble minde, as well to punish offendors, as to reward well doers: and yet he did exceede more in geving, then in punishing. Now for his outragious manner of railing he commonly used, mocking and flouting of everie man: that was remedied by it selfe. For a man might as boldly exchaunge a mocke with him, and he was as well contented to be mocked, as to mock others. But yet it oftentimes marred all. For he thought that those which told him so plainly, and truly in mirth: would never flatter him in good earnest, in any matter of weight. But thus he was easely abused by the praises they gave him, not finding howe these flatterers mingled their flatterie, under this familiar and plaine manner of speach unto him, as a fine devise to make difference of meates with sharpe and tart sauce, and also to kepe him by this franke jeasting and bourding with him at the table, that their common flatterie should not be troublesome unto him, as men do easely mislike to have too muche of one thing: and that they handled him finely thereby, when they would geve him place in any matter of waight, and follow his counsell, that it might not appeare to him they did it so muche to please him, but bicause they were ignorant, and understoode not so much as he did. Antonius being thus inclined the last and extreamest mischiefe of all other (to wit, the love of Cleopatra) lighted on him, who did waken and stirre up many vices yet hidden in him, and were never seene to any: and if any sparke of goodnesse or hope of rising were left him, Cleopatra quenched it straight, and made it worse then before. The manner how he fell in love with her was this. Antonius going to make warre with the Parthians, sent to commaunde Cleopatra to appeare personally before him, when he came into Cilicia, to aunswere unto suche accusacions as were layed against her, being this: that she had aided Cassius and Brutus in

Antonius simplicity.

Antonius maners.

Antonius love to Cleopatra whom he sent for into Cilicia.

their warre against him. The messenger sent unto Cleopatra to make this summons unto her, was called Dellius: who when he had thoroughly considered her beawtie, the excellent grace and sweetnesse of her tongue, he nothing mistrusted that Antonius would doe any hurte to so noble a Ladie, but rather assured him selfe, that within few dayes she should be in great favor with him. Thereupon he did her great honour, and perswaded her to come into Cilicia, as honorably furnished as she could possible, and bad her not to be affrayed at all of Antonius, for he was a more curteous Lord, then any that she had ever seene. Cleopatra on thother side beleving Dellius wordes, and gessing by the former accesse and credit she had with Julius Cæsar, and Cneus Pompey (the sonne of Pompey the great) only for her bewtie: she began to have good hope that she might more easely win Antonius. For Cæsar and Pompey knew her when she was but a young thing, and knew not then what the worlde ment: but nowe she went to Antonius at the age when a womans beawtie is at the prime, and she also of best judgement.

The wonderfull sumptuousnes of Cleopatra, Queene of Ægypt, going unto Antonius.

So, she furnished her selfe with a world of gifts, store of gold and silver, and of riches and other sumptuous ornaments, as is credible enough she might bring from so great a house, and from so wealthie and rich a realme as Ægypt was. But yet she caried nothing with her wherein she trusted more then in her selfe, and in the charmes and inchauntment of her passing beawtie and grace. Therefore when she was sent unto by divers letters, both from Antonius him selfe, and also from his frendes, she made so light of it, and mocked Antonius so much, that she disdained to set forward otherwise, but to take her barge in

Cydnus fl.

the river of Cydnus, the poope whereof was of gold, the sailes of purple, and the owers of silver, which kept stroke in rowing after the sounde of the musicke of flutes, howboyes, cithems, violls, and such other instruments as they played upon in the barge. And now for the person of her selfe: she was layed under a pavillion of cloth of gold of tissue, apparelled and attired like the goddesse Venus, commonly drawen in picture: and hard by her, on either hand of her, pretie faire boyes apparelled as painters doe set forth god Cupide, with little fannes in their hands, with the which they fanned wind upon her. Her ladies and gentlewomen also, the fairest of them were ap-

parelled like the nymphes Nereides (which are the mer-
maides of the waters) and like the Graces, some stearing
the helme, others tending the tackle and ropes of the
barge, out of the which there came a wonderfull passing
sweete savor of perfumes, that perfumed the wharfes
side, pestered with innumerable multitudes of people.
Some of them followed the barge all alongest the rivers
side: others also ranne out of the citie to see her comming
in. So that in thend, there ranne such multitudes of
people one after an other to see her, that Antonius was
left post alone in the market place, in his Imperiall seate
to geve audience: and there went a rumor in the peoples
mouthes, that the goddesse Venus was come to play with
the god Bacchus, for the generall good of all Asia. When
Cleopatra landed, Antonius sent to invite her to supper
to him. But she sent him word againe, he should doe
better rather to come and suppe with her. Antonius
therefore to shew him selfe curteous unto her at her
arrivall, was contented to obey her, and went to supper
to her: where he found such passing sumptuous fare, that
no tongue can expresse it. But amongest all other thinges,
he most wondered at the infinite number of lightes and
torches hanged on the toppe of the house, geving light in
everie place, so artificially set and ordered by devises,
some round, some square: that it was the rarest thing to
behold that eye could discerne, or that ever books could
mencion. The next night, Antonius feasting her, con-
tended to passe her in magnificence and finenes: but she
overcame him in both. So that he him selfe began to
skorne the grosse service of his house, in respect of Cleopatraes sumptuousnes and finenesse. And when Cleopatra found Antonius jeasts and slents to be but grosse,
and souldier like, in plaine manner: she gave it him
finely, and without feare taunted him throughly. Now
her beawtie (as it is reported) was not so passing, as unmatchable of other women, nor yet suche, as upon present viewe did enamor men with her: but so sweete was
her companie and conversacion, that a man could not
possiblie but be taken. And besides her beawtie, the good
grace she had to talke and discourse, her curteous nature
that tempered her words and dedes, was a spurre that
pricked to the quick. Furthermore, besides all these, her
voyce and words were marvelous pleasant: for her tongue

The sumptu-
ous prepara-
tions of the
suppers of
Cleopatra
and
Antonius.

Cleopatraes
beawtie.

was an instrument of musicke to divers sports and pastimes, the which she easely turned to any language that pleased her. She spake unto few barbarous people by interpreter, but made them aunswere her self, or at the least the most parte of them: as the Æthiopians, the Arabians, the Troglodytes, the Hebrues, the Syrians, the Medes, and the Parthians, and to many others also, whose languages she had learned. Whereas divers of her progenitors, the kings of Ægypt, could scarce learne the Ægyptian tongue only, and many of them forgot to speake the Macedonian. Nowe, Antonius was so ravished with the love of Cleopatra, that though his wife Fulvia had great warres, and much a doe with Cæsar for his affaires, and that the armie of the Parthians (the which the kings Lieutenauntes had geven to the onely leading of Labienus) was now assembled in Mesopotamia readie to invade Syria: yet, as though all this had nothing touched him, he yeelded him selfe to goe with Cleopatra into Alexandria, where he spent and lost in childish sports, (as a man might say) and idle pastimes, the most pretious thing a man can spende, as Antiphon sayth: and

An order set up by Antonius and Cleopatra. The excessive expences of Antonius and Cleopatra in Ægypt.

that is, time. For they made an order betwene them, which they called Amimetobion (as much to say, no life comparable and matcheable with it) one feasting ech other by turnes, and in cost, exceeding all measure and reason. And for proofe hereof, I have heard my grandfather Lampryas report, that one Philotas a Physition, born in the citie of Amphissa, told him that he was at that present time in Alexandria, and studied Physicke: and that having acquaintance with one of Antonius cookes, he tooke him with him to Antonius house, (being a young man desirous to see things) to shew him the wonderfull sumptuous charge and preparation of only one supper. —When he was in the kitchin, and saw a world of diver-

Eight wilde boares rosted whole.

sities of meates, and amongst others, eight wilde boares rosted whole: he began to wonder at it, and sayd, Sure you have a great number of ghests to supper. The cooke fell a laughing and answered him, No (quoth he) not many ghests, nor above twelve in all: but yet all that is boyled or roasted must be served in whole, or else it would be marred straight. For Antonius peradventure will suppe presently, or it may be a pretie while hence, or likely enough he will deferre it longer, for that he hathe dronke well to day, or else hath had some other great matters in hand: and therefore we do not dresse one supper only, but many suppers, bicause we are uncerteine of the houre he will suppe in.

. . . .

But now againe to Cleopatra. Plato wryteth that there are foure kinds of flatterie: but Cleopatra devided it into many kinds. For she, were it in sport, or in matter of earnest, still devised sundrie new delights to have Antonius at commaundement, never leaving him night or day, nor once letting him go out of her sight. For she would play at dyce with him, drinke with him, and hunt commonly with him, and also be with him when he went to any exercise or activity of body. And sometime also, when he would goe up and downe the citie disguised like a slave in the night, and would peere into poore mens windowes and their shops, and scold and brawle with them within the house: Cleopatra would be also in a chamber maide array, and amble up and downe the streets with him, so that oftentimes Antonius bare away both mockes and blowes. Now, though most men misliked this maner, yet the Alexandrians were commonly glad of this jolity, and liked it well saying verie gallantly, and wisely: that Antonius shewed them a commicall face, to wit, a merie countenaunce: and the Romanes a tragicall face, to say, a grimme looke. But to reckon up all the foolishe sportes they made, revelling in this sorte: it were too fond a parte of me, and therefore I will only tell you one among the rest. On a time he went to angle for fish, and when he could take none, he was as angrie as could be, bicause Cleopatra stood by. Wherefore he secretly commaunded the fisher men, that when he cast in his line, they should straight dive under the water, and put a fishe on his hooke which they had taken before: and so snatched up his angling rodde, and brought up fish twise or thrise. Cleopatra found it straight, yet she seemed not to see it, but wondred at his excellent fishing: but when she was alone by her selfe among her owne people, she told them howe it was, and bad them the next morning to be on the water to see the fishing. A number of people came to the haven, and got into the fisher boates to see this fishing. Antonius then threw in his line and Cleopatra straight commaunded one of her men to dive under

Marginal notes:

Plato writeth of foure kinds of flatterie. Queene of all flatterers.

Antonius fishing in Ægypt.

water before Antonius men, and to put some old salte
fish upon his baite, like unto those that are brought out
of the contrie of Pont. When he had hong the fish on his
hooke, Antonius thinking he had taken a fishe in deede,
snatched up his line presently. Then they all fell a laughing. Cleopatra laughing also, said unto him: Leave us
(my Lord) Ægyptians (which dwell in the contry of
Pharus and Canobus) your angling rodd: this is not thy
profession: thou must hunt after conquering of realmes
and contries. Nowe Antonius delighting in these fond
and childish pastimes, verie ill newes were brought him

The warres
of Lucius
Antonius
and Fulvia,
against
Octavius
Cæsar.

from two places. The first from Rome, that his brother
Lucius, and Fulvia his wife, fell out first betwene them
selves, and afterwards fell to open warre with Cæsar, and
had brought all to nought, that they were both driven to
flie out of Italie. The second newes, as bad as the first:
that Labienus conquered all Asia with the armie of the
Parthians, from the river of Euphrates, and from Syria,
unto the contries of Lydia and Ionia. Then began
Antonius with much a doe, a litle to rouse him selfe as if
he had bene wakened out of a deepe sleepe, and as a man
may say, comming out of a great drunkennes. So, first of
all he bent him selfe against the Parthians, and went as
farre as the contrie of Phœnicia: but there he received
lamentable letters from his wife Fulvia. Whereuppon he
straight returned towards Italie with two hundred saile:
and as he went, tooke up his frendes by the way that fled
out of Italie, to come to him. By them he was informed,
that his wife Fulvia was the only cause of this warre: who
being of a peevish, crooked, and troublesome nature, had
purposely raised this uprore in Italie, in hope thereby to

The death
of Fulvia
Antonius
wife.

withdraw him from Cleopatra. But by good fortune, his
wife Fulvia going to meete with Antonius, sickened by
the way, and dyed in the citie of Sicyone: and therefore
Octavius Cæsar, and he were the easelier made frendes
together. For when Antonius landed in Italie, and that
men saw Cæsar asked nothing of him, and that Antonius
on the other side layed all the fault and burden on his
wife Fulvia: the frendes of both parties would not suffer
them to unrippe any old matters, and to prove or defend
who had the wrong or right, and who was the first pro-
curer of this warre, fearing to make matters worse betwene them: but they made them frendes together, and

devided the Empire of Rome betwene them, making the sea Ionium the bounds of their division. For they gave all the provinces Eastward, unto Antonius: and the countries Westward, unto Cæsar: and left Africke unto Lepidus: and made a law, that they three one after another should make their frendes Consuls, when they would not be them selves. This seemed to be a sound councell, but yet it was to be confirmed with a straighter bonde, which fortune offered thus. There was Octavia the eldest sister of Cæsar, not by one mother, for she came of Ancharia, and Cæsar him self afterwards of Accia. It is reported, that he dearly loved his sister Octavia, for in deede she was a noble Ladie, and left the widow of her first husband Caius Marcellus, who dyed not long before: and it seemed also that Antonius had bene widower ever since the death of his wife Fulvia. For he denied not that he kept Cleopatra, but so did he not confesse that he had her as his wife: and so with reason he did defend the love he bare unto this Ægyptian Cleopatra. Thereuppon everie man did set forward this mariage, hoping thereby that this Ladie Octavia, having an excellent grace, wisedom, and honestie, joined unto so rare a beawtie, that when she were with Antonius (he loving her as so worthy a Ladie deserveth) she should be a good meane to keepe good love and amitie betwext her brother and him. So when Cæsar and he had made the matche betwene them, they both went to Rome about this mariage, although it was against the law, that a widow should be maried within tenne monethes after her husbandes death. Howbeit the Senate dispensed with the law, and so the mariage proceeded accordingly. Sextus Pompeius at that time kept in Sicilia, and so made many an inrode into Italie with a great number of pynnasies and other pirates shippes, of the which were Captaines two notable pirats, Menas, and Menecrates, who so scoored all the sea thereabouts, that none durst peepe out with a sayle. Furthermore, Sextus Pompeius had delt verie frendly with Antonius, for he had curteously received his mother, when she fled out of Italie with Fulvia: and therefore they thought good to make peace with him. So they met all three together by the mount of Misena, upon a hill that runneth farre into the sea: Pompey having his shippes ryding hard by at ancker, and Antonius and Cæsar their

Marginal notes:

All the Empire of Rome devided betwene the Triumviri.

Octavia, the halfe sister of Octavius Cæsar, and daughter of Ancharia which was not Cæsar's mother.

A lawe at Rome for marying of widowes. Antonius maried Octavia, Octavius Cæsar's halfe sister.

Antonius and Octavius Cæsar, doe make peace with Sextus Pompeius.

armies upon the shoare side, directly over against him. Now, after they had agreed that Sextus Pompeius should have Sicile and Sardinia, with this condicion that he should ridde the sea of all theeves and pirats, and make it safe for passengers, and withall that he should send a certaine [quantity] of wheate to Rome: one of them did feast an other, and drew cuts who should beginne. It was Pompeius chaunce to invite them first. Whereupon Antonius asked him: And where shall we suppe? There, said Pompey, and shewed him his admirall galley which had six bankes of owers: That (sayd he) is my fathers

Sextus Pom-
peius taunt
to Antonius.

house they have left me. He spake it to taunt Antonius, bicause he had his fathers house, that was Pompey the great. So he cast ankers enowe into the sea, to make his galley fast, and then built a bridge of wodde to convey them to his galley, from the heade of mount Misena: and there he welcomed them, and made them great cheere.

Sextus Pom-
peius being
offered won-
derfull great
fortune:
for his
honestie and
faithes sake,
refused it.

Now in the middest of the feast, when they fell to be merie with Antonius love unto Cleopatra: Menas the pirate came to Pompey, and whispering in his eare, said unto him: Shall I cut the gables of the ankers, and make thee Lord not only of Sicile and Sardinia, but of the whole Empire of Rome besides? Pompey having pawsed a while upon it, at length aunswered him: Thou should-est have done it, and never told it me, but now we must content us with that we have. As for my selfe, I was never taught to breake my faith, nor to be counted a traitor. The other two also did likewise feast him in their campe, and then he returned into Sicile. Antonius after this agreement made, sent Ventidius before into Asia to stay the Parthians, and to keepe them they should come no further: and he him selfe in the meane time, to gratefie Cæsar, was contented to be chosen Iulius Cæsars priest and sacrificer, and so they joyntly together dispatched all great matters, concerning the state of the Empire. But in all other maner of sportes and exercises, wherein they passed the time away the one with the other: Antonius was ever inferior unto Cæsar, and always lost, which grieved him much. With Antonius there was a soothsayer or astronomer of Ægypt, that coulde cast a figure, and judge of mens nativities, to tell them what should happen to them. He, either to please Cleopatra, or else for that he founde it so by his art, told Antonius plainly that his fortune (which of it selfe was excellent good, and very great) was altogether bleamished and obscured by Cæsars fortune: and therefore he counselled him utterly to leave his company, and to get him as farre from him as he could. For thy Demon, said he, (that is to say, the good angell and spirit that kepeth thee), is affraied of his: and being coragious and high when he is alone, becometh fearefull and timerous when he commeth neere unto the other. Howsoever it was, the events ensuing proved the Ægyptians words true. For, it is said, that as often as they two drew cuts for pastime, who should have any thing, or whether they plaied at dice, Antonius alway lost. Oftentimes when they were disposed to see cocke-fight, or quailes that were taught to fight one with an other: Cæsars cockes or quailes did ever overcome. The which spighted Antonius in his mind, although he made no outward shew of it: and therefore he beleved the Ægyptian the better. In fine, he recommended the affaires of his house unto Cæsar, and went out of Italie with Octavia his wife, whom he caried into Græce, after he had had a daughter by her. So Antonius lying all the winter at Athens, newes came unto him of the victories of Ventidius, who had overcome the Parthians in battel, in the which also were slaine, Labienus, and Pharnabates, the chiefest Captaine king Orodes had. For these good newes he feasted all Athens, and kept open house for all the Græcians, and many games of price were plaied at Athens, of the which he him selfe would be judge.

Antonius told by a Soothsayer, that his fortune was inferior unto Octavius Cæsar.

Antonius unfortunate in sport and earnest, against Octavius Cæsar.

Orodes king of Parthia.

.   .   .   .

In the meane time, Ventidius once againe overcame Pacorus, (Orodes sonne king of Parthia) in a battell fought in the contrie of Cyrrestica, he being come againe with a great armie to invade Syria: at which battell was slaine a great number of the Parthians, and among them Pacorus, the kings owne sonne slaine. This noble exployt as famous as ever any was, was a full revenge to the Romanes, of the shame and losse they had received before by the death of Marcus Crassus: and he made the Parthians flie, and glad to kepe them selves within the confines and territories of Mesopotamia, and Media after they had thrise together bene overcome in severall battells. Howbeit Ventidius durst not undertake to follow

Ventidius notable victorie of the Parthians.

The death of Pacorus, the king of Parthiaes sonne.

them any further, fearing least he should have gotten Antonius displeasure by it.

. . . .

Ventidius
the only man
of the Ro-
manes, that
triumphed
for the
Parthians.

Ventidius was the only man that ever triumphed of the Parthians untill this present day, a meane man borne, and of no noble house nor family: who only came to that he attained unto, through Antonius frendshippe, the which delivered him happie occasion to achieve to great matters. And yet to say truely, he did so well quit him selfe in all his enterprises, that he confirmed that which was spoken of Antonius and Cæsar: to wit, that they were alway more fortunate when they made warre by their Lieutenants, then by them selves. For Sossius, one of Antonius Lieutenauntes in Syria, did notable good service: and Canidius, whom he had also left his Lieu-

Canidius
conquests.

tenaunt in the borders of Armenia, did conquer it all. So did he also overcome the kinges of the Iberians and Albanians, and went on with his conquests unto mount Caucasus. By these conquests, the fame of Antonius power increased more and more, and grew dreadfull unto all the barbarous nations. But Antonius notwith-

Newe dis-
pleasures
betwext An-
tonius and
Octavius
Cæsar.

standing grewe to be marvelously offended with Cæsar, upon certaine reportes, that had bene brought unto him: and so tooke sea to go towards Italie with three hundred saile. And bicause those of Brundusium, would not receive his armie into their haven, he went further unto Tarentum. There his wife Octavia that came out of Græce with him, besought him to send her unto her brother: the which he did. Octavia at that time was great with child, and moreover had a second daughter by him, and yet she put her selfe in jorney, and met with her brother Octavius Cæsar by the way, who brought his

The wordes
of Octavia
unto
Mæcenas
and Agrippa.

two chiefe frendes, Mæcenas and Agrippa with him. She tooke them aside, and with all the instance she could possible, intreated them they would not suffer her that was the happiest woman of the world, to become nowe the most wretched and unfortunatest creature of all other. For now, said she, everie mans eyes doe gaze on me, that am the sister of one of the Emperours and wife of the other. And if the worst councell take place, (which the goddes forbidde) and that they growe to warres: for your selves, it is uncertaine to which of them two the goddes have assigned the victorie, or over-

throwe. But for me, on which side soever victorie fall, my
state can be but most miserable still. These words of
Octavia so softned Cæsars harte, that he went quickely
unto Tarentum. But it was a noble sight for them that
were present, to see so great an armie by lande not to
sturre, and so many shippes aflote in the roade, quietly
and safe: and furthermore, the meeting and kindenesse
of frendes, lovinglie imbracing one an other. First,
Antonius feasted Cæsar, which he graunted unto for his
sisters sake. Afterwardes they agreed together, that Cæsar
should geve Antonius two legions to go against the
Parthians: and that Antonius should let Cæsar have a
hundred gallies armed with brasen spurres at the prooes.
Besides all this, Octavia obteyned of her husbande,
twentie brigantines for her brother: and of her brother
for her husbande, a thowsande armed men. After they
had taken leave of eache other, Cæsar went immediately
to make warre with Sextus Pompeius, to gette Sicilia into
his handes. Antonius also leaving his wife Octavia and
litle children begotten of her, with Cæsar, and his other
children which he had by Fulvia: he went directlie into
Asia. Then beganne this pestilent plague and mischiefe
of Cleopatraes love (which had slept a longe tyme, and
seemed to have bene utterlie forgotten, and that Antonius had geven place to better counsell) againe to kindle,
and to be in force, so soone as Antonius came neere unto
Syria. And in the ende, the horse of the minde as Plato
termeth it, that is so hard of rayne (I meane the un-
reyned lust of concupiscence) did put out of Antonius
heade, all honest and commendable thoughtes: for he
sent Fonteius Capito to bring Cleopatra into Syria.
Unto whome, to welcome her, he gave no trifling things:
but unto that she had already, he added the provinces of
Phœnicia, those of the nethermost Syria, the Ile of
Cyprus, and a great parte of Cilicia, and that contry of
Iurie where the true balme is, and that parte of Arabia
where the Nabatheians doe dwell, which stretcheth out
towardes the Ocean. These great giftes muche misliked
the Romanes. But now, though Antonius did easely geve
away great seigniories, realmes, and mighty nations unto
some private men, and that also he tooke from other
kings their lawfull realmes: (as from Antigonus king of
the Iewes, whom he openly beheaded, where never king

Octavia pacifieth the quarrell be-twixt Antonius, and her brother Octavius Cæsar.

Plato calleth concupis-cence: the horse of the minde.

Antonius sent for Cleopatra into Syria.

Antonius gave great provinces unto Cleopatra.

Antigonus king of Iurie, the first king beheaded by Antonius.

before had suffred like death) yet all this did not so much offend the Romanes, as the unmeasurable honors which he did unto Cleopatra. But yet he did much more aggravate their malice and il wil towards him, bicause that Cleopatra having brought him two twinnes, a sonne and a daughter, he named his sonne Alexander, and his daughter Cleopatra, and gave them to their surnames, the Sunne to the one, and the moone to the other. This notwithstanding, he that could finely cloke his shamefull deedes with fine words, said that the greatnes and magnificence of the Empire of Rome appeared most, not where the Romanes tooke, but where they gave much: and nobility was multiplied amongest men, by the posterity of kings, when they left of their seede in divers places: and that by this meanes his first auncester was begotten of Hercules, who had not left the hope and continuance of his line and posterity, in the wombe of one only woman, fearing Solons lawes, or regarding the ordinaunces of men touching the procreacion of children: but that he gave it unto nature, and established the fundacion of many noble races and families in divers places.

Antonius twinnes by Cleopatra, and their names.

．　．　．　．　．　．　．　．

Now whilest Antonius was busie in this preparation, Octavia his wife, whome he had left at Rome, would needes take sea to come unto him. Her brother Octavius Cæsar was willing unto it, not for his respect at all (as most authors doe report) as for that he might have an honest culler to make warre with Antonius if he did misuse her, and not esteeme of her as she ought to be. But when she was come to Athens, she received letters from Antonius, willing her to stay there untill his comming, and did advertise her of his jorney and determination. The which though it grieved her much, and that she knewe it was but an excuse: yet by her letters to him of aunswer, she asked him whether he would have those thinges sent unto him which she had brought him, being great store of apparell for souldiers, a great number of horse, summe of money, and gifts, to bestow on his friendes and Captaines he had about him: and besides all those, she had two thowsand souldiers chosen men, all well armed, like unto the Prætors bands. When Niger, one of Antonius friends whome he had sent unto Athens, had brought these newes from his wife Octavia, and

Octavia, Antonius' wife, came to Athens to meete with him.

withall did greatly prayse her, as she was worthy, and
well deserved: Cleopatra knowing that Octavia would
have Antonius from her, and fearing also that if with her
vertue and honest behavior, (besides the great power of
her brother Cæsar) she did adde thereunto her modest
kind of love to please her husband, that she would then
be too stronge for her, and in the end winne him away:
she suttelly seemed to languish for the love of Antonius, **The flickering**
pyning her body for lacke of meate. Furthermore, she **enticements**
every way so framed her countenaunce, that when **of Cleopatra**
Antonius came to see her, she cast her eyes upon him, **unto**
like a woman ravished for joy. Straight againe when he **Antonius.**
went from her, she fell a weeping and blubbering, looked
rufully of the matter, and still found the meanes that
Antonius should oftentymes finde her weeping: and then
when he came sodainely uppon her, she made as though
she dryed her eyes, and turned her face away, as if she
were unwilling that he should see her weepe. All these
tricks she used, Antonius being in readines to goe into
Syria, to speake with the king of Medes. Then the flatterers that futhered Cleopatraes mind, blamed Antonius,
and tolde him that he was a hard natured man, and that
he had small love in him, that would see a poore Ladye
in such torment for his sake, whose life depended onely
upon him alone. For, Octavia, sayd they, that was
maryed unto him as it were of necessitie, bicause her
brother Cæsars affayres so required it: hath the honor to
be called Antonius lawefull spowse and wife: and Cleopatra, being borne a Queene of so many thowsands of
men, is onely named Antonius Leman, and yet that she
disdayned not so to be called, if it might please him she
might enjoy his company, and live with him: but if he
once leave her, that then it is unpossible she should live.
To be short, by these their flatteries and enticements,
they so wrought Antonius effeminate mind, that fearing
least she would make her selfe away: he returned againe
unto Alexandria, and referred the king of Medes to the
next yeare following, although he receyved newes that
the Parthians at that tyme were at civill warres amonge
them selves. This notwithstanding, he went afterwardes
and made peace with him. For he maried his Daughter
which was very younge, unto one of the sonnes that
Cleopatra had by him: and then returned, beeing fully

The occasion
of civil warres
betwixt An-
tonius and
Cæsar.

The love of
Octavia to
Antonius
her husband,
and her wise
and womanly
behavior.

Antonius
arrogantly
devideth
divers
provinces
unto his
children by
Cleopatra.

Cæsarion, the
supposed sone
of Cæsar, by
Cleopatra.
Alexander
and Ptolomy,
Antonius
sonnes by
Cleopatra.

bent to make warre with Cæsar. When Octavia, was
returned to Rome from Athens, Cæsar commaunded her
to goe out of Antonius house, and to dwell by her selfe,
bicause he had abused her. Octavia aunswered him
againe, that she would not forsake her husbands house,
and that if he had no other occasion to make warre with
him, she prayed him then to take no thought for her: for
sayd she, it were too shamefull a thinge, that two so
famous Captaines should bringe in civill warres among
the Romanes, the one for the love of a woman, and the
other for the jelousy betwixt one an other. Now as she
spake the worde, so did she also performe the deede. For
she kept still in Antonius house, as if he had bene there,
and very honestly and honorably kept his children, not
those onely she had by him, but the other which her husband had by Fulvia. Furthermore, when Antonius sent
any of his men to Rome, to sue for any office in the common wealth: she received him very curteously, and so
used her selfe unto her brother, that she obtained the
thing she requested. Howbeit thereby, thinking no hurt,
she did Antonius great hurt. For her honest love and
regard to her husband, made every man hate him, when
they sawe he did so unkindly use so noble a Lady: but yet
the greatest cause of their malice unto him, was for the
division of lands he made amongst his children in the
citie of Alexandria. And to confesse a troth, it was too
arrogant and insolent a part, and done (as a man would
say) in derision and contempt of the Romanes. For he
assembled all the people in the show place, where
younge men doe exercise them selves, and there upon a
high tribunall silvered, he set two chayres of gold, the
one for him selfe, and the other for Cleopatra, and lower
chaires for his children: then he openly published before
the assembly, that first of all he did establish Cleopatra
Queene of Ægypt, of Cyprus, of Lydia, and of the lower
Syria, and at that time also, Cæsarion king of the same
Realmes. This Cæsarion was supposed to be the sonne of
Iulius Cæsar, who had left Cleopatra great with child.
Secondly he called the sonnes he had by her, the kings of
kings, and gave Alexander for his portion, Armenia,
Media and Parthia, when he had conquered the contry:
and unto Ptolomy for his portion, Phenicia, Syria, and
Cilicia. And therewithall he brought out Alexander in a

long gowne after the facion of the Medes, with a high copped tanke hat on his head, narrow in the toppe, as the kings of the Medes and Armenians doe use to weare them: and Ptolomy apparelled in a cloke after the Macedonian manner, with slippers on his feete, and a broad hat, with a royall band or diademe. Such was the apparell and old attyre of the auncient kinges and successors of Alexander the great. So after his sonnes had done their humble duties, and kissed their father and mother: presently a company of Armenian souldiers set there of purpose, compassed the one about, and a like company of the Macedonians the other. Now for Cleopatra, she did not onely weare at that time (but at all other times els when she came abroad) the apparell of the goddesse Isis, and so gave audience unto all her subjects, as a new Isis. Octavius Cæsar reporting all these thinges unto the Senate, and oftentimes accusing him to the whole people and assembly in Rome: he thereby stirred up all the Romanes against him. Antonius on thother side sent to Rome likewise to accuse him, and the chiefest poyntes of his accusations he charged him with, were these: First, that having spoyld Sextus Pompeius in Sicile, he did not give him his parte of the Ile. Secondly, that he did deteyne in his hands the shippes he lent him to make that warre. Thirdly, that having put Lepidus their companion and triumvirate out of his part of the Empire, and having deprived him of all honors: he retayned for him selfe the lands and revenues thereof, which had bene assigned unto him for his part. And last of all, that he had in manner devided all Italy amongest his owne souldiers, and had left no part of it for his souldiers. Octavius Cæsar aunswered him againe: that for Lepidus, he had in deede deposed him, and taken his part of the Empire from him, bicause he did overcruelly use his authoritie. And secondly, for the conquests he had made by force of armes, he was contented Antonius should have his part of them, so that he would likewise let him have his part of Armenia. And thirdly, that for his souldiers, they should seeke for nothing in Italy, bicause they possessed Media and Parthia, the which provinces they had added to the Empire of Rome, valiantly fighting with their Emperor and Captaine. Antonius hearing these newes, being yet in Armenia, commaunded Cani-

Accusasion, betwixt Octavius Cæsar and Antonius.

dius to goe presently to the sea side with his sixteene
legions he had: and he him selfe with Cleopatra, went
unto the citie of Ephesus, and there gathered together
his gallies and shippes out of all parts, which came to the

Antonius
came with
eight
hundred
saile against
Octavius
Cæsar.

number of eight hundred, reckoning the great shippes
of burden: and of those, Cleopatra furnished him with
two hundred, and twenty thowsand talents besides, and
provision of vittells also to mainteyne al the whole army
in this warre. So Antonius, through the perswasions of
Domitius, commaunded Cleopatra to returne againe
into Ægypt, and there to understand the successe of this
warre. But Cleopatra, fearing least Antonius should
againe be made friends with Octavius Cæsar, by the
meanes of his wife Octavia: she so plyed Canidius with
money, and filled his purse, that he became her spokes
man unto Antonius, and told him there was no reason to
send her from this warre, who defraied so great a charge:
neither that it was for his profit, bicause that thereby the
Ægyptians would then be utterly discoraged, which
were the chiefest strength of the army by sea: considering
that he could see no king of all the kings their confeder-
ats, that Cleopatra was inferior unto, either for wisedom
or judgment, seeing that longe before she had wisely
governed so great a realme as Ægypt, and besides she
had bene so long acquainted with him, by whom she had
learned to manedge great affayres. These fayer perswasions wan him: for it was predestined that the
government of all the world should fall into Octavius

Antonius
carieth Cleo-
patra with
him to the
warres,
against Oc-
tavius Cæsar:
and kept
great feasting
at the Ile of
Samos to-
gether.

Cæsars handes. Thus, all their forces being joyned together, they hoysed sayle towards the Ile of Samos, and
there gave them selves to feasts and sollace. For as all the
kings, Princes, and communalties, peoples and cities
from Syria, unto the marishes Mæotides, and from the
Armenians to the Illyrians, were sent unto, to send and
bringe all munition and warlike preparation they could:
even so all players, minstrells, tumblers, fooles, and
jeasters, were commaunded to assemble in the Ile of
Samos. So that, where in manner all the world in every
place was full of lamentations, sighes and teares: onely
in this Ile of Samos there was nothing for many dayes
space, but singing and pyping, and all the Theater full
of these common players, minstrells, and singing men.
Besides all this, every citie sent an oxe thither to sacrifice,

and kings did strive one with another who should make the noblest feasts, and give the richest gifts. So that every man sayd, What can they doe more for joy of victorie, if they winne the battell? when they make already such sumptuous feasts at the beginning of the warre?

. . . .

Furthermore, Titius and Plancus (two of Antonius chiefest friends and that had bene both of them Consuls) for the great injuries Cleopatra did them, bicause they hindered all they could, that she should not come to this warre: they went and yelded them selves unto Cæsar, and tolde him where the testament was that Antonius had made, knowing perfitly what was in it. The will was in the custodie of the Vestall Nunnes: of whom Cæsar demaunded for it. They aunswered him, that they would not give it him: but if he would goe and take it, they would not hinder him. Thereuppon Cæsar went thither, and having red it first to him self, he noted certaine places worthy of reproch: so assembling all the Senate, he red it before them all. Whereuppon divers were marvelously offended, and thought it a straunge matter that he being alive, should be punished for that he had appoynted by his will to be done after his death. Cæsar chiefly tooke hold of this that he ordeyned touching his buriall: for he willed that his bodie, though he dyed at Rome, should be brought in funerall pompe through the middest of the market place, and that it should be sent into Alexandria unto Cleopatra.

Titius and Plancus revolt from Antonius, and doe yeld to Cæsar.

. . . .

Nowe, after Cæsar had made sufficient preparation, he proclaymed open warre against Cleopatra, and made the people to abolishe the power and Empire of Antonius, bicause he had before given it uppe unto a woman. And Cæsar sayde furthermore, that Antonius was not Maister of him selfe, but that Cleopatra had brought him beside him selfe, by her charmes and amorous poysons: and that they that should make warre with them should be Mardian the Euenuke, Photinus, and Iras, a woman of Cleopatraes bedchamber, that friseled her heare, and dressed her head, and Charmion, the which were those that ruled the affaires of Antonius Empire.

Antonius Empire taken from him.

. . . .

The Admirall galley of Cleopatra, was called Anto-

An ill signe, foreshewed by swallowes breding in Cleopatraes shippe.

Antonius power against Oct. Cæsar.

Antonius had eyght kings, and their power to ayde him.

The army and power of Octavius Cæsar against Antonius.

Antonius dominions.

Octavius Cæsars dominions.

Antonius too much ruled by Cleopatra.

niade, in the which there chaunced a marvelous ill signe. Swallowes had bred under the poope of her shippe, and there came others after them that drave away the first, and plucked downe their neasts. Now when all things were ready, and that they drew neare to fight: it was found that Antonius had no lesse then five hundred good ships of warre, among the which there were many gallies that had eight and ten bancks of owers, the which were sumptuously furnished, not so meete for fight, as for triumphe: a hundred thowsand footemen, and twelve thowsand horsemen, and had with him to ayde him these kinges and subjects following: Bocchus, king of Lybia, Tarcondemus king of high Cilicia, Archelaus king of Cappadocia, Philadelphus king of Paphlagonia, Mithridates king of Comagena, and Adallas king of Thracia. All the which were there every man in person. The residue that were absent sent their armies, as Polemon king of Pont, Manchus king of Arabia, Herodes king of Iury: and furthermore, Amyntas king of Lycaonia, and of the Galatians: and besides all these, he had all the ayde the king of Medes sent unto him. Now for Cæsar, he had two hundred and fifty shippes of warre, foure score thowsand footemen, and well neare as many horsemen as his enemy Antonius. Antonius for his part, had all under his dominion from Armenia, and the river of Euphrates, unto the sea Ionium and Illyricum. Octavius Cæsar had also for his part, all that which was in our Hemisphære, or halfe part of the world, from Illyria, unto the Occean sea upon the west: then all from the Occean, unto Mare Siculum: and from Africk, all that which is against Italy, as Gaule, and Spayne. Furthermore, all from the province of Cyrenia, unto Æthiopia, was subject unto Antonius. Now Antonius was made so subject to a womans will, that though he was a great deale the stronger by land, yet for Cleopatraes sake, he would needes have this battell tryed by sea: though he sawe before his eyes, that for lacke of water men, his Captaines did presse by force all sortes of men out of Græce that they could take up in the field, as travellers, muletters, reapers, harvest men, and younge boys, and yet could they not sufficiently furnishe his gallies: so that the most part of them were empty, and could scant rowe, bicause they lacked water men enowe.

But on the contrary side, Cæsars shippes were not built for pompe, highe, and great, onely for a sight and bravery, but they were light of yarage, armed and furnished with water men as many as they needed, and had them all in readines, in the havens of Tarentum, and Brundusium. So Octavius Cæsar sent unto Antonius, to will him to delay no more time, but to come on with his army into Italy: and that for his owne part he would give him safe harber, to lande without any trouble, and that he would withdraw his armie from the sea, as far as one horse could runne, until he had put his army a shore, and had lodged his men. Antonius on the other side bravely sent him word againe, and chalenged the combate of him man to man, though he were the elder: and that if he refused him so, he would then fight a battell with him in the fields of Pharsalia, as Iulius Cæsar, and Pompey had done before. Now whilest Antonius rode at anker, lying idely in harber at the head of Actium, in the place where the citie of Nicopolis standeth at this present: Cæsar had quickly passed the sea Ionium, and taken a place called Toryne, before Antonius understoode that he had taken shippe. Then began his men to be affraid, bicause his army by land was left behind. But Cleopatra making light of it: And what daunger, I pray you, said she, if Cæsar keepe at Toryne?* The next morning by breake of day, his enemies comming with full force of owers in battell against him, Antonius was affraid that if they came to joyne, they would take and cary away his shippes that had no men of warre in them. So he armed all his water men, and set them in order of battell upon the forecastell of their shippes, and then lift up all his rancks of owers towards the element, as well of the one side, as the other, with the prooes against the enemies, at the entry and mouth of the gulfe, which beginneth at the point of Actium, and so kept them in order of battell, as if they had bene armed and furnished with water men and souldiers. Thus Octavius Cæsar beeing finely deceyved by this stratageame, retyred presently, and therewithall Antonius very wisely and sodainely did cut him of from fresh water. For, understanding that the places where Octavius Cæsar landed, had very litle store of water, and yet very bad: he shut them in with stronge ditches and trenches he cast, to keepe them from salying

Side notes:

Antonius rode at anker at the head of Actius: where the citie of Nicopolis standeth.

* The grace of this tawnt can not properly be expressed in any other tongue, bicause of the equivocation of this word Toryne, which signifieth a citie of Albaria, and also, a ladell to scoome the pot with: as if she ment, Cæsar sat by the fire side, scomming of the pot.

out at their pleasure, and so to goe seeke water further of.
Furthermore, he delt very friendely and curteously with
Domitius, and against Cleopatraes mynde. For, he being
sicke of an agewe when he went and tooke a litle boate
to goe to Cæsars campe, Antonius was very sory for it,
but yet he sent after him all his caryage, trayne, and men:
and the same Domitius, as though he gave him to understand that he repented his open treason, he died immediately after. There were certain kings also that forsooke
him, and turned on Cæsars side: as Amyntas, and
Deiotarus. Furthermore, his fleete and navy that was
unfortunate in all thinges, and unready for service, compelled him to chaunge his minde, and to hazard battell by
land. And Canidius, also, who had charge of his army by
land, when time came to follow Antonius determination:
he turned him cleane contrary, and counselled him to
send Cleopatra backe againe, and him selfe to retyre into
Macedon, to fight there on the maine land. And furthermore told him, that Dicomes king of the Getes, promised
him to ayde him with a great power: and that it should
be no shame nor dishonor to him to let Cæsar have the
sea, (bicause him selfe and his men both had bene well
practised and exercised in battels by sea, in the warre of
Sicilia against Sextus Pompeius) but rather that he
should doe against all reason, he having so great skill and
experience of battells by land as he had, if he should not
employ the force and valliantnes of so many lusty armed
footemen as he had ready, but would weaken his army
by deviding them into shippes. But now, notwithstanding all these good perswasions, Cleopatra forced him to
put all to the hazard of battel by sea: considering with
her selfe how she might flie, and provide for her safetie,
not to helpe him to winne the victory, but to flie more
easily after the battel lost.

So when Antonius had determined to fight by sea, he
set all the other shippes a fire, but three score shippes of
Ægypt, and reserved onely but the best and greatest
gallies, from three bancks, unto tenne bancks of owers.
Into them he put two and twenty thowsand fighting men,
with two thowsand darters and slingers. Now, as he was
setting his men in order of battel, there was a Captaine,
and a valliant man, that had served Antonius in many

Domitius for-
saketh An-
tonius, and
goeth unto
Octavius
Cæsar.

Amyntas, and
Deiotarus, do
both revolt
from Anton-
ius, and goe
unto Cæsar.

battels and conflicts, and had all his body hacked and cut: who as Antonius passed by him, cryed out unto him, and sayd: O noble Emperor, how commeth it to pass that you trust to these vile brittle shippes? what, doe you mistrust these woundes of myne, and this sword? let the Ægyptians and Phænicians fight by sea, and set us on the maine land, where we use to conquer, or to be slayne on our feete. Antonius passed by him, and sayd never a word, but only beckoned to him with his hand and head, as though he willed him to be of good corage, although in deede he had no great corage him selfe. For when the Masters of the gallies and Pilots would have let their sailes alone, he made them clap them on, saying to culler the matter withall, that not one of his enemies should scape. All that day, and the three dayes following, the sea rose high, and was so boysterous, that the battel was put of. The fift day the storme ceased, and the sea calmed againe, and then they rowed with force of owers in battaile one against the other: Antonius leading the right wing with Publicola, and Cælius the left, and Marcus Octavius, and Marcus Iusteius the middest. Octavius Cæsar on thother side, had placed Agrippa in the left winge of his armye, and had kept the right winge for him selfe. For the armies by lande Canidius was generall of Antonius side, and Taurus of Cæsars side: who kept their men in battell raye the one before the other, uppon the sea side, without stirring one agaynst the other.

Antonius regardeth not the good counsell of his souldier.

Battail by sea at Actium, betwixt Antonius and Octavius

.   .   .   .

Howbeit the battell was yet of even hand, and the victorie doubtfull, being indifferent to both: when sodainely they saw the three score shippes of Cleopatra busie about their yard masts, and hoysing saile to flie. So they fled through the middest of them that were in fight, for they had bene placed behind the great shippes, and did marvelously disorder the other shippes. For the enemies them selves wondred much to see them saile in that sort, with ful saile towards Peloponnesus. There Antonius shewed plainely, that he had not onely lost the corage and hart of an Emperor, but also of a valliant man, and that he was not his owne man: (proving that true which an old man spake in myrth, that the soule of a lover lived in another body, and not in his owne) he was so caried

Cleopatra flyeth.

The soule of a lover liveth in another body.

away with the vaine love of this woman, as if he had bene
glued unto her, and that she could not have removed
without moving of him also. For when he saw Cleo-

Antonius
flyeth after
Cleopatra.

patraes shippe under saile, he forgot, forsooke, and betrayed them that fought for him, and imbarked upon a
galley with five bankes of owers, to follow her that had
already begon to overthrow him, and would in the end
be his utter destruction. When she knew his galley a farre
of, she lift up a signe in the poope of her shippe, and so
Antonius comming to it, was pluckt up where Cleopatra
was, howbeit he saw her not at this first comming, nor
she him, but went and sate down alone in the prowe of
his shippe, and said never a word, clapping his head
betwene both his hands . . . and so lived three days alone,
without speaking to any man. But when he arrived at the
head of Tænarus, there Cleopatraes women first brought
Antonius and Cleopatra to speake together, and afterwards, to suppe and lye together. Then beganne there
agayne a great number of Marchaunts shippes to gather
about them, and some of their friends that had escaped
from this overthrow: who brought newes, that his army
by sea was overthrowen, but that they thought the army
by land was yet whole. Then Antonius sent unto Canidius, to returne with his army into Asia, by Macedon.

Antonius
lycenceth his
friends to
depart, and
giveth them
a shippe
loden with
gold and
silver.

Now for him self, he determined to crosse over into
Africk, and toke one of his carects or hulks loden with
gold and silver, and other rich cariage, and gave it unto
his friends: commaunding them to depart, and to seeke
to save them selves. They aunswered him weeping, that
they would nether doe it, not yet forsake him. Then
Antonius very curteously and lovingly did comfort them,
and prayed them to depart: and wrote unto Theophilus
governor of Corinthe, that he would see them safe, and
helpe to hide them in some secret place, until they had
made their way and peace with Cæsar. This Theophilus
was the father of Hipparchus, who was had in great estimation about Antonius. He was the first of all his infranchised bondmen that revolted from him, and yelded
unto Cæsar, and afterwardes went and dwelt at Corinthe.
And thus it stoode with Antonius. Now for his armie by
sea, that fought before the head or foreland of Actium:
they helde out a longe tyme, and nothing troubled them
more then a great boysterous wind that rose full in the

prooes of their shippes, and yet with much a doe, his navy was at length overthrowen, five howers within night. There were not slaine above five thowsand men: but yet there were three hundred shippes taken, as Octavius Cæsar writeth him selfe in his *Commentaries*. Many plainely sawe Antonius flie, and yet could hardly beleeve it, that he that had nyneteene legions whole by lande, and twelve thowsand horsemen upon the sea side, would so have forsaken them, and have fled so cowardly: as if he had not oftentimes proved both the one and the other fortune, and that he had not bene throughly acquainted with the divers chaunges and fortunes of battells. And yet his souldiers still wished for him, and ever hoped that he would come by some meanes or other unto them. Furthermore, they shewed them selves so valliant and faithfull unto him, that after they certainly knewe he was fled, they kept them selves whole together seven daies. In the ende Canidius, Antonius Lieuetenant, flying by night, and forsaking his campe: when they saw them selves thus destitute of their heads and leaders, they yelded themselves unto the stronger.

. . . .

But now to returne to Antonius againe. Canidius him selfe came to bring him newes, that he had lost all his armie by land at Actium. On thother side he was advertised also, that Herodes king of Iurie, who had also certeine legions and bandes with him, was revolted unto Cæsar, and all the other kings in like manner: so that, saving those that were about him, he had none left him. All this notwithstanding did nothing trouble him, and it seemed that he was contented to forgoe all his hope, and so to be ridde of all his care and troubles. Thereupon he left his solitarie house he had built in the sea which he called Timoneon, and Cleopatra received him into her royall pallace. He was no sooner comen thither, but he straight set all the city of rioting and banketing againe, and him selfe, to liberalitie and giftes. He caused the sonne of Iulius Cæsar and Cleopatra, to be enrolled (according to the maner of the Romanes) amongest the number of young men: and gave Antyllus, his eldest sonne he had by Fulvia, the mans gowne, the which was a plaine gowne, without gard or imbroderie of purple. For these things, there was kept great feasting, banket-

Antonius navy overthrowen by Cæsar.

Antonius rioting in Alexandria after his great losse and overthrow.
Toga virilis.
Antillus, the eldest sonne of Antonius by his wife Fulvia.

ing, and daancing in Alexandria many dayes together. In deede they did breake their first order they had set downe, which they called Amimetobion, (as much to say, no life comparable) and did set up an other which they called Synapothanumenon (signifying the order and agreement of those that will dye together) the which in exceeding sumptuousnes and cost was not inferior to the first. For their frendes made them selves to be inrolled in this order of those that would dye together, and so made great feastes one to another: for everie man when it came to his turne, feasted their whole companie and fraternitie. Cleopatra in the meane time was verie carefull in gathering all sorts of poysons together to destroy men. Now to make proofe of those poysons which made men dye with least paine, she tried it upon condemned men in prison. For when she saw the poysons that were sodaine and vehement, and brought speedy death with grievous torments: and in contrary maner, that suche as were more milde and gentle, had not that quicke speede and force to make one dye sodainly: she afterwardes went about to prove the stinging of snakes and adders, and made some to be applied unto men in her sight, some in one sorte, and some in an other. So when she had dayly made divers and sundrie proofes, she found none of all them she had proved so fit, as the biting of an Aspicke, the which only causeth a heavines of the head, without swounding or complaining, and bringeth a great desire also to sleepe, with a litle swet in the face, and so by litle and litle taketh away the sences and vitall powers, no living creature perceiving that the pacientes feele any paine. For they are so sorie when any bodie waketh them, and taketh them up: as those that being taken out of a sounde sleepe, are very heavy and desirous to sleepe. This notwithstanding, they sent Ambassadors unto Octavius Cæsar in Asia, Cleopatra requesting the realme of Ægypt for her children, and Antonius praying that he might be suffered to live at Athens like a private man, if Cæsar would not let him remaine in Ægypt. And bicause they had no other men of estimacion about them, for that some were fledde, and those that remained, they did not greatly trust them: they were inforced to sende Euphronius the schoolemaister of their children. For Alexas Laodician, who was brought into Antonius house

An order erected by Antonius, and Cleopatra, called Synapothanumenon, revoking the former called Aminetobion.

Cleopatra verie busie in proving the force of poyson.

The property of the biting of an Aspick.

Antonius and Cleopatra send Ambassadors unto Octavius Cæsar.

and favor by meanes of Timagenes, and afterwards was in greater credit with him, then any other Grecian: (for that he had alway bene one of Cleopatraes ministers to win Antonius, and to overthrow all his good determinations to use his wife Octavia well) him Antonius had sent unto Herodes king of Iurie, hoping still to keepe him his frend, that he should not revolt from him. But he remained there, and betrayed Antonius. For where he should have kept Herodes from revolting from him, he perswaded him to turne to Cæsar: and trusting king Herodes, he presumed to come in Cæsars presence. Howbeit Herodes did him no pleasure: for he was presently taken prisoner, and sent in chaines to his owne contrie, and there by Cæsars commaundement put to death. Thus was Alexas in Antonius life time put to death, for betraying of him. Furthermore, Cæsar would not graunt unto Antonius requests: but for Cleopatra, he made her aunswere, that he woulde deny her nothing reasonable, so that she would either put Antonius to death, or drive him out of her contrie. Therewithall he sent Thyreus one of his men unto her, a verie wise and discreete man, who bringing letters of credit from a young Lorde unto a noble Ladie, and that besides greatly liked her beawtie, might easely by his eloquence have persuaded her. He was longer in talke with her then any man else was, and the Queene her selfe also did him great honor: insomuch as he made Antonius gealous of him. Whereupon Antonius caused him to be taken and well favouredly whipped, and so sent him unto Cæsar: and bad him tell him that he made him angrie with him, bicause he shewed him selfe prowde and disdainfull towards him, and now specially when he was easie to be angered, by reason of his present miserie. To be short, if this mislike thee said he, thou hast Hipparchus one of my infranchised bondmen with thee: hang him if thou wilt, or whippe him at thy pleasure, that we may crie quittaunce. From thenceforth, Cleopatra to cleere her selfe of the suspicion he had of her, she made more of him then ever she did. For first of all, where she did solemnise the day of her birth very meanely and sparingly, fit for her present misfortune: she now in contrary maner did keepe it with such solemnitie, that she exceeded all measure of sumptuousnes and magnificence: so that the ghests that were bidden to the

Alexas treason justly punished.

feasts, and came poore, went away riche. Nowe things passing thus, Agrippa by divers letters sent one after an other unto Cæsar, prayed him to returne to Rome, bicause the affaires there did of necessity require his person and presence. Thereupon he did deferre the warre till the next yeare following: but when winter was done, he returned againe through Syria by the coast of Africke, to make warres against Antonius, and his other Captaines. When the citie of Pelusium was taken, there ran a rumor in the citie, that Seleucus, by Cleopatraes consent, had surrendred the same. But to cleere her selfe that she did not, Cleopatra brought Seleucus wife and children unto Antonius, to be revenged of them at his pleasure. Furthermore, Cleopatra had long before made many sumptuous tombes and monumentes, as well for excellencie of workmanshippe, as for height and greatnes of building, joyning hard to the temple of Isis. Thither she caused to be brought all the treasure and pretious things she had of the auncient kings her predecessors: as gold, silver, emerods, pearles, ebbanie, ivorie, and sinnamon, and besides all that, a marvelous number of torches, faggots, and flaxe. So Octavius Cæsar being affrayed to loose suche a treasure and masse of riches, and that this woman for spight would set it a fire, and burne it every whit: he alwayes sent some one or other unto her from him, to put her in good comfort, whilest he in the meane time drewe neere the citie with his armie. So Cæsar came, and pitched his campe hard by the city, in the place where they runne and manage their horses. Antonius made a saly upon him, and fought verie valliantly, so that he drave Cæsars horesmen backe, fighting with his men even into their campe. Then he came againe to the pallace, greatly boasting of this victorie, and sweetely kissed Cleopatra, armed as he was, when he came from the fight, recommending one of his men of armes unto her, that had valliantly fought in this skirmish. Cleopatra to reward his manlines, gave him an armor and head peece of cleane gold: howbeit the man at armes when he had received this rich gift, stale away by night, and went to Cæsar. Antonius sent againe to chalenge Cæsar, to fight with him hande to hande. Cæsar aunswered him, that he had many other wayes to dye then so. Then Antonius seeing there was no way

Pelusium was yeelded up to Octavius Cæsar.

Cleopatraes monuments set up by the temple of Isis.

more honorable for him to dye, then fighting valliantly: he determined to sette up his rest, both by sea and lande. So being at supper, (as it is reported) he commaunded his officers and household servauntes that waited on him at his bord, that they should fill his cuppes full, and make as muche of him as they could: for said he, you know not whether you shall doe so much for me to morrow, or whether you shall serve an other maister: and it may be you shall see me no more, but a dead bodie. This notwithstanding, perceiving that his frends and men fell a weeping to heare him say so: to salve that he had spoken, he added this more unto it, that he would not leade them to battell, where he thought not rather safely to returne with victorie, then valliantly to dye with honor. Furthermore, the selfe same night within litle of midnight, when all the citie was quiet, full of feare and sorrowe, thinking what would be the issue and ende of this warre: it is said that sodainly they heard a marvelous sweete harmonie of sundrie sortes of instrumentes of musicke, with the crie of a multitude of people, as they had bene dauncing, and had song as they use in Bacchus feastes, with movinges and turninges after the maner of the Satyres: and it seemed that this daunce went through the city unto the gate that opened to the enemies, and that all the troupe that made this noise they heard, went out of the city at that gate. Now, such as in reason sought the depth of the interpretacion of this wonder, thought that it was the god unto whom Antonius bare singular devotion to counterfeate and resemble him, that did forsake them. The next morning by breake of day, he went to set those few footemen he had in order upon the hills adjoyning unto the citie: and there he stoode to behold his gallies which departed from the haven, and rowed against the gallies of his enemies, and so stoode still looking what exployte his souldiers in them would do. But when by force of rowing they were come neere unto them, they first saluted Cæsars men: and then Cæsars men resaluted them also, and of two armies made but one, and then did all together row toward the citie. When Antonius sawe that his men did forsake him, and yeelded unto Cæsar, and that his footemen were broken and overthrowen: he then fled into the citie, crying out that Cleopatra had betrayed him unto them, with whom he had made warre for her

Straunge noises heard, and nothing seene.

Antonius navie doe yeeld them selves unto Cæsar. Antonius overthrowen by Octavius Cæsar.

Cleopatra
flieth into
her tombe
or monu-
ment.

sake. Then she being affraied of his fury, fled into the
tombe which she had caused to be made, and there
locked the dores unto her, and shut all the springes of the
lockes with great boltes, and in the meane time sent unto
Antonius to tell him that she was dead. Antonius
beleving it, said unto him selfe: What doest thou looke
for further, Antonius, sith spitefull fortune hath taken
from thee the only joy thou haddest, for whom thou yet
reservedst thy life? When he had sayd these words, he
went into a chamber and unarmed him selfe, and being
naked said thus: O Cleopatra, it grieveth me not that I
have lost thy companie, for I will not be long from thee:
but I am sory that having bene so great a Captaine and
Emperour, I am in deede condemned to be judged of
lesse corage and noble minde, then a woman. Now he
had a man of his called Eros, whom he loved and trusted
much, and whom he had long before caused to sweare
unto him, that he should kill him when he did commaunde him: and then he willed him to keepe his pro-
Eros Anton-
ius servant,
slue him selfe.
mise. His man drawing his sworde, lift it up as though he
had ment to have striken his maister: but turning his
head at one side, he thrust his sword into himselfe, and
fell downe dead at his maisters foote. Then said Antonius, O noble Eros, I thanke thee for this, and it is valliantly done of thee, to shew me what I should doe to my
selfe, which thou couldest not doe for me. Therewithall
Antonius did
thrust his
sword into
him selfe, but
died not
presently.
he tooke his sword and thrust it into his bellie, and so fell
downe upon a litle bed. The wounde he had killed him
not presently, for the blood stinted a litle when he was
layed: and when he came somwhat to him selfe againe,
he praied them that were about him to dispatch him.
But they all fled out of the chamber, and left him crying
out and tormenting him selfe: untill at last there came a
secretarie unto him called Diomedes, who was com-
Antonius
caried unto
Cleopatraes
tombe.
maunded to bring him into the tombe or monument
where Cleopatra was. When he heard that she was alive,
he verie earnestlie prayed his men to carie his bodie
thither, and so he was caried in his mens armes into the
entry of the monument. Notwithstanding, Cleopatra
would not open the gates, but came to the high windowes, and cast out certaine chaines and ropes, in the
which Antonius was trussed: and Cleopatra her owne
selfe, with two women only, which she had suffered to

come with her into these monumentes, trised Antonius up. They that were present to behold it, said they never saw so pitiefull a sight. For, they plucked up poore Antonius all bloody as he was, and drawing on with pangs of death, who holding up his hands to Cleopatra, raised up him selfe as well as he could. It was a hard thing for these women to do, to lift him up: but Cleopatra stowping downe with her head, putting to all her strength to her uttermost power did lift him up with much a doe, and never let goe her hold, with the helpe of the women beneath that bad her be of good corage, and were as sorie to see her labor so, as she her selfe. So when she had gotten him in after that sorte, and layed him on a bed: she rent her garments upon him, clapping her brest, and scratching her face and stomake. Then she dried up his blood that had berayed his face, and called him her Lord, her husband, and Emperour, forgetting her owne miserie and calamity, for the pitie and compassion she tooke of him. Antonius made her ceasse her lamenting, and called for wine, either bicause he was a thirst, or else for that he thought thereby to hasten his death. When he had dronke, he earnestly prayed her, and perswaded her, that she would seeke to save her life, if she could possible, without reproache and dishonor: and that chiefly she should trust Proculeius above any man else about Cæsar. And as for him selfe, that she should not lament nor sorrowe for the miserable chaunge of his fortune at the end of his dayes: but rather that she should thinke him the more fortunate, for the former triumphes and honors he had received, considering that while he lived he was the noblest and greatest Prince of the world, and that now he was overcome, not cowardly, but valiantly, a Romane by an other Romane. As Antonius gave the last gaspe, Proculeius came that was sent from Cæsar. For after Antonius had thrust his sworde in him selfe, as they caried him into the tombes and monuments of Cleopatra, one of his gard called Dercetæus, tooke his sword with the which he had striken him selfe, and hidde it: then he secretly stale away, and brought Octavius Cæsar the first newes of his death, and shewed him his sword that was bloodied. Cæsar hearing these newes, straight withdrewe him selfe into a secret place of his tent, and there burst out with

A lamentable sight to see Antonius and Cleopatra.

The death of Antonius.

Octavius Cæsar lamenteth Antonius death.

teares, lamenting his hard and miserable fortune, that
had bene his frende and brother in law, his equall in the
Empire, and companion with him in sundry great
exploytes and battells. Then he called for all his frendes,
and shewed them the letters Antonius had written to
him, and his aunsweres also sent him againe, during
their quarrell and strife: and how fiercely and prowdly
the other answered him, to all just and reasonable matters he wrote unto him. After this, he sent Proculeius,
and commaunded him to doe what he could possible to
get Cleopatra alive, fearing least otherwise all the treasure would be lost: and furthermore, he thought that if
he could take Cleopatra, and bring her alive to Rome,
she would marvelously beawtifie and sette out his
triumphe. But Cleopatra would never put her selfe into
Proculeius handes, although they spake together. For
Proculeius came to the gates that were very thicke and
strong, and surely barred, but yet there were some
cranewes through the which her voyce might be heard,
and so they without understoode, that Cleopatra demaunded the kingdome of Ægypt for her sonnes: and
that Proculeius aunswered her, that she should be of
good cheere, and not be affrayed to referre all unto
Cæsar. After he had viewed the place verie well, he came
and reported her aunswere unto Cæsar. Who immediately sent Gallus to speake once againe with her, and
bad him purposely hold her with talke, whilest Proculeius did set up a ladder against that high windowe, by
the which Antonius was trised up, and came downe into
the monument with two of his men hard by the gate,
where Cleopatra stoode to heare what Gallus sayd unto
her. One of her women which was shut in her monuments with her, saw Proculeius by chaunce as he came
downe, and shreeked out: O, poore Cleopatra, thou art
taken. Then when she sawe Proculeius behind her as she
came from the gate, she thought to have stabbed her selfe
in with a short dagger she ware of purpose by her side.
But Proculeius came sodainly upon her, and taking her
by both the hands, said unto her: Cleopatra, first thou
shalt doe thyselfe great wrong, and secondly unto
Cæsar: to deprive him of the occasion and opportunitie,
openly to shew his bountie and mercie, and to geve his
enemies cause to accuse the most curteous and noble

*Proculeius
sent by Oc-
tavius Cæsar
to bring Cleo-
patra alive.*

*Cleopatra
taken.*

Prince that ever was, and to appeache him as though he were a cruell and mercielesse man, that were not to be trusted. So even as he spake the word, he tooke her dagger from her, and shooke her clothes for feare of any poyson hidden about her. Afterwardes Cæsar sent one of his infranchised men called Epaphroditus, whom he straightly charged to looke well unto her, and to beware in any case that she made not her selfe away: and for the rest, to use her with all the curtesie possible.

.   .   .   .   .   .

Shortly after, Cæsar came him selfe in person to see her, and to comfort her. Cleopatra being layed upon a litle low bed in poore estate, when she sawe Cæsar come in to her chamber, she sodainly rose up, naked in her smocke, and fell downe at his feete marvelously disfigured: both for that she had plucked her heare from her head, as also for that she had martired all her face with her nailes, and besides, her voyce was small and trembling, her eyes sonke into her heade with continuall blubbering: and moreover, they might see the most parte of her stomake torne in sunder. To be short, her bodie was not much better then her minde: yet her good grace and comelynes, and the force of her beawtie was not altogether defaced. But notwithstanding this oughly and pitiefull state of hers, yet she showed her selfe within, by her outward lookes and countenance. When Cæsar had made her lye downe againe, and sate by her beddes side: Cleopatra began to cleere and excuse her selfe for that she had done, laying all to the feare she had of Antonius. Cæsar, in contrarie maner, reproved her in every poynt. Then she sodainly altered her speache, and prayed him to pardon her, as though she were affrayed to dye, and desirous to live. At length, she gave him a breefe and memoriall of all the readie money and treasure she had. But by chaunce there stoode Seleucus by, one of her Treasorers, who to seeme a good servant, came straight to Cæsar to disprove Cleopatra, that she had not set in al, but kept many things back of purpose. Cleopatra was in such a rage with him, that she flew upon him, and tooke him by the heare of the head, and boxed him wellfavouredly. Cæsar fell a laughing, and parted the fray. Alas, said she, O Cæsar: is not this a great shame and reproche, that thou having vouche-

Cæsar came to see Cleopatra.

Cleopatra, a martired creature, through her owne passion and fury.

Seleucus, one of Cleopatraes Treasorers.

Cleopatra bet her treasorer before Octavius Cæsar.

Cleopatraes wordes unto Cæsar.

saved to take the peines to come unto me, and has done me this honor, poore wretche, and caitife creature, brought into this pitiefull and miserable estate: and that mine owne servaunts should come now to accuse me, though it may be I have reserved some juells and trifles meete for women, but not for me (poore soule) to set out my selfe withall, but meaning to geve some pretie presents and gifts unto Octavia and Livia, that they making meanes and intercession for me to thee, thou mightest yet extend thy favor and mercie upon me? Cæsar was glad to heare her say so, perswading him selfe thereby that she had yet a desire to save her life. So he made her answere, that he did not only geve her that to dispose of at her pleasure, which she had kept backe, but further promised to use her more honorably and bountifully then she would thinke for: and so he tooke his leave of her, supposing he had deceived her, but in deede he was deceived him selfe. There was a young gentleman Cornelius Dolabella, that was one of Cæsars very great familiars, and besides did beare no evil will unto Cleopatra. He sent her word secretly as she had requested him, that Cæsar determined to take his jorney through Suria, and that within three dayes he would sende her away before with her children. When this was tolde Cleopatra, she requested Cæsar that it would please him to suffer her to offer the last oblations of the dead, unto the soule of Antonius. This being graunted her, she was caried to the place where his tombe was, and there falling downe on her knees, imbracing the tombe with her women, the teares running downe her cheekes, she began to speake in this sorte: 'O my deare Lord Anton-'ius, not long sithence I buried thee here, being a free 'woman: and now I offer unto thee the funerall sprink-'linges and oblations, being a captive and prisoner, and 'yet I am forbidden and kept from tearing and murdering 'this captive body of mine with blowes, which they care-'fully gard and keepe, onely to triumphe of thee: looke 'therefore henceforth for no other honors, offeringes, nor 'sacrifices from me, for these are the last which Cleopatra 'can geve thee, sith nowe they carie her away. Whilest 'we lived together, nothing could sever our companies: 'but now at our death, I feare me they will make us 'chaunge our contries. For as thou being a Romane, hast

Marginal notes:

Cleopatra finely deceiveth Octavius Cæsar, as though she desired to live.

Cleopatraes lamentation over Antonius tombe.

'bene buried in Ægypt: even so wretched creature I, an
'Ægyptian, shall be buried in Italie, which shall be all
'the good that I have received by thy contrie. If therefore
'the gods where thou art now have any power and
'authoritie, sith our gods here have forsaken us: suffer
'not thy true frend and lover to be caried away alive,
'that in me, they triumphe of thee: but receive me with
'thee, and let me be buried in one selfe tombe with thee.
'For though my griefes and miseries be infinite, yet none
'hath grieved me more, nor that I could lesse beare with-
'all: then this small time, which I have bene driven to
'live alone without thee.' Then having ended these dole-
ful plaints, and crowned the tombe with garlands and
sundry nosegayes, and marvelous lovingly imbraced the
same: she commaunded they should prepare her bath,
and when she had bathed and washed her selfe, she fell
to her meate, and was sumptuously served. Nowe whilest
she was at dinner, there came a contrieman, and brought
her a basket. The souldiers that warded at the gates,
asked him straight what he had in his basket. He opened
the basket and tooke out the leaves that covered the
figges, and shewed them that they were figges he brought.
They all of them marvelled to see so goodly figges. The
contrieman laughed to heare them, and bad them take
some if they would. They beleved he told them truely,
and so bad him carie them in. After Cleopatra had dined,
she sent a certaine table written and sealed unto Cæsar,
and commaunded them all to go out of the tombes where
she was, but the two women, then she shut the dores to
her. Cæsar when he received this table, and began to
read her lamentation and petition, requesting him that
he would let her be buried with Antonius, founde
straight what she ment, and thought to have gone thithe
him selfe: howbeit he sent one before in all hast that
might be, to see what it was. Her death was very sodaine. The death
For those whom Cæsar sent unto her ran thither in all of Cleopatra.
hast possible, and found the souldiers standing at the
gate, mistrusting nothing, nor understanding of her
death. But when they had opened the dores, they founde
Cleopatra starke dead, layed upon a bed of gold,
attired and araied in her royall robes, and one of her two
women, which was called Iras, dead at her feete: and her
other woman called Charmion halfe-dead, and tremb-

Cleopatraes
two waiting
women dead
with her.

ling, trimming the diademe which Cleopatra ware upon
her head. One of the souldiers seeing her, angrily sayd
unto her: Is that well done Charmion? Verie well sayd
she againe, and meete for a Princes discended from the
race of so many noble kings. She sayd no more, but fell
downe dead hard by the bed. Some report that this
Aspicke was brought unto her in the basket of figs, and
that she had commaunded them to hide it under the
figge leaves, that when she shoulde thinke to take out the
figges, the Aspicke shoulde bite her before she should see
her: howbeit, that when she would have taken away the
leaves for the figges, she perceived it, and said, Art thou
here then? And so, her arme being naked, she put it to

Cleopatra
killed with
the biting of
an Aspicke.

the Aspicke to be bitten. Other say againe, she kept it in
a boxe, and that she did pricke and thrust it with a
spindell of golde, so that the Aspicke being angerd withall, lept out with great furie, and bitte her in the arme.
Howbeit fewe can tell the troth. For they report also,
that she had hidden poyson in a hollow raser which she
caried in the heare of her head: and yet was there no
marke seene of her bodie, or any signe discerned that she
was poysoned, neither also did they finde this serpent in
her tombe. But it was reported onely, that there were
seene certeine fresh steppes or trackes where it had gone,
on the tombe side toward the sea, and specially by the
dores side. Some say also, that they found two litle pretie
bytings in her arme, scant to be discerned: the which it

The image
of Cleopatra
caried in
triumphe at
Rome, with
an Aspicke
biting of her
arme.

seemeth Cæsar him selfe gave credit unto, bicause in his
triumphe he caried Cleopatraes image, with an Aspicke
byting of her arme. And thus goeth the report of her
death. Now Cæsar, though he was marvelous sorie for the
death of Cleopatra, yet he wondred at her noble minde
and corage, and therefore commaunded she should be
nobly buried, and layed by Antonius: and willed also
that her two women shoulde have honorable buriall.